W9-BAW-958

OPERATION KINETIC

OPERATION KINETIC
STABILIZING KOSOVO

Sean M. Maloney

Foreword by Sir Mike Jackson

Potomac Books
An imprint of the University of Nebraska Press

All rights reserved. Potomac Books is an imprint of
the University of Nebraska Press.
Manufactured in the United States of America.

⊗

Library of Congress Cataloging-in-Publication Data
Names: Maloney, Sean M., 1967– author. |
Jackson, Mike, 1944– writer of foreword.
Title: Operation Kinetic: Stabilizing Kosovo /
Sean M. Maloney; Foreword by Mike Jackson.
Description: Lincoln, Nebraska: Potomac Books,
An imprint of the University of Nebraska Press, [2018]
| Includes bibliographical references and index.
Identifiers: LCCN 2017038813
ISBN 9781612349640 (cloth: alk. paper)
ISBN 9781640120457 (epub)
ISBN 9781640120464 (mobi)
ISBN 9781640120471 (pdf)
Subjects: LCSH: Kosovo War, 1998–1999—
Participation, Canadian. | Kosovo War,
1998–1999—Peace. | Canada—Armed
Forces—Kosovo (Republic) | KFOR
(Organization) | Canada—Military policy.
Classification: LCC DR2087.6.F652 C376 2018 |
DDC 949.7103/15—dc23 LC record available at
https://lccn.loc.gov/2017038813

Set in Minion Pro by Mikala R Kolander.

For my students at RMC, *future leaders all*

CONTENTS

ILLUSTRATIONS

FIGURES

FOREWORD

SIR MIKE JACKSON

I had the privilege to command NATO's Allied Command Europe Rapid Reaction Corps (ARRC) from early 1997 to the end of 1999. My headquarters was multinational, with the United Kingdom as lead nation; I was fortunate enough to have Canadian officers on my staff. After nearly a year of stop/start planning and preparation in relation to the Kosovo crisis, the ARRC headquarters was finally deployed to the Former Yugoslav Republic of Macedonia (FYROM) in February 1999. At this stage our role was the coordination of various NATO troop contingents in FYROM—then still under national command—with a view to the possible rapid implementation of any agreement that might have emerged from the Rambouillet talks.

The failure of those talks led quickly to the commencement of NATO air strikes against Yugoslavia on 24 March 1999. As the embryonic Kosovo Force (KFOR), we saw our role change dramatically to the conventional ground defense of northern FYROM while preparing for entry into Kosovo—either by agreement following Yugoslav concession or, if need be, by ground offensive. It was a challenging and uncertain time during which KFOR grew in size and multinationality.

Yugoslavia conceded on 3 June 1999, and I conducted the Kumanovo talks with a Serb military delegation over five days (5–9 June). Those talks ended with agreement on the manner and timing of KFOR's entry into Kosovo and the Serb security forces' withdrawal. Our entry commenced at first light on Saturday, 12 June; the Serb withdrawal was complete, a few hours before their deadline, on Sunday, 20 June. It was a hectic, confused, and dangerous nine days during which KFOR had to stamp its authority on both the Serb forces and their opponents, the Kosovo Liberation Army (KLA), while assuring so far as we could the safety of the civilian population, of whatever ethnic origin.

Having secured the Serb withdrawal, we had as our next urgent security task the demilitarization of the KLA. Following parallel negotiations conducted mainly in Albania, the KLA leadership presented me with their official understanding to demilitarize over the following ninety days. This was done in my tactical headquarters just outside Priština in the wee hours of 21 June.

KFOR spent the following weeks and months on a myriad of challenging tasks: ensuring that the KLA held to their program of demilitarization; establishing a secure environment for a volatile and angry population; restarting public utilities, including hospitals, power generation, and communications; providing support to UNMIK, the UN civil administration; assuring freedom of movement; demining; assisting with the return of refugees; and deterring any reoccupation of Kosovo by Former Republic of Yugoslavia (FRY) forces.

The whole operation was a demanding, challenging, and exciting task for the soldiers of KFOR, drawn as they were from many countries, both NATO and non-NATO. Among them was the Canadian contingent, based initially on a reconnaissance squadron from Lord Strathcona's Horse (Royal Canadians) with its very effective Coyote vehicles, supported by Griffon helicopters. Time was against the Canadian deployment, and the determination shown to make the line of departure on time was most impressive. Indeed it was a tour de force. With the subsequent arrival of 1st Battalion, Princess Patricia's Canadian Light Infantry (1 PPCLI), the Canadian contingent developed into a strong and impressive battle group under 4 (UK) Armoured Brigade and provided a very significant element of KFOR's combat power.

Sean Maloney has described most vividly these extraordinary events from the Canadian perspective. It is a fascinating account, wide in its international context, putting together as it does the pieces of a most complicated jigsaw; the book portrays a very rapidly moving political and military situation with great clarity. Indeed I have discovered things of which I was not aware at the time!

The author also provides us with rich descriptions of the human aspect of these dangerous and uncertain events. The personal narratives of Canadian soldiers are a vibrant picture of the demands placed on soldiers by their nations, as well as of the quite admirable way in which they responded.

Three years before these events in Kosovo, during the first half of 1996, I was commanding NATO's Multinational Division Southwest in Bosnia-Hercegovina during the first phase of implementing the Dayton Agreement. There were two brigades under command: 4 (UK) Armoured Brigade (again!) and the Canadian Multinational Brigade. During this time I got to know the Canadian Army very well and also to admire their professionalism and cheerful, can-do approach to soldiering.

It was therefore a great honor and pleasure once more to have Canadian soldiers under my command in Kosovo. They rose superbly to the challenges and uncertainty of the rapidly changing situation before, during, and after KFOR's entry. No general is of any value whatsoever without the soldiers whose task it is to translate intent into reality; I owe an enormous debt of gratitude to the Canadian soldiers of KFOR who did just that in 1999, along with the soldiers of my own and other nations. My thanks go to them all.

ACKNOWLEDGMENTS

The origin of this book dates back to the early 1990s and my initial involvement in the Balkans. I served as the historian for 4 Canadian Mechanized Brigade (4 CMB), which was the Canadian Army's NATO ground force commitment in West Germany during the Cold War. When the Wall went down and trouble started in Slovenia, the Organization for Security and Cooperation in Europe asked Canada to contribute observers to the European Community Monitor Mission (ECMM). The ECMM later expanded its activities into Croatia and Bosnia. While I was working on the Canadian brigade history, 4 CMB was tasked to deploy ECMM observers and then units—the first Canadian UN contingent—to Croatia. These events were incorporated into the final chapter of the brigade history, later published as *War without Battles: Canada's NATO Brigade in Germany, 1951–1993*.

On repatriation to Canada I retained a growing interest in the Balkan conflicts. I cowrote, with my friend and colleague John Llambias, an oral history of Canadian soldiers in the Balkans, *Chances for Peace*. In 1995 I traveled to Croatia and Bosnia and observed UNPROFOR I and II operations. I then wrote a short history of the ECMM, *Operation BOLSTER*.

During my work with the ECMM and UNPROFOR I met and interviewed Maj. Gen. Mike Maisonneuve, who was the chief operations officer at UNPROFOR HQ during the Medak Pocket operation in 1993. I was teaching in the War Studies Program at Canada's Royal Military College (RMC) and providing input into the Directorate of Army Doctrine (DAD) and Army Lessons Learned Center organizations when Canada was asked to deploy observers with the Kosovo Verification Mission (KVM). General Maisonneuve asked me for a copy of my Operation Bolster study so they could apply lessons learned to KVM as it prepared to deploy. Sure, I said, but I wanted to come over and write the history of the KVM too, to which he readily agreed. Mike and his boss, Lt. Gen. Marc Caron, deployed in late 1998. They were working on getting me over to Kosovo to accompany KVM when the mission was ejected from the province and Operation Allied Force's bombardment started, in March 1999.

From there the project turned into something much larger and more complex. Who was going to capture the history of the army's involvement in Kosovo Force? There was no easy answer to this, as the structure that was supposed to be established in DAD to do this had its "person years" and position numbers removed in a reshuffling. Because time was of the essence, I took on Operation Kinetic as a Canadian Forces–supported research project in my capacity as a professor at RMC. I eventually got to Kosovo to conduct research once KFOR was on the ground.

The events of 11 September 2001 and the war that followed overshadowed my efforts and unfortunately ensured that *Operation Kinetic* did not see light of day at the time. The Balkans had seemingly become irrelevant, and publishers made that point clear. That state of affairs was not only frustrating to me, the author, but it was also frustrating for the soldiers who had enthusiastically explained to me in detail what they accomplished in Kosovo and who wanted their successes known, particularly after all of the Balkan and African failures during the 1990s. It was with a heavy heart that I communicated with many disappointed troops and had to explain the reality of the situation.

I am thus doubly grateful that Tom Swanson at Potomac Books took a strong interest in the exploits of Operation Kinetic, and I thank him not only on my own behalf but for those who served on this operation and entrusted their experiences to me. I would like to thank Generals Maisonneuve and Caron for supporting me in my efforts to document our operations in the Balkans, as this cooperation led directly to the volume in your hands. Another key individual was Col. Jamie Cade, then working in the DCDS's J-3 International shop (the predecessor to Canadian Expeditionary Forces Command and its successor, Canadian Joint Operations Command). With General Caron's concurrence I was able to identify primary source material from army records and have it vetted for use in this publication through the good offices of Colonel Cade and his staff. I would like to thank them all for taking a liberal view on what could and could not be used, as this positively contributed to the narrative of *Operation Kinetic*. Indeed a security review of the manuscript resulted in no demanded or requested changes.

There were four combat arms and two helicopter units that contributed forces to Op Kinetic: Lord Strathcona's Horse (Royal Canadians); Royal Canadian Dragoons; 1st Battalion, Princess Patricia's Canadian Light Infantry; 1st Battalion, the Royal Canadian Regiment; 408 Tactical Helicopter Squadron; and 430 Escadron Tactique d'Hélicoptères. Back in 1999–2001 all of these organizations assisted me openly and fully with documentation, and the unit leadership in all six cases facilitated my interviewing a cross section of their personnel who served in Kosovo. Thanks especially to all of the interviewees.

I would be remiss if I did not recognize the crucial assistance of Dr. Jason Ridler, who at the time was a graduate student and my research assistant during the initial phases of this project. Jay's dedication, hard work, and outside-the-box thinking were most appreciated on many occasions. I'd like to also thank my colleague Maj. Tanya Grodzinski, who was at the time editor of the *Canadian Army Journal* and highly supportive of contemporary army history and still is today. Thanks also to Maj. Terry Turner and his wife, Jenny, for assisting me when I was undertaking research in the United Kingdom.

Finally I would like to thank my agent and friend Fritz Heinzen for his support and patience over the years. When we were constantly told by publisher after publisher post 9/11 that the Balkans were as passé as the Cold War, we could only smile to ourselves and wait it out, because we knew that when it comes to eastern Europe, the wheel always turns.

INTRODUCTION

On the sweltering night of 12 June 1999 Canadian Coyote reconnaissance vehicles pulled out of the Krivolak training area south of Skopje, Macedonia, and headed for the tactical assembly area on the international border around 2300 hours. Four hours before British airmobile troops were scheduled to board their helicopters and seize the strategic Kačanik passes leading into Kosovo, men and women wearing black berets on their heads and maple leaf flags on their left shoulders swarmed onto the sleek eight-wheeled armored vehicles, attaching equipment, mounting machine guns, tightening bolts, and filling jerry cans with that precious fluid, water. Not all of the feverish activity was due to the humid, 40-plus degrees Celsius atmosphere: NATO's Kosovo Force (KFOR) was preparing to enter that eponymous Yugoslav province, and the timelines were tight. The soldiers of the Lord Strathcona's Horse Reconnaissance Squadron sweated out their last-minute tasks as radios and vehicle intercoms crackled back and forth. There was a hum of purposeful activity, but it was tempered by uncertainty. Despite all of the assurances made by the diplomats, KFOR might not be actually be invited guests.

The Yugoslav army might decide at the last minute to play the spoiler in this latest drama in the little shop of horrors called the Balkans. The Canadian code name for this mission was Operation Kinetic, and like that physics-based name NATO was prepared to use its energy to punch a hole into the heart of Kosovo. Canada and its allies were not going to stand idly by and observe the wholesale ethnic cleansing of yet another Balkan minority group. This new conflict had potentially huge repercussions in the volatile region, especially in recently stabilized Bosnia. And the Russians were now threatening to intervene.

Even though it was front-page news for more than a year, in 1998–99, "Kosovo" even today is a name barely spoken outside of a tight ring of Balkans specialists. In the nearly two decades after al Qaeda's 9/11 attacks and the subsequent wars in Afghanistan and Iraq it is easy to forget that a NATO-led coalition intervened in Serbia to protect the population from state-sponsored genocidal violence and then established a statelet administered by the international community to stabilize the affected province. At that time the air campaign NATO conducted against Serbia was massively controversial. Boris Yeltsin's Russia even conducted a nuclear "flourish" directed at North America.

Why exactly have the dramatic events of the Kosovo campaign receded into collective amnesia? There are many reasons, none of them good.

During the war against al Qaeda and its allies in the 2000s the Balkans region, along with its discontents, became a strategic backwater. There was media fatigue, as well as compassion fatigue, after almost a decade of protracted violence in the region. In the reordering of the world after 9/11 the campaign in Kosovo had no relevance to the al Qaeda propaganda machine: indeed the "Crusader" West's rescue and protection of one million Muslims in what had been Yugoslavia was a liability to Osama bin Laden as he attempted to mobilize his constituents against his enemies near and far, including NATO members. Although he decried Serb barbarities in Bosnia, he was silent on Kosovo in his expositions.[1] Bin Laden's opponent, Donald Rumsfeld, the U.S. secretary of defense, was scathing about Kosovo and "offered the Balkans as a model of a postwar policy gone wrong," one that had generated a "'culture of dependence' that made it hard for the Kosovars to stand on their own feet."[2] Nothing good, it seemed, could be derived from those experiences. Counterinsurgency was the way of the future for the 2000s, not failed 1990s "peacekeeping" operations. And if one wanted to progress upward in Rumsfeld's Pentagon, one did not mention Kosovo or the Balkans.

The Kosovo intervention is today obscured or otherwise distorted by the virulent "hybrid warfare" propaganda that accompanies Russian adventures in Ukraine, the Baltic states, and Syria.

Vladimir Putin, viewing the geopolitical stage through the kaleidoscope of Kosovo, justifies Russian interventions in these regions on the basis of NATO's intervention in the Balkans. With tired old Communist Party propaganda techniques employing moral equivalence, the simplistic argument is made that what happens in Ukraine is acceptable because it somehow balances what NATO did in the Balkans, particularly in Serbia.[3]

Arguments employed in the service of current Russian objectives similarly include the assertion that all NATO operations since the 1990s are either failures, have questionable legitimacy, or both and that they generate regional chaos in each case. The logic is this: if all NATO operations are failures and illegitimate, then the Kosovo operation was a failure and illegitimate. The argument has no further utility except as a club with which to beat NATO and excoriate its membership. Normally this sort of simplistic argument remains in the realm of propaganda, but now some members of the academic community use it in public forums, and the facts about what happened in Kosovo are in some cases actively suppressed.[4]

The criticism does not stop there. For Serb nationalists it was the intervention that unleashed ethnic cleansing and genocide directed against the Kosovar Serb population, who suddenly morphed from perpetrator to victim status. Therefore NATO was held to be at fault. For extremist Kosovar Albanians the intervention force got in the way of the final victory against the Serbs. Therefore NATO was held to be at fault.

The cumulative effect of these criticisms over nearly twenty years is a tendency to unfairly ignore or even vilify the successful actions and activities of those who participated in the complex Kosovo intervention. In 1999 Kosovo was the breakpoint in a decade of problematic and failed interventions by international organizations in locations around the globe: Somalia, Rwanda, Haiti, Croatia, and Bosnia. Kosovo cannot and should not be taken out of its historical context. The intervention was the first time in the 1990s that ethnic cleansing was arrested while it was in progress and the effects reversed. That fact alone should merit historical recognition if not praise for those who conceived and carried out those operations. They should no longer be subjected to one-sided excoriation by those critics in the comfortable and safe surroundings of the human rights industry, academia, the legal profession, the internet, and the diplomatic cocktail party. Somebody had to carry out the operation on the ground, dig up the mass graves, prevent the destruction of cultural property, and forestall mob violence.

The expulsion of an estimated 850,000 Kosovar Albanians to Albania and Macedonia and Serbian security forces' internal displacement of some 400,000 more out of a population of two million residents was unparalleled in post–World War II western Europe.[5] This humanitarian outrage included Serb forces murdering an estimated 10,000 Kosovars, many of whose remains were later excavated, pulverized, and transported to multiple sites in Serbia when it became clear that NATO forces would enter the province (these transportations were dubbed "sanitation" operations by Serbian special security forces). Mass graves of Kosovar Albanians were still being found in Serbia as late as 2010.[6]

Indeed the deliberate destruction of archives, libraries, land ownership documentation, and other cultural artifacts undertaken in 1998–99 by Serb elements appears to have been an attempt to expunge Kosovar Albanians from the history of Kosovo.[7] In essence the combined effects of these events constituted genocide in its original 1948 definition, despite attempts by elements in the UN to shy away from seriously discussing it.[8] The wanton destruction of Serb Orthodox monasteries, churches, art, and religious facilities by Kosovar Albanians during violence that surged in March 2004, as well as any other revanchist activity undertaken subsequently against Kosovar Serbs, while equally abhorrent, does not retroactively justify the large-scale actions Belgrade implemented in Kosovo during 1998–99.[9] For rational human beings history is chronological, not concurrent.

Ultimately the unwillingness of the peoples of Kosovo to reconcile over real and imagined grievances related to Josip Broz Tito's management of Yugoslavia and the exploitation of those grievances during the Slobodan Milošević years, coupled with the inability of the peoples of Kosovo as a whole to grip those who profit from advocating and employing prejudice and ethnic violence are some of the problems that baffle the international community today in the region. Those problems perhaps have no short-term solution. Certainly the economic limitations owing to Kosovo's small size and divided status aggravate those conditions, not the fact of the 1999 intervention by the international community to restore a million and half people to their homes, reroof or rebuild those homes, and generate a comparatively secure environment so the people could remain in those homes.

Operation Kinetic: Stabilizing Kosovo is an in-depth examination of how the international community transitioned from a small observer force on the ground, where it monitored the deteriorating situation, to the NATO-led Kosovo Force (KFOR) building up in Macedonia and then deploying into Kosovo and on subsequent operations. It does not deal with the air campaign, Operation Allied Force. The highly tactical nature of KFOR operations was generated by the relatively small operating area coupled with the complex human and ethnic terrain laid like a web in the hills and valleys of the province. KFOR divided the province up into lead-nation sectors: British, French, German, American, and Italian. Other NATO members and even Russia contributed additional forces and subordinated them to those sectors.

Canada's contribution to KFOR started off as augmentation to the British-led sector, with a tactical helicopter squadron, an armored reconnaissance squadron, and a mechanized infantry battle group. However, the mobility of the Canadian units plus their unique technical surveillance capabilities led them to be employed throughout the province. As a result, the activities of the Canadian sub-units provide us insight into the problems of stabilizing Kosovo as a whole, not just within the British sector.

Reflecting the broad activity of the Canadian participation, this book is divided into several sections. The complexities of the conflict in Kosovo and why Canada chose to become involved form part 1. The deterioration of the situation, its monitoring by the international observer missions, the Kosovo Force buildup, and its entry into Kosovo constitute the material in part 2. The operational context of the sector known as Multinational Brigade (Center) begins part 3. From there, there are four functional chapters that cover the tactical activities of the reconnaissance squadron, the tactical helicopter squadron, and the mechanized battle group for the period 1999–2000. It is here that the collision of stabilization methodology with the specific local problems of the province takes place and leads us to examine the limits of stabilization operations in this particular ethnic and cultural arena.

The all-or-nothing approach taken by numerous propagandists, commentators, and some academics in critiquing the operation in Kosovo does not assist us at this level. It is best to let the practitioners explain what was within the realm of the possible and why they thought so at the time. Only then can we really determine how to measure the viability of this stabilization operation. It was a series of small, local successes, sustained over the short term, that presented a foundation for long-term success, not grandiose, publicly proclaimed, short-attention-span projects. And one must be prepared for setbacks like the violent events of 2004, contain the emotionally driven criticism that follows from all players, and incrementally move forward. There is no decisive battle. This will not be solved quickly or overnight. *Operation Kinetic* describes one particular phase of the Kosovo stabilization project, something that remains in progress nearly two decades later but without the bloodshed that occurred in 1998–99.

A note on conventions. Kosovo place-names come in two versions: Serbian and Albanian. This orthographic difference was a point of contention at times between the local populations and the KFOR troops, since the Kosovar Albanian majority in the region had had their language and culture suppressed under the Belgrade regime. They preferred to abandon anything Serb-related, and that included place-names: even road signs written in Serbian were defaced so that a visitor to the region could not tell where the destinations were, even though the arrows remain. I have elected to use the Serbian place-names simply because the NATO contingent's maps used them, as did the personnel I interviewed for this project. This should not be taken as an indication of partiality on their part or mine.

ABBREVIATIONS

ABCA	America-Britain-Canada-Australia–New Zealand army standardization agreements
ACE	Allied Command Europe
ALCE	air logistics control element
AOR	area of operations
APC	armored personnel carrier
APOD	aerial point of debarkation
ARRC	ACE Rapid Reaction Corps
ASD	alternate service delivery
ASZ	air safety zone
ATGM	antitank guided missile
AVLB	armored vehicle launched bridge
AWACS	airborne warning and control system aircraft
CBC	Canadian Broadcasting Corporation
CDS	chief of the Defence Staff
CFIOG	Canadian Forces Information Operations Group
CIDA	Canadian International Development Agency
CLS	chief of the Land Staff
CO	commanding officer
COMKFOR	Commander, Kosovo Force
CP	command post
DAD	Directorate of Army Doctrine
DCDS	deputy chief of the Defence Staff
DFAIT	Department of Foreign Affairs and International Trade (Canada)
DLFR	Directorate of Land Force Readiness
ECMM	European Community Monitor Mission
EOD	explosive ordnance disposal

FARK	Freedom Army of Kosovo
FLIR	forward looking infrared system
FRY	Former Republic of Yugoslavia
GPMG	general purpose machine gun
GSZ	ground safety zone
HEAT	high explosive antitank
ICTY	International Criminal Tribunal for the Former Yugoslavia
IFOR	Implementation Force (NATO)
IMP	individual meal pack
ISTAR	intelligence, surveillance, target acquisition, and reconnaissance
ITC	international training center
JIAS	joint interim administrative structure
JIC	joint implementation commission
JNA	Yugoslav National Army
JSO	Jedinice za Specijalne Operacije (special operations unit)
KDOM	Kosovo Diplomatic Observer Mission
KFOR	Kosovo Force (NATO)
KRWAU	Kosovo Rotary Wing Aviation Unit
KTA	Krivolak training area
KVCC	Kosovo Verification Coordination Center
KVM	Kosovo Verification Mission
LDK	Lidhja Demokratike e Kosovës (Democratic League of Kosovo)
LKÇK	Lëvizja Kombëtare për Çlirimin e Kosovës (National Movement for the Liberation of Kosovo)
MAWS	missile attack warning system
MFO	Multinational Force and Observers
MIF	military implementation force
MNB	Multinational Brigade
MRP	Ministria e Rendit Publik (Ministry for Public Order)
MSR	main service route

MTA	military technical agreement
MUP	Ministarstvo unutrašnjih poslova (Yugoslav interior ministry police forces)
NATO	North Atlantic Treaty Organization
NDHQ	National Defence Headquarters (Canada)
NGO	nongovernmental organization
NLA	National Liberation Army (of Albanians in Macedonia)
NORAD	North American Aerospace Defense Command
NVGS	night vision goggles
OPO	operations order
OSCE	Organization for Security and Cooperation in Europe
PGOK	Provisional Government of Kosovo
PJP	Posebne Jedinice Policije (special police units)
PSYOPS	psychological operations
PU	Policia Ushtarake (Kosovar Albanian "police")
QRF	quick reaction force
RCD	Royal Canadian Dragoons
RCMP	Royal Canadian Mounted Police
RGJ	Royal Green Jackets (UK)
ROE	rules of engagement
RO-RO	roll-on/roll-off ship
ROWPU	reverse osmosis water purification unit
RRB	remote rebroadcast site
RS	Republika Srpska
SACEUR	Supreme Allied Commander Europe (NATO)
SAJ	Specijalna Antiteroristicka Jedinica (Special Antiterrorist Police)
SDB	Služba Državne Bezbednosti (State Security Service,Serbia's secret police)
SFOR	Stabilization Force (NATO)
SHAPE	Supreme Headquarters Allied Powers Europe
SOF	special operations forces
SUP/OUP	Sekretariat Unutrašnjih Poslova/Odeljenje Unutrašnjih Poslova (ordinary police units)

SWSS	secure weapons storage sites
TAG	Tactical Air Group
TMK	Trupat e Mbrojtjes së Kosovës (Kosovo Protection Corps)
TUA	TOW under armor (antitank missile system)
UÇK	Ushtria Çlirimtare e Kosovës (Kosovo Liberation Army)
UÇPMB	Ushtria Çlirimtare e Preshevës, Medvegjës, dhe Bujanocit (Liberation Army of the Presevo, Medvedja, and Bujanovac)
UDB	Uprava Državne Bezbednosti (Yugoslav security police)
UN	United Nations
UNMIK	United Nations Mission in Kosovo
UNPROFOR	United Nations Protection Force
UNPREDEP	United Nations Preventive Deployment
UNSCOM	United Nations Special Commission
VCDS	vice chief of the Defence Staff
VCP	vehicle checkpoint
VJ	Vojska Jugoslavije (Yugoslav Army)
WAC	weapon authorization certificate
WEU	Western European Union

OPERATION KINETIC

1

BACKGROUND

ONE

The Balkans

A Quick and Dirty Primer

The UN, through the Security Council, could not guarantee the
peace. . . . Collective security could not, in fact, be organized on a basis
of world-wide agreement. We knew that this hard fact must lead to changes
in our policies. While we actively supported the UN, we had no illusions
about its weaknesses, especially about the growing tendency to
substitute propaganda for constructive debate and action.

—LESTER B. PEARSON, Canadian secretary of state for external affairs,
on why Canada helped form NATO in 1949

Throughout the 1990s it was commonplace in streets, hockey rinks, and bars to hear Canadians ask in wonderment why Canada maintained such a large military commitment to the pieces of the former Yugoslavia. The most common remark was, "Why do we bother? They've been killing each other for hundreds (or thousands) of years anyway." Such resignation was understandable, particularly when UN forces in the region were hamstrung, or when Canadian soldiers serving as UN military observers were roughed up and handcuffed to poles at Bosnian Serb installations to act as human shields, or even when Canadian soldiers were disarmed and forced to undergo a mock execution.

Yet successive governments deemed it necessary that Canadian soldiers be deployed to these places. The answers to those questioning such measures were of course extremely complex ones, and it is not a stretch to suggest that Canadian decision makers did not and could not have had all of the facts available when committing the Canadian Army to the Balkans. Indeed the decision to participate in KFOR was based on better information than the decision makers had back in 1991, when Canada joined the European Community Monitor Mission (ECMM), the first Balkans peacekeeping operation. Twenty years later we are in a better position to look back at the events that led up to Operation Kinetic. In essence the violent collapse of Yugoslavia produced fragmentation over time. The situation prompted Canada to commit forces at each stage of that fragmentation to contain the violence, to prevent spillover effects on adjacent countries, and to forestall aggressive Russian intervention in the region that would affect NATO and therefore Canada. In 1999 KFOR was the latest step in that process.

Topography of Terror, Crossroads of Empires

Yugoslavia was a European country located next to the Adriatic Sea in the heart of the Balkans. The territory that modern-day Yugoslavia controlled in the twentieth century had historically been an area over which a variety of empires had fought. The Balkans region was the dividing zone between the Roman and Byzantine Empires until parts of it were absorbed by the Ottoman Empire in the 1000s. It was the battleground between the Hapsburgs and the Ottomans and then between their nineteenth-century successor empires—the Austro-Hungarian Empire and the Turkish-controlled Ottoman Empire.

In terms of religion the Balkans region was pagan until around AD 500 and then Christian, both in its Eastern Orthodox and Roman Catholic forms. Once the Ottomans had overrun significant portions of the Balkans in 1300s, some groups occupying what would become Albania and Bosnia-Hercegovina converted to Islam. This is how the region developed its ethnic matrix. The situation was not clear-cut, however, in that the conflicts in the region at that time were not conducted solely on religious grounds: Christian troops fought for the Ottomans, while troops from Islam-oriented societies in the region fought for Christian princes. Christian sold out Christian, as well as their converted Muslim cousins, and the Ottoman Turks took every advantage of these divisions and exerted control through fear and by threatening forcible assimilation of all ethnic and religious groups.[1]

The Balkans region was like a seismic fault zone where the "tectonic plates" of the Eastern world, the Western world, and the Muslim world uneasily encountered each other for the next five hundred years. The nature of the conflicts that erupted involved temporary alliances, proxy wars, and jockeying for position. Given that the Balkans region consists mostly of mountainous terrain and is thus highly defensible, there was a certain utility to dominating the region. Control of the Balkans or key portions of it prevented attack and also provided a secure base from which to attack a rival.

The collapse of the Austro-Hungarian and Ottoman Empires in the wake of World War I permitted a growing Yugoslav nationalist movement to blossom. This movement had started in the mid-1800s among Croatian intellectuals who viewed the French Revolution with interest and saw the economic possibilities of a multiethnic, modern state: this was called the "Yugoslav idea." Similar concepts were generated inside Serbian intellectual circles at the same time. The outside control exerted by the Austro-Hungarian and Ottoman Empires did not, however, allow these ideas to be realized until the 1920s, when the first modern multiethnic state called Yugoslavia was formed. Notably, the formation of the first Yugoslavia at that time had been predicted back in the 1870s, when the Ottoman Empire was having economic difficulties and there was a belief that the bonds holding it together would eventually be loosened.[2]

Two new empires, Nazi Germany and fascist Italy, then took control of the region during World War II and used ethnic division to divide and conquer Yugoslavia, pitting Croatian and Albanian against Serb and Bosnian Muslim. As the Germans and Italians were losing ground in the war, a young communist named Josip Broz changed his name to Tito and led a war of liberation (with Allied help) against the Axis powers. At the same time, however, Tito fought another war against those ethnic-based groups seeking autonomy—groups that had been suppressed by the Yugoslav government in the 1930s. Tito instituted a totalitarian police state that kept the lid on such ethnic-nationalist aspirations throughout the long Cold War.[3]

Prior to its demise in 1991 Yugoslavia consisted of eight administrative divisions: Slovenia, Croatia, Macedonia, Montenegro,

Vojvodina, Serbia, and Kosovo. The last three had a slightly different relationship in that Kosovo and Vojvodina were "autonomous provinces," but politically they were appendages of Serbia. All eight had a varied ethnic matrix, though usually one ethnicity was in the majority due to sheer numbers. The ethnic matrix in Yugoslavia by the latter part of the twentieth century included Croatians, Slovenes, Serbians, Albanians, Bosnian Muslims, and Hungarians. These ethnic groups were generally based on religious groupings. The Slovenes, Croatians, and Hungarians were mostly Roman Catholic, while the Serbians were Eastern Orthodox. Albanians and Bogomils or their descendants, the Sandzak Muslims from Bosnia, followed Islam. Over hundreds of years, particularly during Tito's time, ethnic groups were transplanted from one region to another for political reasons so that by 1991 no one region was populated by a single ethnic group.[4]

The concept of the Balkans as the "crossroads of empires" continued into the 1940s. What was Canada's general position on Yugoslavia? Canada displayed little interest in the region until World War II, when Canadian covert operators working with the Special Operations executive supported Tito in his fight against Nazi Germany. These operations supported the main Allied effort on the Italian front, which included I Canadian Corps, by drawing off German and other Axis forces that would otherwise be used against the Allies. The British also had plans to land in Yugoslavia and move north through Hungary and into Germany to cut off the Soviets and thus stop them from seizing control of eastern Europe.[5]

The Cold War emerged out of the smoking ashes of 1945 as the Soviets became more and more expansionistic. Canada joined the North Atlantic Treaty Organization (NATO), formed in 1949 to deter communist aggression and if necessary defend western Europe from communist attack. It was assumed for many years, with complete justification, that Yugoslavia was a Soviet ally and thus antagonistic toward the Canadian way of life and interests. In time Tito broke with Stalin and declared Yugoslavia to be nonaligned, though it remained communist. Despite this realignment, NATO remained concerned about Yugoslavia throughout the Cold War, and, since Canada was part of that organization, NATO concerns tended to be

Canadian concerns, particularly since Canada had dedicated significant air and land forces to NATO in central Europe.[6]

It was conceivable that the Balkans region might fulfill its traditional role as a crossroads of empires if the Cold War turned hot, though in this case the heat would have been caused by nuclear weapons. The Ljubljana Gap in Slovenia was considered by NATO planners to be a likely point of entry by Soviet forces targeting Italy and Austria; they would then have access to NATO's rear area in West Germany. NATO developed several defense scenarios, some of which had Yugoslavia resisting the Soviet advance and others where they facilitated it.[7] NATO on the whole remained pessimistic about Yugoslavia's ability to remain nonaligned and generally treated it as a potential adversary.

A 1965 NATO intelligence estimate concluded that "despite 17 years of the regime's best efforts to instill a Yugoslav consciousness, most of the population still consider themselves primarily Serbs, Croats, Montenegrins or the like. The practical consequences of this psychology are a reluctance on the part of the more advanced areas of the country[,] such as Slovenia or Croatia, to be forced to contribute to the development of backwards areas in the south and an indifference to problems outside one's constituent republic. In time of war the tensions between the various people called Yugoslavs probably again would be the cause of disunity."[8]

Why Yugoslavia Collapsed

Since the outbreak of hostilities in 1991 and the subsequent deployment of European Community, United Nations, and NATO operations within the former boundaries of Yugoslavia, the media and scholars have expended considerable effort in trying to determine exactly what prompted the country to collapse so violently. There is no single or easy answer: such events always have many causes, and, depending on which side one takes, the reasons will always be controversial with any given opposing group. Professional Balkans observers tend to fall into three groups: journalists, political scientists, and historians. Broadly speaking, journalists blame nasty people, while political scientists blame failed political structures. Historians tend to look at both but also to examine those factors over the long term and then place today's events in that context. Put another way, Yugoslavia collapsed either because it was never structurally sound in the first place, that is, the nineteenth-century "Yugoslav idea" was unrealistic, or it collapsed from a more immediate and malevolent agenda initiated in the 1980s. Finally there is an argument to be made that Yugoslavia collapsed for both reasons. Let us examine each of these views carefully, since all of these reasons have a direct bearing on the place of Kosovo and the need to deploy NATO forces there in 1999.

One argument suggests that the collapse was a victory of aggressive nationalism brought about by conflicting nineteenth-century nationalist identities that were reborn in the 1980s. When Yugoslavia was formed in the 1920s, not all ethnic groups, particularly the Croats, Albanians, and Slovenes, bought into the idea of a federal Yugoslav state. Some members of these groups did buy into the "Yugoslav idea," but those who dissented also covertly kept their dreams of independent states alive. These nationalisms were not fully developed, that is, there was division and argument as to what a Croatian or Slovenian state would look like, how it would work, and so on. Serb nationalism and identity were, however, more developed than other identities before Yugoslavia existed and more resilient when federal authorities crushed nationalist groups in the 1930s. Therefore it was in a better and stronger position when the breakup occurred in the 1990s. Consequently the other groups wanted to balance things out rapidly to right the wrongs of the past that had been inflicted on them by the communist federal Yugoslav system, which they viewed as dominated by Serbs. There was a tendency to overreact to the situation, particularly when communism in other countries collapsed at the end of the Cold War in the early 1990s.[9]

A similar view agrees that the end of the Cold War promoted a revival of nationalism among several ethnic groups in Yugoslavia but that the number of people within each ethnic group demanding their own independent state and identity was much higher, that is, nationalism was more developed all around, not just among the Serbs. The problems in the region therefore were the result of a collision between fully formed cultural and religious values. The values within each ethnic group produced social expectations that in turn affected the interactions between groups.[10]

What does this mean? One group defines itself as not being like the others. The differences are in language, religion, culture, and territory. Part of defining oneself as not being another may lie in the fact that long ago those who are not yours committed some transgression, possibly violent, against yours, which in turn assists in defining the difference between the two groups. Therefore the seeds of hatred in the Balkans were sewn in the very distant past. Historical memory is long in that part of the world, and wounds are carried from one generation to the next. Further atrocities in later years, particularly during World War II, were committed partly because of the situation at the time and partly because of something that occurred decades or even centuries before.[11]

In modern Canada we use television, radio, and the internet to transmit ideas and information. In the medieval Balkans region religion and religious organizations were used to broadcast ideas to populations with limited education. Many Balkan cultures use disturbing, apocalyptic, and violent religious imagery: for example, Ottoman Turks are portrayed as demons in religious artwork. Fairy tales reminiscent of the Grimm brothers' stories depict Serbs as monsters. Atrocity stories from hundreds of years earlier are handed down in an oral tradition. It is not surprising that they serve as fuel for ethnic violence. Revenge is then exacted for perceived as much as for real historical violence. When civilizing controls like representative government are removed, terrorism and anarchy result.[12] One observer believes that the Serbian Orthodox Church "deserves credit for having done much to embitter Serbs against Albanians [and] Croats."[13] Similar remarks could be made about the religious authorities in each ethnic group.

Moving away from religion and ethnicity, one finds another view on the collapse, one arguing that all ethnic groups bought into the "Yugoslav idea" in the 1920s in hopes of external security, the promise of a representative government, and improved economic prosperity. This system worked until it was replaced by Tito's communist system. Communism's institutions and governmental structures just didn't work in the long term, since communism could only compromise so much between the ethnic groups. There was "widespread disillusionment and bureaucratic chaos." It was then undermined by individuals pushing their own nationalistic agendas.[14]

The Yugoslav economy was already in trouble by 1979: economic trouble produces uncertainty among citizens of any country. Tito, the man who had created the communist state and held Yugoslavia together, died in 1980. Competing strongmen then moved onto the scene to exploit the uncertain situation even further, for their own benefit. One observer noted in 1991 that "if we were to judge the six presidents of the former Yugoslav republics by their characters of twenty years ago, then Slovenia would have a Stalinist head of state; Croatia, a raving anti-Semite; Serbia, a blood-thirsty Bolshevik; Montenegro an adolescent; and Macedonia another Stalinist."[15]

Franjo Tudjman was fomenting unrest in Croatia as early as 1984, in part because he told his people that there were more Serbs in power positions throughout the late 1980s than any other ethnic group and that this affected Croatian aspirations. When violence broke out between Kosovo's ethnic Albanian population and the Serbian minority in 1987, Slobodan Milošević emerged as the Serbian leader after traveling to Kosovo to reassure Serbs that "no one shall dare beat you."[16] The effects of the speech he delivered on that occasion and the role of Kosovo as the "Serbian Jerusalem" will be explored in a later chapter.[17]

In recent years more and more attention has been focused on the roles of the key leaders in the tragedy that followed. Indeed one view is that Yugoslavia didn't fall: it was pushed. The country "was deliberately and systematically killed off by men who had nothing to gain and everything to lose from a peaceful transition from state socialism and one-party rule to free-market democracy."[18] Milan Kučan, a political opportunist in Slovenia, was part of this effort, while Tudjman in Croatia wanted to create a Croatian state at the expense of the Bosnian Serbs and Bosnian Muslims.

In the 1980s the central government in Belgrade had, for example, been cracking down on Croatian nationalists for some time. Belgrade thought that Croatia and Slovenia were too closely tied to the West, while the nationalists argued that the East was backward and that there were too many Serbs in control. Tudjman used the old ethnic horror stories to create his mass movement demanding Croatian sovereignty. Bosnian Muslims were, in his view, Islamized Croats and therefore Croatia had to expand in the direction of Bosnia, or, alternatively, they were the tools of the global Muslim conspiracy that wanted to use Bosnia as a springboard into Europe.[19]

Serb nationalists and Belgrade intellectuals (who drafted a memo in 1986 demanding the protection of Serbs in Kosovo from "Albanian genocide") were also part of the mix. Slobodan Milošević used both groups in a bid to seize power in Serbia first and then continue to control the rest of Yugoslavia as Tito's successor. In 1991, when that agenda disintegrated in the face of Slovenian and Croatian resistance, Milošević shifted his aim to creating as large a Serbian state as possible at the expense of the other ethnic groups. Serb groups in Albania, Bosnia, Slovenia, and Croatia therefore had to be supported since they were Serbian footholds in those areas.[20]

Control over the Yugoslav National Army (JNA) and other coercive components of the state apparatus was key to these endeavors. The armed forces of any communist state were part of huge bureaucracies that were horizontally and vertically integrated into one big state plan. The elimination of communism would produce efficiencies that would entail the elimination of a vast part of that bureaucracy. Thus the livelihood of those people working in that bureaucracy was put at risk. The Yugoslav army's leadership targeted enemies who perhaps were not there as part of a bid to retain power. Slovenia was singled out as the first scapegoat, an action that produced the Ten-Day War in June 1991.[21]

Tito's communist system of control over Yugoslavia was based on a federal state in Belgrade that controlled the Communist Party, the police, and the army. When he died in 1980, the balance between the three could not be held in check because that balance was based on the charismatic control of one man. Throughout the 1980s the Yugoslav army was becoming a state within a state, with 60 percent of its officers drawn from Serbia and Montenegro. The Yugoslav army also had the Kontraobaveštajna služba (KOS), its own counterintelligence service, and the army also controlled the massive Yugoslav arms industry. Yugoslavia sold weapons to whomever would pay, offering everything from AKM assault rifles to T-72 tanks (called the M-84 in Yugoslav army service). Hard currency flowed into Belgrade, and the arms factories concentrated in Bosnia flourished under JNA control.[22]

The political police (UDB) were predominantly Serbian and highly decentralized into each province. The UDB conducted covert overseas terror campaigns against Croatian and Slovenian émigré nationalist groups located in Germany, Italy, and Austria. This naturally increased the animosity between Croatia and Belgrade.[23]

Legislative weaknesses compounded the problem. Were the leaders of the republics and provinces representative of all of the different ethnic groups in their particular province or were they supposed to represent only their own ethnic group members? Proportionate representation was no longer guaranteed. In Kosovo, for example, the Albanian majority did not want the minority Serbian population to determine their destiny. Belgrade bureaucrats did not like the closer Slovenian economic relationship with the West and instituted controls that in turn irritated the Slovenians. The Serb population in Croatia was agitated by the pro-Nazi wartime record of the Croatians. Anti-Croatian rhetoric increased, as did demands for less Croatian control over the Serb population. Meanwhile an Islamic revival in Bosnia, fueled by increased contact between Bosnian Muslim expatriates working in the Middle East, prompted Belgrade to initiate a virulent propaganda campaign that even included Stalinesque show trials.[24]

A serious aggravating factor that would appear later in the Balkan wars of the 1990s was the presence of the Territorial Defense Forces. Under Tito small arms and heavy weapons had been stockpiled in decentralized depots. In the event of external attack on Yugoslavia a trained partisan organization would collect the weapons and conduct guerrilla warfare against the invader. With a collapsing federal system, the security of the depots could not be guaranteed, and the partisan organizations were politically unreliable since they consisted of the various ethnic groups in each republic or province. The existence of such an organization was a critical factor in the rush to violence: the partisan groups could fight the JNA with sophisticated weapons.[25]

The collapse of Soviet communism and the resultant instability in eastern Europe are other critical factors in the collapse of Yugoslavia. In essence the Soviet empire was Yugoslavia writ large: the Union of Soviet Socialist Republics consisted of more than one hundred ethnic groups, which were kept in check by a combination of military might, secret police organizations like the KGB, and the structure of the Communist Party of the Soviet Union. The early movements toward a more democratically representative system initiated under Mikhail Gorbachev in the mid-1980s loosened the bonds enough to allow chafing at the edges. In 1986 there were mass riots and deaths in Kazakhstan. In 1987 Crimean Tatars demonstrated in Moscow. By 1988 Nagorno-Karabakh had exploded into violence, followed by Georgia and Azerbaijan in 1990.[26]

By 1989 the Warsaw Pact system was disintegrating. The first indications were mass demonstrations in Rumania and the occupation of the Berlin Wall. Poland, already isolated within the Warsaw Pact system in the wake of the shipyard strike and subsequent Solidarity movement of 1980, was ready to change governments. Then the fervor spread to the Baltic states. This was a little too close to home for Moscow, and troops were dispatched to Lithuania in February 1990. In January 1991 there was nearly a war with Latvia. In August 1991 Communist Party hardliners, led by the head of the KGB, attempted a coup against Gorbachev. Thus the mighty Soviet Union was destabilized, and the situation was suddenly very, very unclear. Although the Berlin Wall had been torn down by this time, there were still half of a million Soviet troops in the former East Germany. Peace in newly freed eastern Europe was by no means secure.[27]

It is no coincidence that the breakup of Yugoslavia that began in 1990 and 1991 occurred at the same time the Warsaw Pact was dissolved and the future existence of the Soviet Union thrown into doubt. Like the collapse of the Ottoman and Austro-Hungarian Empires after World War I, the collapse of the Soviet system at the end of the Cold War provided nationalist groups in the Yugoslav republics and provinces with new opportunities. There was no lon-

FIG. 1. Kosovo

ger a strong communist federal structure to hold them in check as there had been at the end of World War II. The first republic to go was Slovenia, and that was where Canada first got involved in the Balkans.

Why the Canadian Army Deployed to the Balkans, 1991–1999

The Ten-Day War between Slovenia and the federal government in Belgrade resulted in a Yugoslav defeat and produced the Brioni Agreement, which called for the withdrawal of Yugoslav army troops from the new country. The Conference for Security and Cooperation in Europe (now called the OSCE) was asked to mediate the ceasefire, and the European Community was subcontracted to provide an observer force to do just that. The parties to the agreement, however, wanted American or Canadian observers on the newly formed European Community Monitor Mission so that the European members would be kept honest. When fighting started between the Yugoslav army and the Croatians in the aftermath of the Ten-Day War, the ECMM was expanded so that it could broker ceasefires. The first Canadian peace observation troops arrived to serve with the ECMM in the fall of 1991.[28]

Canadian involvement at this point was motivated by several factors. First, Canada had developed a credibility problem with its closest allies in NATO. After the Berlin Wall was brought down late in 1989, the Canadian government abruptly announced that its NATO forces stationed in Europe—4 Canadian Mechanized Brigade and 1 Canadian Air Group—would be brought home and the bases in Germany closed. This move was a purely bureaucratic one and made without consideration of the damage it could cause to Canada's relations with the new Europe. Meanwhile war broke out in the Persian Gulf when Iraq invaded Kuwait. This dangerous situation had the potential to drastically affect the European economy and thus Canada's economy, not to mention the fact that the Iraqi regime was reported to be developing nuclear weapons that could threaten other Canadian interests in the region. The Canadian government made a minimalist contribution to fight Iraq and refused to send ground troops. For all intents and purposes it appeared that Canada was adopting an isolationist stance in the new world order.[29]

The decisions behind these two actions require further study. There is one school of thought suggesting that some in the Canadian foreign policy establishment were convinced that the United Nations would come into its own now that the world order was no longer based on superpower influence and NATO was therefore less important as a pillar of Canadian security. Canada could thus cater to the third world and not the first. Such views, as the 1990s bore out, were naïve and optimistic. Be that as it may, Canada's decision to participate in the ECMM operation was an attempt to regain some influence with European allies.[30] Why was this important?

Canadian participation in the ECMM and the other Balkan operations, including Operation Kinetic in Kosovo, are the result of a long-standing Canadian strategic tradition called Forward Security.

In the most fundamental terms the purpose of the Canadian government is to physically protect Canadian citizens. This protection takes many forms: health care, pensions for the elderly, and law enforcement. Canadians also require and demand a certain standard of living and opportunities for self-improvement. Therefore the protection of the means by which these things are provided is critical. Canada has never been and cannot be completely self-sufficient. Consequently the economic health of the country and the protection of it is necessary so that Canadians can enjoy prosperity. These factors have remained the same since Canadian Confederation in 1867.[31]

In essence these are the predominant Canadian values on which the nation is based. The primary threat to these Canadian values since 1867 has been totalitarianism, which is, according to the *Canadian Oxford Dictionary*, a political philosophy that demands "a centralized dictatorial form of government requiring complete subservience to the state." Such a political system is inherently violent and seeks to destroy individual liberty. Individual liberty is fundamental to having a personally fulfilling and economically prosperous society.

So when Canada's closest cultural connections and trading partners in Europe were threatened by Nazi, Italian, and Japanese totalitarianism during World War II and Soviet totalitarianism during the Cold War, Canada deployed troops to Europe. In the first case Canadian troops fought against the Nazi and fascist forces, while in the second Canada was a member of NATO seeking to deter the Soviets in Europe and supporting UN peacekeeping to prevent the Soviets, the Chinese, and their surrogates from forays into the developing world.

In the post–Cold War world there are still some totalitarian states that have the potential to threaten Canadian interests. The Russian "kleptocracy" that emerged from the totalitarian Soviet Union may in fact be more dangerous than the former Soviet Union.[32] Those totalitarian states have, however, been supplemented by other emergent threats. Technological and media developments have produced new weapons that groups of people without allegiance to any state can use to affect a country's interests. Thus the level of violence can be quite high and disproportionate to the numbers of people involved. An individual can kill three hundred people with a truck bomb. A religious cult can use nerve gas against commuters. A local warlord decides to kill off the competing clan for control over humanitarian aid. A small nation of one million people can acquire a nuclear capability and the means to deliver it. Tribal loyalties may override weak national governments, and huge, forced population movements might affect the economic and political status quo of neighboring states. In other words, widespread effective violence and chaos in the post–Cold War world is as much a threat to Canadian interests in some regions as totalitarian states.[33]

Forward security is then a strategic tradition that seeks to keep violent conflict away from North America and to keep crises overseas from developing into conflicts that can affect Canada's allies and trading partners. Both assure the physical and economic protection of Canadian citizens.

Forward security was operating in the background when Canada joined the European Community mission in 1991. As the situation in the Balkans deteriorated later that year, however, forward security again was reestablished as the prime Canadian motivator when the UN asked members to deploy troops in Croatia, particularly when KFOR was created in 1999.

The sheer geographical proximity of the collapsing Yugoslavia to Canada's European neighbors might have been enough to trigger Canadian involvement: this was not some remote African or Asian slaughterhouse. Indeed it boggled the mind that the front lines in Croatia and the massacres in Bosnia were less than a day's drive from the bases of Canadian Forces in Lahr and Baden-Soellingen, Germany.

By the end of 1991 the instability in the disintegrating Yugoslavia was associated with political and economic uncertainty in the former communist states in eastern Europe and in the former Soviet Union (which was dissolved that year). Potential instability north of Yugoslavia came in two varieties. First, there was no guarantee that the newly freed states of the new Russia would not succumb to some new form of totalitarian control. It was possible, as the events of August 1991 demonstrated, that Communist Party hardliners could mount coups d'état. There was also the problem of who had control of the estimated twenty-six thousand Soviet nuclear weapons, many of which were pointed at Canada and the United States.[34] Second, there was serious concern about the future of the united Germany in the new Europe. Would Germany follow the old paths that had led to World Wars I and II? Would the new Germany remain a stalwart ally of the West? Would the fever pitch of nationalism reach into the new Germany, too?[35] These were important questions for Canada since it had an estimated eighty thousand war dead buried in Europe as part of the effort to stop German totalitarianism during the course of the twentieth century, plus several hundred Canadian soldiers and airmen who had died while serving with NATO forces in Europe during the Cold War.

Placed in the historical context of World War I, the situation in Yugoslavia in the early 1990s appeared to some to be shaping up into a German-Russian proxy fight that could drag in allies on either side. Croatia was cultivating Germany with pleas of help for Catholic Croatians beset by "atheistic" Serb communists, while Belgrade was appealing to Moscow out of pan-Slavic unity to contain "German-sponsored fascism."[36] As one journalist noted, "This was utter nonsense, but it was nonsense which a large number of men with heavy weaponry believed."[37] If the situation was not contained, it could easily get out of control and put the world back to the pre-1990 status quo or worse.

After the European Community decided that a western European peacekeeping force was out of the question, the United Nations spent most of the spring of 1992 setting up and deploying a United Nations peacekeeping force to Croatia. The United Nations Protection Force (UNPROFOR) was designed to implement the Vance Agreement, whereby the UN would guarantee the security of four ethnic Serbian enclaves in a newly independent Croatia and police the demarcation lines between the belligerents in those areas. Canada deployed a composite battalion group from 4 Canadian Mechanized Brigade in Lahr, Germany, to UNPROFOR; this was called Operation Harmony.[38]

Soon after the Canadian Battalion (CANBAT) settled into its positions in May and June 1992, Bosnia-Hercegovina was the next Yugoslav republic to disintegrate. UNPROFOR's logistic airhead and headquarters were situated in Sarajevo, which was quiet at the time. Now UNPROFOR's "rear area" was a triethnic battle zone between Bosnian Serbs, Bosnian Croats, and Bosnian Muslims. CANBAT 1 was then tasked to redeploy to Sarajevo to secure the airport for the UN in July 1992. This was the start of the next phase of the Balkan wars.[39]

Thus far Slovenia was out of the conflict: the federal forces were gone and nobody was harassing ethnic minorities. Croatia was frozen in place, albeit temporarily. Now pent-up murderous rage broke out in Bosnia. It was as if each Yugoslav republic was lining up in turn to confront anarchy and violence. The lines in Bosnia stabilized, and a second UN force, UNPROFOR II, was established to provide armed protection to humanitarian relief operations in the region.[40] Canada then deployed a battle group (CANBAT 2) as part of this effort in the winter of 1992. This operation was called Cavalier. In addition, Operation Air Bridge was also mounted. This mission involved the use of a specially modified Air Command CC-130 transport and ground support deployed to work alongside other NATO members flying in humanitarian air relief to Sarajevo.

UNPROFOR II's mandate was unclear and resulted in some mutation throughout 1993. CANBAT 2 therefore wound up not only escorting convoys but maintaining the line between the belligerents in its area of operations and rotating into one of three established UN safe areas to deter Bosnian Serb attacks against predominantly Bosnian Muslim populations. To make matters worse, Croatia stepped up support for the Bosnian Croats against both the Serbs and the Bosnian Muslims, which in turn increased Belgrade's assistance to the Bosnian Serbs. Strategically the situation in Bosnia, combined with the situation in Croatia, remained explosive in that it could prompt Germany, Russia, and others to increase their support to the belligerent forces, perhaps in other areas. The Russians were particularly upset with the events in Bosnia, particularly NATO air support for UN forces, and even rattled their nuclear sabers on at least one occasion.[41]

The situation once again turned critical in 1993. Macedonia, another of the Yugoslav republics, declared independence. This move increased fears that the violence in Croatia and Bosnia would continue its march south. Macedonians feared that Belgrade, as well as Albania or Bulgaria, might take advantage of the situation and take over. The government in Skopje requested deployment of a UN force to act as a trip wire on its borders with these three states. Thus the United Nations Preventive Deployment (UNPRE-DEP) was formed. A Canadian company group from CANBAT 2 deployed in January 1993 as part of this operation. In addition the European Community mission deployed Canadian observers to Albania, Bulgaria, and Macedonia to act as listening posts so that any move by those states toward the use of force could be countered diplomatically.[42]

Instability dominoing south in the Balkans was as detrimental to Canadian interests as the instability that could affect relations to the north. The most important problem here was the poor state of relations between Greece and Turkey. These two NATO members had nearly gone to war four times in the 1960s over ethnic cleansing and intolerance on the island of Cyprus. Canada was instrumental in establishing a NATO-backed UN peacekeeping force, UNFICYP, in 1964.[43] The Greeks and Turks remained at loggerheads over Cyprus well into the 1990s. Turkey, where Islam predominated, had an affinity with the Muslims in Bosnia, Macedonia, and Albania, while the Greeks were Orthodox Christians, like the Serbs. To complicate matters even further the Greeks were extremely upset with the Macedonians over what they viewed as the appropriation of the name "Macedonia." Macedonia could be caught in a squeeze play that in turn could domino into a war between Greece and Turkey. Turkey abutted members of the Russian Federation, which supported the Serbs in Belgrade. It was not in Canada's best interests to step back and allow this conflagration to proceed any further, particularly if the possibility of aggressive Russian involvement existed.

The Canadian contribution to peace operations in the Balkans was significant: there were military observers working with the European Community, military observers working with the UN, two battle groups and a logistics battalion attached to the UN forces, and a transport aircraft. In time practically every unit in the Canadian Army would rotate through the former Yugoslavia. To apply even more pressure to belligerents, Canada also participated in

Operation Sharp Guard, a combined NATO–Western European Union (WEU) naval interception force designed to enforce UN economic sanctions against Belgrade. As with the army and its units in UNPROFOR, practically every Canadian naval ship would rotate through this mission, as would a number of Air Command Aurora maritime patrol aircraft.[44]

By 1995 UNPROFOR was in serious trouble. It was outgunned and understrength. The force suffered from obsolete rules of engagement and a convoluted command system. Elements of UNPROFOR were unreliable, and some took to covertly supporting one or more belligerents. On the whole the force lacked credibility, and the belligerents sensed this. In time the Dutch battalion from UNPROFOR II guarding the Srebrenica UN protected area surrendered to Bosnian Serb forces, and most of the Muslim population were massacred. UNPROFOR I forces, including a Canadian infantry battalion covering the southern Krajina areas, were then overrun by Croatian forces while the Krajina Serb population fled for their lives. The only UN forces left in Croatia were in the Serb-dominated rump of Eastern Slavonia, which the Croatian army was incapable of kicking out. UNPROFOR I and II were disbanded, and a small UN force remained in Eastern Slavonia.

A series of American-led peace initiatives supported by NATO consensus and threats to bomb Serb military targets were able to bring all parties in Bosnia to meet and agree on a ceasefire. The resulting mechanism to secure the peace was a NATO peacekeeping force, Implementation Force (IFOR). Operation Joint Endeavor was supposed to last for one year, starting in December 1995. Its mandate was to separate the belligerent forces and enforce the ceasefire. Unlike UNPROFOR, IFOR was fully capable of using a wide range of military force to accomplish its mandate: IFOR had attack helicopters, tanks, massed air support, and plenty of infantry. Even more important was that IFOR commanders had the will to use these tools to intimidate the belligerent forces from all sides and thus pressure them into complying with the ceasefire.[45]

Canada decided to contribute several discrete units that would fit into a British division controlling one of the IFOR sectors. Unlike the UNPROFOR contributions, the Canadian IFOR troops were not whole units. For example, the first IFOR rotation (Operation Alliance) consisted of a brigade headquarters, a reconnaissance squadron, an infantry company, an engineer squadron, and a small hospital unit.[46]

IFOR, however, was not without its problems. The mandate made it a tougher and more effective version of UNPROFOR. According to some observers, however, the limit on IFOR's mandate, one year, gave the belligerents time to wait it out and continue fighting once the NATO troops left. In addition IFOR was not designed to address the underlying problem that had ignited the conflict in the first place: ethnic nationalism. There was a great deal of debate over whether or not IFOR should or even could do anything in that regard. In time belligerent forces from all sides challenged IFOR in areas that it was not equipped to deal with: the arrest of indicted war criminals, the question of electoral control, and even road construction.[47]

IFOR essentially dampened the fires that could spread elsewhere in the Balkans but did not extinguish them. Some problems with the IFOR mandate were addressed, and after its one-year term IFOR was replaced with the NATO-led Stabilization Force (SFOR) in 1997. SFOR was supposed to last for eighteen months. Canada sent a similar force, Operation Palladium, to serve in Bosnia, again under British control.[48] SFOR was smaller in numbers than IFOR but still had to cover the same amount of ground. It was also more dependent on the goodwill of the belligerent factions in Bosnia than IFOR had been, though SFOR could still call up significant combat power if necessary. In time SFOR settled into a routine that was not unlike UNFICYP's first ten years in Cyprus back in the 1960s: hours of boredom followed by minutes of sheer terror during weapons cache searches in Serb areas and border confrontations with Croatian forces.[49]

Politically Operation Palladium became Canada's new NATO commitment, in the same way 4 Canadian Mechanized Brigade had been during the long Cold War. In addition to its immediate stabilizing functions on the ground, Palladium demonstrated to NATO that Canada would remain effectively engaged in containing violence that could have detrimental effects on European and North American interests. National prestige was a factor in that the damage caused by attempts at more isolationist Canadian policies in the early 1990s was in many ways under repair by continued Canadian commitment to Balkans operations. These factors were part and parcel of NATO's need to maintain credibility in the region. The UN was demonstrably inadequate as a stabilization tool, and NATO was the solution. If NATO failed in Bosnia, the results would probably be another wave of terror and ethnic violence to rival the 1991–95 bloodshed. NATO credibility in the Balkans and Canada's credibility in NATO were one and the same.

By 1996 western Europe was more stable in many ways than it had been five years earlier. It appeared as though Russia was progressing toward a free-market economy with resultant social and political benefits, fears of a more aggressive Germany were shelved for the time being, and moves were made for Poland, the Czech Republic, and Hungary to join NATO. There was less uncertainty in the region north of the former Yugoslavia. The southern regions, however, still seethed, particularly as Macedonian-Greek relations remained tense, Cyprus remained divided, and the Albanian economy thundered into chaos because of a failed pyramid scheme. Watchful eyes shifted from the Balkans to the Caucasus "tar baby"—Russia's brutal war against Muslim fundamentalist-backed rebels in Chechnya.[50]

It seemed for many that some form of relative and uneasy peace in the Balkans had been secured. Yet the seeds of the Kosovo crisis had been laid long before, and they started to germinate during the 1995 peace process. While all of this was happening, however, the Canadian Army was undergoing a painful process of reorganization to respond to the needs of forward security and to deal with the new variants of post–Cold War conflict. The "decent interval" between the uncertain and violent days of 1995 and 1999 was a busy one for Canada's soldiers.

TWO

Kosovo

Cradle of Conflict, 1389–1999

However effective the leader, he cannot develop a passionate, unified
movement unless powerful dissatisfaction already exists. The moment
must be ripe; the feelings simmering. Of course, an important quality
for a leader is to "ripen" an issue. When a foundation of discontent is
present, a traumatized group can powerfully exert "role suction"—that
is, the group can induce the leader to behave in a paranoid or caretaking
manner. The two postures, paranoia and caretaking, are not in opposition,
for one can take care of a group by protecting it against the enemy. The
swirling currents of paranoid fears, irrational dependency, self-righteous
aggression, and unrealistic expectations of a millennium are
manifest in extreme form.

—ROBERT S. ROBINS, MD, and JERROLD M. POST, MD,
Political Paranoia: The Psychopolitics of Hatred

While the Canadian Army evolved in the 1990s, the situation in the
southern Balkans continued to deteriorate. This chapter examines
the historical problems related to the piece of territory that we now
call Kosovo and the part it played in the collapse of Yugoslavia. As
the situation in the northern Balkans stabilized in 1995, instability
emerged farther south, in Albania and Macedonia, which in turn
affected the status of the Kosovar Albanians. The harsh policies
implemented by the Milošević regime in Kosovo for clearly domestic political purposes prompted a cycle of violence that escalated and
appeared to have no end. These events were the immediate trigger
of the conflict in Kosovo that prompted NATO intervention in 1999.

A word of caution: the players and events surrounding progress toward the air war and the introduction of NATO forces into the region are as numerous as are the ulterior motives for their behavior. The drama that developed over Kosovo was influenced by an intricate series of relationships, many of them submerged deeply in the background and some of them of an arcane economic nature. As we have seen in chapter 1, there are no easy or straightforward explanations to anything that happens in the Balkans.

Be that as it may, Canadian forces were still committed to operate in Kosovo, and they had to do so with this high level of complexity as a backdrop to their actions. The larger Canadian objectives remained the same as they had in previous Balkans interventions: to prevent the increasingly violent situation in Kosovo from spreading and affecting Canadian interests elsewhere in Europe.

Kosovo: Setting the Stage

The Yugoslav province of Kosovo is twice the size of Prince Edward Island (about ten thousand square kilometers) and was populated by approximately 2.1 million people, that is, half the size of the population of Toronto or the same number of people who reside in Arkansas in the United States. The British forces note in their briefings that Kosovo bears an uncanny resemblance to Northern Ireland in terms of size and population numbers.

Any visitor to the province of Kosovo approaching by land is confronted with a rugged natural fortress that is castlelike in many ways. The "outer walls" surround two wide, flat, and fertile valleys as if they were open marketplaces. These walls consist of a ring of mountains: the Massif of Prokletije in the southwest, the Mokra Gora, the Ravna Planina to the north, then the Goljak Mountains and the Crna Gora to the east. The "marketplace" is bisected by two more "battlements": Mount Čičavica from the north and Mount Crnoljevo from the south, which nearly come together like a pincer in the center. There are a few small rivers like the Ibar, but none has the stature of the Rhine or Ottawa; the Rubicon for Kosovo is actually the Šar Planina, a mountain range to the south that borders Macedonia. Although not by any means the Alps or the Rockies, the natural battlements of Kosovo are steep, tree covered, and split by gorges.

In the interior everything is wreathed with a light, damp haze, perhaps from coal emissions given off by the architecturally Stalinesque Obilić power plants. The juxtaposition of green land and the orange clay roofs of the houses in the outlying towns can be jarring to those acclimated to North American suburban color coordination. Phallic minarets on the mosques dominate the Kosovar Albanian areas, competing with weird concrete Communist Party–erected sculptures and solid, squat Orthodox churches, which give every indication that they are built like God's bunkers to last till Armageddon. The urban areas, like Priština, Prizren, and Mitrovica, are different: their edifices were once white concrete, now turned gray. Garbage clogs the streets and the crumbling sidewalks. The corpses of rats and domestic pets are in evidence. Haphazard solid waste clutters the fields: huge rusting bulldozers sans tracks are immovable objects with no irresistible force to challenge them. Kosovo in 1999 resembled those in all other formerly communist eastern European territories: a decayed, polluted, and crumbling industrial dump.

Yet Kosovo was once important to Tito's government. The province was a road and rail hub that linked Belgrade in the north to Albania on the Adriatic, as well as through the Yugoslav province of Macedonia to Greece. The brutalist Kosovo A and Kosovo B power station monstrosities, fueled by the coal extracted from seams near Kosovska Mitrovica (hereafter, simply Mitrovica) and elsewhere, provided power to all adjacent countries and thus hard currency for Belgrade's coffers. Antimony, copper, lead, zinc, nickel, gold, and chrome were extracted from the mines north of Zvečan and Mitrovica. Kosovo was an important link necessary not only to sustain Tito's empire but to keep its southern reaches connected to it. At another level, those connections, coupled with the ruggedness of the territory, also served criminal purposes, particularly for the transshipment of illegal narcotics from Turkey to Albania and beyond.

A traveler may also be struck with a hint of suspicion, a borderline feeling of menace, a tempered, sullen hostility among the residents. And it is the fate of those residents that concerns us here.

Historical Background to 1981

As with other artificial Yugoslav boundary lines that ignored the presence of ethnic groups, the debate over who first occupied Kosovo developed into a cottage industry in the 1980s. Essentially there have been since the beginning of time many back-and-forth migrations of the occupants of the territory we call Kosovo. What can be said for certain is that some of the pagan people in the region converted to Christianity, which then split into the Roman Catholic and Eastern Orthodox variants before the 1300s. When the Muslim-dominated Ottoman Empire seized control, some of those people converted to Islam. One group of people occupying part of the region—the Serbians professing the Orthodox faith— fought the Ottoman invaders in a climactic battle at Kosovo Polje in 1389 and lost. The importance of that battle, at the Field of the Blackbirds, can hardly be overestimated in Serbian culture. As Tim Judah explained in *The Serbs*, "In all of European history it is impossible to find any comparison with the effect of Kosovo on the Serbian national psyche. The battle changed the course of Serbian history. . . . Its real, lasting legacy lay in the myths and legends which came to be woven around it, enabling it to shape the nation's historical and national consciousness."[1]

In essence the Serbian consciousness is entwined with a masochistic death cult in which the Serbian leader Prince Lazar, who died during the battle, became a Christ figure representative of the entire Serbian people. The area we call Kosovo became the front line of the Ottoman Empire in Europe, lying adjacent to a series of small buffer states that sat between Istanbul (then known as Constantinople) and the Holy Roman Empire.[2] Similar events also occurred in the regions we now call Bosnia and Macedonia: both Istanbul and Rome exerted varying degrees of control at different times.[3]

The entire area of Kosovo was thus subjected to control by the Ottomans in Istanbul. Ottoman policies were fairly liberal and sought the development of a multiethnic, multilingual empire, though it was run by those professing the Islamic faith. Social advancement, however, was dependent on conversion, and many took advantage of it. In time groups of people both from the region and from elsewhere settled in Kosovo; some of them were Muslim, some of them were not. Indeed there was a fair amount of collaboration between the Orthodox Christian population and the Ottomans, including the provision of Christian military units for service to the empire.[4]

The region we call Albania was the last Christian barrier between the Ottomans and the Adriatic Sea. The people who occupied that mountainous region were led by Skanderberg, the "Champion of Christ," and were more successful at fighting off the Ottomans than the Orthodox Christian populations elsewhere. Istanbul invaded in 1466, but Skanderberg put up fierce resistance. Although he died in 1467, over the next sixteen years the Ottomans fought bloodily for every inch of land controlled by Skanderberg's followers. The usual Ottoman policies were put into effect in Albania, and some people converted to Islam, while others remained Christian.[5]

Over the next six hundred years the area of Albania, Kosovo, and Macedonia became increasingly Muslim, while the Orthodox Serbian population farther north consolidated its position vis-à-vis the Ottoman Empire. The Orthodox Serbians were permitted more and more autonomy and functioned as a proxy state rather than as a province of the empire. During the sometimes three-way wars between the Catholic Hapsburgs, Orthodox Russia, and the Ottomans, the Serbians "were more inclined to seek Russian protection against the Catholic Austrians, who sought to convert them from the Orthodox to their own faith, rather than against the [Muslim] Turks, who did not seek to make converts."[6]

During the 1800s the Ottoman Empire's internal contradictions and refusal to modernize weakened its position in the world. More and more ethnic groups had more and more educated people, and educated people demanded independence. The Serbians, Croatians, Albanians, and others could by this time not be completely categorized as uneducated serfs. Consequently nationalist movements emerged while at the same time, as mentioned in chapter 1, a federal pan-ethnic Yugoslav movement came into being. The Serbian intellectuals of the day latched onto the 1389 battle in Kosovo and portrayed it as the Orthodox Serb knights fighting valiantly against the Ottoman Islamic hordes; this became the touchstone of their new movement. The nationalist movement was cultlike and spread widely within Serbian communities, and it was then legitimized and supported by authorities of the Orthodox Church.[7]

In Bosnia Catholics revolted against the Ottomans. Istanbul used this revolt to generate an Islamic reawakening in the Balkans in a bid to maintain the Ottoman position. Istanbul orchestrated an effort to keep the Serbian population in its place by inciting the Muslim Albanian population to violence and repression against them. Albanians were encouraged to settle in the Kosovo region as part of this effort. The Serbians invaded Kosovo in 1877, forced out large numbers of Albanians, and seized the Gračanica Monastery, which will figure in the Canadian Kosovo story in later chapters. An Orthodox liturgy was held here to commemorate the events of 1389 and the "liberation" of the sacred ground where the battle was fought. Peć, a sizable city in western Kosovo, effectively became the Canterbury of the Serbian Orthodox Church. These areas and the Mitrovica area were ceded to Serbia when the Ottomans realized that the Russians were backing the Serbs. The remaining Albanians in Kosovo formed secret defense societies, while Istanbul encouraged Albanians in the region to provide financial and military support to them.[8]

In 1878 a peace treaty forced a Serbian withdrawal from Kosovo. At this point there was a lot of activity among Albanian nationalist groups intending to form a single Albania that would include Kosovo and part of Macedonia. Istanbul was unwilling to support this, as the government there did not want to trigger a Russian invasion. Even the Albanians were split: some wanted to retain a close relationship with Istanbul, while others wanted a truly independent and modern nation-state like Great Britain and France had become in Europe. To prevent an Albanian civil war, Istanbul encouraged the factions to take out their frustrations on the Serbian population in areas under their control, which included Kosovo.[9]

By 1900 the "sick man of Europe" called the Ottoman Empire was taken over from within by the Young Turk movement, which sought to modernize and secularize the empire-controlled areas. Albanians supported these men in their efforts. The quid pro quo for this support was the sanctioned use of the Albanian language in Albanian-dominated areas. Albanian nationalist culture flourished, though there tended to be a split between the more liberal Albanians on the Adriatic coast and the conservative Albanians in the Kosovo region. In 1908 the Austro-Hungarian Empire annexed Bosnia, which irritated the Young Turks after stories of the repression of the Muslim population reached Istanbul. The Albanians covertly supported the Bosnian Muslims, and Albanians in Kosovo repressed the Serbian population. Russia then backed the Serbs, who were fired up by nationalist rhetoric and itching to retake Kosovo. The following year Albanian nationalists revolted against the Turks and the Turk-supported Albanians. The Serbs then sent arms to the Albanians to fight the Turks. Kurdish troops from the eastern reaches of the Ottoman Empire were brought in to crush everybody in 1910.[10]

By this time Greece had shrugged off Ottoman control and gained independence. The Greeks tended to support other Orthodox groups, including the Serbs. The Serbs worked out an alliance with the Greeks and the Bulgarians (who hated the Turks in any event) and in 1912 started the First Balkan War. The Serbs entered Kosovo with a vengeance and declared this action another revenge trip for 1389. According to one observer, "The worst [atrocities] were committed not by the regular army but by the paramilitary Četniks. Among them were intellectuals, men of ideas, nationalist zealots. . . . The rest were just thugs, robbers."[11] It was commonplace for Ottoman troops captured by Serbians and their Montenegrin allied forces to have their lips and noses cut off. In 1912 peace was declared. An independent Albania was established by the Austro-Hungarians, and Kosovo was split between it and Serbia. Serbs in the Serb-controlled part again exacted savage revenge on the Albanian inhabitants.[12]

The peace was short-lived, and the Second Balkan War started in 1913. The situation on the ground was so confusing that the exact borders between the entities were not clear. When peace was again established, the Northern Frontier Boundary Commission and its southern counterpart were formed. These commissions consisted of British, French, German, and Dutch officers whose job was to delineate the international borders. No faction was satisfied with the boundary proposals, and various actors interfered with the commission's work.[13] The Albanians continually announced that "we will manure the plains of Kosovo with the bones of Serbs."[14] The boundary commissions were "unable to complete any survey or erect beacons in place where no accurate map or any civil registration or ownership of property existed."[15] Then World War I began when a Serb nationalist shot Archduke Franz Ferdinand in Sarajevo.

Kosovo became a battle zone between Serb and Albanian guerrilla groups. The Austro-Hungarians and Bulgarians occupied Kosovo in their war against Serbia, while the Serbs, with British and Greek support, conducted a fighting withdrawal through Kosovo, which was then occupied and split by the Bulgarians and Austrians. Kosovo Albanians joined Austro-Hungarian forces to repress the Serbians on their side, while the Kosovo Serbians joined the Bulgarians to suppress the Kosovo Albanians on their side.[16]

The Austro-Hungarian and Ottoman Empires were carved up during the World War I endgame. Officers from the Italian-British-French peace commission sought to sort out the boundary issue in 1919–20. The result was a situation in which "the boundaries were intended to weaken or destroy traditional loyalties, but they were in fact gerrymandered so that Serbs would form a majority in six provinces, Croatians in two, Slovenians in one, and the Muslims and Albanians in none."[17]

Yugoslavia emerged out of the ashes and the pan-nationalist proponents won out. In 1921, however, the Albanians in Kosovo petitioned the government for the boundary to be redrawn so that Kosovo could become part of Albania. Serbian groups reacted violently. Kosovo Albanians activated dormant resistance groups, and the Kachak movement emerged to demand integration. The Kachak movement was not a coherent force: it consisted of outlaw groups as well as national liberation activists. It was essentially the prototype of the Kosovo Albanian uçk resistance movement in the 1990s. The Yugoslav government in Belgrade ruthlessly suppressed the Kachaks in the 1920s and 1930s.[18]

During World War II fascist Italy and Nazi Germany invaded Yugoslavia. Germany was particularly interested in controlling the

Mitrovica region of Kosovo because of its rich natural resources and mines. These resources were desperately needed by the Nazi war effort after the Allies blockaded German ports. The Germans established an Albanian protection force for this area, and it promptly took revenge on the local Serbs for anti-Kachak activities ten years earlier. The Italians then organized Albanian units for service with the Italian army: a "Kosovar" unit was formed specifically to crush any opposition in Kosovo. Kosovo was for all intents and purposes part of the Albanian puppet state. In a similar fashion the Nazis established the SS Division Skanderberg, which was used for counterpartisan operations. It was a particularly vicious formation, one that worked closely with the Croatian SS division.[19]

In 1945, with the Axis forces losing on all fronts, Albanian communist forces successfully seized control in Albania. Tito's communist Yugoslav Partisans were triumphant against Axis forces throughout the Balkans (in part due to considerable British and Soviet support). The situation devolved whereby the Albanians were fighting against each other, and the Kosovo Serbs were fighting Kosovo Albanians. Tito backed the Albanian communists, who fought everybody and won. Tito then attacked Albanian nationalists in Kosovo, as well as the remnants of the Albanian SS division, and then integrated Kosovo into Yugoslavia. Between 1944 and 1946 thousands of Kosovo Albanians died at the hands of Tito's Partisan army and secret police. Tito's forces were assisted in their efforts by the Albanian Communist Party–led government.[20]

During the Tito years the Yugoslav government placed Serbs and Montenegrins in dominant Communist Party and security forces positions within the province of Kosovo. The political status of the region was unclear for some time. Tito was from the north, he believed in the "Yugoslav idea," and he was somewhat unbiased on the Kosovo problem. He wanted to counter any threat to Communist Party power, and it just happened that Albanian nationalism was the threat de jour. The best means available to counter that threat was to control the Albanians, using Serbs to keep them in line.[21]

Tito similarly forbade any Kosovo Serbs who had left the region during the war to return there. This in turn irritated Serb nationalists, but they were in no position to do anything about it since their position in the new Yugoslavia would be compromised. This position was rather fragile since in some cases Serb nationalists had collaborated with the Nazis. To alleviate potential problems, Tito then permitted those who had not sided with Germany during the war or who had not been part of the prewar gendarmerie to return to Kosovo.[22]

Albanian schools and the Albanian language, which had been suppressed in the 1920s and 1930s in Kosovo, were slowly allowed back in the 1950s. Since the political and security controllers were Serbo-Croat speakers, legal and government business was conducted in that language. This increased friction among the Albanian intelligentsia. As of 1945, 74 percent of Kosovo Albanians were illiterate.[23]

Despite Tito's commitment to communism, he broke away from Stalin's domination during the 1950s. His communist ally in Albania, Enver Hoxha, remained a Stalinist. Hoxha initiated a subversion campaign against Yugoslavia by covertly supporting anti-Belgrade Kosovo Albanians. In time the other groups in Kosovo, particularly the Serbs, became increasingly suspicious. The security forces, namely the UDB, conducted cordon and search operations on a regular basis. There were show trials, interrogations, and deportations of Kosovo Albanians to other parts of Yugoslavia.[24]

In terms of political representation Serbs made up 27 percent of the population in Kosovo but held 50 percent of the leadership positions. Among factory workers in the barely industrialized region 50 percent were Serb. In industrial terms Tito gave preferential treatment to the Croatians and Slovenes. By the late 1960s Tito had lightened up on state apparatus repression, but he did little to improve Kosovo's economy or provide balanced ethnic representation. A better education system was implemented, however. Still, the Kosovo Albanians produced more children, and thus by the 1980s 90 percent of Kosovo's population was Albanian and only 10 percent were Serb or Montengrin.[25]

It is essential at this point to note the presence of another ethnic group in Kosovo: the Roma, previously referred to as Gypsies. Amounting to possibly 5 percent of the population, the Roma in

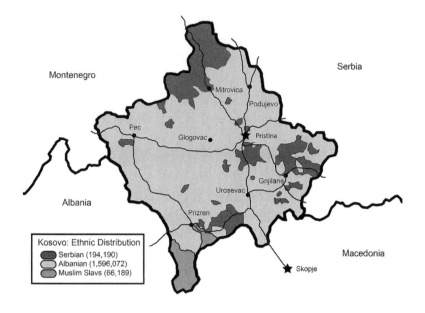

FIG. 2. Ethnic distribution in Kosovo, 1999–2000. Based on 1991 UNHCR data.

Kosovo, like their people elsewhere in the Balkans, had an "allegiance [that] was familial, and at the outer limit tribal but never national."[26] Usually characterized as nomadic, the Roma populations in the former Yugoslavia were for the most part sedentary as a result of long-term Communist Party policies of forced assimilation. Antagonism between the Roma and Albanians goes back to World War II, when Albanian ss units assisted Nazi Germany in deporting the bulk of the Roma population to Auschwitz. Their ethnic distinctiveness, independence, and ability to operate on the fringes of the law was ultimately to place the Roma of Kosovo in an unenviable position between the Kosovar Serbians and Kosovar Albanians after the air war was completed and NATO forces entered the region in 1999, particularly in the Canadian area of operations.[27]

Flashpoint, Crucifix, and Dollar Sign, 1981–1997

One of the first events to contribute to the collapse of Yugoslavia was Slobodan Milošević's 1989 declaration to the Kosovo Serbs that they would not be beaten again. The origins of that speech lay in

1981, when Kosovo Albanian students rioted at the University of Priština over perceived inequalities related to the food served in their residences. Demonstrations spread like wildfire and prompted work stoppages. Yugoslav security forces moved in, and in days a thousand people were dead and more than four thousand arrested. Investigations by Belgrade authorities determined that the party officers in Kosovo were incompetent and responsible for a dysfunctional economy. The fact that the poor economy in Kosovo was a symptom of larger problems with Yugoslavia's communist system could not, naturally, be admitted by anyone involved.[28]

Among some Kosovo Albanians the new repression generated renewed interest in uniting with Albania. Serbian nationalists, once they got wind of the happenings in Kosovo, used the situation to further their own position. In 1986 a group of leading Serbian intellectuals and academics in Belgrade concocted a memo that established the basis for the new Serbian nationalism. In their view the creation of Yugoslavia in the 1920s and its maintenance by Tito until his death in 1980 was a conspiracy to repress the Serbian people. Croatians, Slovenes, and now the Kosovo Albanians were behind that conspiracy. The Kosovo Albanians, they stated, wanted "genocide." For the authors of the memo, genocide in part meant control over the "holy" portions of Kosovo that related to the 1389 battle.[29]

Over the next three years Slobodan Milošević took control of the Serbian nationalist movement. Milošević's parents were from Montenegro, though he had been brought up in a small town outside of Belgrade toward the end of World War II. His main hero was Tito, but instead of leading partisans Milošević became a lawyer. Ivan Stambolić, the prime Communist Party leader in Serbia, was an important mentor who ensured that Milošević became the president of Serbia without an election. In time Milošević sought to supplant Stambolić's charismatic hold in Belgrade. The opportunity presented itself when Stambolić sent Milošević to Kosovo to reassure the Kosovo Serb population after the 1987 riots. Milošević saw a nationalistic fervor in the crowd. If it could be connected to the influence that the academics had in Belgrade, such a movement could become a potent political force. Milošević orchestrated Stambolić's demise as party chief, and he then rose to power on a wave of Serb nationalism. By harnessing this renewed Serbian nationalism, Milošević could become the new Tito, except this time the Serbs would dominate the structure. Control of the "holy" sites in Kosovo was the trigger.[30]

An important event in this effort occurred in 1990. The Serbian parliament agreed to and implemented a six-point pogrom that included the following:

1. Encouraging Serb resettlement of Kosovo

2. Removing Albanians from government and industry

3. Purging the Kosovo police forces of Albanians

4. Coercing Albanian professionals to leave their jobs

5. Eliminating Albanian-language media and publishing

6. Eliminating Albanian schools and driving Albanians out of universities[31]

These measures were ruthlessly implemented. Tens of thousands were driven into unemployment.

Between 1989 and 1992 Milošević consolidated power in Belgrade, which remained the capital of "Greater" Serbia once Yugoslavia ceased to be. One consequence of the wars in Croatia and Bosnia was the imposition of international sanctions, which had detrimental effects on how Serbia was governed. Milošević and his supporters walked a fine tightrope in this game. As in any dictatorship, the next dictator is always waiting in the wings once the normal civilized structures such as the judicial and legislative systems are corrupted in a totalitarian state and unable to deflect the use of force. To assure control, Milošević permitted a number of small and weak opposition parties and used his secret police forces against them selectively, to keep them alive but off balance. He therefore gave the appearance of a representative state that could keep the masses quiet.[32]

The Orthodox Church was another component. Though split over their support for Milošević, the fact that ethnic Serbs were under attack elsewhere in the former Yugoslavia and the fact that their "holy sites" in Kosovo were threatened led the church to go along with the Milošević program.[33]

The only other possible internal threat facing Milošević was his own people, burdened as they were by economic sanctions. The Serbian population could revolt against Milošević if the economy reached a state in which the basics were unavailable. Milošević co-opted the families of those who could provide basic goods and services by building on existing communist-era patronage and nepotism. This included organized crime figures. These men were needed because of their expertise in the use of covert means to break the sanctions placed on Serbia, and they consequently became part of the power structure, thus corrupting it further. This amounted to "official crime," and it had essentially undermined the economic system by 1999.[34]

Prior to the imposition of peace in Bosnia after the Dayton Accords of 1995, Serbia developed a series of other economic relationships that overlapped with the smuggling enterprises. The Greek government was sympathetic to the Serbs for historical and religious reasons. Attempts were made to thwart NATO interceptions of smuggling vessels in the Adriatic (attempts that were unsuccessful in part due to Canadian naval ships and maritime patrol aircraft operating off Montenegro). Greek companies also invested heavily in Serbia's telecommunications and media systems, which in turn permitted Milošević to use modern propaganda techniques to attack his enemies at home and abroad.[35]

In addition to sanctions-busting with covert loans to Serbia amounting to $100 million, Greek companies were also involved in exchanging supplies and equipment for Serbian natural resources such as chrome and zinc. One of the mines in question, the Trepča mine, is located in northern Kosovo. The Trepča mine and its associated sites in Kosovo were critical to the economic survival of internationally isolated Serbia. The health of Serbia's economy was therefore based in large part on control over Kosovo and thus directly related to Milošević's ability to maintain power.[36] The Greeks were not the only ones involved in the Serbian mining business: at least one French consortium had a stake in the flow of metals from Kosovo. These factors would become important for the Canadian contingent in KFOR once it started operating in that region in 1999.

Throughout the 1990s Milošević's power preservation tactics continued to include agitating the Serbian population to target the Kosovo Albanians with periodic riots and low-level violence. This strategy gave the Serbian population a useful scapegoat for the poor economic situation.[37] Unfortunately for the Serbs, other Albanians outside their control had a stake in Kosovo too, and this factor lay behind the behavior of the Kosovo Albanian population.

Trouble in the Neighborhood: The Southern Balkans, 1990–1997

The Albanian response to the Serbian parliament's systematic repression of that ethnic group was the formation of the LDK, a political party led by Ibrahim Rugova. Rugova believed that passive resistance was the best way to go, as there was no military option available once Serb security forces had confiscated the Territorial Defense Forces' weapons from the depots. Rugova and others favored a Sinn Fein–like approach to the situation: they would beat the Serbian government by ignoring it and forming a virtual government. This virtual government declared independence in 1991. The objective was to wait out the Serbs until they collapsed under their own weight. This might take years, but the intellectuals of the Elida Café Group determined that this was a morally correct course of action. The LDK won 76 percent of the votes in the secret process; there were other, smaller parties, but the covert nature of the situation attenuated their efforts and it was not clear how much legitimacy the LDK actually had with the Kosovo Albanian population at large. In any event Rugova was no saint: his main backer was Bujar Bukoshi, the LDK "finance minister," who handled collections from the Albanian diaspora and had significant connections in Turkey.[38]

The shadow government, however, needed money. There was the semblance of a government in exile located in Switzerland and Germany whose purpose was to run the parallel economy. Five hundred thousand Kosovar Albanians worked throughout Europe as *Gastarbeiter* (guest workers). Money was continuously collected from these people and was to be used to support the covert edu-

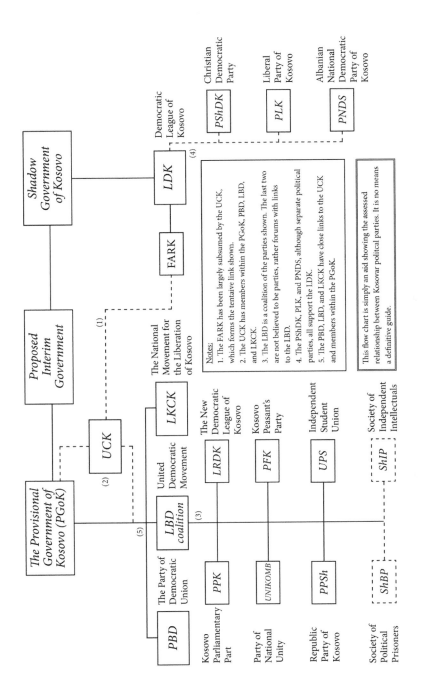

FIG. 3. Kosovar Albanian political relationships.
Author's collection, from 1 **PPCLI**.

cational and medical systems. The underground Kosovo Albanian government had the means to carry out its policies, which were ultimately directed toward supplanting the existing Serbian-dominated governmental structure in Kosovo. As it did so, legitimacy was transferred to the underground government from the government in Belgrade. This was a rather sophisticated and time-proven insurgency strategy dating back to the Irish attempts to form an independent state during and after World War I and modified in successive insurgencies throughout the twentieth century.[39]

What of military policy? Kosovo Albanians trapped in Croatia and Bosnia during the collapse of the Yugoslav army had served with Croatian and Bosnian Muslim units. These men, a number of whom committed war crimes as serious as any committed by Serb paramilitaries, were called back to Kosovo late in 1994–95. Bosnian and Croatian military leaders hoped that the Kosovo Albanians would develop an armed insurgency that would in turn draw off Serbian military resources and thus assist the Croatian and Bosnian military efforts. It is possible that the appointment of Agim Çeku (a major general with the Croatian army) as UÇK chief of the General Staff was related to this planning. This "second front" did not happen, in part due to the Dayton Accords in 1995 and in part due to Rugova's decision to use passive resistance.[40]

The passive resistance policy soon collapsed for a number of reasons. The first of these was the Kosovo Albanian perception that the Dayton Accords did not go far enough and that Kosovo Albanians had been sold out by the West. The reality, however, was that the Dayton deal was specifically designed to address the problems in Bosnia and was not supposed to be a panacea for all of the problems in the Balkans.[41]

The Kosovar Albanians, who were not as unified as they appeared, developed splinter groups that opposed the LDK's passive policy. Some of these splinter groups broke off along family and clan lines, while some groups, like the LKCK, were ideologically opposed to the LDK and wanted an independent, communist Kosovo. Yet another overlap was the presence of organized crime. Some of these groups operated lucrative narcotics-smuggling enterprises that operated in parallel to the covert, "legitimate"

Kosovo Albanian nonmilitary aid effort. Kosovo's central location and its geography facilitated the movement of heroin from Turkey to Albania. From Albania, smugglers moved Turkish heroin and Albanian-grown cannabis to ports in Italy (which hosts about one hundred thousand guest workers) and then through the Albanian diaspora to communities in Switzerland (two hundred thousand Albanian expats), Germany (four hundred thousand), and beyond (e.g., North America, with a half million). In addition to trafficking in drugs, Albanian organized crime was involved in illegal immigration and also specialized in stolen cars. Like the Italian Mafia of North American lore, the Albanian mafia was family or clan based. Some personalities moved seamlessly in and out of criminal, nationalist, and family circles.[42]

Even more sinister were the links some Kosovar Albanians developed with organized crime groups based in Lebanon. Initially this was related to drug-smuggling sources (like the Bekaa Valley) and means of supply, but these links could not be kept separate from the activities of Iranian-backed terrorist movements like Hezbollah, which were also involved in such activity. The lure of weapons training proved too great for some young Kosovar Albanians, and a number made their way to Taliban-dominated Afghanistan to train with the al Qaeda terror network run by Osama bin Laden. These men would later return to Kosovo, Macedonia, and Albania and join the nascent Kosovar Albanian guerrilla groups.[43]

Another reason for the folding up of the passive resistance policy was the economic crisis and imminent collapse of Albania. Communist rule in Albania continued after the despotic Enver Hoxha died in 1985. Yugoslavia remained a close trading partner, but the UN sanctions imposed on Serbia after the Bosnian war began produced another situation in which black market and smuggling-based economic pressures undermined the Albanian government. To make matters worse, Greece cut off economic relations with Albania because Albania supported Macedonia's independence. In 1992 Greece increased its troop strength on the Albanian border. This generated fears of a Greek invasion, which Albania could not have withstood.[44]

Once the communists lost power, Albania underwent a religious revival involving all three faiths: Islam, Catholicism, and Orthodox. This revival was not as virulent as it was elsewhere in the Balkans: there was more religious tolerance in Albania. A cultural revival accompanied the religious revival, which unfortunately brought back the blood feud, a less than savory Albanian tradition.[45]

As the Albanian economy screamed when the Ponzi pyramid scam on which it was based collapsed in 1997, Kosovo Albanians had more and more influence on the remnants of Albanian politics. Albanian nationalist groups in Albania wanted unification with Kosovo, though the motives of those pushing such a scheme were in question. It was clear that a lot of money could be made selling Albania's armory to the Kosovo Albanians for their fight against the Serbs. Similarly the more romantic notions that some Kosovar Albanians had for Albania were shattered by the avarice generated by the economic collapse, which in turn produced a certain amount of economic and political cynicism on their part. Indeed some Kosovar Albanians looked down on Albanians because of their inability to get their house in order, which may be a reflection of the 1950s split between Albania and Yugoslavia.[46]

The situation affected NATO members, particularly Italy. A mass migration of economic refugees from Albania began in 1994 and threatened detrimental effects on not only the Italian economy but Europe's as a whole. Illegal immigration rings flourished, and the NATO maritime interdiction force in the Adriatic, which was enforcing sanctions against Serbia, was drawn into deterring human smuggling. Another complicating factor was the possibility of an Albanian civil war fought on political grounds as opposed to ethnoreligious ones.[47]

To forestall Albania's collapse, NATO and the WEU held discussions in early 1997 about intervening with some form of stabilization force. The members of both organizations could not come to an agreement, so Italy took the lead, got UN support, and executed Operation Alba in April 1997. Op Alba was an eleven-nation, six-thousand-member multinational force that deployed right before national elections were held. The force succeeded in backing up the Albanian security forces, providing medical aid, and ensuring that humanitarian relief could be delivered amid the chaotic conditions.[48]

Stability was also restored by the possibly rigged reelection of Sali Berisha, who, on American, German, and Italian urging, downplayed pan-Albanianism: the carrot in this case was American aid. The Americans' ulterior motive was to establish a base for reconnaissance flights over the Balkans. The problem with Berisha was that he used the same unpalatable and repressive methods as his predecessors.[49]

None of this boded well for Kosovar Albanian attempts to organize themselves into the semblance of a country. Meanwhile Milošević was having trouble keeping his only ally, Montenegro, in line. A political rival, Milo Djukanović, appeared to threaten Slobodan Milošević's precarious existence. Djukanović attempted to make Montenegro function as an offshore banking haven to attract investors while at the same time he facilitated black market activity and smuggling throughout the region. There was a small Albanian population in Montenegro that had good relations with his regime, but now Milošević used that against Djukanović in the political arena while he attempted to get his own man into a position of power. Djukanović then announced that Milošević had instigated problems in Montenegro by pushing Kosovar Albanian refugees onto his turf. The situation escalated to the point where NATO authorities considered militarily assisting Montenegro if Milošević's forces intervened. It should come as no surprise that Montenegro and Albania were not on the best of terms during this period.[50]

Another complicating factor was the disjointed American approach to the situation, particularly with regard to the emergent Ushtria Çlirimtare e Kosovës, or UÇK, known in the West as the Kosovo Liberation Army (KLA). In some ways the UÇK could trace its lineage back to a small terrorist faction called the MNLK, a Marxist Albanian nationalist group formed in 1978. It would be a mistake, however, to assume that in the mid-1990s the UÇK was some form of coherent successor organization. The fragmented nature of underground Kosovo Albanian politics was mirrored within the guerrilla organizations as well. At this time there was probably no centralized control over UÇK cells. The links between UÇK groups and the overseas fundraising and organized crime groups constitute a web of intrigue so intricate that it taxed the resources of some Western intelligence agencies.[51]

In any event, an American State Department spokesperson announced that the UÇK was a terrorist organization. This reflected a severe split within the American foreign policy community as to the utility of what some saw as a group with connections to anti-American terrorist groups in Lebanon and elsewhere that were supported by Iran. It is possible that Milošević saw this as a sign the United States would not intervene. The Serbian Resistance Movement (SRM) was formed by Kosovar Serbs with official backing from Belgrade. Efforts to counter Kosovar Albanian nationalism were stepped up in 1997. The SRM and other groups like it had a large number of Krajina Serbs who were ethnically cleansed by Croatia in 1995 and resettled by Belgrade in the Mitrovica region. They proved to be the most militant of the Kosovar Serbian population, which was perfectly understandable since they were not going to allow themselves to be ethnically cleansed a second time.[52]

Belgrade's continuing campaign against the Kosovar Albanians then activated further unrest, this time in Macedonia. The situation in that country remained relatively stable with the introduction of UNPREDEP (which included American and Canadian troops) in 1993. There was an Albanian party in the Macedonian government. Albanian nationalists from Kosovo, however, started agitation in the ethnic Albanian towns in western Macedonia. Suddenly there were demands to fly the Albanian flag in a town called Gostivar, and the Macedonian government sent in tanks as a show of force. The mayor of Gostivar was subsequently sentenced to fourteen years in jail. Unlike his counterparts in other former Yugoslav regions, Macedonian president Kiro Gligorov was able to maintain intercommunal peace, albeit with significant Western investment and support. This stability was now endangered in the early months of 1998.[53] To make matters worse, China eventually vetoed further funding and mandate extensions for UNPREDEP in Macedonia. UNPREDEP had to disband, which meant that there was no international "trip wire" force deterring incursions against Macedonia from all sides.[54]

Tension then developed between Macedonia and Greece. The Greeks viewed the use of "Macedonia" as a country name by a group of non-Greek peoples to be an affront to Greek history and sovereignty. As one observer noted, "The territory of the Macedonian state that had become independent in 1991 represents nothing more than a historical accident. . . . It is, like Bosnia, an artificial creation of history, a cartographic relic of the Treaty of Bucharest, possessing neither an ethnic homogeneity, nor a population that uniformly recognizes the validity of the state. And like Bosnia this confusing heterogeneity is pushing the region towards war."[55]

2

CRISIS IN KOSOVO

THREE

Clash of the Damned

UÇKs and MUPs in the Land of Kos, 1998

"Blood calls for blood," he says. "According to the *Code of Leke Dukagjini*
(who lived in the 15th century), land problems could also be solved by
payment in gold or by changing boundaries, but people seldom had
money and they did have guns."

—LINDA WHITE et al., *Albania* (1995)

Consider the old doctrine of "an eye for and eye, and a tooth for a tooth."
In relations with individuals, that doctrine is now generally regarded . . .
as primitive and barbarous. So it is from the viewpoint of *higher* moral
standards. But it is well not to forget that there are also *lower* levels, more
primitive and more barbarous than that doctrine of equivalents. . . .
The doctrine that only a limited use of force, proportionate to the
circumstances and strictly necessary to accomplish specific objectives,
can be justified as self-defence is, I think, inherent in the
principles of natural law.

—LESTER B. PEARSON, *Democracy in World Politics* (1955)

Developments, January–August 1998

The full catalog of UÇK guerrilla activity from 1996 to 1999 is too
lengthy for examination here.[1] The UÇK groups grew bolder in
the scope and intensity of their activities. By early 1998 the groups
had changed tactics and targeted economic facilities like the huge
Belaćevac coal mine. Belaćevac is important since it is adjacent
to the main power stations in Kosovo. These facilities also supply
power to grids outside the province, including in Greece, Mace-

donia, and Albania. The vital Trepča mine in the north was next. Serbian forces responded with the deployment of more and more interior ministry police forces (Ministarstvo Unutrašnjih Poslova, or MUPs). Five days later the mines were retaken by force. Rhetoric from Belgrade's propaganda mills lashed out at Macedonia for supporting UÇK operations and "refusing" to crack down on Albanian groups northwest of Skopje: this was clearly an inversion of reality.[2]

Notably Milošević sent in the infamous paramilitary leader known as Arkan and his Tiger paramilitary group to operate against the UÇK. Arkan was Belgrade's point man in the initial ethnic cleansing operations on the Serbia-Bosnia border in early 1992, and his ruthless unit operated throughout Bosnia later on. Arkan was also a black marketeering warlord who had significant economic (read: smuggling) interests in Kosovo. The Tiger deployment was deliberately made public, which sent a titter throughout the Western press corps: was this Belgrade's signal that Kosovo could become the next Bosnia?[3]

The first notable Serbian offensive operation was conducted in the Drenica Valley in late February and early March 1998. Small-scale UÇK ambushes directed against local police generated combined responses from Belgrade's plethora of security forces.[4] A digression is important here given the confusing alphabet soup of Yugoslav security force designators. Belgrade's forces in Kosovo consisted of the following:

- VJ (Vojska Jugoslavije, or Yugoslav Army), regular military forces, with the Border Guards (BG) equipped with APCs and heavy weapons as a separate organization under army control
- MUP (Ministarstvo Unutrašnjih Poslova), interior police, paramilitary in structure, which had several suborganizations: the PJP, the SAJ, the SUP/OUP and the SDB:
  - PJP (Posebne Jedinice Policije), special police units equipped with heavy weapons
  - SAJ (Specijalna Antiteroristicka Jedinica), special antiterrorist police, highly mobile and equipped with helicopters

- ○ SUP/OUP (Sekretariat Unutrašnjih Poslova and Odeljenje Unutrašnjih Poslova), ordinary police units at the regional and precinct levels
- ○ SDB (State Security Service), essentially Belgrade's KGB-type secret police, which also had a special operations unit called the JSO (Jedinice za Specijalne Operacije) (aka Frenki's Boys, named after the JSO's creator, Franko Simatović)

- Paramilitaries (essentially under command of the MUP):
  - ○ Arkan's Tigers (based on a football supporter organization)
  - ○ White Eagles
  - ○ Republika Srpska Delta Force
  - ○ Pitbull Terriers
  - ○ Tulips
  - ○ Hawks
  - ○ Black Star
  - ○ Black Hand

The role of the paramilitary groups appears to have been, based on the Bosnian experience, a means to empty Belgrade's rather full jails and create "legions of the doomed" to handle plausibly deniable dirty work like ethnic cleansing. Many overlapped with organized crime groups and carried out the systematic looting of Kosovar Albanian areas. Note that all of these organizations had reservist units, drawn from local populations, that were noted for their lack of professional behavior.[5] There were also, according to some reports, a number of Roma groups that assisted the paramilitary units in their activities.[6]

The UÇK organization, though not as diverse or well equipped, continually evolved under fire throughout 1998. Divided into some seven operational zones, the UÇK maintained active guerrilla forces at the village level, with each force consisting of about ten men, with a roving hundred-man companylike structure of a more conventional nature commanded by the zonal leadership. At the "theater" level the UÇK had a battalion-sized (seven hundred to eight hundred men) mobile force that could be employed in any operational zone as necessary, plus the "Atlantic Brigade," which was made up of ethnic Albanians from Canada, the United States, and the United Kingdom who had come to Kosovo to fight. Some operational zones extended into Macedonian and Albanian territory, as well as the Preševo Valley, the ethnically Albanian–dominated portion of Serbia to the east of Kosovo. There was also a village militia system that was more defensive in orientation and essentially consisted of lightly equipped military-age men. Estimates as to the size of the UÇK suggest that there were between three thousand and five thousand active members, depending on the time of year. As a guerrilla organization, the UÇK was dependent on a supporting network of some twenty thousand to forty thousand civilians for logistics, shelter, and intelligence. It is critical to understand that the UÇK was family and clan based, loosely commanded, and extremely decentralized, particularly in its early period.[7]

The Drenica operations were carried out by the MUP and VJ without restraint or discrimination. Three villages in the Drenica Valley suspected of harboring UÇK forces were surrounded by VJ mechanized troops, while MUP units conducted extremely violent house-to-house clearance tasks. Some eighty-three people were killed, including the entire family (twenty persons) of a politically prominent Kosovar Albanian, Adem Jashari. These events were relayed by European Community Monitor Mission observers to their respective governments.[8] Meanwhile analysts in the CIA warned of escalating violence in the region throughout 1998 that would result from Belgrade's crackdown in Kosovo.[9]

The elimination of the Jashari family produced unexpected effects: hundreds flocked to the UÇK, and guerrilla operations dramatically increased. More and more bellicose propaganda from Belgrade implicated Albania and Macedonia in rhetoric that seriously concerned Pres. Kiro Gligorov in Skopje. Discussions between Gligorov and Gen. Wesley Clark, NATO's Supreme Allied Commander Europe (SACEUR), during his visit to UNPREDEP refocused Clark's attention on the region. Clark, a man who had previous

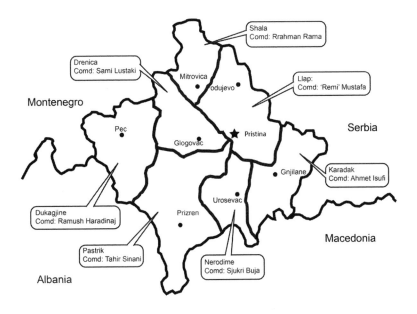

FIG. 4. The K V M Fusion Center's understanding of what ground was held by the UÇK as of 1 July 1999. Based on K V M data.

personal experience dealing with Milošević, determined that "we can't let this get out of hand."[10]

In March 1998 the Albanian government sent a formal request to NATO to ask for assistance in guaranteeing its borders. These requests were initially rebuffed: some NATO leaders thought that the UN or OSCE should carry out that mission, though various means of assisting the Albanian military to help itself were seriously explored. The reluctance of some NATO members to get involved may have been connected to revelations that Iran was supporting the Kosovo Albanians through intermediaries in Albania.[11] In any event the UN passed a vaguely worded Security Council resolution, UNSCR 1160(1998), which implied that Chapter VII military operations for humanitarian purposes might be acceptable in the region, with the OSCE functioning as the lead international organization.

The imprecision in the wording of the UN resolution and the

UN's poor track record in using coercion in the Balkans, combined with increasingly effective UÇK guerrilla operations, prompted another major security operation by the MUP and VJ in May 1998. This time the operations expanded to cover the entire province and were not limited to the Drenica Valley: some operations were conducted in border areas and even into Albania. During the course of these operations an estimated fifteen thousand Kosovar Albanians fled to Albania, while another thirty thousand decamped for Macedonia.[12] The Albanian chief of defense was forced to consult with Clark under the auspices of the Partnership for Peace program, which allowed for expanded bilateral talks between Albania and NATO. NATO then reconsidered sending a thirty-thousand-member armed "Albanian Force" (AFOR) to prevent violence in Kosovo from spilling over into the now more stable Albania. There were problem areas, however. If, for example, Belgrade decided to attack UÇK sympathizers or support areas in Albania, what would NATO troops do about it? Would they fight? Some elements within the Canadian government backed a UN solution like UNPREDEP instead of establishing AFOR, but the obstacles to it were gigantic, particularly in UN circles.[13]

Then there was the issue of Bosnia, which is highly nuanced and cannot be divorced from any explanation regarding NATO's desire to prevent spillover violence in the southern Balkans. Throughout 1998 peace in Bosnia was maintained by the NATO-led Stabilization Force (SFOR). Recall that NATO was brought in to stabilize the region when the UN force, UNPROFOR, lost its credibility and proved incapable of containing the violence to acceptable levels. From 1991 to 1995 the European and North American members of the international community endured massive media-driven condemnation for not performing effectively in Somalia, for not preventing the Rwandan massacres, or, more particularly, not preventing the Srebrenica massacre of seven thousand people in Bosnia in 1995.[14] Criticism of the ineffective UN-NATO command and control relationship in Bosnia particularly stung in NATO circles, since air strikes might have deterred Bosnian Serb forces from taking Srebrenica and thus could have averted the massacre.[15]

CLASH OF THE DAMNED

Consequently NATO forces were better employed in 1995, when they supported the UN in Bosnia (Operation Deliberate Force), which was the primary factor in bringing the belligerents to the negotiating table in Dayton, Ohio. The NATO-led IFOR and successor SFOR were products of the Dayton Accords. These stabilization operations replaced the UN forces and used much more robust and coercive methods to maintain the peace between the Bosnian belligerents. The perception was essentially that NATO had succeeded in closing down the Bosnian slaughterhouse while the UN and European organizations, such as the WEU and OSCE, had failed to do so. NATO was the last resort for the international community in Bosnia. There could be no other organization or means to prevent further war in that country.[16]

It was understood by those nations contributing troops to IFOR and SFOR that the military forces were deployed to stabilize the situation as a precondition for seeking a long-term solution, which was to be carried out by other agencies in coordination with NATO. The forces were not solutions unto themselves, yet media and academic commentators continued to criticize and portray them in such a way. This generated heightened expectations, perhaps unrealistic ones, of what the force was capable of achieving.[17]

At the same time, belligerent elements in Bosnia, including Bosnian Serbs supported by Belgrade, conducted an elaborate campaign throughout 1998 to undermine SFOR's credibility. This move was a precursor to the creation of an extremist independent Republika Srpska (RS), which would effectively lay the groundwork for another Bosnian war. Two factions vied for power, one portrayed as extremist and the other moderate, though they varied merely in their degree of extremism. For example, there was a pattern of noncompliance with the Dayton Agreement by the Police Anti-Terrorism Brigade (another special police unit), the rather virulent SRT (a Serbian media outlet), a number of RS armored units that regularly deviated from established exercise parameters, and elements of the Federal Rapid Reaction Brigade, which conducted unauthorized movements.[18]

In another case the UN Office of the High Representative declared the extremist deputy prime minister of Serbia, Vojislav

Šešelj, persona non grata for "meddling in Bosnian politics"; SFOR forces escorted him out of the country.[19] There also remained the thorny problem of the Brčko salient, a critical piece of terrain where the Bosnian Serb population interfered with the return of non-Serb residents.

By 1998 SFOR appeared to be failing and was increasingly portrayed by belligerent propaganda as a Western imposition on the population. In a land where perception quickly becomes reality these developments were dangerous for all concerned. SFOR conducted Exercise Dynamic Response from March to April, ostensibly to "test the capability of SFOR to deploy strategic reserve forces into Bosnia-Hercegovina."[20] This two-thousand-person exercise, which included three marine units (American, Italian, and Dutch) and a Polish airborne battalion, had clear signaling overtones.[21] In another operation SFOR deployed forces to the FRY-Bosnia border to prevent the illegal transfer of weapons from RS-controlled storage sites to the FRY, where it was feared they would be used by Serb paramilitary forces in Kosovo.[22] The influx of ten thousand Kosovar refugees strained resources, created friction among the Bosnian entities, and greatly concerned humanitarian organizations already contending with the Bosnian problem.[23]

The importance of NATO's presence in Bosnia went beyond the explicit stabilizing functions, however. Western leaders and diplomats such as Javier Solana, Richard Holbrooke, and Robin Cook believed that Western success in Bosnia was necessary to demonstrate that democratization worked in eastern Europe in the post-communist, post–Cold War world.[24] If the West failed in Bosnia, the prospects for continued stability and peace throughout eastern Europe could be endangered, along with NATO expansion. The European Union integration process could also be paralyzed by further conflict, with obvious detrimental economic effects on members and potential members.

For the Americans NATO participation was critical to demonstrate continued U.S. engagement in Europe and to indicate that NATO was an indispensable instrument of American policy. Any pullout from Bosnia undermined both principles and permitted too much French or even German control, which could in turn could antagonize an already wounded and seething Russia. Despite the rhetoric of cooperation throughout the 1990s NATO was still needed as a hedge against renewed aggressive Russian behavior if the Far Right perhaps took control in Moscow, either by coup or election.[25]

One cannot discount entirely the role of personality and pride in decision-making. For example, a NATO collapse in Bosnia would call into question Richard Holbrooke's Dayton triumph. For Madeleine Albright, the U.S. secretary of state, a NATO collapse would disprove her assertions that U.S. military force could be used effectively to further a humanitarian agenda. For Canada's Lloyd Axworthy, a NATO failure in the Balkans would call into question his "soft power" and "human security" agendas. Personal credibility was not necessarily the driving force for NATO intervention, but it certainly was a contributing factor.

Western credibility was therefore at stake when the Kosovo situation escalated in 1998. A NATO failure in the southern Balkans had the potential to affect the gains that had been made in Bosnia. It is vital to understand that the situation was not as politically or morally clear-cut as those who were critical of NATO's actions would have us believe.[26] The Western members of the international community were in a real quandary. To maintain the relative peace in the region, particularly in Bosnia and Eastern Slavonia, the West needed to retain credible means of sending a message not only to Milošević in Belgrade but to Serbian leaders in Bosnia. The difficult terrain in each part of the former Yugoslavia and vacillations by the Italian government meant that secure base areas for the launching of any military activity against belligerents in Bosnia or Serbia were in short and unpredictable supply. Similarly, if NATO was asked to protect Macedonia or Albania, secure port and base infrastructure was an absolute prerequisite.

The strategic effects of spillover violence in the region and a consequent loss of Western credibility could resonate in important lands far away from the Balkans. It was not inconceivable that increased Greek-Turkish tensions, including the forty-year-old problem of Cyprus, which nearly destroyed NATO in 1964 and 1974, could be brought out of suspended animation like some horrible Frankenstein's monster.[27] The Greeks reestablished a religious-cultural affinity and economic ties with Milošević's Orthodox Serbia, which was perceived to be threatened by Islam, the dominant religion of their long-term antagonists, the Turks. There were also the economic links being forged between Belgrade and Athens, which could be threatened by a conflict in the region. Turkey, for its part, did not want to be physically isolated from Europe and the two million expatriate Turks residing there, something that would result from a Balkans-wide war. Such a situation could also encourage Turkey's adversaries in the Middle East to make moves at its expense.[28]

One potential effect of a Greco-Turkish split could have been a degradation in containment efforts directed against Saddam Hussein's Iraq and a decreased ability to deter threats to Turkey, from Iraq and those emanating from instability in the Caucasus.[29] Turkish participation was critical to containing Iraq, and the French had recently delivered a blow to that project by withdrawing from the no-fly zone enforcement operations Northern Watch and Southern Watch. A lot of Anglo-American prestige was riding on this controversial decade-long effort. A loss of credibility over NATO's handling of the Milošević regime could have repercussions in Baghdad. Saddam Hussein might even resort to conducting activity detrimental to Western interests in the Persian Gulf region if he believed he could get away with it. Indeed the Hussein regime continued to aggressively test Western resolve over the United Nations Special Commission inspectors seeking out weapons of mass destruction in Iraq throughout this period.[30]

NATO's immediate objective therefore was to stabilize Albania and Macedonia. This approach was not without complications. There were two means: either sit back and allow Belgrade to beat up on and contain the UÇK, which might spark violence among the Albanian communities in Macedonia and Albania, or to pressure both Milošević and the Kosovar Albanians to moderate and deal. These courses of action presented NATO with a dilemma.

The UÇK groups had questionable legitimacy in the eyes of the West: they used drug money, engaged in organized criminal activity, had unsavory connections with Middle Eastern terrorists, and were possibly led by strongmen as unstable as their Serbian ene-mies. The UÇK groups were, however, a fact of life on the ground and could not be ignored. NATO had to find a means to support them but not overly support them: Kosovo was not a sovereign state under international law and was part of Serbia. NATO also needed congruence with its other Balkans stabilization activities: if consistency was ignored in Kosovo, it could blow the Bosnian peace sky high. On the other hand the Serbs could not be allowed to conduct ethnic cleansing operations against an ethnic minority, particularly after the events in Bosnia and Croatia in the early 1990s. It would be even more difficult to not intervene if the situ-ation was cast in the context of the events in Rwanda during 1994 or Srebrenica in 1995.

Yet "public opinion" (i.e., media commentators and cultural elites) in NATO countries would probably not support an all-out war aimed at crushing Milošević and Serbia or even a more lim-ited one aimed at "liberating" Kosovo on behalf of the Kosovo Albanians, which had a morally questionable leadership from a Western philosophical perspective and, as intelligence agencies revealed, had connections with anti-American terrorist groups. Worse, the "CNN factor," which forced NATO's hand in Bosnia and the West's hand in Somalia, might push NATO members into proceeding into the Kosovo quagmire without thinking about the long-term effects of an intervention on the region. There was also the question of obtaining UN legitimacy for offensive NATO oper-ations in the region. Would this be forthcoming?

The reality of the situation was that the Kosovo Serbians, their supporters in Belgrade led by Milošević, Kosovar Albanians, and Albanian nationalists wanted a decisive fight. The UÇK groups knew they could not succeed without outside help and thus pres-sured for NATO intervention, which was assisted by the CNN effect. The situation was complicated by the fact that there were serious splits within the UÇK and their political organizations. This was the situation as it stood in the summer of 1998, with Bal-kans observers warning that "the permanent prevention of a new Balkan war remains contingent upon a long-term political solu-tion to the Kosovo crisis."[31]

There was therefore a moral imperative that NATO first demonstrate concern for the situation and explore methods short of war. A SHAPE planning conference in May 1998, which served as the genesis of Canada's eventual involvement with land forces in Kosovo, came up with several options. These included a force to take control of Albania, a peacekeeping force for Kosovo, a no-fly zone directed against the Milošević regime, and a series of exercises to signal NATO resolve without actually resorting to air strikes or a ground campaign. One of the options discussed at that time included the deployment of NATO's ACE Mobile Force (Land).[32] This was a multinational brigade for Albania commanded by British a major general, John Reith, and it included the possible participation of a Canadian infantry battalion group. Options also existed to increase the size of this force, so NATO's ACE Rapid Reaction Corps (ARRC), led by Sir Mike Jackson, a British lieutenant general, was also brought into the loop. In time ARRC would take over the planning from which the NATO-led Kosovo Force would evolve.[33]

The options developed by NATO planners for a ground campaign by this time included:

1. Option A: NATO enforcement of a ceasefire agreement in Kosovo with a force of fifty thousand, with air and naval support patterned on IFOR but to be deployed without waiting for a peace settlement to be reached.

2. Option A(−): NATO enforcement of a peace settlement in Kosovo with a force able to monitor and enforce a peace settlement. The force for this option is lighter and smaller than Option A and similar to IFOR. Size: thirty thousand to forty thousand.

3. Option B: NATO forced entry, with a peace enforcement operation, without the consent of the parties. Operations would be conducted throughout Yugoslavia and not limited to Kosovo. Size: two hundred thousand.

4. Option B(−): NATO forced entry into Kosovo, with a peace enforcement force, without the consent of the parties and limited to the Kosovo area. Objective of Option B(−) would be to

defeat the army and police and neutralize the UÇK in order to create conditions for the negotiation of a ceasefire agreement or a peace settlement. Size: seventy-five thousand.[34]

Canada's interest in the unfolding events was initially demonstrated by the deployment of Canadian CF-18 fighter-bombers to Italy in June 1998, a move that emerged after two inputs. First, Canada's ambassador to Belgrade, Raphael Girard, had undertaken a tour of Kosovo earlier that month and reported to Ottawa that the MUP and VJ were using disproportionate levels of force, including the widespread destruction of civilian infrastructure, and that a humanitarian crisis was in the offing as refugees clogged the roads.[35]

Second, the North Atlantic Council and the NATO defense ministers met to explore the SHAPE alternatives.[36] One of these alternatives, backed by Britain, Canada, and the United States, was to deploy limited numbers of troops to Macedonia and Albania for exercises. This would serve two purposes: it would sent a message that NATO was observing developments closely and that the troops on exercise could form the basis of a preventive deployment force to keep the conflict from spilling over into Albania and Macedonia. Variants of this proposal were explored and rejected. More and more attention was then focused on the use of air strikes instead. The result of these discussions was the activation of Exercise Determined Falcon (which included Canadian CF-18 aircraft) on 15 June.[37]

The coercive effects of this air exercise on Belgrade were negligible. Renewed VJ and MUP operations used even more disproportionate force, so much so that intelligence reports discerned a pattern of deliberate "village-busting" and refugee flow generation. By the end of June the United Nations envoy Elisabeth Rehn was publicly arguing for NATO intervention in Kosovo, to little effect. By this point the UN was debating the issue but incapable of developing any real solution to the problem, as its credibility had been badly damaged during its involvement in Bosnia and Croatia.[38]

Milošević had by this time met with Pres. Boris Yeltsin in Moscow in mid-June, a move that seriously concerned the NATO leadership. What if Russia backed the Serbs? Many NATO members wanted Russian consensus with any moves taken against Belgrade, which possibly slowed the process. Consequently diplomatic moves led by Richard Holbrooke in June and July produced the Kosovo Diplomatic Observer Mission (KDOM), which included Russian participation alongside British, American, and Canadian observers. It was as much a sop to the Russians to massage their wounded national pride as it was an opportunity to get Western eyes on the ground to find out what was going on. Milošević's motives for permitting KDOM to operate in Kosovo were clearly self-serving: the unarmed observers would be at the whim of the VJ and MUP, and thus their perceptions could be manipulated.[39] KDOM was operational by 6 July 1998 and initially included one Canadian army officer.[40]

Albania started to destabilize even further when a number of political assassinations rocked the pro-Western government of Fatos Nano, which had by this time replaced Sali Berisha, who was off leading pro-Kosovar Albanians in northern Albania. To make matters worse, media reports in the West accused the Italian government of plotting to replace Nano with Pandeli Majko. NATO then deployed a seventeen-hundred strong portion of ACE Mobile Force (Land) to Albania ostensibly as an exercise, though the forces involved in Operation Collaborative Assembly had other stabilizing and signaling purposes in addition to exerting presence. Any observer of the Albanian situation could be excused for being confused at this point, but the effects on the rest of the region were obvious: the Albanian and Kosovo problems were linked. Action in one related to action in the other.[41]

Canada's activities at this stage of the crisis require some explanation. On 8 August 1998 Lloyd Axworthy condemned Belgrade's actions in Kosovo and labeled them a threat to world peace. Axworthy urged the UN Security Council to hold Yugoslavia accountable and to act.[42] It is unclear how much faith he put in the UN as an institution capable of doing those things at that point, though many thought NATO needed a green light from the UN to proceed against Belgrade and mute Russian objections to unilateral NATO action. As discussed earlier, NATO credibility was riding on success in Bosnia, and a NATO failure in the southern Balkans would be detrimental to NATO's ability to achieve its aims in Bosnia. The trans-Atlantic nature of NATO is highlighted by Canada's participation in the alliance as part of the North American "pillar." To not participate would erode Canada's hard-won credibility in the alliance, and it would also erode the effectiveness of using the European "pillar" as a counterweight to American power, which was a long-standing Canadian strategic tradition. European stability—another Canadian strategic goal, one dating to World War I—was placed at risk by the events in the Balkans yet again, as had been the case throughout the 1990s. NATO credibility therefore equaled Canadian credibility and affected Canadian interests.

The UÇK meanwhile shifted from pure guerrilla operations to a series of conventional small-unit attacks at the end of July. This in turn generated a massive influx of VJ and MUP forces aiming to contain and then retake areas held by the UÇK. It took Belgrade's forces most of August and the bulk of September to regain the initiative.

The nature and effects of these offensives were instrumental in coalescing Western action in the fall of 1998, particularly the disproportionate use of force.[43] The VJ/MUP forces, operating in a clockwise fashion around Kosovo, systematically cleaned out UÇK-held areas, while the VJ border guard forces attempted to seal the borders and block any UÇK retreat. The methods used followed a discernible pattern that could even be considered doctrine: VJ forces would shell villages to drive out the civilian population, who would run for the hills once the men of military age were arrested. Mechanized units would then sweep through the target area, while the PJP and SAJ mopped up the remaining resistance and burned any residential dwelling left standing. Canadian observers noted that the creation of a humanitarian crisis was deliberate: if the Albanian population was focused on basic human survival in the coming winter months, it was less likely to conduct or support guerrilla operations. Since the borders were closed, there was nowhere for refugees to flee, so they were forced to rebuild their shattered villages as best they could.[44] At this point there were an estimated 250,000 internally displaced persons in addition to the thousands who already had fled to Albania and Macedonia.[45] The FRY security forces' methods clearly contravened international law.

While the final VJ/MUP offensive into the UÇK-held Drenica Valley region was in progress in September 1998, the United Nations Security Council passed resolution 1199, which called for a ceasefire in Kosovo. NATO ministers met at this time, issued an ultimatum to Belgrade to cease and desist its operations in Kosovo, and approved a phased air campaign. Canada publicly pledged a CF-18 fighter-bomber force as part of this campaign.[46] The situation started to deteriorate further when Russia sent a delegation to Belgrade in October. This move bolstered Serbian morale to the point that its defense minister threatened to attack NATO forces elsewhere in the region with the Yugoslav air force if any move was made against Serbia.[47]

The situation by late September 1998 was precarious. NATO air forces were poised to attack targets in Serbia if Belgrade did not stop operations in Kosovo. The Russians tacitly backed the Serbs, while the UÇK was apparently under no centralized control. Despite the ultimatum, NATO members could not agree on the provision of ground troops to forcibly evict Serbian forces from Kosovo, in part because their respective publics did not appear to favor an out-and-out ground war. More and more Serbian air defense units were then moved into Kosovo in anticipation of the promised air strikes during this debate. Russia subsequently initiated a military aid program, and air defense systems started to flow into Serbia from former Soviet republics. China then sided with Russia and pressured NATO members in UN circles to back off.[48]

The problem of ground troops was a significant factor. It was clear that there was serious confusion in the American camp brought on by the need to contain Saddam Hussein, Slobodan Milošević, and Monica Lewinsky all at the same time. A number of senior American policy makers continually equated everything in the Balkans to the Vietnam War and shied away from involvement at every opportunity, while statements emerged from the White House asserting that there would be no ground campaign.[49] There were other NATO members wavering, particularly France. Time and again some NATO members and some of Secretary General

Solana's closest advisors deluded themselves into believing that air exercises would eventually coerce Milošević into desisting. Gen. Maurice Baril, Canada's CDS, noted,

> I certainly remember very emotional discussions among the uniforms at [NATO's] Military Committee. If we were asked to go to Kosovo, we knew it might mean going all the way to Belgrade. That's the way it was. If we start going by air you're not going to sort this crisis out, you've got to go in on the ground. How far do you go if Milosevic doesn't agree? So everybody thought that you have to go to Belgrade, nobody got political direction to do it, or the political will to do that. [People thought] we would start bombing and they would cry "Uncle!" It didn't happen that way, of course. It was difficult to sell that to the governments, that we were going to have to put troops on the ground, that we're going to have to fight.[50]

It took the chair of the Military Committee, Gen. Klaus Naumann, to lecture the North Atlantic Council and remind its members that an air plan was not feasible without a ground plan. He was overridden, and another inconclusive air exercise was conducted.[51]

All of this dithering did not alter the thrust of VJ and MUP operations in Kosovo. On 28 September Canadian observers reported that after a three-day siege of two UÇK villages near Mount Čičavica, north of Priština, KDOM personnel saw fourteen dead, including two old men, four women (one of whom was pregnant), and six children. All had been tortured and mutilated with knives before being killed. The houses and crops in the area had been destroyed and the farm animals killed and mutilated. The Canadian observers were convinced that Belgrade's moves to accept political conciliation were merely "a smokescreen to avoid military intervention and keep the Alliance off balance until such time as they have achieved all of their objectives on the ground to do with suppression of the UÇK and the terrorization of any communities that would shelter them."[52]

On 1 October the United Nations held an emergency session after sketchy reports of the massacre emerged in the media. Kofi Annan, the UN secretary general, condemned the atrocity, but little was accomplished in New York. Even Lloyd Axworthy was exasperated and publicly warned, in preparation for a debate in the House of Commons, that non-UN options would have to be considered to stop the killing. Prodded by media criticism that its reputation was hurt by empty posturing, the North Atlantic Council approved an activation order (ACTORD) on 12 October 1998 so that NATO air operations could be authorized and executed against Yugoslavia. This move, coupled with a Holbrooke-Milošević meeting and then a Clark-Solana-Milošević meeting in which SACEUR threatened the Serbian leader with air strikes if VJ and MUP forces were not withdrawn from Kosovo, resulted in the creation of the Kosovo Verification Mission (KVM) under the auspices of the OSCE. A belated UN Security Council resolution provided additional legitimacy to the KVM.[53]

Essentially the KVM was a much larger and better organized mission than the KDOM, which then merged into KVM. The KVM, unlike other peace observation missions, was designed for the intrusive verification of the reductions of VJ and MUP force levels in accordance with the agreement, that is, the KVM verifiers were more like UNSCOM inspectors in Iraq than UN military observers in Bosnia. In general the KVM was supposed to assist in the maintenance of the ceasefire in accordance with OSCE and UN resolutions and NATO-FRY agreements, verify compliance with the agreements, and improve the humanitarian situation. This entailed the return to cantonment of all weapons larger than 12.7mm, the return of all VJ and MUP units to barracks, the reduction of VJ and MUP forces to pre-1998 levels, the removal of all roadblocks, and the return of refugees and displaced persons. Investigation and reportage of human rights violations was another KVM task.[54]

It took some time to organize and deploy the KVM: Milošević assented on 16 October, and the first contingent of the planned two thousand verifiers deployed in mid-November. Canada was a critical member of the KVM and provided one of five regional center commanders (Brig. Gen. Michel Maisonneuve) and twenty-three verifiers.[55]

NATO military planning was in a state of flux that resulted from the dithering of late September. SHAPE was ordered to produce an operations plan (OPLAN 10411), which was supposed to han-

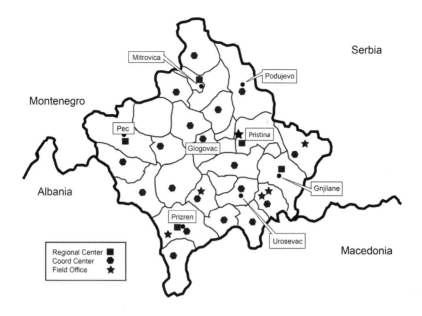

FIG. 5. The deployment of the Kosovo Verification Mission in Kosovo by late February 1999. Based on KVM data.

dle the monitoring, verification, and enforcement of any ceasefire agreement in Kosovo. The North Atlantic Council then suspended this planning. This was in part due to increased OSCE involvement and the creation of the KVM. NATO's role, as part of the agreement with Milošević, was to handle aerial observation to assist the KVM with the establishment of the Kosovo Verification Coordination Center (KVCC) and its associated reconnaissance aircraft and unmanned aerial vehicles provided by the Germans, Americans, and British (Operation Eagle Eye). The KVCC, located outside of Skopje in Macedonia, was essentially an intelligence fusion center.[56]

The evolution of the ground option continued, however. Sir Mike Jackson at the ACE Rapid Reaction Corps and others were pessimistic, believing that Holbrooke "had bought us a winter at best, but no longer," that this was all a grand game being played out by Milošević, whose objective was to fragment NATO's will to act. Ultimately many NATO military commanders knew that the politicians would have to call for a ground option if they wanted to resolve the crisis, and anticipatory planning would facilitate that when the time came. ARRC conducted a series of command post exercises (CPX) that fall, to explore various options just in case: Should ARRC prepare for an IFOR-like mission or some form of war-fighting? From what location would it operate? And what of the twelve hundred or so KVM verifiers who had already deployed? What if they were used as human shields and had to be rescued?[57]

While ARRC was considering the options, the problem of how to handle a possible hostage-taking situation in Kosovo was under consideration. Out of these discussions emerged the Extraction Force (or Ex For, also known as "The Dentists"). Because of the political sensitivities in NATO relating to the debate over ground forces, the Ex For was established in Macedonia on an ad hoc basis under national command, not NATO command. It consisted of two airborne battalions (French and Dutch), three mechanized infantry companies (British, German, and Italian), an Italian attack helicopter battalion, and two medium transport helicopter squadrons (French and Dutch), all under the command of a French brigade headquarters. Ex For was designed to extract the KVM verifiers in a "permissive environment" and to conduct medical evacuation and hostage rescue missions with Belgrade's permission.[58]

The relationship between Ex For and ARRC was initially circumspect, or as Sir Mike Jackson put it, "We all looked rather sideways at this concept because with the small amount of combat power present, you needed consent to enter Kosovo, and if there was consent, why did you need to extract? It all seemed rather circular." Indeed there was some speculation that Ex For was a foot in the door to provide stability, possibly to make up for the withdrawal of UNPREDEP. For example, the American battalion remained in Macedonia after the closure of that mission (the Scandinavian battalion packed up and went home). When all was said and done, NATO members now had four infantry battalions and significant helicopter support on the ground in the region.[59]

In time a connection was made between ARRC and Ex For. As ARRC deployed into the region in early 1999, it assumed what were called Tier III responsibilities. Ex For would handle Tier I and II situations, that is, incidents in which a small group of verifiers was caught in the middle of a firefight and unable to get out, or if verifiers were blocked into regional centers by belligerent forces and unable to perform their tasks. Tier III extraction would be conducted by ARRC in a nonpermissive environment where uncontrolled belligerent forces targeted the KVM, the UÇK took KVM personnel hostage and used them as shields, or if plausibly deniable Serbian irregular forces pretended to be UÇK and started to kill verifiers to generate provocation.[60]

Canada's contribution to all of these efforts was diverse. There were Canadian liaison officers in ARRC monitoring planning and developments in that headquarters.[61] There were Canadian verifiers with KDOM and KVM (Operation Perseverance and Operation Kimono). Canadian CF-18s based in Aviano were tasked to provide air support to combat search-and-rescue missions if an Eagle Eye reconnaissance aircraft was brought down, as well as to support the Tier III missions if necessary. Canadian intelligence personnel served in the KVCC, while fifty airfield engineers supported the Ex For and the KVCC (Operation Guarantor).[62] Taken together, Canada had representatives embedded into all levels of activity related to the Kosovo situation, which in turn permitted Canadian policy makers access to timely and accurate information necessary for their deliberations on future Canadian involvement.

In November planners in the Land Staff received word from Canadian officers in ARRC that NATO was working up a "hot entry" plan for Kosovo in parallel with the earlier planning for an ACE Mobile Force (Land) deployment. As Lt. Col. David Fraser, a DLFR planner, explained,

> There was a bunch of us just talking about it and looking ahead. We can see the buildup, we can see what is going on, and it was only a matter of time before it was going to drag us in. So we continued our discussions and then all of a sudden we got the executive okay to go out and start planning. It was tightly controlled; we couldn't even talk to the [Land Force] Areas [across the country]. The prime concern at that time was that speculation in the press might force the political people to truncate the decision process, which would force us, the planners, to cut corners.[63]

Cutting corners in the planning process had contributed to the Somalia fiasco. The planning for Operation Cordon (Somalia) in 1992–93 was too constrained; the planners and the policy makers quickly became locked into one option and did not leave enough flexibility when the situation on the ground dramatically changed.[64] On another occasion, during the run-up to Operation Toucan in East Timor, a part of the planning estimate made its way into the press and the government felt compelled to send the forces the estimate called for, not what the planners ultimately recommended.[65] Nobody wanted a repeat performance, not with a crisis this important. There was also concern that the media, not au fait with the Canadian planning process, would simplistically misinterpret anticipatory planning as some form of rogue activity on the part of the armed forces—a misperception that had occurred during Operation Broadsword planning for the Gulf War in 1990, with negative consequences. With these concerns in mind the staffs in National Defence headquarters quietly initiated the process that would produce Operation Kinetic in 1999.[66]

Events in Kosovo did not remain static once the KVM deployed. As some VJ and MUP units withdrew from Kosovo, the UÇK moved in and reoccupied those areas. From there UÇK units launched new attacks to deliberately provoke the VJ and MUP, with predictable results. Remaining Serbian forces responded as well in a predictable, disproportionate fashion, and the situation escalated once again. This time, though, Belgrade's ability to react with the level of force it wanted to use was hampered by the presence of the KVM and KDOM. Canadian observers had noted earlier in the fall that MUP personnel were returning to Kosovo in civilian clothes in significant numbers: this activity continued into December. Rather than exercise restraint, Milošević replaced his Belgrade-based head of security, Jovica Stanišić, a man who opposed the Kosovo crackdown, with Radomir Marković, an extremely vicious character. It was clear to analysts that Gen. Vlastimir Djordjević's continued tenure as the head of public security in Kosovo was a signal that nothing would change. More and more restrictions were placed on the KVM and KDOM personnel. When these fac-

CLASH OF THE DAMNED

tors were tabulated, it was hard to accept that either Milošević or the UÇK leadership was adhering to the spirit of the October agreement.[67]

Events outside the region may have played a role in Milošević's decision to continue the Kosovo cat-and-mouse game. Increased media scrutiny of the UÇK, for example, led to more and more questions being raised about the presence of mujahhedin from Osama bin Laden's al Qaeda organization in Albania, Kosovo, and Macedonia after al Qaeda personnel were intercepted and arrested in Tirana, Albania, in late November 1998.[68] Milošević could now, for example, appeal to the Russians for support by portraying his fight against the UÇK as akin to the Russian fight against local ethnic groups' Muslim forces in Chechnya (who were also supported by al Qaeda).[69] It was an appeal that resonated among the Russian population after several terrorist attacks by Chechen groups against civilian targets took hundreds of lives.

There were other distractions for the West. On 16 December Britain and the United States commenced the aerial bombardment of targets in Iraq as a coercive tool to get the Hussein regime to meet its commitments to the disarmament process and to stop obstructing the UNSCOM verification unit from carrying out its tasks. Operation Desert Fox involved more than just air strikes: two infantry brigades were flown to Kuwait, Patriot missiles were deployed, and U.S. Navy carrier battle groups and B-52 aircraft were all assigned to missions in the region. In other words this was a significant commitment of forces to the Persian Gulf, not the regular reactive and spasmodic bombing by Southern Watch forces.[70] Saddam Hussein's behavior and policies may have suggested to the Milošević regime that dedicated incremental and covert measures taken to achieve national aims in the face of overwhelming Western military force and in the presence of shaky Western political will could in fact succeed. The aftermath of the operation may also have convinced Milošević that Russia would back diplomatic moves designed to thwart the allegedly "unrestrained" exercise of American power, as it had in the UN during the period leading up to the December air strikes.

On 14 December 1998 the VJ conducted a successful ambush of UÇK forces crossing the Albanian border, killing some thirty-five fighters.[71] UÇK retaliation was swift and deadly, and a new cycle of violence started, resulting in a VJ/MUP offensive near Podujevo on Christmas Eve. By New Year's Day Belgrade was sending in more and more reinforcements, and there was little the KVM could do but report developments and try to act as a "conscience" to the MUP and OUP as it swept through Kosovar Albanian villages hunting for the men of the UÇK.

FOUR

In NATO's Vanguard

KFOR and the Canadian Commitment

The Parties to this Treaty reaffirm their faith in the purposes and principles
of the Charter of the United Nations and their desire to live in peace
with all peoples and all governments.
They are determined to safeguard the freedom, common heritage and
civilization of their peoples, founded on the principles of democracy,
individual liberty and the rule of law.
They seek to *promote stability* and well-being in the North Atlantic Area.
They are resolved to unite their efforts for collective defence *and for
the preservation of peace and security.*
They therefore agree to this North Atlantic Treaty.

ARTICLE 1

The Parties undertake, as set forth in the Charter of the United Nations,
to settle any international dispute in which they may be involved by
peaceful means in such a manner that international peace and security and
justice are not endangered, and to refrain in their international relations
from the threat or use of force *in any manner inconsistent with the
purposes of the United Nations.*

—North Atlantic Treaty, Washington DC, 4 April 1949 (emphasis added)

Prudent observers in 1998 knew deep down that force would be
needed to resolve the situation in Kosovo. The question really centered on the levels of force to be used. As the previous chapter has
shown, nonviolent attempts to generate a settlement included diplomacy, NATO military exercises to signal and demonstrate resolve,
and the introduction of not one but two peace observation forces

into Kosovo, supported by a third in the air. Yet both belligerents sought ways and means to accomplish their objectives anyway, weaving in and out through solutions provided by those outsiders interested in Balkans stability. By early 1999 the second observation force, the Kosovo Verification Mission, had encountered more and more intransigence, yet the internal diplomatic debate only increased in pitch. As hundreds of thousands of people fled Kosovo, pressure continued to build in adjacent countries, particularly Macedonia, whose ethnic Albanian population seethed. Canada was instrumental in convincing some of the more skeptical NATO members that any attempt to successfully coerce the belligerents into achieving some form of peace lay in the application of military force. Canada eventually committed substantial military force, not only in the air but also and especially on the ground, as part of the NATO effort. This chapter examines the progress of the Kosovo crisis throughout 1999, how Canada decided to send ground forces to join the NATO-led Kosovo Force (KFOR), and how KFOR's mission evolved.

The Bloody Road from Račak, January–March 1999

Led by an American diplomat, Ambassador William Walker, the KVM continued in its efforts to verify the October agreements. The first half of January 1999 consisted of a tit-for-tat cycle of violence. On 8 January UÇK ambushed and killed three MUP personnel in the Dulje Pass, while another UÇK unit kidnapped eight VJ troops near Mitrovica. The MUP retaliated, killing two UÇKs at Decane, while VJ and SAJ units from Vučitrn deployed to retake the hostages. The eight soldiers were subsequently released through KVM mediation led by Maj. Gen. John Drewienkiewicz, a British officer known as DZ. The UÇK increasingly obstructed KVM movement into their areas, so it was more and more difficult to maintain the ceasefire.[1]

The event that ultimately catalyzed Western action over Kosovo was the so-called Račak massacre of 15–16 January 1999. What exactly occurred at Račak, a Kosovar Albanian village near Stimlje, remains obscure. An initial KVM report indicated that, after fighting occurred between the UÇK and the VJ and MUP forces

Montenegro

Serbia

Mitrovica
•
Podujevo
24 Dec 98

Drenica Valley ⬡ Mt Cicavica
Sep 1998 Sep 1998
Pec
•● ★ Pristina
17 Dec 98 Glogovac •
⬡ Kosovo Polje
3 Jan 99

Racak ⬡
Rogovo 15-16 Jan 99 Gnjilane
29 Jan 99 ⬡
Urosevac •
19 Jan 99

Albania

Prizren
•

Macedonia

★ Skopje

FIG. 6. Kosovo flashpoints, 1998–99.

in the area, twenty-five civilian bodies were discovered in and around Račak. Most of these people appeared to have been executed. Ambassador Walker was alerted, and he arrived later in the day. He was subsequently shown another twenty bodies, males between twenty and sixty years of age. Ten of these appeared to have been mowed down first, then shot in the head. In Račak itself there were four more dead: two children and two men. Walker, clearly shaken by the discoveries, immediately held a press conference condemning the FRY security forces.[2]

Old Balkan hands among the KVM were more cautious. Veterans of UN operations in Bosnia were quite familiar with incidents that had been staged by the belligerents to garner media attention and sympathy for their particular causes. Although Račak looked like a straightforward massacre based on the victims' ethnicity, there was always a lingering suspicion that not all was aboveboard. Who, exactly, committed the killings? Were they under orders from high up in Belgrade's chain of command? Or did the UÇK or even elements embedded within it decide to kill their own in order to provoke the MUP to respond disproportionately in order to generate NATO action? The best information available suggests that MUP forces based out of Uroševac carried out the killings on orders from Belgrade.[3]

Claim and counterclaim resonated through the media, and ultimately the specifics did not matter. Račak took on an importance that transcended the cold, hard investigative facts that might eventually emerge over time. With no time to spare Walker was on the phone to SACEUR (Gen. Wesley Clark) to inform him that "I have them where I want them." Secretary of State Madeleine Albright, who was isolated within the Clinton administration for advocating military action against Belgrade, developed more support almost immediately. Milošević then declared Walker persona non grata, arguing that Walker had acted prematurely, and Louise Arbour, chief prosecutor for the International Criminal Tribunal, was denied entry into the FRY to investigate. Both decisions earned Milošević international condemnation.[4]

Between 21 January and 28 January the UÇK kidnapped five elderly Serbs near Mitrovica while another five were grabbed near Vučitrn. In another incident five Kosovar Albanians were killed by an unidentified group, after which the UÇK attacked an MUP station in Podujevo. The MUP and VJ poured out of their barracks and initiated another sweep operation, looking for the culprits. And then there was Rogovo.[5]

On 29 January SAJ forces supported by the PJP assaulted a suspected UÇK base area after chasing a UÇK group from the Albanian border to Rogovo. The SAJ and PJP achieved complete surprise, and twenty-six people were killed. Only twelve were armed, and there were only two survivors who got away. There were no wounded captured, which led KVM personnel to conclude that excessive force had been used by units that were not even supposed to be deployed in Kosovo according to the agreements. The operation was deemed too efficient to have been conducted by the irregulars or even regular MUP forces. A series of tit-for-tat bombings followed in which four people were killed and nine injured. Two MUP police officers were subsequently kidnapped.[6]

Taken together, Račak and Rogovo gave the international community impetus to force the belligerents to the negotiating table and to generate more public support for military operations to halt further violence and to prevent spillover into Macedonia and Albania. Ultimately Secretary General Kofi Annan of the United Nations met with Secretary General Javier Solana of NATO at the end of January in Brussels to discuss Kosovo, the first time in history that a UN secretary general had visited NATO HQ. Annan praised NATO efforts in Bosnia, declared Račak a crime against humanity, and publicly stated that he supported the use of force to head off another Bosnia. Prime Minister Jean Chrétien and Art Eggleton, the minister of national defence, were not far behind, stating that Canada was prepared to commit troops to a Kosovo endeavor.[7]

The North Atlantic Council (NAC) then announced on 31 January that NATO "stands ready to act and rules out no option" and that "the crisis in Kosovo remains a threat to peace and security in the region." NAC warned that if the "excessive and disproportionate use of force" was not curbed, NATO would "take whatever measures are necessary . . . to avert a humanitarian catastrophe by compelling compliance with the demands of the international community," including the use of air strikes if UÇK and Belgrade did not meet for talks.[8] In due course delegations from UÇK and Belgrade flew into Rambouillet, France, for talks on the future of Kosovo.

Expectations were high. Rambouillet could be another Dayton, and everybody could go home except the stabilization force troops. The OSCE and KVM worked up a plan for the Kosovo Implementation Mission (KIM), in which there would be a military implementation force (MIF) like IFOR in Bosnia and a civilian implementation force (with an Office of the High Representative and police and civil structures). While the Rambouillet talks went forward in early 1999, the KIM concept was worked into the agenda: the relationship between the MIF and NATO remained a sticking point both in Belgrade and in Moscow. There were enough problems just getting the delegations to Rambouillet and carrying on a civilized conversation.[9]

Canadian diplomats at NATO, including Ambassador David Wright, were concerned that too much attention was focused on the FRY security forces and not enough on UÇK when it came to verification of the ceasefire and reduction of units in Kosovo.[10] There was a possibility that any results of the talks could would be portrayed in Belgrade and Moscow (and even Paris) as a humiliating one-sided imposition on FRY. Old Balkans hands in both the Canadian Forces and Foreign Affairs staff knew from experience that impartiality was critical in any such effort, particularly in the arenas of propaganda and world opinion. If, for example, Belgrade's forces were to withdraw, what was the equivalent UÇK action? Stop cross-border operations? Disarm? How would they be handled if UÇK didn't disarm? Would NATO aircraft bomb them too? How would irregular and terrorist forces be identified and handled? What about extremist groups with no uniform or plausibly deniable killer groups with loose affiliations to Belgrade or Tirana? Unlike the NATO-MIF "sticking point," the lack of proportional impartiality could completely undermine the Rambouillet talks and result in more fighting.

NATO was even split internally: France wanted any MIF to report not to NATO but to the Contact Group, which was set up back in 1993–94 to coordinate international diplomacy in Bosnia. Canada was extremely opposed, having been excluded from the Contact Group despite the fact that Canada contributed significant military forces to UNPROFOR, ECMM, Operation Sharp Guard, Operation Deny Flight, Operation Air Bridge, IFOR, and SFOR from 1991 to 1999. In the Canadian view the Contact Group was inefficient, had no legitimacy, and lacked credibility. The Americans backed the Canadian position, though for their own reasons: they did not want to establish a situation in which only the UN could authorize the use of force. France also demanded explicit UN authorization for an MIF. The Russians backed this as well, in part because they didn't want NATO running the show in the Balkans, and both countries were looking for a way to thwart what they viewed as too much American control. The Americans, however, were still split on whether they would contribute to an MIF: many in Washington did not want any part of it, and sparks flew between SACEUR and the American military establishment.[11]

As the talks commenced in Rambouillet, Canadian planners were working with their NATO partners to fashion a ground force.

On 1 February 1999 SACEUR was instructed by the North Atlantic Council to reactivate planning that had been suspended in the fall of 1998 and to draft a military plan to support the implementation of the peace process in Kosovo. As noted earlier, Canada was taking the lead in ensuring that impartiality was built into the process and that the implementation force's terms of reference would not be lopsided in favor of the UÇK agenda.[12]

On 5 February a draft of OPLAN 10413 Joint Guardian was delivered to the Land Staff in Ottawa for their perusal. Joint Guardian was based on the Option A and Option A(−) thinking generated in the summer and fall of 1998 by the SHAPE planners. The NATO process for generating forces requires some explanation. Generally the NATO military headquarters responsible for a given operation creates a draft plan, which is usually accompanied by a statement of requirements (SOR). The SOR is a list of unit types, equipment, and capabilities the NATO commander needs to carry out the mission. Nations interested in participating then negotiate with the NATO commander's staff and commit forces to fulfill the SOR as required, according to their national interests. In some cases a nation with a unique capability may be asked to provide it. In the case of Joint Guardian no SOR accompanied the draft plan because it was still being prepared.[13] And the situation remained in flux, or as Lt. Gen. Bill Leach, chief of the Land Staff, put it, "Every time somebody goes to a NATO meeting in Brussels, or Washington, or London, the nature of the issue itself is a little different, depending on who has decided to opt in or opt out, or who has decided to play in a particular way or not to play."[14]

There was only sketchy political guidance, mostly along the lines of "Canada will contribute to the NATO-led force implementing the cease-fire agreement." Consequently the planners generated a series of options based on what the army was currently doing, what it could do, and what it wanted to do. For example, the army was still committed to Operation Palladium, the SFOR commitment in Bosnia, and could not withdraw from it. Another operation, Prudence, was under way in the Central African Republic. Other units were preparing to rotate with the deployed forces and were trained and equipped specifically for those missions.[15]

The most important assumption was that the mission would be like IFOR, that is, a NATO stabilization operation as opposed to a UN peacekeeping operation. The difference, as explained by Brig. Gen. Andrew Leslie, commander of 1 Canadian Mechanized Brigade Group (1 CMBG), was that IFOR-type organizations "bring to the table well-disciplined, well-trained soldiers who operated with a common operational picture, a common lexicon, etc. NATO commanders understand each other's intent and are backed with a sophisticated, robust war-fighting system. That's something the UN didn't have. If the former warring factions know that you can't actually use force against them, they will push you and push you and be obstructionist up to the point where your mission will fail because they know you can't do certain things."[16]

Another assumption was that the mission would last three years. This allowed planners to address the options in terms of the size of force needed: Canada has a relatively small army and thus is limited in how large a force it can deploy at any one time. To sustain the commitment—that is, to prevent the soldiers from burning out—the deployed unit must be rotated regularly, usually every six months. Four options emerged at this time: a mechanized infantry company, along with a reconnaissance troop and a helicopter flight; a reconnaissance squadron and a helicopter flight; a towed artillery battery and a helicopter flight; or a helicopter squadron.[17]

A complicating factor was the saliency principle. The force that Canada deploys has to be both large enough and useful to the operation or else it becomes mere symbolism. Symbolism does not permit Canada to wield political influence in NATO circles and in fact puts the force at risk since Canada has no right to fill influential NATO command positions under which the Canadian force must operate. Operational influence is necessary so that Canadian soldiers are not misused, as they were at Hong Kong in 1941 and Dieppe in 1942. Therefore, the deployed force has to matter, it has to fill some role that others cannot or will not take on, or it has to have some unique capability that is needed and nobody else has. Saliency drove the first phase of the Operation Kinetic process in early 1999.[18]

The option that looked like it would fit the bill was the reconnaissance squadron/tactical helicopter combination. A new type of Canadian reconnaissance, or recce, vehicle—the Coyote—was supposed to be available for the upcoming Palladium rotation to Bosnia. Coyote is a completely unique vehicle, possessing surveillance capabilities no other nation in NATO has in their force structures. As the chief of the Land Staff put it, "It was just shit house luck, to be very blunt. Coyote was already sitting there, sort of already in the shop window."[19] Coyote was brand new at this point, and bureaucrats in the Department of National Defence materials acquisition fiefdom raised some timid queries about supportability. General Leach told the planners that this was all "bullshit," that the problems could be overcome with enough money, and that passing up an opportunity like this was "absolutely stupid." Leach and the CDS, Gen. Maurice Baril, placed so much pressure on the Materiel section people "that it just set the world on edge."[20]

By this point the Joint Guardian plan was fleshed out by Gen. Sir Mike Jackson's staff at ACE Rapid Reaction Corps, who were also generating the SOR. The ARRC planners were informed about the Coyote and its capabilities and insisted on a briefing. Maj. Paul Fleury, who commanded the Lord Strathcona's Horse (Royal Canadians) Recce Squadron, was flown in to give it. The British, particularly Brig. Bill Rollo of 4 (UK) Armoured Brigade, were duly impressed, and Coyote was incorporated into the SOR.[21]

The air force was conducting a similar exercise and attempting to deploy its new CH-146 Griffon helicopters. Working with the Land Staff, the air planners were able to increase the planned size of the unit from a flight of two or three machines to a squadron of eight. These Griffons would be equipped with a surveillance capability, something the ARRC planners needed but no other NATO country was willing to provide.[22]

Two days after a House of Commons debate on Kosovo on 17 February the national defence minister, Art Eggleton, told the media that Canada was going to participate but that the force composition was still under consideration. After the SOR was received from ARRC on 18 February, Cabinet met and agreed to the deployment of a recce squadron and a tactical helicopter squadron.[23]

"Warning Order 01–Operation KINETIC" was issued on 4 March 1999. Operation Kinetic was based on the premise that "all parties have agreed to an international agreement and that the environment would be permissive." The order took into account that "some rogue elements would not accept all provisions of the agreement" and that "there may be an escalation in violence by the parties." The assumption was that the UÇK "would have their capabilities degraded" by the agreement but that the VJ would not, since the agreement would only cover Kosovo and not adjacent parts of Serbia. Therefore "the VJ would retain significant armoured resources close to Kosovo" while the UÇK "would also retain significant numbers of weapons . . . presumably in northern Albania." Consequently "Canada would be prepared to contribute forces to demonstrate the Government's resolve in support of the establishment of a stable environment in Kosovo so that a long-term peaceful settlement to the political problems in the region can be achieved."[24]

While the planners planned and diplomats talked, the KVM was still monitoring waves of violence throughout Kosovo. The UÇK shot up an MUP helicopter, established roadblocks near Studecane, and blew up a bank in Uroševac. FRY security forces then found demolitions on two major bridges, one near the Macedonian border and another on the Kosovo-Serbia boundary. Three Serbs were kidnapped, an event that prompted extensive KVM negotiations. The VJ brought in additional forces from Serbia and deployed them to a "training area" south of Mitrovica "temporarily," for "winter warfare training," a clear violation of the agreement.[25]

The diplomatic ins and outs of Rambouillet are far too detailed for a complete description in this study. In the end the Kosovar Albanian delegation remained as intransigent as the FRY delegation. Canadian experience in similar mediation over the issues of ethnic violence in Israel/Palestine, Cyprus, and the Congo indicates that it is impossible to achieve a timely and 100 percent diplomatic solution once blood has been spilled and centuries-old grievances are brought to the surface. Despite the fact that the Kosovar Albanians signed the agreement on 18 March, neither side really wanted a solution that would involve any form of compromise. Milošević refused to withdraw ground forces. The Kosovo Verification Mission was then withdrawn from Kosovo to Macedonia and Albania on 20 March without incident. Another attempt by Richard Holbrooke to persuade Milošević to relent failed two days later. The line had finally been crossed and there was no more room to maneuver: diplomacy had failed and the war was on.

NATO planning conducted throughout 1998 envisioned various types of air campaigns, each with different objectives depending on what was required at the political level. One of these options was selected, the activation order was approved, and Operation Allied Force commenced on 24 March 1999. Six USAF B-52H bombers initiated the attack with some thirty-six conventional air-launched cruise missiles, while the Royal Navy submarine HMS *Splendid* fired Tomahawk cruise missiles and two USAF B-2 Spirit strategic bombers unloaded thirty-two satellite-guided joint direct attack munitions over FRY targets in an attempt to strip away the FRY air defense system. Aircraft from eight other NATO members, including Canada, saw action on day one.[26]

Cabinet had previously approved Canadian participation on 20 March. Operation Echo was the Canadian code name for the employment of six, then twelve, and eventually eighteen CF-18 fighter-bombers in Allied Force. Canadians would remain in the forefront of the Allied Force campaign, conducting some 224 missions (between two and eight aircraft each): 57 combat air patrol and 167 ground attack missions. Task Force Aviano's CF-18 pilots led more than 50 percent of the missions assigned to them for the seventy-day air campaign.[27]

Allied Force remains controversial, particularly with regard to its effectiveness in coercing Milošević in Belgrade to adhere to a ceasefire and withdrawal agreement in Kosovo. NATO planners worked on the assumption of a short air war, hoping that the Belgrade regime would capitulate in days. This did not happen, and Allied Force had to be expanded and its original assumptions reexamined within a week of its initiation.[28] In any event, Allied Force altered the character and tempo of Operation Kinetic planning during March and April 1999.

Second Fronts, a New Cold War, and Harboring the Allies

The effects of the Kosovo crisis were wide-ranging and dangerous. Ultimately they affected Canadian interests not only in the Balkans and Europe but in North America as well. The most immediate problem was the refugee flow out of Kosovo into Macedonia and Albania. After the withdrawal of the KVM, Belgrade reintroduced VJ and MUP forces into Kosovo and initiated another campaign similar to the one conducted in the fall of 1998 but much larger in scale. The day the KVM withdrew, the first VJ and MUP operations started against established rural UÇK base areas, particularly those in the Drenica Valley. By 24 March the security force operations had escalated into an orgy of destruction in the populated, built-up areas throughout the entire province. This generated a mass exodus of Kosovar Albanians, estimated to have included 450,000 people, for a grand total of 850,000, into Albania and Macedonia.[29] Atrocities that would have been unheard of with the KVM present were widespread: a list of reported atrocities during this period, conducted by both sides, runs some fifty-one pages.[30] Several thousand Kosovar Albanians were deported to Serbia proper, and an estimated 2,000 of them disappeared.[31] The physical destruction of housing appears to have been systematic and deliberately designed to discourage the inhabitants from returning.[32]

At the time, simplistic analysis fueled by anti-NATO propaganda blamed Allied Force for the exodus. The reality is far more complex. ARRC analysis determined that Belgrade had two objectives. The first was to completely destroy the UÇK both through direct attacks against identifiable units and by indirect attacks against its infrastructure and support system in the population. The second and far more insidious goal was the deliberate generation of instability in Albania and Macedonia with the express purpose of disrupting NATO's buildup. Not only did NATO now have to contend with caring for and feeding 850,000 people, but Macedonia now had to deal with further agitation within its Albanian population, suddenly increased a hundredfold, who were still angry about the Gostivar incidents back in the mid-1990s. Alba-

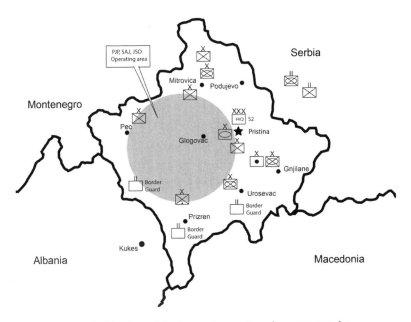

FIG. 7. Serbian forces' deployment, 1999. Based on 1 PPCLI data.

nia, already an economic basket case, could ill afford the influx of some 200,000 additional people. ARRC commander Sir Mike Jackson viewed this as an FRY "deep battle element" and "had no doubt that Milošević hoped that by putting 250,000 refugees into Macedonia . . . he would destabilize the country, which was the ARRC assembly and support area."[33]

Another problem was the possibility of a "second front" in Bosnia. The Serbian population reacted with hostility toward the international community in the RS area, which prompted the withdrawal of international personnel from those areas. Mobs in Banja Luka sacked several liaison offices and attacked vehicles containing personnel from international organizations engaged in Bosnia. A car bomb killed the Bosnian deputy interior minister (a Croat), while the RS 311th Infantry Brigade had to be forcibly disbanded by SFOR, ostensibly for smuggling weapons near Brčko but probably because it was involved in even more nefarious activity. A number of RS radar vehicles were confiscated for "unauthorized radar activity." Even the Republika Srpska president, Nikola Poplašen, was removed by the Office of the High Representative for attempting to destabilize the RS entity.[34]

During the air campaign twelve FRY MiG-29 fighter-bombers flew in to attack SFOR positions in Bosnia: two were downed by Dutch F-16 fighters, and the others retreated before they could deliver any ordnance.[35] Recall that Canada had an eleven-hundred-member contingent deployed to Bosnia as part of SFOR. Although the Palladium forces occupied an area dominated by the Croatians and Muslims, Bosnian Croat agitation blossomed once Bosnian Serb elements demonstrated they could flout SFOR and the Office of the High Representative. These developments potentially put Canadian forces at risk, since Bosnia could explode. They also complicated a KFOR deployment: the Op Kinetic force could not just be re-rolled Palladium forces deployed south. Op Kinetic units would have to come from Canada.[36]

A complicating factor in the Joint Guardian buildup was the Greek problem. Greek sympathies lay with the Serbs in Belgrade, yet ARRC needed the port of Thessaloniki to deploy into the interior of land-locked Macedonia. The ten-year Macedonian-Greek dispute over the poor treatment of the Macedonian minority population in northern Greece and the use of the Star of Vergina on the Macedonian flag threatened to spin out of control on several occasions.[37]

With NATO pouring resources into an adversary and bombing Greek commercial enterprises in Serbia, including the communications system and the power grid, the Communist Party in Greece generated a wave of labor agitation directed against Thessaloniki and the lines of communication to the north. For example, the Irish Guards loaded their armored vehicles onto Greek trains. On several occasions the engineers stopped the trains in built-up areas and encouraged locals to strip the vehicles of external kit and vandalize them. A plethora of anti-NATO graffiti appeared, with NATO's compass rose emblem twisted into a crude swastika. A Canadian officer traveling to Skopje via Thessaloniki was even greeted at the airport by well-dressed young women shouting, "NATO, today you die!"[38]

The most dangerous factor by far, however, was the Russian problem. The collapse of the Soviet Union in 1991 and the subsequent damage caused by Russia's lurch into full-contact capitalism had left in its wake a crisis in national confidence. As Russian president Boris Yeltsin explained in his memoirs, "It was then in 1995 that Russia was infected with a new disease: a total negativity, a complete lack of confidence in ourselves and our strengths. We Russians had come to dislike ourselves. And that is a historical dead end for a nation."[39] It was also a nation possessing twenty-six thousand nuclear weapons.

As we have seen elsewhere, the role of national pride in the acceleration of violent and murderous events is significant. Essentially the Russian economy melted down in August 1998 from a combination of the devaluation of the ruble, debt repayment, and the effects of a proliferation of pyramid savings schemes like the MMM investment pyramid (similar to those that doomed the Albanian economy), which collapsed and thus destroyed the life savings of millions of people. The keystone of the Russian economy, oil, was threatened in that pipelines necessary for the expansion of that industry could not be built because the routes from the Caspian Sea to the Black Sea were interdicted by the war in Chechnya, which was supported by Muslim fundamentalists. The Chechnya war also threatened neighboring Ingushetia, which acted as Russia's "offshore" banking haven without which Russia's economy could not function effectively.[40]

The only way out was for Russia to ask the International Monetary Fund (IMF) for a series of loans. The IMF complied but demanded restructuring of the Russian economy. The nationalists and former communists, already suffering from loser syndrome, escalated their old rhetoric—that Russia was now controlled by hostile elements in the West, that the IMF loans were a national humiliation. This monetary assist, in addition to the war in Chechnya, where Russian military might was defeated, did not bode well for the future of Russia's struggling democracy. In response to the instability generated by the nationalists, foreign investors backed out in the fall of 1998, which further exacerbated the economic crisis. The IMF then held back some of the loans.[41]

The nationalists then made connections between the economic crisis and NATO expansion. Since the end of the Cold War, certain former Warsaw Pact countries that had met rigid criteria relating to decommunization had become eligible to join NATO and ultimately the European Community, with its attendant economic benefits. The Russian nationalists screamed that there was a plot to destroy Russia, that Allied Force was a dress rehearsal for a NATO attack on Russia.[42] Combined with the economic problems, Russia was on the verge of a coup d'état or worse, even another civil war. Yeltsin recalled, "I could not rule out mass disorder and unconstitutional actions. In the final analysis, wars have always provoked revolutions. That was what irritated me most. Did the NATO leaders really not understand? I had met with these leaders dozens of times! Some of them called me their friend. Wasn't it obvious to them that each missile strike against Yugoslavia was an indirect strike against Russia?"[43]

Yeltsin's rhetoric notwithstanding, the media reported that Russia was preparing to transport MiG fighters to Serbia. These aircraft were, however, impounded in Azerbaijan after American diplomatic pressure was brought to bear. Rather than working with NATO to end the conflict in Kosovo, Yeltsin's government undertook a variety of moves that ran counter to NATO objectives. First, Russia threatened to pull out of SFOR in Bosnia and then withdrew their representative at SHAPE. Russian SFOR troops refused to take orders from SFOR HQ, and rumors started that they would assist the RS in its efforts to destabilize Bosnia. Then the Russians informed Turkey that a naval force would transit through the Bosporus Strait. This force consisted of a Kara-class cruiser, a Kashin-class destroyer, a Kynda-class cruiser, two Krivak-class frigates, an Alligator-class amphibious assault ship, and an AGI (intelligence-gathering ship). These naval moves worried SACEUR. These ships could move into the Adriatic and provide early warning for the FRY air defenses and gather signals intelligence for Belgrade. Worse, by using their surface-to-air missiles or even just their search-and–fire control radars, they could harass the Allied Force strike forces operating from Italy against the FRY and seriously interfere with the operation. For SACEUR "it was an unmistakable signal."[44] The situation was reminiscent of the Cold War and had the potential to become a miniature version of the Cuban Missile Crisis if not handled properly.

The Canadian view on Russian developments, according to the CDS, was that "Russia was a big very proud giant that was badly wounded, badly humiliated in Afghanistan, Chechnya, and all over the place, economically shattered and totally unstable with this vodka-drinking guy at the head. You never knew when and what would trigger a desperate move. I think the danger was that somebody who is cornered and wounded will bite. He'll die, but he'll bite and can hurt you a lot. They were extremely difficult to deal with, they were getting bad instructions. It was the worst mess you could have with a powerful but beaten nuclear foe."[45]

The Russian problem would continue to plague NATO throughout the crisis, as we will see later.

The most immediate of the problems was the refugee situation in Albania and Macedonia. On 5 April 1999 SACEUR put ACE Mobile Force (Land) on seventy-two hours' notice to deploy to Albania. The AMF(L) exercise Collaborative Assembly held the previous fall facilitated the process, and by 10 April the core staff of AMF(L) had arrived in Albania. The NATO-led Albania Force (AFOR) officially stood up on 16 April and was given the code name Operation Allied Harbor. More than twelve thousand NATO and allied troops poured into Albania. NATO objectives in Allied Harbor operated at several levels. First, the operation was designed to provide shelter and medical support for refugees, assist in their movement by coordinating the nongovernmental relief organizations, and improve the flow of humanitarian aid by improving Albania's decrepit infrastructure. This included improving the Tirana airport and the port of Durrës and repairing roads throughout the country. Another agenda point was "to maximize positive publicity for NATO." Op Allied Harbor was part of the information warfare campaign as much as it was a humanitarian effort.[46] The objectives of the information warfare campaign were as follows:

1. Reducing the combat capability and the will of the VJ and MUP to fight

2. Neutralizing the internal media and other components of the Milošević propaganda machine

3. Expanding support and assistance for NATO actions by front-line states

4. Isolating Milošević from his economic, industrial, and political power base

5. Enabling Russian support of NATO/Western initiatives and soliciting positive Russian involvement in conflict resolution and regional stability

6. Enabling the creation of a stable, democratic, and regionally integrated FRY[47]

The obvious benefits of Allied Harbor to NATO, however, lay in the need to develop a secure base and communications zone for any military action taken against Kosovo and Serbia. Indeed one of AFOR's specific tasks was "to be prepared to enable the flow of KFOR forces through Albanian Lines of Communications."[48] The combination of stabilization, facilitation, and information was fortuitous. Canada's contribution to Allied Harbor consisted of two C-130 Hercules aircraft, which handled humanitarian aid movement to and within Albania and Macedonia.[49] As an aside, it was clear to NATO military authorities that only NATO resources could be used effectively to handle the humanitarian crisis. As Gen. Klaus Naumann noted,

> The United Nations High Commissioner for Refugees, which had promised wonderful things, was never able to deliver. . . . Had we lost this part of the campaign, we may have seen a destabilization of [Macedonia] and Albania which could have resulted in toppling the [pro-NATO] governments. . . . Had this happened, Milosevic had strategically won the conflict since with that we had been deprived of the potential launching pad for a ground campaign. Had he had this final assurance that we could never come in [on the ground] he may have felt encouraged to sit the air campaign

out knowing that some nations would sooner or later under the influence of the media say[,] "Okay, stop it."[50]

ARRC, meanwhile, was using its engineering, logistics, and medical resources to assist Kosovar Albanian refugees in Macedonia. There were other pressing concerns, which included a number of drive-by shootings at NATO installations and at least one occasion when a rocket-propelled grenade was fired at an ARRC vehicle. Sophisticated propaganda leaflets, professionally printed on water-resistant paper, were also distributed. These featured a picture of a target over a British soldier and a NATO compass rose emblem turned into a Nazi swastika.[51]

Sir Mike Jackson was concerned that these and other operations could generate conditions in which ARRC would be attenuated in its ability to conduct a nonpermissive entry into Kosovo: "There were special forces coming over the border and there was indigenous terrorism within Macedonia itself from the Serb minority which amounted to about fifty thousand people. We took military precautions against all of that."[52] There were also conventional threats to ARRC:

> Here we are, a tiny force of five battalions, each with five one-star headquarters. We had plenty of command and control and bugger all else. We were an embryo peace implementation force, we didn't have an ACTORD or the funding that went along with it. There was a series of threats. All of our infrastructure was within artillery range of the VJ forces in Kosovo. We were also in range of their airpower, if any of it was still flying. There was even the improbable but not impossible threat of a mechanized ground incursion in the open terrain near Kumanovo in the east, not to take the whole territory, but as a propaganda exercise. Recall the Iraqi Khafji operation during the Gulf War. We constructed a General Defence Plan with our little force, using the Ex For units and our one battery of British 155mm guns.[53]

ARRC also used Allied Force airpower against VJ forces in the Preševo Valley across the border from Kumanovo. ARRC had thirty-five Phoenix unmanned aerial vehicles (UAVs) and access to imagery from American Predator and German CL-289 UAVs. The Phoenix vehicles were used over the Preševo Valley to locate VJ mechanized units and then air attacks were called in from Allied Force units based in Italy. Several main battle tanks were subsequently destroyed in an effort to discourage any ground incursion.[54]

Canadian Planning from Kinetic to Fortitude and Kinetic Plus

The debate over a ground war to accompany Allied Force continued well into April 1999. Options A and A(−) were off the table, and thinking shifted to the Option B and B(−) categories. Option B was the controversial one, since it meant conducting a war throughout Yugoslavia with a force of two hundred thousand and going straight for Belgrade. It was impossible to consider either Option B or B(−) without American participation, and the Clinton administration was wavering. Canada and the United Kingdom pressured the United States to make some commitment after Art Eggleton, Canada's minister of national defence, and the British defense minister met with SACEUR in early April. Media reports suggested on 10 April that this pressure was a significant factor in the American decision-making process. The fact that 70 percent of Canadians favored NATO intervention was a nice exclamation mark to the Anglo-Canadian argument about the need to prevent another Rwanda, retain NATO credibility, and stop Bosnia's collapse.[55]

By the time the NATO summit began on 23 April the members had finally reached an agreement on objectives. NATO objectives were now defined as follows:

1. Ensuring a verifiable end to all military action and the immediate ending of violence and repression

2. Ensuring the withdrawal from Kosovo of the military, police, and paramilitary forces

3. Agreeing to the stationing in Kosovo of an international military presence

4. Agreeing to unconditional and safe return of all refugees and displaced persons, and humanitarian aid organizations' unhindered access to them

5. Providing credible assurance of Milošević's willingness to work, on the basis of the Rambouillet Accords, in conformity with international law and the charter of the United Nations[56]

So which planning option would be the best means to achieve these objectives and what were the forces capable of doing? Sir Mike Jackson at ARRC was instructed by Gen. Wesley Clark, head of SACEUR, to "be prepared to establish KFOR to implement and, when necessary, enforce compliance with the military provisions of an interim [peace or ceasefire] agreement." Three plans were under way: peace implementation; peace implementation (with constraints), which both corresponded to Options A and A(−); and forced entry, which corresponded to Option B(−).[57]

By this time ARRC was in the process of deploying to Macedonia two mechanized infantry brigades (French and Italian), two armored brigades (German and British), and an American armored cavalry battalion. Other units from the Netherlands, Norway, and the Czech Republic were also inbound. This force totaled approximately fourteen thousand people in mid-May, or roughly the requirements for Option A. ARRC planners figured that this was less than the minimum number of personnel necessary to implement Option A, though they developed various "thin-spread" deployment plans with increased levels of risk attached to them. ARRC simply needed more troops and more units if it was to carry out any of the options.[58]

As the air campaign dragged on through April and May, it appeared more likely that a forced-entry ground offensive would be needed. Fortunately Land Staff planners had been conducting anticipatory planning for such a move back in March, and there had been discussions in London with the British on expanded Canadian participation within the context of ARRC. The British were interested in a third maneuver element for 4 (UK) Armoured Brigade, which was deploying to Macedonia.[59]

On 1 April the deputy chief of the Defence Staff (DCDS), Lt. Gen. Ray Henault, informed the planners that "Canada will be expected to contribute ground forces in addition to the CF-18s already deployed in support of NATO's air campaign to demonstrate Canadian resolve to expedite an end to the crisis in Kosovo." The DCDS further directed that the army plan for the "training and preparation for an infantry battle group of 1400–1500 personnel" in case another NATO request came in for additional forces. The DCDS further instructed army planners to prepare a force that would include three mechanized infantry companies, a tank squadron, a combat engineer squadron, a TOW antitank platoon, a mortar platoon, a recce platoon, and an air defense troop. The initial plan was called Operation Fortitude. Operation Kinetic forces (the Coyote squadron and the Griffon squadron) were to be prepared to re-role to operate as part of the forced-entry plan. All Canadian ground forces were to operate within the context of a British brigade as opposed to operating independently, something that would be necessary for a ground offensive since mechanized battalion- and squadron-sized units do not operate alone in such an environment.[60]

The Op Fortitude warning order introduced a number of complications, however. The first involved "rice bowls" within National Defence headquarters. A common problem among Western militaries with scarce financial resources is the prevailing belief that if a capability, be it engineers, military police, dentists, lawyers, or whatever, is not used or *seen* to be used, it will become dispensable during the inevitable round of budget cuts the following year. Consequently each branch or corps makes demands on the planners trying to put together a force for an operation, and in some cases some proponents exaggerate the requirement for their services in an attempt to get a larger group to go. These debates can get quite emotional and acrimonious, with everybody elbowing their way to the table to justify their existence. This is not surprising or always devious in intent: these are all professional people, proud of what they do, and wanting to serve their country.[61]

In the case of Kosovo the planners in DLFR had to contend with such a situation. Simply put, not everybody could go. The level of Canadian involvement was set at the unit (battle group and helicopter squadron) and sub-unit (recce squadron) level, not the formation level (brigade group). If Canada committed a brigade group (which usually contained about five thousand persons), then there would have been no problem, since all branches and corps would have their place. The decision to operate within a British formation meant that many capabilities would be provided by them, not Canada. The danger was that the "rice bowl" problem would force the planners to create a miniature self-sufficient brigade group out of a fifteen-hundred-strength battle group. This would increase the number of service support people, which would in turn reduce the combat capability of the unit, which in turn would make it less useful to the British brigade, and ultimately Canada's operational and political influence would wane. This drama played itself out through April and May 1999.[62]

The question of which brigade group would provide the additional forces also concerned the Land Staff. There were three mechanized brigade groups in Canada, 1 CMBG, 2 CMBG, and 5 GMBC (5e Groupe-brigade mécanisé du Canada), all of which were trained and structured differently, depending on the personal vision of the brigade group commander. In the past, 1st Canadian Division HQ served as the focal point for standards and training for the brigades, but the decision to convert the divisional headquarters into a pseudo joint force headquarters wiped this out.[63]

It is important to understand that brigade groups are no longer the stable formations they were during the Cold War. The cuts introduced by the Brian Mulroney and Jean Chrétien governments went far beyond the fat and sliced deep into the meat. The high operational tempo in the 1990s produced high levels of burnout that increased the recovery time of units after they returned from overseas tours. In many cases brigade groups had to rob nondeployed units for personnel and equipment so that one unit could deploy, say, to Op Palladium in Bosnia or Op Stable in Haiti. The proliferation of UN missions and Foreign Affairs' demands that Canada send something to almost all of them gobbled up large numbers of signals and service support personnel, so much so that they were burning out as thoroughly as those in combat units.[64]

As fate would have it, the right man was in the right place at the right time, and he had done the right things. Col. Andrew Leslie, the commander of 1 Canadian Mechanized Brigade Group in Edmonton, was that man. Colonel Leslie's philosophy and training plan, which he implemented in 1997 when he took command of 1 CMBG, gave the units of that brigade group the combination of skills and experience that would be critical if Canada was to include a unit in the ARRC forced-entry operation. These facts should not be taken as denigration of the professionalism of the men and women of 2 CMBG and 5 GMBC: the other two brigade groups were more heavily committed to peacekeeping and stability operations and were not prepared for the type of mid-intensity operations envisioned by ARRC staff.

Colonel Leslie's experiences in the Balkans during the UNPRO-FOR period dramatically affected how he wanted 1 CMBG trained:

> In February 1995 I went overseas as the Chief of Staff for Sector South, which was a brigade-sized formation, and suffered through a variety of war-fighting operations initiated by the Croats, the Serbs, and the Muslims. The one that really struck me and made me change the way I look at my business as a professional soldier was the Croatian attack on the Krajina in August of 1995, Operation Storm. Our lightly armed, relatively impotent, poorly commanded UN force was made redundant by the Croatian army. I saw, from a brigade perspective, what happens when lightly armed soldiers were put under massive amounts of hostile fire. The UN force collapsed. A whole bunch of people lost their lives. What was apparent was the lack of confidence, the lack of combined armed skill sets, and the lack of heavy weaponry to protect the UN soldiers. I had a sense of failure. I resolved to do everything in my power to ensure my soldiers were as well trained as possible for the types of missions they may encounter.[65]

In 1997 Colonel Leslie established his training objectives:

> When I took command of 1 Brigade I went with a very clear idea of what I wanted to do and how I wanted to get it done. I wanted to focus on combined arms war-fighting skills, live fire, because it didn't take a rocket scientist to figure out that something else was going to happen in the Balkans. The operational tempo of the Canadian Army is such that it is too easy to fall into the trap of focusing uniquely on constabulary activities, and armies can quickly become

used to a routine and never bring it up to the level where actual live fire training was conducted at the unit and formation level. . . .

It's a lot harder to train for the high end, it's a lot more dangerous, it takes more focus. But once soldiers know what they can do and know just how good they are, a well-trained, war-capable Canadian soldier has no fear and once they're trained for the high end it is something they will never lose: confidence. If you train for the low end and just hope to God they'll do well at the high end, they'll lose confidence. If you see a bunch of confident, professional-looking soldiers with up-to-date equipment rumbling around in tanks or Coyotes or APCs, they will project an aura of ability to do what has to be done and guess what? The local bad guys won't do anything.[66]

This approach put Leslie on a collision course with the chief of the Land Staff. To save money, formations were apparently instructed not to conduct combined arms training above the sub-unit level (company and squadron), nor were they to conduct live-fire exercises unless the units were about to deploy on a mission. 1 CMBG therefore conducted forty simultaneous sub-unit live-fire maneuver exercises directed toward the same objectives in the same training area.[67]

Initial Op Fortitude plans envisioned a light infantry battalion, 3 PPCLI, drawn from 1 CMBG. Then the Department of Foreign Affairs got involved. Foreign Affairs professionals understood the need to achieve saliency in the alliance effort and wanted to ensure that Canada deployed a sizable enough force so they could use it for political influence. The problem was that another Foreign Affairs faction was interested in a contribution that was "nonviolent," that is, not combat capable, in order to preserve the mythology that Canada just "did peacekeeping," not war.[68] The Defence Staff deputy chiefs were adamant, and the CDS agreed, saying that "all NATO nations have invested so heavily in Kosovo that there is no option but to ensure that KFOR succeeds. Contributing the wrong capabilities or insufficient capabilities will not contribute to the KFOR mission success. It is not a matter of what any nation can afford to provide, but rather what it must provide to contribute to mission success. Canada's contribution should be robust and meaningful for Canada to be seen to be sharing the risks."[69]

The options rejected by the planning staffs included a transport battalion, medical facilities and ambulance platoons, an air defense battery, an engineer regiment, an MP company, and staff augmentation. None of these options was considered salient enough to be a meaningful contribution. The salient options included a mechanized infantry battalion, an artillery regiment with M-109 self-propelled guns, and a brigade headquarters, all in addition to the planned Kinetic forces.[70] Indeed the deployment of noncombat units would have been the equivalent of offering a logistics division to back up the Normandy invasion instead of having the 3rd Canadian Division storm the beaches.

A meeting was then held with senior army planners and the CDS and DCDS to determine which force option was the best. The artillery regiment and brigade headquarters were rejected. After serious debate relating to firepower, mobility, and force protection issues, the army was told to plan for two organizations: a mechanized battle group with three infantry companies and a tank squadron, and a mechanized battle group with two infantry companies and a tank squadron. A National Support Element (NSE) was also to be formed to handle the logistics.[71] Around this time the code word Fortitude was dropped and the additional units were referred to as Operation Kinetic (+).

The DCDS favored the two-company and tank squadron option. The tanks and armored personnel carriers were not deemed to have enough protection and needed upgrading, a process that would take time to get through the bureaucracy of the Materiel section at National Defence HQ. Time was of the essence, and it would be quicker to deploy two companies instead of three, as well as easier to sustain.[72]

While Lt. Gen. Bill Leach and his staff pounced on Materiel and accelerated the uparmoring of the Leopards and Grizzlies, Cabinet was briefed on the Kinetic (+) force structure on 1 June. The briefing officer was adamant that the CDS had recommended "in his best military judgment that the soundest contribution for Canada would be to deploy a battle group consisting of a mechanized infantry battalion, a tank squadron of 19 Leopards, and an engineer unit . . . and that tanks were a necessary component of the force."[73] Cabinet did not want tanks to go, for whatever reason: the planners were told that "a political review of the Op KINETIC (Plus) Battle Group has raised concerns over costs. The CDS has directed that the Battle Group option be reviewed to include an option excluding the armoured squadron."[74]

When NATO ARRC was told Canada was going to remove tanks from the plan, the ARRC planners "made it clear that what they wanted was a unit, capable of ensuring its own freedom of movement and its own self-protection, a unit that could be assigned to tasks without attachments from the remainder of the brigade. . . . [The planners] were noticeably disappointed in the possible reduction of capability and therefore utility of [the] Canadian contribution. They indicated that an infantry battalion on its own would be relegated to secondary roles and tasks."[75]

The problem therefore was that if Canada didn't deploy tanks, "Canada will not be seen to be doing its share"; there would be no saliency and thus reduced operational and political influence.[76] The DCDS and CDS believed that "if Canada were to decide not to make an additional contribution, we could expect criticism from the media and commentators. Our allies will note our small contribution and make future decisions based on our indicated level of commitment." Every other NATO army was deploying tanks to Macedonia, and there was a significant FRY armored and mechanized threat. Additionally "NATO's peace implementation force must possess the firepower and force protection to ensure its ability to enforce compliance with the terms of the ceasefire agreement. In this instance the presence of tanks in the peace support role will demonstrate NATO's resolve to expedite the peace process and provide a heightened degree of security to the peacekeepers in a volatile environment. The deterrent effect of the tank is much greater than any other vehicle in theatre."[77]

This debate over the deployment of a mere 19 tanks (out of total of 550 other Kinetic-tasked vehicles) is strange but very important. The only conceivable explanation relates to the absurd perception generated during the Trudeau era of the 1970s that tanks are "offensive" and therefore not in keeping with Canada's mythological peacekeeping image, something that must have lingered like some bizarre virus in the dark corners of the Canadian government. Tanks therefore became a symbol of Canada's continued commitment to the existence of an army as opposed to a constabulary force. These 19 tanks also ultimately symbolized Canada's continued commitment to and desire to be an effective player in NATO.

Word came down from the DCDS operations staff to the army planners that the battle group was to be cut to five hundred persons, from one thousand. The phone call came ten minutes before the minister of National Defence was about to go on television to announce the Kinetic deployment. The army planners had to figure out in ten minutes what was going to go and it boiled down

> to three Post-It notes. That's what we had to give them. On three Post-It notes I told them they could have a combat team (an infantry company and half of a tank squadron of ten Leopards), a big company group (an infantry company and a tank troop of four Leopards), and a small battalion (two infantry companies and a tank troop). They picked the third option. This "process" bypassed [the chief of the Land Staff] and it came as a complete surprise.... People are screaming at us, "What have you done!" right after the minister announced we were going to Kosovo with four tanks.[78]

Ultimately the decision to deploy a troop instead of a squadron reflected a compromise between those in the political ranks who thought tanks were too "offensive" from a public relations perspective and soldiers who understood the needs of the operational environment, where Canadian troops might have to fight an enemy equipped with main battle tanks, mechanized infantry combat vehicles, and self-propelled artillery.[79]

The decision-making process over the National Command Element (NCE) and National Support Element (NSE), though equally acrimonious for the branch and corps contenders, did not receive the high-level attention of the tank issue. The problem now shifted to getting the Kinetic and Kinetic (+) force to Kosovo, since Canada did not own any strategic lift. As part of cost-cutting measures introduced in the 1990s, a doctrine of alternate service delivery

(ASD) was developed whereby logistics functions were contracted out as much as possible, not only to save money but to reduce the burnout in service support personnel.[80] The logistics staff in NDHQ now sought out a roll-on/roll-off (RO-RO) transport ship suitable for the operation. The pressure was on after someone on the logistics staff suggested that the Kinetic and Kinetic (+) forces might, in fact, not be deployable until November 2001 because of the strategic lift situation. There were serious political ramifications, since "the arrival of the [battle group] in November would have the unpalatable appearance of Canada making an increased contribution only after the potential threat had largely been removed by its Allies."[81] Events in Kosovo were evolving and with them the need to get the Canadian force into the operational theater and acclimatized as rapidly as possible.

FIVE

Into the Breach, Dear Friends

KFOR Enters Kosovo

> From camp to camp, through the foul womb of night,
> The hum of either army stilly sounds,
> That the fixed sentinels almost receive
> The secret whispers of each other's watch.
> Fire answers fire, and through their paly flames
> Each battle sees the other's umbered face.
> Steed threatens steed, in high and boastful neighs,
> Piercing the night's dull ear. And from the tents
> The armorers accomplishing the knights
> With busy hammers closing rivets up
> Give dreadful note of preparation.
>
> —SHAKESPEARE, *King Henry V*, Act 4

The media focused their attentions on the air campaign throughout May and June 1999. In time the war of perceptions and the air war became indistinguishable, as commentators dissected the tone of voice and word usage of NATO spokespersons, attempted to decipher hidden, subliminal messages, and facilitated Belgrade's attempts to distort reality for their purposes. The deaths of people caught in the crossfire in Kosovo, minuscule in number compared to the figures for those killed in the great campaigns of World War II or by the various belligerent factions in Bosnia in the early 1990s, were now elevated to the status of weapons. The reality of the situation, however, was different. Almost no media attention was directed to the NATO land force buildup beyond a few stories about the role of KFOR and AFOR in assisting the refugees.

The FRY could not fail to see from its extensive espionage apparatus in the region that the NATO forces in Macedonia and Albania were preparing for a nonpermissive entry, and it was only a matter of time before they would be unleashed. Perhaps the VJ leadership was confident that they could make a fight of it: certainly the terrain favored the defense and there were fissures in NATO's resolve that could still be exploited. Perhaps they could hold out until the Russians intervened to save them. The pessimism among the media commentators, however, could not compete with the resolve and grim professional determination that resonated throughout the NATO forces deployed in Macedonia as they prepared for that day. Canada, meanwhile, grappled with the complexities of deploying the Op Kinetic forces and the tight timelines imposed by the situation as it developed.

Political and Military Developments, May 1999

The larger political drama over Kosovo was dominated by ongoing problems with the Russians, since there were many policy makers in the West who believed that Russia had to be included in some fashion and perhaps believed that Russia had some peculiar sway over Belgrade because of pan-Slavism. Russia, on the other hand, was coy. One view, espoused by Boris Yeltsin in his memoirs, was that the Clinton administration "found it necessary to stimulate North Atlantic solidarity by any means," that there was some form of "crisis of post-war values" in the United States, and that the Americans feared growing European influence. NATO, in Yeltsin's view, should not be allowed to be a "world policeman." Such a posture would create more instability and rekindle the Cold War, neither of which was good for Russia economically and either of which would be politically exploited by communists and nationalists alike. NATO's objectives of containing Milošević and fighting for national minorities and human rights were not real and were a cover for other objectives relating to an American global agenda inimical to Russian interests.[1]

Boris Yeltsin's ex post facto explanation for Russian actions during the Kosovo crisis is too pat and fails to explain subsequent Russian behavior. It also neatly avoids any Russian culpability for delaying an end to the conflict. A number of NATO nations, the United States included, were desperate to have Russia participate in solving the Kosovo problem. Yet the aggressive actions taken by the Russians in all areas proved to be impediments to this. For example, at Rambouillet the Russian delegation continuously pushed for the protection of FRY sovereignty, used every opportunity to discredit the Kosovar Albanians, and at every turn demanded that NATO's role in the enforcement of a peace be extremely limited.[2] At the same time, Russian representatives in the OSCE demanded to inspect NATO forces deployed in Italy, Macedonia, and Albania under the provisions of the Cold War–era Treaty on Conventional Forces in Europe (CFE), something that obviously would compromise AFOR and ARRC's operational security (in any event the Macedonia government interfered with an attempted Russian visit). Russia then suspended its involvement in Partnership for Peace activities.[3]

To make matters worse, the Russian general Viktor Chechevatov declared that this was all the start of World War III, and he attempted to form a volunteer airborne battalion from his command to serve with the VJ. In telephone conversations with President Clinton, Yeltsin even made veiled threats about nuclear war.[4]

Fate threw another wild card into this volatile mix. Louise Arbour and the ICTY indicted Milošević as a war criminal. In NATO circles the indictment was believed to have hardened Milošević's will to resist and to have disrupted attempts at direct negotiations, though ultimately it did shore up political support for Allied Force in some wavering member countries.[5] The Russians somehow interpreted this as a sabotage attempt against Russian peacemaking efforts to "prevent Yeltsin from achieving a very public diplomatic triumph [which was] necessary to boost his domestic political situation."[6]

The back-and-forth diplomatic game with the Russians continued concurrently with Allied Force. By 1 June the German-Russian-American talks in St. Petersburg were highlighting the specific obstacles to Russian cooperation in diplomatically pressuring Belgrade. The Russian delegation said "Nyet!" to a withdrawal of VJ and MUP forces from Kosovo, demanded a geographical sector in Kosovo under Russian command not subject to NATO command in any way if peace implementation forces went in, demanded UN

INTO THE BREACH, DEAR FRIENDS

political control of the operation, and insisted on a series of unrealistic modifications to any command and control arrangements. The talks stalled.[7]

Any separate Russian sector in Kosovo was unacceptable to those in NATO who were intimately familiar with similar problems encountered in Bosnia. If the Russians occupied their own sector free from KFOR control, there was a belief in some NATO quarters that the Kosovar Serbian population would flock to that sector and thus ethnically partition Kosovo and plant the seeds for long-term problems similar to those encountered in Cyprus. KFOR's stabilization mission would be ultimately ineffective and the principle of impartiality compromised, since the Russians and the Serbians would wind up in a de facto face-off against NATO and the Kosovar Albanians.[8]

The Russian position was not as inflexible as it appeared at the time, however; indeed there were serious splits between the Ministry of Defense negotiators led by Leonid Ivashov and the foreign affairs negotiators led by Viktor Chernomyrdin. The Russian military, as we will see, was not under the positive control of the Yeltsin government and took independent action that nearly started a war with NATO.

Chernomyrdin successfully wrested control of the negotiations from Ivashov and agreed that a joint Finnish-Russian delegation would visit Belgrade bearing a joint proposal of the G-8 to end the fighting. Essentially this proposal was the same as the proposed UN Security Council Resolution 1244, which demanded a full VJ and MUP withdrawal and the demilitarization of the UÇK, a resolution that was based on G-8 principles established back in April.[9]

Mounting the Belgrade trip took some time, and the war inside Kosovo continued. The VJ and MUP forces dramatically increased the tempo of their operations over a forty-eight-hour period, probably in response to the possibility that a political settlement might be reached in the near future. FRY operations on the border near Kukës and Ilias, Albania, which involved significant cross-border incursions accompanied by the use of artillery, prompted the UÇK to conduct Operation Arrow, which produced fighting in the Paštrik Mountain area.[10]

In general there are conflicting accounts about the degree of coordination between UÇK operations in Kosovo and operations conducted by NATO forces involved in ARRC, Allied Harbor, and Allied Force. Planners at SHAPE wanted the UÇK to flush out VJ mechanized forces (which were dispersed in the mountains and forests) so that NATO aircraft could target and destroy them.[11] The only time this appears to have worked effectively was in the later stages of the air campaign, when NATO air power and Albanian army artillery were used to support UÇK forces during Operation Arrow.[12]

Indeed it is generally assumed that a number of NATO nations introduced special operations forces into Kosovo to work with the UÇK and to designate targets for Allied Force. It is probable that the numbers involved were much smaller than those reported by the media.[13] It is also probable that there was a greater reliance on unmanned aerial vehicles, or UAVs, to provide surveillance and targeting data. For example, at least eight Predator UAVs were shot down by FRY air defenses during Allied Force, in addition to an equal number of German CL-289s.[14] Media reports that Canadian special operations forces were designating targets for NATO aircraft in Kosovo during this time are believed to be inaccurate.[15] NATO-member special operations forces were gathering information on the UÇK as much as observing the VJ and MUP dispositions, though their primary role was to liaise with the UÇK during and after the air campaign.[16]

Successful psychological operations were also conducted at this time. The Kosovar Albanian refugee flow into Macedonia was kept under close observation from American air resources, even at night. For several days running MUP and auxiliary police at a border control point would pull women and girls from the crowd, take them away, and rape them. These actions were recorded by the crew of an AC-130 Spectre gunship. A decision was made to kill the perpetrators, who could be individually identified by their hats, insignia, and weapons. The rapists were each killed with an individual 40mm round from the AC-130. Nonperpetrators, some of them within two meters of the targets, were left unharmed, at least physically. The rapes stopped and the psychological effect of the operation on Serb forces was measurable.[17]

KFOR Planning and Operation Agricola

Gen. Sir Mike Jackson and his staff at KFOR continued to grapple with the uncertainty of the political situation throughout May 1999. The main dilemma centered on how to get the force deployed on the ground in Macedonia and prepare it for operations so that it could function as both a credible tool to threaten Belgrade and a potential stabilization force. Jackson was hampered by the lack of understanding in NATO political circles regarding the relationship between the strategic ends and the military means. The types of forces necessary to implement an IFOR-like operation were not necessarily the same types of forces needed to conduct a forced entry mission. Yes, both force types included mechanized infantry combat vehicles, main battle tanks, attack helicopters, and self-propelled artillery, but the types of support structures necessary to handle the logistics of a protracted campaign were very different from those needed for an IFOR-like stabilization mission. Larger amounts of ammunition, more tanks, larger intelligence organizations, battle casualty handling units, and other elements necessary to carry the war to the VJ were all needed if the forced-entry option was to be implemented.

Preparing the troops was just as important, Jackson believed: "It was a period of uncertainty and many people had to live with that. I spent a lot of time talking to soldiers and told them this was a very dynamic situation and we will handle whatever comes of it, but I couldn't tell them what the end game was. They were pretty good about it, actually."[18]

On some days it was acceptable for NATO planners to plan for a forced entry, while on others it was not acceptable, particularly when options involving attacking toward and then occupying Belgrade were considered. KFOR, for example, was part of one contingency plan in which forces in Macedonia would conduct a spoiling operation in the south to pin down VJ forces, while other NATO forces operating from countries adjacent to Serbia would move on Belgrade. The debate at SHAPE revolved around the best means to end the conflict: forced entry into Kosovo or outright occupation of Serbia. Again, these were not rogue planning exercises conducted by NATO's military leadership. They were prudent, detailed operational plans designed to be available to provide NATO politicians with options.[19] The "Belgrade option" remained in the planning cells and was not actively considered by NATO political authorities in an official manner.[20]

KFOR's options were therefore considerably reduced. If pressed to conduct a forced-entry option, KFOR had only so many axes of advance. NATO forces could move to Kukës in Albania and then advance through the mountain pass toward Prizren, reinforcing the ongoing UÇK Operation Arrow to prepare the ground. KFOR could also conduct a right hook through the Preševo Valley north of Kumanovo and then to Gnjilane and on to Kosovo's interior. Neither of these options was optimal: moving KFOR through the mountainous region separating Macedonia and Albania and then logistically supporting the force through a network of extremely poor roads before assaulting through defensible terrain was risky. The other option was problematic for other reasons. Even though the terrain was much more open and lent itself to maneuver, the Preševo Valley hook would introduce NATO forces into Serbia proper, something that was considered akin to the "Belgrade option," with the accompanying associated political ramifications and the specter of unwelcome Russian involvement.

This left only one option: straight in the front door through the Kačanik defile. The Kačanik defile was the only substantial cut through the hills bordering Macedonia. It is about fifteen kilometers long and consists of a two-lane highway that parallels a railway line. The road hugs the right side of the pass, passing over several bridges and through numerous tunnels. The rail line lies below the level of the road along what amounts to a small river (depending on the season) and traverses it over a major bridge at one point. To further complicate things, there is a significant, built-up area two-thirds of the way through the defile: the town of Kačanik itself. The hills on either side of the road and rail line are increasingly forested the deeper one penetrates into the zone. All the road verges, tunnels, and bridges were mined. Clearly any trained and equipped military unit seeking to defend the Kačanik defile would have ample opportunity to make life hell for any attacking force by blowing up the tunnels and bridges and conducting a fighting withdrawal.

Defending forces in the immediate vicinity included a Border Guard battalion of eight hundred troops equipped with light armor and heavy weapons, and it was tasked with the immediate defense of the Kačanik zone. Backing up this unit was the VJ's 243rd Mechanized Brigade, based mostly in and around Uroševac, though a T-54/55 tank company, a mechanized infantry company, and a towed artillery battery were forward-deployed to Kačanik proper. The 243rd Mechanized Brigade was assessed to be 75 percent combat effective, with declining morale, poor command and control (there had been a "friendly fire" incident that had resulted in some deaths and a loss of confidence in the brigade leadership), and a logistics system that nearly forced the brigade to live off the land. Available reinforcements included the 252nd Armored Brigade and 15th Armored Brigade deployed in and north of Priština, forty-five to fifty kilometers away. These formations were believed to be in better shape from a morale and logistics standpoint.[21]

There were significant time pressures mounting in the summer of 1999. If the nearly one million refugees were not to suffer the deprivations of winter in their nearly open refugee camps, then they would need to return to their homes no later than mid-November. The end of October was a safer bet, as most houses had been torched and needed roofing. It would take a month just to repatriate these people. A military campaign to remove the VJ and MUP from Kosovo would therefore have to be completed by the end of September. In early May not enough NATO forces had arrived in Macedonia to implement such an operation (there were 13,900 as of 9 May), so Sir Mike Jackson and his staff pushed for an accelerated deployment in early May. When the facts were made available, "events changed gear from first to seventh," particularly after the G-8 meeting on 6 May. The effect of this shift was the discussion and development of concrete means to implement a ceasefire and withdrawal plan, as opposed to the vague ideas circulating in NATO, the G-8, and elsewhere.[22]

Between 5 and 16 May Canadian participation was limited to command liaison visits and a strategic/tactical recce as the Task Force Kosovo commander, Col. Mike Ward, and his staff sorted out myriad issues prior to the arrival of the first Canadian troops. As the situation stood on 9 May, all three options remained on the table: peace implementation, peace implementation with constraints, and forced entry.

So far ARRC had four reduced mechanized or armored brigades—French, German, Italian, and British—while the Americans supplied a reconnaissance battalion. KFOR was short of engineers, armored reconnaissance, medical support, and attack helicopters. The German, French, and British forces were prepared to double in size on short notice, particularly the Germans, who pre-positioned equipment for such a move. KFOR's mission was still to "monitor, verify and, when necessary, enforce compliance with the provisions of a cease-fire, provide humanitarian assistance to UNHCR, and establish initial basic law and order enforcement and core civil functions in order to facilitate peace and stability within Kosovo."[23]

Did KFOR wait to build up to five fully equipped brigades before conducting a forced entry or other operation, or should the existing deployed forces create a "foot in the door" through the Kačanik defile, which could then be held and expanded once reinforcing units were brought into Macedonia? It all depended on Belgrade's willingness to comply. All options were laden with risk. There was no safe, no-risk option. The timelines were tight and the geographic and political constraints severe.[24]

Determining the status of forced entry was necessary so that planning for Op Fortitude, by now called Kinetic (+), could continue, and the timing of the arrival and the exact role of the Kinetic recce and tactical helicopter squadrons needed clarification. Indeed "KFOR and the [intelligence staff of 4 (UK) Brigade] are very eager to see the Coyote vehicles arrive as they represent a considerable boost to the Brigade and force capabilities."[25]

As for the Lord Strathcona's Horse troops and the 408 Tactical Helicopter Squadron, the decision was made to place them under the operation control (OPCON) of 4 (UK) Brigade. Operation command (OPCOM) remained with Commander Task Force Kosovo (TFK). This is an extremely important distinction in that Canadian unit commanders under the OPCON of an allied commander retain the right to take orders from the Canadian task force commander if there is a belief that Canadian forces may be misused or otherwise improperly employed. Sovereign command of Canada's forces remains in Canadian hands at all times.

Colonel Ward was therefore to "supervise the administration, discipline, and operational readiness of TFK" and "to monitor" for the CDS "the day-to-day operations of the Canadian contingent." The operational chain of command went from the units (the Strathcona's troops and 408 Squadron) to the brigade commander of 4 (UK) Armoured Brigade to Commander KFOR. Commander TFK was to "continually monitor the situation in Kosovo, taking the necessary action to ensure that Canadian policy and Canadian interests are represented and respected."[26]

Canada had a number objectives that were to be met by participating in Operation Joint Guardian: "Canada's overall desired end-state for KFOR is a secure environment and a self-sustaining peace, adequate for the continued consolidation of peace without the need for NATO-led military forces in Kosovo. Canada's expectation is that it will be called upon to contribute to the mission for approximately a three-year period . . . you shall ensure that OP KINETIC personnel, as part of KFOR, maintain a deterrent posture to ensure compliance with a negotiated peace accord."[27]

On 20 May SACEUR briefed NATO military commanders that the ground force option as developed by KFOR would consist of entry into a "semi-permissive environment," a situation in which there was no detailed political agreement between Belgrade and NATO but one in which well-organized Serb resistance had collapsed. This move essentially rationalized an intervention with a force level substantially less than that recommended by the planners: twenty-six thousand instead of fifty thousand, though the environment was considered to be slightly more benign.[28]

The situation for the Canadian forces on 29–30 May was as follows: the air logistics control element (ALCE) of seventeen personnel was in position to handle the air movement of personnel into

Macedonia and/or Thessaloniki. Thirty members of the National Command Element (NCE) and fifty-five members of the National Support Element (NSE) were in Skopje. The first eighty-three members of 15th Engineer Squadron were in theater, preparing living space and facilities for the NCE and NSE at the Sveti Nikole factory site. The twelve-person Strathcona's recce party led by Maj. Paul Fleury was seeking working-up facilities and liaising with 4 (UK) Brigade HQ. Counterintelligence indicated that Serb assets were observing the Canadian deployment and trying to assess the size and equipment of the force. In Macedonia the espionage threat was rated as high, while the terrorism threat level was placed at moderate. In Greece, particularly the communist political stronghold of the Thessaloniki port, where the Op Kinetic forces would unload, the same alert levels applied. Greek demonstrators continued to interfere with KFOR troop movements: in one case, four hundred demonstrators delayed the Italian contingent's off-load for forty-eight hours.[29]

The problem of the Kačanik defile was addressed when Sir Mike Jackson asked NATO for a light infantry brigade, preferably one that had an airmobile capability. The nature of the terrain in the defile made it problematic for a direct armored thrust, and KFOR planners believed that an airmobile coup de main designed to simultaneously secure the bridges and high ground was the best means. Numerous NATO governments declined to provide light infantry forces, so the British government prepared to dispatch nineteen hundred members of Five Airborne Brigade to Macedonia at the last minute in a rather rushed deployment. Five Airborne Brigade, commanded by Brig. Adrian Freer, included 1st Battalion, Parachute Regiment, and 1st Battalion, Royal Gurkha Rifles, plus several Chinook and Lynx helicopters.[30]

The entire planning and deployment situation was thrown a curve by a diplomatic breakthrough and the abrupt start of the endgame for Belgrade's war. One can speculate endlessly about exactly how Slobodan Milošević decided to cease and desist. Ultimately it was probably a combination of factors. On 2 June Viktor Chernomyrdin of Russia and Martti Ahtisaari of Finland delivered an ultimatum on behalf of the international community: withdraw from Kosovo or face a NATO ground invasion accompanied by an expanded bombing campaign. Chernomyrdin added that Russia would do nothing to interfere with a NATO ground offensive and that Milošević was now on his own. Any rational calculus on Milošević's part should have included a combination of NATO's demonstration of resolve, the understanding that the UÇK could not be defeated, and the efforts of Serbia's political opposition, as exemplified by Radio B92 and the anti-Milošević OTPOR group. Whether it did or not, there was the added ignominy of Arbour's ICTY indictment of Milošević, which made it all too personal. According to intelligence sources, Milošević's decision making throughout May was punctuated by continual screaming at aides, temper tantrums, and the hurling of papers and small items across his office—clear signs that the NATO campaign had had a significant psychological impact on the Serb leader.[31]

On 3 June Belgrade media announced that the Serbian parliament had accepted and Milošević had ratified the G-8's terms for a ceasefire in Kosovo. Those terms included a UN interim administration for Kosovo, a NATO-led international force, and the total withdrawal of VJ and MUP forces. Sir Mike Jackson told KFOR contributors to be prepared for an agreement that might permit KFOR to enter Kosovo within five days.[32] This did not necessarily mean that the forced-entry option was shelved; indeed it was unclear what action the VJ and MUP, let alone the Kosovar Serbs themselves, might take.

Reporting that there was "an air of prudent expectation throughout KFOR," Col. Mike Ward urgently asked the DCDS to accelerate the Canadian deployment. With the existing timelines and the ongoing problems with the Greeks, the Op Kinetic forces would be declared ready no earlier than 22 June, which meant that "our troops would be assigned to 4 (UK) Brigade a minimum of twelve days after it had potentially commenced operations into Kosovo. This would leave the Commander 4 (UK) Brigade short handed and would deny him resources that he has factored into his plans for the operation."[33]

Translation: if Canada is not on the ground in time, the reliability of Canada's armed forces would once again be questioned in NATO political circles, with a resultant decrease in influence and prestige, as had been the case in the Persian Gulf in 1990, in Bosnia and Croatia in 1995, and in Zaire in 1996, not to mention the potential for professional embarrassment at the military level, which had to be avoided to maintain army self-esteem.

On 7 June 4 (UK) Armoured Brigade issued its warning order and contingency plan for Operation Agricola, "Entry into Kosovo."[34] In keeping with the uncertain nature of the political and tactical situation, the planners believed that "the VJ will probably be generally compliant" but that "the potential threat from Serb terrorists and paramilitary groups could be high." There was also a significant mine threat. The situation could easily shift in that "Serb compliance could change quickly if Serb forces or civilians in Kosovo are attacked by the UCK and NATO is unable to intervene or guarantee adequate protection." As for the Albanian population, they would "initially welcome NATO but relations could deteriorate if KFOR attempts to disarm the UCK or neutralize their influence." The intelligence staff anticipated that the UÇK would attack withdrawing MUP and VJ forces.[35]

KFOR was therefore to "deploy available forces as rapidly as possible to establish an initial presence in Kosovo to fill the vacuum created by withdrawing VJ/MUP forces . . . and create a secure environment." A "robust reaction in those areas where we may face difficulties" was mandated "to pre-empt escalation and avoid recurrences." A detailed phased withdrawal scheme was formulated for the VJ and MUP forces. There were three zones: Zone I would be cleared by day three, II by day five, and III by day seven.[36]

Op Agricola was set to go, pending final negotiations between Belgrade and the international community that would create the interim agreement (IA), as well as final negotiations between KFOR and the senior VJ commanders, which would form the basis for a military technical agreement (MTA). Canada was still not ready: "Commander 4 (UK) Armd Bde is urgently waiting to receive additional resources ASAP. Four (UK) Armd Bde continues to produce contingency plans to enforce the [international agreement] for peace with what they physically and currently have on the ground

INTO THE BREACH, DEAR FRIENDS

and ready to deploy with two hours north into Kosovo. To date, other than 15 Engineer Squadron, CANADA cannot and has not been considered a 'player' until they are under OPCON to 4 (UK) Armd Bde and ready to deploy within 2 hours [notice to move]. Time is of the essence as operational tempo remains relentless."[37]

Clearly the presence of 111 engineers working on rear-area facilities and the 117 members of the NCE and NSE occupying them did not constitute enough of a credible force to represent Canada in this endeavor. Commander Task Force Kosovo's intent was to accelerate, by any means necessary, the deployment of the Coyote recce squadron.[38]

Like a Stream of Light, Canada Arrives Just in Time

Canada was confronted with two problems: Greek intransigence over landing Kinetic, as well as Canadian political approval for Kinetic (+). In addition to its barely concealed sympathy for the Belgrade regime, the Greek government was involved in elections throughout this period and didn't want the Kosovo issue to disproportionately interfere with the political campaign. Consequently Greece imposed a ban or embargo on NATO troop movements through Thessaloniki from 5 June to 15 June. This embargo was announced at the end of May and appeared to be an extension of the "unofficial" harassment of KFOR forces that had been under way in the port area for some time.[39]

As we have seen, the indicators on 4 June that the Belgrade regime would cave in had accelerated KFOR planning, and Canada struggled to catch up, having set a date of 15 June to land the Kinetic forces in Thessaloniki and having found that date not acceptable. Canada then entered into a "very delicate diplomatic dance" with the Greeks.[40] Through the efforts of Col. Geoff St. John and others, the Greek defense ministry was persuaded to support a Canadian exception to the embargo in the face of the Greek foreign affairs ministry's demands that there be no special treatment unless Canadian pressure was brought to bear in NATO councils to stop Operation Allied Force or a ceasefire agreement was signed, sealed, and delivered by Belgrade. Worse, it appeared to some that the Russians were influencing the Greeks to slow down KFOR, since any delay gave the Russians time to deploy a force into Kosovo before NATO could do so.[41]

Salami tactics were then employed by the Canadian representatives: Could the non-military-looking sea containers on the ship perhaps be off-loaded, since the embargo applied to obvious military equipment? Could the helicopters be assembled out of sight and fly north under cover of darkness? What if the 25mm gun barrels were not mounted on the Coyotes to reduce their aggressive appearance? Was there an out-of-the-way quay near Thessaloniki where the ship could unload away from the prying eyes of the activist mayor? The local stevedores and dockworkers did not need to be involved: could Canadian drivers drive the vehicles off the ramps themselves?[42]

While the Kinetic forces were preparing to unload at Thessaloniki, Gen. Maurice Baril was finally able to secure Canadian government approval for Op Kinetic (+). On 11 June the CDS issued a warning order for the departure of the 1 PPCLI battle group.[43] The Kinetic (+) deployment initially was not considered as urgent as Kinetic, since it would take some time for the battle group to deploy, and the recce squadron and tactical helicopter squadron were sufficient to guarantee significant participation in the early stages of Op Agricola. The 1 PPCLI battle group was, however, integral to 4 (UK) Armoured Brigade's plans once KFOR entered Kosovo's interior.

Gen. Sir Mike Jackson and the KFOR staff meanwhile remained involved in intense negotiations with VJ representatives in Kumanovo, Macedonia. Despite the high-level agreement with Belgrade, the war in Kosovo continued and would do so until a comprehensive agreement was made to implement an actual ceasefire on the ground. For example, on 8 June the VJ were preparing an offensive against the UÇK in western Kosovo along the Albanian border. The next day American B-52 bombers unloaded tons of bombs on the VJ forces in the west, killing some 225 personnel and effectively blunting the offensive. MUP counterinsurgency operations continued near Komorane in the Drenica Valley.[44]

The interconnectedness between all levels (political, strategic, tactical) is best captured by a Canadian assessment on 8 June 1999:

> G8 ministers have agreed on a draft resolution for a peace as negotiations continued in Bonn. Initial reports indicate that successful talks resulted in a submitted proposal to the [UN Security Council]. If the UN Security Council agrees to it formally, Russian President Yeltsin [has] told his foreign minister to sign. Assuming [European Union] envoy Ahtisaari succeeds in persuading China to co-operate, this could happen today. However, China and Russia say they will not agree to a formal [UN Security Council] resolution until NATO's bombing campaign stops. Sequencing therefore next involves NATO-Yugoslavia agreement on a [military technical agreement]. This is to be followed by Yugoslav troop withdrawals and a bombing pause.[45]

One part of the MTA problem involved the command and control arrangements with the proposed Russian KFOR contingent. The Russians, as discussed earlier, wanted their own zone, and SACEUR wanted to deny them this. Jackson, however, was dealing with the specifics of the VJ/MUP withdrawal plan, which essentially were similar to those of the 7 June Agricola contingency plan discussed above. On 9 June at 2106 hours the KFOR commander and the VJ leadership signed the MTA and agreed that the withdrawal would commence on 10 June (for a detailed examination of the MTA and its specific effects on the KFOR concept of operations, see below). Hašim Thaçi from the UÇK belatedly announced to Madeleine Albright that the UÇK would cooperate with the VJ/MUP withdrawal.[46]

On 10 June 1999 the bombing stopped (though it could readily be turned on again at any time) and the UN Security Council passed Resolution 1244 (1999) authorizing the creation of the United Nations Mission in Kosovo (UNMIK) as the civilian pillar. It also recognized the NATO-led KFOR as the military pillar in administering and controlling Kosovo.[47] There was yet another delay in introducing KFOR into Kosovo: the Russians were starting to change their minds on supporting the MTA, so KFOR was now scheduled to go in on 12 June.[48]

Maj. Paul Fleury of the Lord Strathcona's Horse Recce Squadron meanwhile was trying to convince Brigadier Rollo and the staff of 4 (UK) Armoured Brigade that the squadron would arrive in time to participate in the first day of operations:

> They figured we weren't going to get in there and the brigadier had other fish to fry, but he hadn't said no we couldn't come with them, so I went right to the staff officers and said I wanted in and I didn't care where. We just had to get in there someplace on the big day. No one remembers who comes in on D +1 or D +3 or D +40. We had to be able to say we were in the first wave of allied troops. In fact, only us and the Brits got in the first day; all the other nations came after. It was a prestige thing for Canada and we had worked so bloody hard to get there. We needed to get in there. We thought we had something to offer which the British didn't have and they eventually came to see it that way.[49]

The Coyotes, however, were still on the ship that was approaching Thessaloniki, and their crews hadn't yet left Canada by air. The efforts of Colonel St. John and others finally succeeded: the first chartered 747 flight came in at 1030 hours and the GTS *Katie* docked at 2030 hours, 9 June. The ordeal continued, however:

> There was a demonstration. We had difficulty with the port police, who were actually working on behalf of the rioters and the Communist Party, and they did everything they could to shut us down or disrupt the offloads so that we couldn't meet our timings. . . . We had to get the packets ready to go because the Greeks didn't want convoys on the roads. We also wanted to keep a low profile because convoys that were detected were often stoned and had windows broken and troops injured. About midway through the morning a Greek colonel responsible for the logistics in the port started playing games with us and gave us two hours to unload. We had seven hours to go, so our attaché ran interference. I would turn to him and pose the problem, he would turn back to me and vehemently say it couldn't be done, and I would turn to the intermediary who was a major working for the colonel and say, "You know, I'm sorry, we're doing the best we can," and he would go back

to his colonel who was smoking a cigarette Napoleon-style with one arm behind his back, and he would insist that this was unacceptable and so on. It became apparent to him he couldn't stop the offload, so it became a face-saving game. It was very Peter Sellers: he'd wave his finger at us for the benefit of his subordinates and sternly tell us to get going.[50]

The Strathcona's battle captain, Trevor Gosselin, coordinated the offload and move north to Macedonia:

> The guys landed at the airport and we were escorted everywhere by Greek national police till we got to some Greek barracks for about twelve hours, then down to the port at midnight, start unloading, first convoys leave at 0430, the sun comes up, we stop operations, put the guys to ground, and do the same thing again. There was some chaos: our guys had never unloaded a boat before. There was just obstacle after obstacle being thrown up. As soon as we get the Greek police on side, someone else said we can't do this or that. It was hurdle, after hurdle, after hurdle just getting out of Thessaloniki.
>
> Then we started to run out of fuel. The Coyotes were not full up because of expansion, blah, blah, blah, federal shipping regulations, yadda yadda yadda. On the way, Major Fleury took the squadron through a gas station on the highway which had a single pump running.[51]

Capt. Mark Connolly, the recce squadron second in command (2IC), commented,

> We arrived in the Krivolak training area [Macedonia] at 0700 hours, and it was 40 degrees [104 Fahrenheit] and dusty as hell. Some of the sea containers came forward with us, but basically our vehicles were packed with everything we could throw in and it all had to be reorganized. Then test the surveillance equipment, stow the ammunition. This all had to be done by 1700 since the squadron was leaving to go to Skopje, where the brigade assembly area was. We needed fuel and the NSE trucks were caught in a traffic jam, so somebody from the NSE showed up with a bag of money, and with the one diesel pump working, we took two hours to refuel and finally pulled into the assembly area at Petrovac around midnight.[52]

Members of 408 Tactical Helicopter Squadron, led by the squadron aircraft maintenance engineering officer (SAMEO), Capt. Barbara Palmer, also had their trials with bureaucracy and politics at Thessaloniki as they tried to reassemble their Griffon helicopters:

> Because of the political climate, we had to work at night and leave at night. We couldn't even travel during daylight on the streets. After we unloaded the ship at night, which was unique, our stuff was all over the port and we had a time just finding and opening the sea containers. We were lucky we had our special equipment vehicles. Our technicians, thankfully, thought ahead and did "illegal" things like smuggling in baggies of cotter pins and other items from Thessaloniki. . . . We had to do some serious improvisation. We then had to pass a Greek inspection to fly through Greek airspace, so a Griffon had to be assembled and ferried to the inspection site before the rest could leave. We then had to reconfigure the aircraft for the mission equipment in 45 degree [113 Fahrenheit] heat with no sleep.[53]

Then the Greeks claimed that the Griffons did not have diplomatic clearance to fly over Greek airspace, which necessitated further negotiations. More time was lost.[54]

At 0500 hours, 12 June 1999, Gurkhas from the 1st Battalion, Royal Gurkha Rifles, and airborne soldiers from the 1st Battalion, Parachute Regiment, departed for the Kačanik defile aboard large twin-rotor Chinooks and smaller single-rotor Puma helicopters. Capt. David Travers, a Canadian serving with 4 (UK) Armoured Brigade's intelligence staff, was "astonished by the sight of all of this power. There were six AH-64 Apache gunships in the lead, with another six Apaches on each flank. Every transport helicopter available to NATO forces in Macedonia was in the air at once flying the men of 5 Airborne Brigade to their objectives." The initial plan was to have the Gurkhas move on and seize the Priština airport, but reports were coming in that the Russians were on the move, with that area as a probable objective, so the Kačanik defile was split into two battalion areas of operation: one for the paratroopers in the south and the other for the Gurkhas to the north, closer to the deserted town of Kačanik. Both battalions, assisted by combat engineers, cleared the route of demolitions and secured the bridges and tunnels so that 4 (UK) Armoured Brigade could pass through.[55]

The Priština Airport Standoff

While KFOR was preparing to seize and penetrate the Kačanik defile, the ongoing negotiations with the Russians with regard to their role in KFOR and how they would be commanded continued to simmer. The Russians refused to budge on a number of issues, particularly their demand for a separate sector. This was significant domestic issue in Moscow, with the Duma calling on Yeltsin to fire Viktor Chernomyrdin on 10 June.

On Friday, 11 June, the day before Five Airborne Brigade moved on the Kačanik defile, a Russian mechanized infantry company of 150 troops with some fourteen BTR-80 APCs and another fourteen support vehicles left their SFOR area of operations in Bosnia and headed for Belgrade in Serbia. The column then proceeded to enter the outskirts of Priština at 0300 hours, 12 June, or two hours before the KFOR entry plan was launched. By the time the Gurkhas and paratroopers were clearing the defile, the Russian contingent, led by the newly promoted Col. Gen. Viktor Zavarzin, moved on to the Priština airport. Zavarzin incidentally was the Russian NATO representative who had been recalled back in March, and therefore this appointment had a symbolic or signaling function as much as a command function. Russian foreign minister Ivan Ivanov issued a statement that the deployment was a mistake, but within hours he told Madeleine Albright that it was an advance party for a larger follow-up force. The Kremlin then publicly contradicted Ivanov and said that Yeltsin had ordered the troops in.

The Russian move has been the subject of much controversy and speculation, particularly with regard to Russian motives and NATO's response. Many of the events surrounding the airport standoff occurred concurrently, so it is best to handle the incident and its implications one step at a time.

NATO planners and intelligence staffs at SHAPE and KFOR were well aware of the Russian move into Serbia while it was occurring on 11 June but had problems interpreting it. In his memoirs Gen.

Wesley Clark presents the case that the Russians were attempting to secure an enclave for the Kosovar Serbs, embarrass NATO, and disrupt KFOR's ability to carry out its operations or, as he put it, "put the whole premise of KFOR at risk," since the Russian force would not behave in an impartial fashion and act in a pro-Serb manner, as it had in Bosnia.[56] He therefore ordered KFOR to assemble a force to conduct an airmobile landing at the Priština airport ahead of them.

The insertion of special operations forces was prepared and mounted, but the SAS force was unable to get in because its C-130 transport crashed at an airfield near Kukës in Albania on the night of 10 June.[57] KFOR HQ told SHAPE that there was not enough helicopter lift, that the two light infantry battalions were spread thin and had deployed for the Kačanik defile task. The U.S. Marine Corps force committed to KFOR the 26th Marine Expeditionary Unit (26 MEU), and its helicopters were not yet ready, since they were encountering the same problems as the Canadian contingent in Thessaloniki. Although there were two company-sized French airmobile units, their commander was apparently not sympathetic to SACEUR's plan after he consulted with KFOR HQ.

Canadian officers in 4 (UK) Armoured Brigade and in KFOR HQ suggested that elements of the Coyote squadron could, if necessary, race through the Kačanik defile at high speed to reach the Priština airport, since the Coyote was an eight-wheeled armored car with a top speed of more than 100 km/h (60 mph) and significantly faster than the British Scimitar recce vehicle's 80 km/h (50 mph). This option was turned down by KFOR HQ.[58]

Sir Mike Jackson did not agree with SACEUR's view of the situation: "I remember saying 'For fuck's sake, who needs this state of affairs?' There was a real sort of friction with this complication, but it was a reality. These boys were going to be part of KFOR; they would be on the ground."[59] Indeed the senior Canadian on the ground, Col. Mike Ward, noted,

> I think General Jackson stayed with his original time frame, very
> wisely, on the basis that we had created a very difficult negotiated
> settlement [the MTA with the Serbs] and there was real concern

about confidence building in the wake of eighty days of bombing them. We didn't want to disrupt that, unless there was a real requirement. [We had] aviation assets which we could have put in, but they would have been at risk from Serb air defense. An unpredicted, unplanned, and undeclared event would have resulted in a catastrophe, for no greater gain. The Russian issue [at that point] was really a distraction, but it could have completely unraveled the entire diplomatic process.[60]

Unfortunately the situation was starting to spin out of control on the US-Russian diplomatic front, with attendant implications for NATO. Strobe Talbott, the designated American negotiator with Russia on the talks relating to the inclusion of Russia in KFOR, left Moscow when he made no headway. He was turned around in midflight and ordered to get the Russians talking again. Russian media reports stated that chief of the Russian general staff, Anatoly Kvashnin, ordered in the Priština force and bypassed the defense minister, Igor Sergeyev. Intelligence and media reports that IL-76 transport aircraft were warming up at Severnaya airfield and preparing to embark Russian airborne forces for deployment to the Priština airport generated heightened concern in Brussels, Mons, and Washington. Who was in control of the Russian government? Who was giving these orders? And why?

Combined NATO diplomatic activity worked to physically block any attempt by the Russians to intervene. Hungary, Romania, and Bulgaria were asked in turn to resist Russian demands to allow their airborne forces to pass through their airspace (Turkey was already on board with this effort). These three nations agreed to deny any incursion, despite the fact that two of them were not NATO members and did not technically fall under Article 5 protection if they were attacked by the Russians. American policy makers considered the ramifications of shooting down the Russian transports.

General Clark instructed KFOR to enter the Priština airport and block the runways with vehicles and helicopters. In a personally tense discussion General Jackson, backed by the British CDS, according to the media, basically told SACEUR that he was not going to start World War III for him. Indeed KFOR was engaged in negotiations with Zavarzin, and the VJ and MUP had sealed off the airport. Elements of 4 (UK) Brigade (including the Strathcona Coyotes) and 5 Airborne Brigade had by this time reached Priština and conducted a show of force to let the Russians and VJ know they were cut off and surrounded.

Pres. Bill Clinton and Pres. Boris Yeltsin discussed the matter on the phone on Sunday, 13 June, and agreed to allow the local commanders to solve the details of the Russian presence in Priština. Brig. Adrian Freer was appointed (Brigadier Rollo noted that "when we found the Russians, the vodka and whisky bottles came out and I thought one British brigadier engaged in this exercise was quite enough").[61] Freer worked out an arrangement with Kvashnin to split the airport into a British zone and a Russian zone, though this took some time.

The higher-level negotiations about what role Russian troops would play in KFOR and where they would operate continued for several days. By this point the U.S. secretary of defense and his Russian counterpart were meeting in Helsinki to develop a written agreement. The situation remained tense, and Gen. Maurice Baril, the CDS, ordered the Operation Kinetic (+) deployment to accelerate on 16 July. Within ten days the vanguard company from the 1 PPCLI battle group had left from Edmonton by air, heading for Kosovo.

By 19 June the BBC was reporting that there was some sort of power struggle in progress in Moscow. Word was leaking out that the Bosnia-to-Kosovo deployment of Russian troops and the preparations to deploy an airborne battalion from Russia had been made by senior Russian military officers without the knowledge of the prime minister, foreign minister, Yeltsin's Balkans envoy, or the defense minister. Yeltsin in his memoirs claims that this operation was planned and his concurrence given on the night of 4 June: "I decided that Russia must make a crowning gesture, even if it had no military significance. It was not a question of specific diplomatic victories or defeats: it was a question of whether we had won the main point. . . . This last gesture was a sign of our moral victory in the face of the enormous NATO military, all of Europe, and the whole world. I gave the order: GO."[62]

On the surface these admissions appear to tell the story. However, they do not explain the extremely troublesome and dangerous events of 25 June. At 0220 hours Zulu two Bear-H bombers and two TU-160 Blackjack bombers, all Russian aircraft, flew into an identification zone controlled by NORAD. The Bear-H aircraft were intercepted southwest of Iceland and monitored by American F-15 fighter aircraft, while Canadian CF-18 aircraft were deployed to back up the F-15s. The Blackjacks were not intercepted, having exited the identification zone before the Bears.[63]

The types of aircraft and what they were capable of carrying was significant. There are many versions of Bear aircraft. The most common seen by NORAD during the Cold War were the electronic intelligence–gathering variants trying to gauge the strength of Canadian air defenses. The TU-142 Bear-Hs deployed against North America in June 1999 were specifically designed to each carry eight AS-15 cruise missiles. The TU-160 Blackjacks were each capable of carrying twelve AS-15s. There are no non-nuclear or reconnaissance variants of the TU-160. The total number of nuclear cruise missiles carried by these four aircraft was approximately forty. Each AS-15 has a three-thousand-kilometer range and yield of 250 kilotons, that is, more than ten times the yield of the weapons exploded at Hiroshima and Nagasaki.[64]

During the Cold War this event would not have evoked a high level of concern and might even have been considered routine. Lt. Gen. George Macdonald, the Canadian deputy commander in chief of NORAD, was on duty in the Cheyenne Mountain Complex in Colorado that morning: "This was very unusual. There had been an eight- or nine-year hiatus since the previous flight into the Alaska/Northern basin, so this was unique. This was not a deployment to a forward base but rather a single flight. We did not at the time directly link it to events in Kosovo but took the initiative to actively assess whether it was a threat or not. We knew what was happening but not why."[65]

If the bombers had continued on course for another five hundred kilometers, they would have had the entire northeast portion of the United States and most of industrialized Canada in range. It is impossible to interpret this deployment as anything other than an attempt to intimidate NATO with a nuclear threat.

The exact motives for the Bear and Blackjack flight remain obscure, however. The next day a Russian IL-76 was permitted by KFOR to fly into the Priština airport and offload Russian "technicians" to help "repair" the airfield. The three-thousand-strong follow-on force was then grounded en route as negotiations were once again broken off. SACEUR refused to compromise on the Russians' demands for their own sector in Kosovo. Russian military representatives publicly sputtered that this was "provocation," but on 5 July a deal was finally concluded in Helsinki and the first Russian troop contingent arrived by air on 6 July.

What are we to make of this state of affairs? Commander KFOR in retrospect believes that "we should not underestimate the degree of genuine anger, not just posturing, but genuine anger felt in Moscow when NATO went bombing without a UN Security Council resolution. It was a bit hypocritical given what was going on in Chechnya. . . . [It might have been a situation where] I'm sitting in Moscow on the twenty-fourth of March, the West put a finger into each of my eyes, and I say, okay, here's one coming back. Just a little dig."[66]

The Canadian CDS, Gen. Maurice Baril, was aware that the Russian interest in the Priština airport had additional motives: "They went for the big tunnel. Everybody was worried about what the hell was in there. The intervention stopped something very big or could have started something much bigger. . . . We wanted NATO to take the airport right away, [and] Jackson refused to stop the Russians because the Russians were going to fight to go in. That could have started a war."[67]

Priština airport was much more than a civilian airport. The north-south oriented runways that paralleled the high features were supplemented by two long taxiways that ran through blast doors into a huge aircraft storage area and bunker system under Mount Goleš. Prewar Yugoslavia had had several similar bases, like the one located in the Canadian SFOR area of operations near Bihać in Bosnia. The initial Russian force with its hastily applied KFOR insignia immediately secured this facility. Several trucks were loaded up and driven off to the north in the confusion of the KFOR advance. Once the Russians were permitted landing rights in July, empty IL-76 transports regularly landed at the Priština airport to remove whatever else was stored under Mount Goleš.[68]

Some believe that the Russians had given the VJ chemical weapons or even tactical nuclear weapons. Such a move is unlikely, though the Russians had had experience in using chemical weapons against insurgencies in the past. Turning over nuclear weapons to Belgrade is beyond the realm of reality. Others believe that parts from a crashed USAF F-117 Stealth fighter were stored there.

The best explanation is that the bunkers were used to house Russian signals intelligence, electronic warfare, and air defense systems either operated by Russian "advisors" or by the VJ or some combination thereof. Perhaps some of these systems had some role in the destruction of the USAF's F-117 aircraft. Mount Goleš had a number of "golf ball" radar domes on it and numerous antennas and aerials that matched equipment used for signals intelligence and electronic warfare. These were put out of action by NATO air attacks. Canadian reconnaissance resources were able to see SA-2 and SA-6 antiaircraft missiles being removed after the Russians took over the complex.[69]

It is obvious, given the extremely tense relationship between Russia and NATO during the whole Kosovo crisis, that explicit proof of Russian military support to Belgrade—support that posed a direct threat to the lives of NATO pilots (including Allied Force's Canadian CF-18 pilots)—could not have been allowed to fall into NATO hands. The political repercussions would have been enormous and would probably have contributed to a second Cold War or, as we have seen above, worse. It is perhaps better that the Russians were permitted to save face in this instance.

As of the summer of 2001, no non-Russian member of KFOR had been allowed into the Mount Goleš bunker complex.[70]

3

CANADA AND KFOR OPERATIONS

SIX

Warrior Politics
Multinational Brigade (Center) Operations

Allowing flagrant aggression to succeed is always dangerous, even if the immediate consequences seem limited, because of the precedent it sets.

—LADY MARGARET THATCHER, *Statecraft*

The Military Technical Agreement, the Undertaking, and KFOR's Concept of Operations

It is necessary to delve into the specifics of the political agreements and the military concepts of operations designed to implement them before moving on to examine Canadian operations and where they fit. The umbrella document was UN Security Council Resolution 1244 (1999), passed on 10 June. Paying the usual lip service to previous resolutions, 1244 (1999) basically provided UN endorsement of the G-8 foreign ministers' principles adopted at the St. Petersburg meeting of 6 May. To wit, the general principles for a political solution to the Kosovo crisis included:

- Immediate and verifiable cessation of violence and repression in Kosovo
- Withdrawal from Kosovo of military, police, and paramilitary forces
- Deployment in Kosovo of effective international civil and security presences, endorsed and adopted by the United Nations, capable of guaranteeing the achievement of common objectives
- Establishment of an interim administration for Kosovo to be

decided by the Security Council of the United Nations to assure conditions for a peaceful and normal life for all inhabitants in Kosovo

- The safe and free return of all refugees and displaced persons and unimpeded access to Kosovo by humanitarian aid organizations
- A political process toward the establishment of an interim political framework agreement providing for substantial self-government for Kosovo, taking full account of the Rambouillet accords and the principles of sovereignty and territorial integrity of the Federal Republic of Yugoslavia and the other countries of the region, and the demilitarization of the [UÇK]
- Comprehensive approach to the economic development and stabilization of the crisis region[1]

Several aspects of the security presence were also laid out:

- Verifiable withdrawal from Kosovo of all military, police, and paramilitary forces according to a rapid timetable
- Deployment in Kosovo under UN auspices of effective international civil and security presences, acting under chapter VII of the charter
- International security presence with substantial North Atlantic Treaty Organization participation deployed under unified command and control and authorized to establish a safe environment for all people in Kosovo and to facilitate the safe return to their homes of all displaced persons and refugees[2]

Resolution 1244 (1999) also recognized the military technical agreement (MTA) signed on 9 June 1999 by Gen. Sir Mike Jackson, representing KFOR, and Col. Gen. Svetozar Marjanović, representing the VJ, and Lt. Gen. Obrad Stevanović of the MUP. The MTA emphasized that the Serbian parliament agreed to KFOR's presence and that the UN "permitted" KFOR "to operate without hindrance within Kosovo and with the authority to take all necessary action to establish and maintain a secure environment for all citizens of Kosovo and otherwise carry its mission." An air safety zone (ASZ) of twenty-five kilometers and a ground safety

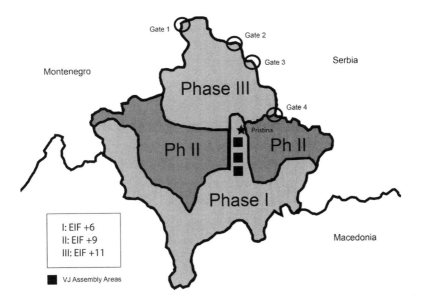

FIG. 8. The military technical agreement withdrawal phase lines and timeline for federal Serbian forces to quit Kosovo.

zone (GSZ) of five kilometers were established extending from the Kosovo provincial border into the rest of Serbia. No VJ, MUP, or any other Yugoslav forces were permitted into the ASZ or GSZ without KFOR approval so that "a durable cessation of hostilities" could be achieved.[3]

Entry into Force (EIF) Day was the "D-Day" for the withdrawal schedule. The phased withdrawal consisted of three phases over an eleven-day period: all VJ and MUP forces had to be clear of the GSZ by day eleven. KFOR "shall retain, as necessary, authority to enforce compliance." Withdrawing VJ and MUP forces using designated routes "will not be subject to air attack." As for air activity, "no FRY aircraft, fixed wing or rotary, will fly in Kosovo airspace or over the ASZ without prior approval from [KFOR]" and "all air defence systems, radar, surface to air missile and aircraft of the Parties will refrain from acquisition, target tracking or otherwise illuminating [KFOR] air platforms operating in Kosovo or over the ASZ." By EIF plus three days, all air defense systems, including troop-portable antiaircraft missiles, had to withdraw beyond the ASZ.[4]

Commander KFOR was permitted great latitude in the MTA: "[KFOR] commander shall have the authority, without inference or permission, to do all he judges necessary and proper, including the use of military force, to protect [KFOR], the international civil implementation presence, and to carry out the [MTA]." In other words the UN-style ambiguity that got peace support operations and their personnel into so much trouble in the Balkans and elsewhere throughout the 1990s would not be tolerated.[5]

The KFOR concept of operations implemented to meet these criteria was based on these intentions:

- Deploying available forces rapidly and dominating the lines of communications to establish an initial presence in Kosovo

- Filling the vacuum created by the withdrawal of VJ and MUP forces

- Securing the Plitković communications site and Priština APOD (the airport) and establishing a presence in Priština

- Ensuring that FRY forces stick to the timelines in the MTA while giving them no excuse not to withdraw

- Reestablishing basic law and order

- Providing humanitarian assistance with UNHCR

(For the phased introduction of KFOR and final dispositions of the formations into Kosovo, see the figures accompanying the text).

As the lead recce unit, the Lord Strathcona's Horse and its Coyotes had specific and critical tasks in this initial plan (the details are covered in a later chapter).

What of the UÇK in all of this? Sir Mike Jackson and the KFOR staff had by no means neglected the Kosovar Albanian factor. Simply put, "the raw and abrupt shift of power that followed the deployment of KFOR was accompanied by civil disorder. Retribution and criminal activity led to an atmosphere of fear and created wide public insecurity." Until UNMIK could establish a functioning police and judicial system, "KFOR will retain the task of maintaining law and order." Once the VJ and MUP were gone, the main point of effort would shift, since "the UÇK, while outwardly complying with the terms of the Undertaking, are exploiting the absence of any civil authority." The shadow government, which was not democratic by any stretch of the imagination, was emerging, "and the presence of UCK/Kosovar Albanian Police (PU) is increasing. There is a danger that this will lead to tension between the UCK and KFOR, as UNMIK attempts to re-gain control of these functions." The problem was that the Kosovar Albanians, in the majority, would then commit reprisals against the Kosovar Serb communities. Ultimately, if the problem was not controlled, "this may increase the likelihood of Serb non-compliance with the [MTA]."[6]

COMKFOR's intent and the "UÇK undertaking" formed the basis for all Canadian operations conducted over the next year:

> My intent is to establish a stable and secure environment throughout Kosovo, while operating in a firm, fair and even-handed manner. To achieve this KFOR must have a thorough understanding of the complex situation in Kosovo. . . . Our role is principally one of creating the conditions within which UNMIK [international organizations and nongovernmental organizations] can bring about political, economic, and humanitarian renewal. . . . We will achieve success by synchronising our work along complementary lines of operation, co-ordinating deep, close and rear operations. This . . . is not a series of watertight compartments, but a conceptual approach. . . . Deep operations will focus on the will and perceptions of the people in order to maintain popular support for KFOR and the renewal process. Close operations will be directed at establishing and maintaining a stable and secure environment. Rear operations will ensure force protection and assistance to UNMIK, IOs and NGOs.[7]

The equivalent of the military technical agreement for the UÇK was known as the "UCK Undertaking of Demilitarization and Transformation," also known as the "undertaking." The exact process by which Hašim Thaçi, commander in chief of the UÇK, was compelled to sign the undertaking is much more obscure than the case of the FRY and the MTA. A Canadian officer at KFOR HQ observed that "Thachi probably didn't speak for all of them; however, he had credibility and was the only person prepared to enter into some kind of agreement with NATO. . . . It was a loose coalition at best. It's been suggested to me that that their best people, which were dedicated to achieving a greater Kosovo, were among those killed outright very early on and some of the elements that took over later were criminal elements as opposed to those ideologically driven."[8]

In any event the undertaking was signed by Thaçi and Jackson on 21 June and served as the basis for the UÇK-KFOR relationship. Essentially the undertaking was based on UNSCR 1244 (1999) and portions of the Rambouillet agreement.[9]

Fundamentally the UÇK renounced the use of force and agreed to comply with KFOR directives and cooperate with the international community (UNMIK, IOs, and NGOs). The UÇK would not hinder KFOR operations and would "refrain from all hostile or provocative acts, hostile intent, and freeze military movement" everywhere, including into or from Serbia, Albania, and Macedonia. Given the UÇK's nebulous nature, the undertaking recognized that the UÇK included "all personnel and organisations within Kosovo, currently under UÇK control, with a military or paramilitary capability," as well as "any other groups or individuals so designated by Commander KFOR."[10]

The UÇK was obligated to stop firing weapons and placing explosive devices and to mark its minefields. It was also prohibited from establishing movement control mechanisms and required to tear down defensive positions. The UÇK was not to "engage in any military, security or training related activities" and was prohibited from "attack[ing], detain[ing] or intimidat[ing] any civilians." Furthermore, the UÇK agreed not to carry weapons near VJ or MUP forces while withdrawing, or within built-up areas or main service routes designated by KFOR, or near the borders of Kosovo. A joint implementation commission (JIC) was also to be established between the UÇK, UNMIK, and KFOR.[11]

Subsequent to this the UÇK agreed to accept a phased demilitarization plan that included registering and placing weapons in storage sites controlled by KFOR and that within seven days automatic small arms would be allowed only in assembly areas. Significantly, within thirty days all "individual advisors, freedom fighters, trainers, volunteers and personnel from neighbouring states and other States shall be withdrawn from Kosovo." It was time for the mujaheddin to go home.[12]

The thorny question of what to do with the UÇK once the VJ and MUP were gone was by no means overlooked. The undertaking provided the basis for demilitarization and what was referred to as transformation. KFOR's special operations forces had up to this point provided liaison functions with the UÇK: the Joint Implementation Commission then took over. Secure weapons storage sites (SWSS) were established: the weapons contained therein were to be registered with KFOR, and KFOR was to verify the contents by K plus seven days. KFOR's multinational brigades would take control by K plus thirty. UÇK units were to make their way to assembly areas (AAs) by K plus seven for registration: UÇK identity papers would be issued and any details of nonautomatic long-barreled weapons that the fighters would retain would also be registered. Prohibited weapons, heavy and automatic, were to all be in the SWSSs by K plus thirty. A close protection party for Thaçi was authorized to retain several automatic weapons, but that was it. Then the fighters were to go home. The MNBs were responsible for encouraging the UÇK fighters "to return to normal civilian life in civilian clothes. . . . Dispensation should not be given to wear uniform longer than necessary and in no cases beyond K + 90."[13] Needless to say, the SWSSs and AAs were not to be co-located. According to Lt. Col. Shane Brennan, who was involved in this process at the KFOR HQ level,

> I personally went around on the 20 August deadline and later on the 19 September deadline to each SWSS. We went by helicopter and took the chief logistics officer of the UÇK. We physically had them count them all. We determined that they'd reached 100 percent of their declared weapons holding. There were more, however, cached outside Kosovo, but after some negotiation they were brought in and secured. There were heavy weapons, ATGMs, mortars of all calibers, including 120mm; there were surface-to-air mis-

siles held in sites off to the west and thousands and thousands of mines, warehouses full of them. A *lot* of RPGs.[14]

The obvious unstated problem for KFOR was to compare the numbers of weapons the UÇK declared it had to an informal estimate of what they did not turn in: "What was their actual weapons holdings? I would suggest to you they probably didn't know what they owned and weapons were still arriving after the undertaking was signed."[15]

Transformation, on the other hand, was a longer-term program. Transformation, as understood by KFOR and the UÇK, was the evolution of the UÇK into "one or more other organizations or institutions, appropriate to Kosovo's changed status and acceptable to its people and the IC [international community]." The UÇK wanted "some of its members, as individuals, to form the backbone of any new police force and civil administration in Kosovo; and also to turn itself as a body into an Army or National Guard, perhaps on US lines." There were dangers: "failure to sustain this vision, in co-operation with the IC, could lead to fractures in the organization . . . if the IC cannot accept the aspiration as espoused by the UCK, it would be wise to articulate an alternative." KFOR planners figured they had until late September to decide how to proceed before the UÇK reformed its clandestine groups and started attacking KFOR.[16]

The problems of transformation were obvious: Kosovo was not an independent country, it was still part of Yugoslavia, and it still contained Kosovar Serbs. Creating a national guard implied that a separate nation existed. Several options were proposed, such as the establishment of a paramilitary gendarmerie as an adjunct for the planned Kosovo Police Service (sort of a riot control/SWAT team). Another, which was adopted, was the development of the Kosovo Civil Defense Corps, later called the TMK, or Kosovo Protection Corps. The TMK was at one level designed to handle disaster relief, mine clearance, and forest fire fighting. At another, it was designed to keep former UÇK fighters under observation and provide them with a quasi-military organization and outlet for aggression.[17]

There was some controversy at the time about how transformation should be approached. What did emerge was that the UN

WARRIOR POLITICS

administration in Kosovo was to play a key role in transformation and in keeping the former UÇK under control and that they would have to be included in the JIC. Another sticking point was the weapons issue, as Sir Mike Jackson pointed out: "Time is not on our side. . . . UCK endorsement of the Kosovo Corps is by no means certain. You will see that although Ceku has moved a long way from his original proposal he remains concerned over numbers and weapons. The latter is a matter of culture, and we must recognize that without a holding of weapons the proposed organization would be viewed as sterile by the UCK."[18]

Desert Rats and Puking Panthers: Multinational Brigade (Center) Concept of Operations

Once the larger political framework was in place, the specific means for KFOR units to implement it on the ground had to be established.[19] MNB(C) essentially had two broad tasks: to deter the VJ from further operations (overt or covert) within Kosovo and to contain the UÇK or other armed entities from carrying on ethnic warfare. There was an obvious symbiotic relationship between the two: failure in one area would generate intervention from the other and vice versa. As Operation Kinetic progressed, the emphasis shifted back and forth.

The concept of operations for Multinational Brigade (Center) evolved within these arcs while the Canadian contingent was present. Initially the Operation Kinetic forces fell under the control of Brig. Bill Rollo's 4 (UK) Armoured Brigade. By August 1999 it had been replaced with Brig. Peter Pearson's 19 (UK) Mechanised Brigade; by that time the Operation Kinetic (+) battle group had arrived. When the Kinetic and Kinetic (+) units rotated late in 1999, the units in MNB(C) were then controlled by Brig. Richard Shirreff's 7 (UK) Armoured Brigade. Each brigadier brought a different concept of operations, which were based on the KFOR commander's original intent and adjusted according to the changing circumstances of the situation in Kosovo. The degree of Canadian input into how the MTA and undertaking were implemented at the MNB (Center) level varied. In most cases the British brigade commanders subscribed to a command philosophy similar to that espoused by Canadian doctrine, one that was not as antagonistic to Canadian sensitivities as that employed during World Wars I and II. Consequently the need for Canadian intervention in the decision-making process was not great, except in some specific cases discussed later in this work.

Four (UK) Armoured Brigade was commanded by Brig. Bill Rollo, an armored recce officer from the Blues and Royals. The bulk of his Cold War experience was with the British Army of the Rhine (BAOR) in West Germany, in addition to some time in Northern Ireland. He had previously served with UNPROFOR in Bosnia, where he had a close working relationship with 2nd Battalion, the Royal Canadian Regiment battle group (CANBAT II), which at the time was based on the Royal Canadian Dragoons.

Four (UK) Armoured Brigade with the Canadian contingent was to conduct a forward passage of lines through 5 (UK) Airborne Brigade, establish liaison with the VJ and MUP, and then secure Route Hawk, which was the main highway from Skopje to Priština. After securing the airport, 4 (UK) Brigade was to expand its influence within its area of operations, particularly into the critical Podujevo area north of Priština, and then transform into Multinational Brigade (Center) and await the arrival of additional allied battalions. During this time, 5 (UK) Airborne Brigade was the KFOR force reserve but was located in the MNB(C) area (at the Priština airport) and worked with MNB(C) units.[20] At this point MNB(C) consisted of elements of an armored recce regiment (Household Cavalry Regiment), an armored regiment (King's Royal Hussars), two mechanized infantry battle groups (1st Battalion Irish Guards and 1st Battalion Royal Irish Regiment), plus the Lord Strathcona's Horse Recce Squadron and 408 Tactical Helicopter Squadron.

Brigadier Rollo's priority was to ensure that there was no power vacuum: "I wanted to make sure that we were established in the police stations and the government buildings rather than the UÇK because I wanted to be quite clear that I was in charge, that the United Nations, on whose behalf we were operating, was going to provide the government rather than anybody else with an AK-47 who happened to walk into a police station at that particular moment." There was a danger that "local heroes" would set themselves up as warlords: "My previous experience in Bosnia said very clearly that there are only two relationships in the Balkans, and one is that somebody is in charge and others are not. I wanted to make it quite clear that KFOR was in charge. . . . We were responsible for law and order. Period." Brigadier Rollo brought his previous Balkans experience to bear in other areas: "[I also learned that] the first information you get is always wrong, often by 180°, and it takes time for the truth to come out. You need to get people on the ground to find out what it is, and even then it will take time for the facts to emerge. Therefore, you want to avoid jumping to conclusions about what's going on in a particular place."[21]

Brigadier Rollo also had no illusions about the UN: "Don't expect anything from anybody else. We learned that in Bosnia too. Don't have too great an expectation for what the UN can provide in the early stages [of an operation]. Or NGOs, for that matter. Later, perhaps. So: phase one, get [the Serbs and UÇK] out and get ourselves in. Provide a measure of security, and then restoration of the infrastructure, then the necessities of government." MNB(C)'s initial deployment, therefore, was to put infantry companies into the principal towns, which would get KFOR's presence established, and then a larger force into the ghost town of Priština, after 600,000 people walked in and occupied this city designed for 250,000. MNB (Center) was also responsible for a fair chunk of the provincial border region, which included a lot of small villages in mountainous terrain; the British Scimitar recce unit (Household Cavalry Regiment) and a Czech recce unit were to handle this area.[22]

Rollo's Canadian units at this point included the Coyote squadron and the Griffon squadron. These highly mobile assets became the MNB (Center) reserve, ready to react and support any other operation. When the Kinetic (+) battle group arrived, Rollo and his staff decided that the area west of Priština, which included the vital Drenica Valley, was a suitable area of operations. Most of Rollo's British units had Northern Ireland experience, which was critical for operations in and around Priština. The Canadians had experience with rural areas in Croatia and Bosnia, had a smaller structure since there was an infantry company missing, and were deployed to the Glogovac area partly because they were mechanized (1st Battalion, Parachute Regiment [1 Para], and the Gurkhas, for example, were light infantry, had no vehicles, and would be hard pressed to patrol such a large area). Rollo was well aware that the Drenica Valley, which controlled a vital east-west main service route (MSR) from Priština to Peć and Djakovica, was a hard-line UÇK stronghold physically separated by Mount Goleš from his other areas in MNB (Center). The brigade commander therefore wanted a relatively self-contained and intimidating KFOR presence permanently located there: the Canadian battle group with its tanks and APCs was well suited to that role. The other MNB(C) armored units were deployed to cover the Podujevo zone behind the recce screen on the provincial boundary, since this was a likely incursion area for the VJ.[23]

The Canadian Army's insistence that Op Kinetic (+) forces be mechanized and equipped to fight came into play when the planners at KFOR HQ and MNB (Center) examined the possibility of continued hostilities with the Belgrade regime: "In the beginning, it was quite clear that [the VJ] wasn't capable of offensive operations: they were too battered. But after we'd been there a while we started to think about contingency planning." Arrayed north and northeast of Kosovo just outside the air safety zone, the VJ retained two armored brigades, two mechanized brigades, a light infantry brigade, and an artillery brigade.[24]

The initial plans, which evolved later, were based on the assumption that the Belgrade regime had the potential to conduct operations against Kosovo and/or Macedonia "in order to embarrass NATO, cut Lines of Communications[,] or exercise leverage by way of an attack on KFOR's cohesion." This did not necessarily amount to a full-scale operation to completely retake Kosovo; rather, "the FRY might wish to challenge the resolve of the International Community to uphold UNSCR 1244 and the MTA by operating forces within [the air and ground safety zones]."[25]

Examples of possible noncompliance activities could include:

1. Air activity or the use of air defense systems to track and illuminate KFOR air platforms operating in Kosovo airspace

2. Deployment of land forces into the GSZ

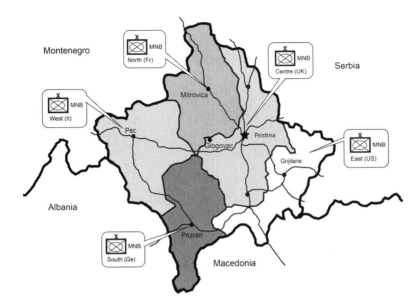

FIG. 9. KFOR deployment, 1999: Multinational Brigade sectors.

3. Provocative action by forces within the GSZ, for example, battalion-size deployment or the use of indirect fire against KFOR units

4. Preparations for brigade-sized incursion into GSZ and/or Kosovo

All such activities were to be met with lethal force by KFOR. In the event of a ground incursion the MNB (Center) forces, including the 1 PPCLI with its TOW under armor antitank vehicles, the Lord Strathcona's Horse Leopards, and the British Challenger tank squadron, were to contain and then fix the enemy in the area called the Podujevo bowl and then defeat it by direct and indirect fire. There were three possible axes of advance the VJ could use in the MNB (Center) area. The northern route from Murgula and southern route through Orlane traversed rugged, defensible terrain and eventually converged on the city of Podujevo. The central route, from the provincial border to the city of Podujevo, traversed much more open terrain. Podujevo lay in a small valley, and the

MSR led southwest twenty kilometers to Priština. This MSR conformed to the valley, with high ground on either side, and thus constituted a canalized killing zone.

MNB (Center) armored units, reinforced by the German Leopard 2s in MNB (South), were to counterattack to restore Kosovo territorial integrity. The self-propelled artillery from the German and Italian sectors would support this attack. In the event of an attack on Macedonia, MNB(C) was to deploy one of its battle groups to Kumanovo as a reinforcement unit behind the Macedonian army while the American AH-64 attack helicopters and airmobile units from MNB (East) attacked the rear of the incursion through Gnjilane.[26]

Brigadier Rollo figures that "it would have been a very expensive attack on Podujevo, particularly if the FRY attack flowed into open ground, where it would have been susceptible to air power. Our plan was to hold the high ground and then batter them to bits. It was like BAOR in West Germany during the Cold War, except in miniature. There were also other plans, much higher, to do other interesting things."[27]

The Kosovar Albanian situation was dire and needed attention, but there were problems in that area too: "[We have to] remember the social context of the Albanian population, which is clan based, diffuse, anarchic by nature, and therefore the extent to which this centralized, unified structure existed [permitted some cooperation] during demilitarization, but I suspect that happened within limits and there were a whole range of other activities conducted by the same people which were not susceptible to civilian control or central control. They had a parallel government and there was a habit of deferral to it [that we had to confront]."[28] An example would be something as "simple" as the Obilić power station: "We put a lot of effort, within our limited abilities, in getting the power station working. There was this armored engineer commander who went in there, he had a brother in the UK who worked in a power station, and with a mobile phone he led the efforts to get it up and running. It took about two months." Obilić was not only critical to providing power to Priština; it also employed people:

"the Albanian workers had been thrown out in '89 and wanted their jobs back . . . the Serbs were there and they hadn't left, so we got everybody back in there and got them working together. Then one of them would be murdered or abducted and they'd go away again." But without lights Priština was difficult to control, so MNB (Center) had to deal with Obilić.[29]

To get Obilić staffed, however, workers insisted on having roofs put back on their houses, but the individual who controlled the only lumberyard with any stock would not release it unless KFOR sorted out a problem about his brother-in-law's hotel being in a poor financial state, since the Serb manager took off with not only the cash but the whiskey supply, and the international press was staying there. A manager with all the right connections was installed (Çeku's brother, perhaps), the UN supplied the whiskey, the wood was delivered, the houses reroofed, and the power station was operating.[30]

Information operations conducted by MNB (Center) in the early phases consisted mainly of low-level activities:

> We ran a leaflet campaign. We had a small ability to do that. For instance, we wanted to emphasize the message that you didn't carry arms, particularly long-barreled weapons, in public. These were distributed in various ways. We emphasized that grenade carriage was a jailable offense. We were really keen on radio; local radio was the main medium to get information to the population. Our message was, NATO's here to help, we're not here to occupy, if you have problems talk to us, don't let these other people influence you. It was all very embryonic in the summer of 1999.[31]

Four (UK) Armoured Brigade handed over to 19 (UK) Mechanised Brigade, led by Brig. Peter Pearson, on 22 August 1999. Brigadier Pearson's career experiences included multiple tours with the Gurkhas, particularly with 5 Airborne Brigade, and some Northern Ireland and BAOR time. He took command of 19 Mech in 1997, just in time for its headquarters to deploy to Bosnia on an SFOR tour during which he worked closely with the Canadian contingent that was part of Multinational Division (Southwest).

In addition to the Canadian Op Kinetic and Kinetic (+) units, 19 Mech included an armored regiment (Queen's Dragoon Guards), an armored recce squadron (Blues and Royals), a mechanized infantry battalion (Second Royal Green Jackets), and a self-propelled artillery regiment (26th Regiment, Royal Artillery). By this point the Finnish Battalion (with four mechanized infantry companies), the Swedish Battalion (three mechanized companies), the Telemark Battalion (Norwegian, also with three mechanized companies), and a Czech recce unit had also deployed and joined 19 Mech to form MNB (Center).[32]

Brigadier Pearson saw that "the main effort was quite clear: we were to stabilize the situation, deterring and preventing, if necessary, aggression from external sources, mainly Serbia, and preventing aggression internally. This meant that we had to continue to disarm the people and get them back to some semblance of normality. The situation was that there was nothing working and no core utilities were operating. There was a possibility of more aggression from the northeast and that kettle was boiling at the time." The UN administration was sluggish in moving in, so Pearson "had Majors running the power stations, Majors running the buses, Majors running the people to get things working. The Serbs, who had all of the leadership positions, had of course disappeared."[33]

To achieve in his area of operations the end-state objectives of a fundamentally peaceful and stable Kosovo, Brigadier Pearson first identified four pillars: the UN, which handled public administration, police, and judiciary; the UNHCR, which was responsible for humanitarian assistance and demining; the OSCE, which dealt with democracy, elections, and civil rights training; and finally the EU, which took over infrastructure and the development of the economy. These pillars didn't appear overnight: "Initially they were a bag of worms. They don't have an expeditionary capability per se, they don't work together, their people arrive with no accommodation, they have to jack up their own vehicles and establish offices. It was all in a big state of flux [for months]. A lot of them are diplomatic people: they're really good at chatting and talking and smoothing [things out] but not so good at saying 'You, fix that.' That's where we came in. [KFOR] was the executive arm in many respects." As with Brigadier Rollo, the formative events that led Brigadier Pearson to adopt this approach were rooted in his experiences with SFOR operations in Bosnia.[34]

If one thinks of the pillars supporting the "roof" of a peaceful and stable Kosovo, the base for all of this was security, provided by KFOR. MNB (Center) headquarters established three lines of operations that formed this base. The first was secure environment operations: "that was to prevent the boys from coming back from Serbia—that was clearly my main effort until we got the plans in line, went on the ground, and so on. Once that was all sorted out, my main activity shifted to the day-to-day business of getting the country running again."[35]

Secure environment operations also involved handling the corrections system:

It was chaos. Of course, the air force had bombed the only prison, which was brilliant, wasn't it. We took over the Lipljan mental hospital, which had cells, and converted it to a prison. Our boys were arresting people, and I was the de facto prison governor. There was no law, so I invoked British military law and these people were treated in exactly the same way as British military prisoners. There were no courts to charge these people, and they were simply arrested and detained at my pleasure. We only locked up the really bad bastards, however, you know, murderers, rapists, people chucking grenades and firing mortars, that kind of thing. It was a really awful system. We did the best we could until we were able to bring over prison guards from the UK to run it. The Canadians were also involved in one rotation as well.[36]

Other aspects of securing the environment included discouraging weapons carriage. The problem was "the general psyche over here that your pistol is the other part of your anatomy."[37] Ultimately it was difficult to keep up with, since the only judges around were Serbs and there was no way that Kosovar Albanians were going to get a fair trial.

Then there were compliance operations with the UÇK. After

the MTA-mandated demilitarization period, MNB (Center) initiated a series of operations to seize the ones remaining at large:

> We controlled movement, vehicle checkpoints on the roads. We blitzed roads and conducted surprise searches with helicopter units. We deterred aggression, we protected the innocent. For example, we had soldiers living in the flat of one Serb old lady who lived in a block full of Albanians and wouldn't move. So we moved in, took her to market, escorted her home. Protecting the innocent was critical. We also protected key sites like Serb Orthodox churches from arson. Some we wired off and boarded up in remote areas. But these things can be used as trigger points to justify violent activity and destabilization, particularly the monastery at Gračanica.[38]

In some areas where there were still Kosovar Albanians and Kosovar Serbs living in close proximity, Pearson had to establish buffer zones.

Compliance operations also involved the transformation of the UÇK into the TMK: "We took this on from [4 (UK)] Brigade and ran the meetings [between KFOR and the UÇK/TMK]. I talked to the brigade commanders. I had to get this particular individual to comply with the [undertaking] and to get his people to stop going around and threatening people and to stop carrying weapons in public and goodness knows what else." Pearson used special operations forces to liaise with the UÇK/TMK brigades since they had independent signals capability and came equipped with a previous relationship to the wartime leaders: "They kept us on the straight and narrow and gave me the inside grit on what was going down with the UCK, who were, generally speaking, naughty boys. . . . As far as they are concerned, they are the Kosovo Liberation Army in Waiting, and their business is an independent Kosovo. They have arms caches. They're playing the game at the moment and do what they really wanted to do quietly. The [TMK] are organized and have weapons cached away."[39]

The third part of the base was civil-military operations. As Brigadier Pearson notes, "These operations are about hearts and minds and gathering information that's needed to prosecute the more difficult tasks of assisting the civil organizations. For example, roofs needed to be fixed, as the winter was approaching. This had to be done at a decentralized level, usually handled at the battalion or battle group because they were the only ones who could conduct a proper survey of the situation and coordinate the UN and NGOs to get the job done in time."[40]

In terms of information operations MNB (Center) managed to change the population's views on a number of critical points:

> There was at one stage a real fear that there were children and young girls being kidnapped and sold off into prostitution and goodness knows what else. We investigated this and it was not happening, but the whole of Priština believed that it was. We sealed off the city, and I ordered that any car with two or more men in it be stopped and searched. We also went on the radio and got into the papers and within days things changed. People were coming out again at night and young girls were seen on the streets. It was completely measurable and the feedback was immediate. This wasn't black PSYOPS by any means. We weren't telling lies here. We didn't need to. I didn't even have to put a spin on it. Information operations was hugely supportive of all the other things we were doing.[41]

Indeed information operations opened up a whole new vista. KFOR intelligence was having problems with collection on certain aspects of the UÇK: "There were things going on, the UCK were doing things, the Mafia were doing things, the criminals were doing things, there was crime, there was extortion, there was duress. And I wasn't inside that loop and I couldn't get in because I wasn't Albanian." The positive relations generated at the local level by operations like the counterkidnapping affair eventually assisted MNB(C), and "we built up very, very good intelligence [and] we built up the ability to get inside that loop, and it started to have a desired effect."[42]

Concerns about VJ intervention continued into the fall and well into the winter of 1999. Indeed it was clear to Canadian and British commanders that there was increased VJ activity directed toward this possibility around September.[43] Consequently MNB

(Center) produced a series of contingency plans based on those created by 4 (UK) Armoured Brigade. Initially called Contingency Plan (CONPLAN) Critical Effort and then Conplan Thunder in its later incarnation, it had Pearson exploiting the unique capabilities of the Coyote:

> They had a very specific role: they were part of ISTAR, the network of observation required to ensure that we not only picked up the enemy when he was coming in but tracked them down to our killing areas. [The recce squadron's] role was a very, very dangerous one, the most dangerous. They were up front, isolated, individual, and they were going to have to rely on their wits. They went up and did their recces. The Coyotes were critical to my plan, bearing in mind I only had thirty-eight tanks. If the bad boys came over the hill, we needed to be able to deal with them. I brought over operations analysis people from England and modeled my plan. [Canadian] Leopards and TOW were critical to covering my left flank, the road coming down from Mitrovica towards Priština. The main killing area was in Podujevo and [I didn't want to get flanked if Multinational Brigade North caved in].[44]

Indeed Canadian officers at MNB (Center) were integral to the planning, given the capabilities that the Kinetic and Kinetic (+) forces brought to the table, as Lt. Col. Shane Brennan described:

> We tend to belittle ourselves in a lot of ways, we don't have all of the most modern equipment, but we certainly had a nice selection and we were prepared. Our objective was to defeat their advance by attrition which was based on early detection and destruction of the VJ forces in kill zones. We were going to go for maximum destruction as early as possible and paralyze them right along the routes. We had good surveillance. We had our tanks, we had TOW, we had ERYX, and we had snipers equipped with .50 cal sniper rifles. We also had two thousand antitank mines with our engineer squadron. It doesn't sound like a great collection, but it would have been an incredible blocking force there. We did a [tactical exercise without troops] and recce'd the ground pretty thoroughly.[45]

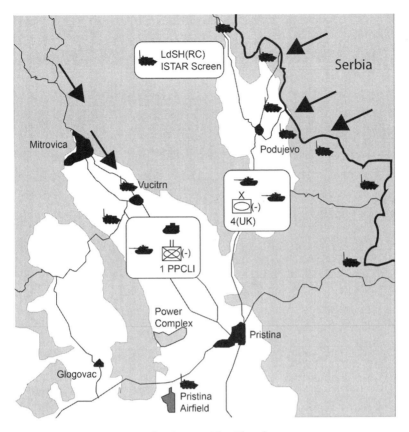

FIG. 10. Contingency Plan Thunder, 1999.

Conplan Thunder was predicated on the 4 (UK) Armoured Brigade planning conducted earlier in the summer of 1999. The threat was determined to consist of three brigade-sized incursions, plus an independent battalion-sized mechanized unit and a helicopter-inserted light infantry battalion. Their mission, according to analysis, was considered limited in nature: embarrass NATO, exercise leverage, and attack KFOR cohesion. There was also the strong possibility that the VJ might mount an infiltration operation through the GSZ to demonstrate capability: if it was not checked, it might lead to further and bolder operations. Ultimately the Conplan Thunder planners believed that the objective of any incursion would be to reestablish authority over northern Kosovo (and not, coincidentally, the mineral resources there) to provide a safe haven for Kosovar Serbs and possibly to create a secure base for further infiltration of Kosovo.[46]

Information operations was also an important aspect of Conplan Thunder. The objective was to deter the VJ from violating the MTA in the first place—that is, convincing the VJ leadership that any attempt to interfere in Kosovo would be "met with full resources and resolve." In the deterrence phase, information operations were to establish KFOR's legitimacy and undermine Belgrade's propaganda efforts. If deterrence failed, information operations were designed to establish the criminality of VJ actions and use whatever means were available to convince the VJ to return to barracks: establishing the primacy of KFOR on the battlefield was key to this. Once KFOR was on the offensive, the plan involved continued demonstration of the futility of further resistance and emphasized that the law of armed conflict would be used by KFOR to mitigate damage and harm to the Serbian people.[47]

Unlike the previous contingency plan, Thunder relied on significant intelligence warning, which would provide time for KFOR and MNB (Center) to mount a demonstration of force along the Kosovo edge of the GSZ to deter any offensive action; Coyote and Griffon were critical components in providing this surveillance. The Queen's Dragoon Guards in their Challengers and the Swedish mechanized infantry battalion were tasked to conduct the demonstration and then would withdraw to fighting positions near Podujevo if deterrence failed. One PPCLI and LdSH(RC) and their successors, 1 RCR and the RCD, were tasked with covering the northern MSR coming in from Mitrovica just north of the Kosovo Polje battlefield with the Leopards, TOWs, and mechanized infantry until the Marines of the 22nd Marine Expeditionary Unit flew in to reinforce from their helicopter carriers in the Adriatic. There was serious concern in KFOR HQ that the French-led MNB(N) would be incapable of protecting the left flank.[48]

All in all Thunder was reminiscent of the role that the Canadian Army had played in NATO's Central Region. Indeed a number of officers and NCOs from the Kinetic and Kinetic (+) units, including the TFK commander, Col. Mike Ward, served with 4 Canadian Mechanized Brigade in West Germany during the Cold War and were familiar with such operations. The training impetus provided by Colonel Leslie and 1 CMBG enhanced this posture. It is clear that an army trained and equipped only for peacekeeping would have been incapable of participating in and contributing effectively to Conplan Thunder.

Although the importance of retaining the ability to conduct mid-intensity mechanized operations was critical for deterrence purposes, the bulk of the activity conducted by the Kinetic and Kinetic (+) units involved stabilization operations. The next three chapters examine each unit's structure and role and then detail the experiences of the participants in operations undertaken to implement the MTA and the undertaking.

SEVEN

The Coyote Howls
Recce Squadron Operations

Spectacular advances in visible light amplification techniques are expected
to make viewing devices available in the post-1970 time from which will
effectively turn night into day. Automatic production and miniaturization
should keep costs low enough that all troops can be equipped with some
form of such devices. Surveillance devices, from aids for the soldier on
patrol to "eyes in the sky" such as the Periscopter, will cover the whole
range of reconnaissance requirements. Improved data handling and
processing techniques will make the results of the increased reconnaissance
capability usable down to the lowest echelon.

—Canadian Army combat development study, 1960

The most spectacular display of Canadian innovation in Kosovo
was the Coyote vehicle. The product of a combination of seren-
dipity, compromise, and foresight, the Coyotes provided KFOR
with an unprecedented surveillance and reconnaissance capability completely unmatched by any other national contributor to
the effort to bring stability to the region. The types of operations
conducted by NATO forces in Kosovo were, as all operations are,
dependent on the provision of timely and accurate information.
A new process for processing information, ISTAR, was the primary engine driven by Coyote operations. The Coyote squadrons were therefore critical means in permitting commanders to
act and react to the constantly changing environment of Kosovo.

This chapter examines Coyote operations in Kosovo. Coyote was
fielded from two regiments: the Lord Strathcona's Horse (LdSH or
Strathcona's) Recce Squadron from June 1999 to December 1999,

led by Maj. Paul Fleury, and then the Royal Canadian Dragoons (the RCD or Dragoons) Recce Squadron from December 1999 to June 2000, led by Maj. Tim Datchko. Where possible, the experiences of both squadrons during Operation Kinetic are combined to avoid repetition. Note that recce squadron operations as they relate to Mitrovica are covered in a later chapter because of the complex combined nature of that multinational operation.

Serendipitous Renaissance in Reconnaissance: Coyote Development

To fully understand why Coyote capabilities were so important, it is necessary to examine how the vehicle was developed and why. During the Cold War, Canadian reconnaissance doctrine was based on a "sneak-and-peek" model: small, lightly armed armored reconnaissance vehicles used stealth to observe and report on enemy movement. Canadian recce forces were not structured to stand and fight. As the Cold War entered its last two decades, other NATO armies shifted to a "blow-and-go" model in which recce forces were equipped with heavier armed and armored vehicles that would fight for information and in some cases delay enemy armored forces. Canada's primary vehicle for sneak-and-peek operations from 1968 to the early 1990s was the tracked Lynx operated by three soldiers and equipped with a .50-caliber machine gun: it had no sensors other than the "Mk 1 Eyeball" with aging night vision goggles and some ingrained sixth sense inculcated by lots of training in West Germany.

In 1984 plans were made to replace Lynx. Two projects were proposed: the armored infantry fighting vehicle, or AIFV (a projected tracked machine), and the Canadian combat vehicle (CCV-90) project, which was to be wheeled. These projects were merged in 1986 into the light armored vehicle (LAV) project, and seventeen hundred vehicles of different variants were deemed necessary, one of which was a recce machine.[1]

The demise of the CCV-90 project in 1989 put the whole idea of a Lynx replacement into suspended animation. There was, however, recognition that the requirement for such a vehicle would not disappear. Therefore the multirole combat vehicle (MRCV) project arose in 1990. The MRCV concept was to have three vehicle types using the same chassis: a fighting vehicle for the infantry, a direct-fire support vehicle, and a Lynx replacement. The MRCV staff, led by Lt. Col. Ross Carruthers, was able to piggyback onto a Norwegian vehicles trial, a project that had the same objectives as the MRCV project. The contending vehicles were all tracked and either mounted or planned to mount a 30mm cannon. These machines were the Bradley, the Warrior, the German Puma, Austria's ASCOD, and the Swedish CV-90. The CV-90 looked good to the MRCV team.[2]

Enter the General Motors Diesel Division, the only producer of armored vehicles in Canada. In addition to employing several thousand Canadians in southern Ontario, GM Diesel also had contracts to build the LAV-25 wheeled family of vehicles for the U.S. Marine Corps. The MRCV team did not think LAV-25 would meet the MRCV requirements, particularly in the areas of armament and protection. The highest levels of DND of the day pestered the MRCV staff to alter their requirements and focus on LAV-25. In 1992 the Materiel section and the DCDS ordered the team to cancel MRCV development. A Lynx replacement project could continue to include 203 vehicles, and it was to be based on the LAV-25. Permission was given to develop capabilities to enhance the vehicle as much as possible, particularly for the surveillance role.[3]

The project staff working with Computing Devices of Canada and Defense Research Establishment Suffield developed a number of sensor packages that could be mounted in different configurations. There were also experiments that mated sensors to a hydraulic mast similar to the type used by television transmitting trucks. Third-generation image intensification for night operations was also emphasized, in addition to a ground surveillance radar. These systems permitted Coyote to deploy its equipment and then detect, identify, and observe enemy activity nearly thirty kilometers away. The Coyote could also be used in a traditional ground reconnaissance role and sported a 25mm gun. The main problem identified before the trials was developing doctrine for the machine's tactical use, finding the balance between surveillance (passive/static) and reconnaissance (active/mobile), and then situating it all within the Canadian Army's overall doctrine.[4] How, exactly, was Coyote supposed to be used? This is where ISTAR came in, fitfully.

RISTA, ISTAR, ERSTA, and Other Weird (but Important) Acronyms

As with any successful concept, there are a hundred fathers: ISTAR (intelligence, surveillance, target acquisition, and reconnaissance) is no exception. In late 1996 the newly established Directorate of Army Doctrine (DAD) became aware of Coyote technical developments. This new vehicle would be able to provide commanders with better information and do so more efficiently. Other information systems were also speeding up, mostly due to geometric increases in computing power. Commanders were increasingly in danger of being overwhelmed: such paralysis could endanger operations. An early attempt to identify the physical and procedural means of fusing incoming information, processing it, and providing commanders with "situational awareness" emerged from a number of American think-tanks. It was called reconnaissance, intelligence surveillance, and target acquisition, or RISTA, an acronym adopted by NATO.[5]

The Canadian Army had to change to keep up with developments, and a reexamination of command and control methods was key to this effort. RISTA information would feed the command and control process, and, since Coyote was one of the information sources, accommodation had to be made. Canadian officers kept an eye on the RISTA concept and in early 1997 the Directorate of Army Doctrine drafted its vision.

RISTA was part of a new idea called "information operations," that is, the melding of command and control warfare (C2W), intelligence and information (I2), and communication and information systems (CIS) so that commanders can impose their will on the enemy using the forces at their disposal. C2W is the integrated use of physical destruction, deception, psychological operations, and electronic warfare to deny information to, influence, degrade, or destroy the enemy's command system. I2 is designed to provide a commander with an accurate understanding of the enemy, terrain, weather, and friendly forces, while CIS comprises integrated digital information networks like the internet, radio, and so on to facilitate operations. RISTA was part of the I2 function and constituted a "system of systems": no single RISTA asset could reliably collect information in all environments and circumstances. The process was designed to allocate, in a headquarters, the appropriate tools as necessary, collect the information coming in from electro-optical, electronic warfare, and radar sensors mounted on airborne and ground based-vehicles, fuse it, and pass it on.[6]

Implementing such a system within an army and then between the army and other services (e.g., the air force) is another matter. Usually the pieces of any nation's RISTA puzzle belong to different, competing, and sometimes politically opposing groups: there is usually never enough money for all of them to be in their desired comfort zone. In March 1997 a RISTA working group brought together all of the players: armored, artillery, infantry, signals, electronic warfare, intelligence, and tactical helicopter communities. The air force, it turned out, was working on a concept that was similar to RISTA: they were using it to justify the acquisition of new sensors for the Griffon helicopters, since the Cold War–era Kiowa recce helicopters had been retired.[7]

ERSTA (electro-optical reconnaissance, surveillance, and target acquisition) was brought back to Canada by an exchange officer serving with the British Army Air Corps. At the same time, other Canadian exchange officers were introduced to a British study paper written by Col. Mike Cronin, who was using the term ISTAR to refer to something that resembled RISTA but was larger and more systematic. The British study was circulated in the Directorate of Army Doctrine and folded into the RISTA discussions. By 1997 RISTA was called ISTAR in Canadian circles after NATO working groups formally adopted the term.[8]

Essentially ISTAR is an information collation matrix that pulls together data from every source imaginable: a soldier on patrol or a clerk driving from point A to B in the area of operations becomes a sensor, in addition to Coyotes or an unmanned aerial vehicle;

everybody is part of the system. Units are given priorities, they feed the matrix, the data are analyzed by intelligence personnel and become part of a decision, new priorities are assigned, and the cycle continues. A historical analogy would be British air defense efforts during the Battle of Britain in World War II. RAF fighter direction depended on the centralized gathering of information from the Observer Corps, the radar stations, Enigma signals intelligence, and antiaircraft artillery units into localized control stations; fighter aircraft were then directed onto enemy bomber formations.

Summed up: the quicker commanders can get the information they need to make decisions on how to allocate their forces to defeat the enemy or achieve aims with minimal distraction, the better. Given the Coyote's capabilities, a lot of different types of information could be rapidly fed into the decision process. No other nation had anything like it.

The Coyote and Its Capabilities: Walk Around

Coyote is an eight-wheeled armored car with a crew of four: driver, commander, gunner, and surveillance operator. It has a turret-mounted stabilized M-242 25mm Bushmaster chain gun capable of firing sabot dart and frangible rounds. Coyote has a top speed of more than 100 kilometers per hour. For crew protection there is a fire suppression system, spall blankets, and an add-on armor kit. Coyote is equipped with a tactical navigation system and global positioning system. In the days of the Lynx the commander would carry a plasticized map with grease pencils and have to decipher eight-figure grid references while being banged about as the vehicle moved: the Coyote's tacnav system provides the commander with this information instantaneously while the crew is being banged about during cross-country movements. The stabilized laser rangefinding system in the turret is linked to the tacnav system: the commander can "lase" a target or geographical feature, and the grid and GPS data are displayed in the turret. There is also a laser warning receiver (LWR). The LWR warns the crew if a hostile laser rangefinding or targeting system is hitting the vehicle: the display provides both distance and direction, which usually prompts radical vehicle maneuvering to avoid any missile or projectile directed against the Coyote.[9]

The main part of the Coyote's surveillance system is mounted on a telescoping hydraulic mast that can extend to ten meters above the ground. Mounted on the mast are a radar that can be used to detect both aerial and ground targets, a thermal imaging system (FLIR), a day TV camera, and a laser rangefinder. A VCR can record the electro-optical feed. The Coyote also has dismountable sensors. According to Cpl. Jason Parteger of the Strathcona's recce squadron, "The remotes are two tripods: one thermal and one radar, like the mast-mounted equipment. We can put them out to two hundred meters away from the Coyote. You can dig the cord in, camouflage the vehicle, and nobody knows you're there. . . . With the FLIR you can see different colors, which show the variations of heat in the body. You can see a guy's cap badge. You can tell if you look carefully how low a vehicle is on gas if you look at the fuel tanks."[10]

The surveillance operator sits in the back of the Coyote and can on the display screen access any of the sensors on command. As Trooper John Nickerson of the RCD explains, "Everything is dependent on a good surveillance operator and how creative he is in how he manipulates the systems. The commander tells the Surv Op what to look for: it is up to the Surv Op to select the means."[11] The surveillance operator usually combines input from the electro-optical and radar sensors and can then establish an invisible "box." This can consist of scan lines and a "radar fence" for the mast sensors to sweep: an alarm can be set to alert the operator if a target or targets enter the box or cross the scan lines. The radar even has an audio track that sounds like a sonar. The radar can be set to provide irregular scanning times to discourage pattern identification and thus targeting by hostile systems.

It takes time to mount the sensors on the mast and then raise it. The turret gun is difficult to employ when the mast is deployed, so careful camouflage and concealment is a critical part of Coyote operations: it requires a clever mind and plenty of initiative to employ Coyote effectively. Another little-known but important capability is the Coyote's nuclear, biological, and chemical detection system based on RADIAC and GRID-3. Cpl. Steven Haynes of the RCD, who served in Somalia, Bosnia with UNPROFOR, and then KFOR, likens the change from Lynx to Coyote as "going from the stone age to the cyber age."[12]

Coyote Squadron Organization

A reconnaissance, or "recce," squadron traditionally acts as the eyes and ears of a brigade group, spreading out along the front of an advance or on its flanks looking for the enemy. Because of the highly decentralized nature of reconnaissance, a premium is placed on flexibility and initiative among recce soldiers. The organization of a recce squadron reflects this. In pre-Coyote days, each squadron had three troops, each of which consisted of seven Lynx vehicles and their crews. Working in pairs called patrols, vehicles would leapfrog down roads until contact was made with the enemy. Strong opposition would be picqueted and bypassed, while specially trained personnel destroyed obstacles to permit greater mobility. Troopers could dismount from the Lynx and conduct foot patrols as needed. A single troop could cover a lot of ground doing "sneak and peek" in a linear battle situation.

Initially the deployment of Coyote did not affect the squadron organization: there were supposed to be three troops of seven Coyotes all equipped with the mast sensor package. With changing budgetary priorities, however, the squadrons were reduced to three troops of five Coyotes under the so-called "equipment rationalization program" ("rationalization" was a 1990s term that meant reductions made due to lack of funds). Indeed in their preparations for Op Kinetic the Strathcona's forces had to make substantial modifications to the organization because of the nature of the mission. The organization remained basically the same for the Dragoons when they rotated to Kosovo in December 1999.

The Sabre, or fighting component of the Coyote recce squadron in Kosovo, consisted of three troops of Coyotes with five Coyotes per troop, plus two additional Coyotes belonging to the squadron headquarters, for a total of seventeen. Each troop had one Coyote command variant, two Coyotes equipped with masts, and two equipped with remotes. One mast Coyote operated with one remote Coyote to form a patrol. The employment of the troop in Kosovo differed from Cold War recce whereby the long-range surveillance capability of the mast Coyote was deployed in place to overwatch a named area of interest (NAI), and the other sensor Coyote and its crew were free to maneuver to acquire specific information. Coyote was flexible enough to be used in both mechanized warfare and stabilization operations.

The recce squadron also had an assault troop. Armoured soldiers with extra demolitions training, assault troop personnel like Cpl. Dave Horne of Strathcona's were deployed "to facilitate the movement of the reconnaissance troops because sometimes you might not be able to get engineer assets from the Brigade quick enough. . . . Our other jobs included patrolling and setting up observation post screens."[13] In addition to blowing up obstacles, the assault troop could function as a mechanized infantry platoon to clear complex defiles that the Coyotes couldn't enter. Cpl. Kevin Malost of the RCD: "We had five Bison APCs, one was the troop leader, and each vehicle had a section of ten men. We had mortars, the ERYX antitank missiles, Karl Gustav antitank rockets, and C-6 machine guns."[14] All told, the assault troop had forty-seven people. The recce squadron also had an attached combat engineer section of four men, with a Bison engineer variant to back up the assault troop in mine clearance tasks.[15]

Supporting the Sabre component was the echelon (called "the esch"). Since the recce squadron was operating alone in Kosovo without a parent armored regiment or Canadian brigade headquarters and its associated logistics system, the echelon was dramatically expanded for Op Kinetic. The recce squadron had four 6,600-liter fuel trucks, some fifteen 10-ton HLVW transport trucks (three of which were the TCV variant plus twelve maintainers to operate them), two mobile kitchens and cooks to staff them, and a light truck for utility purposes. Overall there were forty-five soldiers in the echelon, of which fourteen members were militia augmentees during the RCD tour.[16]

An extremely important aspect of recce is the ability to communicate the acquired information back to the higher headquarters rapidly. The recce squadron's command post (CP), according to Mike Brabant, operations warrant officer from the RCD, consisted of "three Bisons, one of which was used as a radio rebroadcast vehicle, and two command-post variants. We had one hot CP running and one shut down. When the troops are deployed in different areas at long range, some Bisons were used as 'step-ups' so that information could be relayed back."[17] Each CP vehicle was also equipped with an Inmarsat satellite telephone communications system.

Remote rebroadcast or RRB was critical in mountainous terrain: the RRB vehicles were operated by four signal corps personnel. Then the squadron had to communicate with the British brigade, which had different equipment. Maj. Paul Fleury of the Strathcona's ran into problems: "We have a cipher for the radios: you put this stuff in and it scrambles so that anybody listening won't understand it, like the Enigma. The British had one type and we have another, so the British send us a liaison team with their radio and I put one of my guys in with them with a manpack radio who would relay." The obvious problem was that the Land Rover was not armored and thus vulnerable, so other means had to be found to close the gap.[18]

Taken together, the recce squadron was a very flexible unit that could deploy three troop units to different and dispersed areas, support them logistically, and communicate the gathered information from those areas back to the brigade headquarters efficiently.

The Strathconas Go In: Deployment into Kosovo

Once the Strathconas drove off the ship in Thessaloniki, fueled up at the gas station on the way, and reached the forward assembly area on the night of 12 June, they were in a position to enter Kosovo. Squadron Officer Commanding Paul Fleury sets the scene:

The guys were so tired. They had been up hours and days some of them, and I was afraid of a traffic accident because it's so steep and mountainous. Once I saw everybody and they were all there, I didn't worry. The fuel was my only concern: I didn't want to be stuck in Skopje when this thing started. I ordered the echelon forward from the Petrovac training area. We didn't have comms with the Brits, the radio in the Land Rover wasn't working yet, it was horrible. And then I got a commitment from the brigade on the order of march, which I could now get because I was physically there. D Squadron Household Cavalry Regiment [a British recce squadron with Scimitar] was first, then the King's Royal Hussars, the Irish Guards, and then us. Beggars can't be choosers. In the end, my [call sign] 41 with Chris Hunt and his troops went forward very quickly once the battle groups got [through the defile and] out of the way.[19]

Capt. Chris Hunt led his Coyote troop into Kosovo through the Kačanik defile:

We expected that we'd have isolated incidences of combat. I figured we would come across a drunken Serb who would fire off some rounds, we'd fire off some rounds, and it would spread quickly. I passed on to my troops, particularly those who had been in Bosnia before, that it wasn't going to be like that. As it turned out in the long run it was, but we had some interesting times first. I was told that I was going to be the lead element in the squadron, but I was going to be separate. I would move with the Irish Guards battle group, through them, and then race ahead to put up observation in the Obilić area [thirty kilometers into Kosovo]. If we saw something move that was hostile, we could hit it. We fell in with the battle group between 0900 and 1000. The British CO had his whole organization dismount and form around him. He gave a speech: he didn't know what was going to happen but that he had confidence in his troops and he knew this would be a day everyone would remember for the rest of their lives. Then the padre gave a prayer before battle. . . . We could see, in the distance, another British battle group, German tanks forming up, and we had Apache attack helicopters flying over our heads. I have never seen so much firepower put together in one place.

I felt fortunate to be there, and I was anxious about it but excited. At 1100 we got the order to move. We drove through Skopje, through the Albanian neighborhoods, and thousands of people were there cheering, holding signs, and throwing flowers: it was surreal, it was like a World War II movie, the Canadians going through Holland. It was a terrific send-off and a boost to our morale.[20]

Capt. Trevor Gosselin, the battle captain:

When we pulled out of the assembly area, the people from the refugee camps piled out onto the road and were cheering us on. It was pretty exhilarating. We had heard that the Brit columns were stoned by crowds earlier, but here were people on the side of the road throwing flowers at us and chanting "NA-to, NA-to, NA-to." They were in the thousands, kids had NATO painted on their chests. It was almost like the Netherlands during the Second World War. We were being hailed as heroes by these folks. Tactically, it was very slow: we were inching along and then it rained hard. It was spooky going through [the Kačanik defile]. The VJ let the Albanian refugees drive their cars and tractors down to the crossing where they would be abandoned [before entering Macedonia]. There was abandoned farm equipment and cars all over the place. It was a big junkyard. The towns were all blown to shit along there, the windows shot up and all torched. It was ugly. You drive by the big quarry plant at Djeneral Janković and see things covered with a half inch of dust like it's been there fifty years. It's dull, gray, and dreary like East Germany. It's raining and cold.[21]

Capt. Chris Hunt:

The lead call sign was 41 Delta, driven by Trooper Brown, and the crew commander was M.Cpl. Harry Delaney; they were the first into Kosovo. As we moved through the defile, I kept thinking: I was keeping my eyes open in case there were snipers up on the hills, which was a possibility. Our vehicle spacing was fifty to one hundred meters, no longer bumper to bumper. We were passing through tunnels and over bridges, and we could see Gurkhas and Paras sleeping by the side of the road with their sentries up. We had an airborne carpet all the way through the defile. We got to the far side of Kačanik town and it poured rain, which limited our visibility and then we found out that lightning sets off the laser warning receivers! It went BEEEEEEP! and I thought "Oh Jesus!" and started looking around to find the laser. Then I caught on to what was happening. We were cranked up, but you know, if you haven't got a round slamming into your turret, you're good to go.[22]

Capt. Trevor Gosselin:

We had to hold back a bit. The brigade commander found out there were still clashes between the VJ and UCK, and he didn't want us intermingled in there. So we stopped five kilometers south of Priština near Lipljan at around 2000 hours. The OC put the whole squadron tip to tail; we couldn't go off the road because of mines. We posted sentries, pitched our tents between vehicles, fed and shaved and all that kind of jazz, and went to ground. I had to sort out comms with brigade, so I was driving around in the middle of the night in a Land Rover down Route Hawk. We got hit with a spotlight, and we pulled out of the way and all of a sudden I see the end of a barrel and I go right and it's a VJ M-84 going by inches away. I nearly wet my pants, it was that close. There was a platoon of them pulling out nearby. I mean, I'm in a soft vehicle and he's in a tank. . . . So I got the radios reconfigured and wandered back to the squadron around 0200. The OC set reveille for 0400. The squadron piper played "Soldiers of the Queen." . . . I'll never forget that. I wake up at 0400, it's still raining and misty out, and you hear "Soldiers of the Queen" on bagpipes. It's difficult to put into words.[23]

Capt. Trevor Gosselin then was sent to establish an RRB site:

We secured an RRB site and then another one up on Mount Goleš. This was critical because the Russian scenario was playing itself out at the Priština airport and we were watching and sending back information to KFOR. Assault troop secured one of them first, then the Brits brought in their RRB equipment. It was the only way to communicate over the mountains. We had troops in Stimlje, Veliki Belaćevac, and here. We were there to identify the VJ in their withdrawal phase, to make sure they were complying with the MTA. Zone 1 was cleared, except down in Prizren, where the VJ got shot up a bit by the Germans: it was a pretty interesting engagement for Leopard fans. . . . The UCK and Serbs started skirmishing on the Glogovac-Priština road. A motor rifle battalion and a tank company were withdrawing towards Priština. We were collecting the vehicle numbers for brigade. They started taking sniper rounds from the UCK. They were under orders not to return fire, so they buttoned up and kept moving. The situation in the mines was different: there was a lot of fighting until we moved Hunt's troop in to put observation on them and calm things down.[24]

Once the squadron reached the interior, it was employed in an economy of force role on the left flank of the British advance into Priština and to Podujevo. The VJ and MUP withdrawal took eleven days, and there was sporadic payback by the UÇK. The squadron's role within the framework of brigade operations was initially to move into VJ positions to fill the void: the VJ would not leave until KFOR units had done so, mostly to save face. Capt. Chris Hunt:

> We then got orders to establish observation on the Priština airport and also by Veliki Belaćevac, where the mines for the power stations were. I did a quick recce and the one place where we could see both was Ade. . . . Once we got into the area of the mines, we came up to a checkpoint and it looked like MUP (they had blue uniforms), so I dismounted to talk to them. They were in their forties and kind of spooked by seeing us there. This guy in his twenties shows up with a little earpiece radio, and these guys were spooked by him; he had some authority. They led us through a maze of roads to Ade. There were two T-55s dug in, hull down, and a couple of M-80 APCs and twenty infantry. There was no interpreter. The commander of the force there was about my age, but he looked like something out of *Apocalypse Now*. He wore a black cowboy hat with U.S. Cavalry crossed swords, and he had a nylon mesh camouflage covering on his face. He told me his mission was to act as a blocking force and prevent the UCK from getting into Obilić. I told him we had night capability, that we could see, and he could withdraw now. He actually seemed happy to do so. Remember, this mine is huge: it used to be the second-biggest coal mine in Yugoslavia and employed fourteen thousand people at one point. Absolutely massive.
>
> Then the mine manager shows up with media and says the UCK has kidnapped some of his people. There was a UCK position in the next village and they wanted us to do something about it. We called it in and requested British infantry support to han-

dle it. Before it got dark, we noticed puffs of smoke coming from Veliki Belaćevac and then there was artillery going over our heads and then there were numerous firefights going on in Obilić. We watched it all using our sensors and passed it on. We saw a VJ tank company which fired into one of the villages, so the Brits send a squadron of Challengers up and the VJ stopped firing: they were spooked off, but it was a close call. We had 30mm ricochet landing within twenty-five meters of the OP. We heard everything that night: small arms, 30mm from BMPs.

The next day we pushed on through Ade into Grabovac. Ade was smashed: there were four hundred houses and every single one of them was burned. There had been a battle there, two weeks before. The VJ attacked the village the day after the locals finished building their mosque. It was gutted. Grabovac was hit pretty bad too, and then we reached Veliki Belaćevac and made contact with the UCK. Their leader was an anorexic Grizzly Adams, an old guy with a big beard, big bushy haircut, a UCK beret, and a 1914 Webley revolver and bandolier. He was crazy and had bad teeth. Their fifty-man company had taken twelve casualties: guys were missing feet and the stumps were gangrenous.

We asked about the kidnapping and they said no they didn't do it, that there was VJ up ahead. The whole kidnapping story we got was a fabrication and part of a deception plan by the Serbs [so they could justify their attack]. Once we got down the Veliki Belaćevac, we encountered ten T-55s in battle positions and a battery of 2S4 self-propelled guns. Plus two platoons of infantry. They were just waiting for the UCK. We called that in. I started to set up an OP, and he said "I don't give you permission to do that here," and I said, "You don't understand, I am not asking for your permission." He told me he was concerned that the UCK might attack us from the hills and get into Obilić. I told him we were there to ensure that the UCK didn't interfere with his withdrawal by watching UCK movement. I lied and he knew it, but it was all for appearances. We were reinforced with a section from assault troop. The Serbs stayed for another three days and we watched them carefully. We lased all of their vehicle positions to get the ranges [in case they had to be forced out of the area].[25]

Lt. Derek Chenette, troop leader:

The brigadier wanted to know if the Serbs were withdrawing from Sector 2 or if they were still hanging on. So I'm trying to get "eyes on" to see what's going on down the Drenica Valley. Well, I get to Komorane. I'm not allowed to go off the routes because of the mine threat. There's a full company of Serbs dug in, the tower is completely obliterated and very eerie. It's a peace mission, we're supposed to be friendly, so we set up shop near them. We're looking down the valley and then a firefight breaks out between the guys to the north and the UCK down the valley. We're hearing the CRACK-THUMP of the rounds over our heads and we're down in the vehicles going "Oh Jeez, this is great!" It was small arms and heavy machine gun, no artillery. It didn't last long. I think it was more of "We're leaving, screw you, guys," and the Albanians were saying, "Get the hell out." A little bit of "fuck you." We were counting vehicles on their way out. Before we went in we heard that the air campaign destroyed 80 percent of Milošević's armor. This was untrue. I was in Kosovo for six months and I saw one destroyed tank and I was everywhere in the Brit area of operations. When they were pulling out I realized why we hadn't destroyed their armor. The camouflage job they did was extremely effective. They had M-80s buried under garbage: they did a tank scrape, moved the vehicles in, and covered them up so it looked like a dump. They got the word to pull out, so they fling the garbage bags off and out rolls an M-80. This happened all over the countryside. There were hundreds of vehicles, tank column after tank column. I'll probably never see anything like it in the rest of my career. There were T-72s, T-55s, M-80s, and every B-esch vehicle that you could ever imagine. Stolen buses, everything.[26]

VJ protective tactics employed during the air campaign were revealed to the Strathconas as they moved into central Kosovo. Capt. Trevor Gosselin:

I will give the VJ full marks for conducting an orderly withdrawal. They had their antennas on their vehicles, their crew commanders were wearing headsets, they were organized, and when their commander said "Move," they moved. They were by no means a defeated army. They were quite happy to be going home, on the other hand. Their cam and concealment was quite good. We didn't see as many tank hulks as we thought we were going to see. We saw some pieces of equipment abandoned, probably due to lack of fuel or spare parts as opposed to attack. We found, for example, some D-30s [artillery pieces] that were abandoned. During the air campaign the VJ would only light up their radios and transmit once a day, because they knew that if they transmitted, they'd be taken out. That takes disciplined troops to do that. They also built a bridge along Route Dog [the main east-west axis of the province]. It was made out of plywood. They actually put a big piece of black matting on it so overhead it looked like there was damage to it when there wasn't any to the real one. There were tank dummies, mocked up with plywood, coming off the bridge. In another case we were looking at some Serb positions, and they knew that the NATO air recognition signal was an orange panel marker on your vehicle so you don't get bombed. They put them out too, hoping some nervous NATO pilot wouldn't drop. This isn't a group of Iraqis here.[27]

Russian activity was a priority task as well. Cpl. Jason Parteger:

We ended up in a place called Magura watching the airfields from a distance because we weren't cleared to go in there. The Russians were trying to push in there. We had to get "eyes on." They were classified as "enemy" until that whole thing got sorted out. There was actually some shooting in there as well. The Russians were not friendly to the [UÇK] or the [VJ]. We watched them come in and they stopped at a German camp first. The problem was that the Germans had some drive-by [shootings] from a van. We then heard there were UCK people coming back from the mountains. The Serbs then burnt a house on the ground right in front of us, to show us we weren't welcome. It was about eighty to one hundred meters away. The MUP were taking furniture out of the house and then it started smoking. We videotaped it and then they threatened us with the swivel mount on their APC and drove through our position at top speeds. Our guys had to jump out of the way. He did this three or four times until our troop leader got upset. He traversed the main gun to cover the main road and as soon as this gentleman came through, we stopped him with the main gun. We watched the MUP as we drove through some of the towns. We saw soldiers in blue uniforms. These "police" were standing in buildings with their rifles pointed at us. It was tempting to use the 25mm on them. The only reason we didn't was because these guys slowed down to a roll. We even saw a few generals in civilian vehicles go by. By this time the Russians moved in with their BTRs [BTR-80]. They didn't threaten us as much as we thought they might.

We parked in Magura and could hear the EOD teams blowing up 250-pound bombs. We could see the fire going overhead and the guns going off. You could see the charges running through the air. We were glad that these guys had their name on a certain target and it wasn't us. It was the UCK versus the Serbs again. There were flares, there were tracers going by. It was intense. The problem was that the forces [in contact] didn't have radios in their vehicles and it took two days to get them to stop. At another town we entered, a gentleman by the side of the road drew his finger across his throat and pointed at my troop warrant. The message was, "You guys are going to die if you come into town." So we loaded the gun and got ready. I was in the back with my rifle loaded and cracked the top hatch a crack. The whole troop swept in: our two vehicles took the north side, the others took the east. There was nobody with weapons. One gentleman was walking towards our checkpoint: he was gaunt and shaking; he told us this was the first time he'd been out in six months. We went around the bend in the road and we were surrounded by about four hundred children carrying flowers. Our vehicles looked like daisy flower caravans. Getting down from the vehicle, you were swarmed immediately. It was the best feeling in my life to know that I saved this town. We didn't have any gifts, so I ripped open whatever rations we had and I threw out candy bars. I was totally surprised.[28]

Lt. Derek Chenette led his troop into Glogovac, the central town in the strategic Drenica Valley:

Liberating Glogovac was the highlight of the whole tour for my guys. When we pulled in there, it was like we'd liberated Holland.

We pulled into the town square and thousands of people came out of nowhere. They came out of basements of blown-up houses. They were coming down from the hills and within ten minutes all of our vehicles were swarmed with crying Kosovars; they were throwing flowers at us, bouquets of roses. There were UCK soldiers everywhere. We didn't have an interpreter, but Trooper Joey Dalduke spoke Italian, and one of the UCK guys spoke Italian and we wound up talking to the UCK commander for the Drenica Valley. It was a good feeling. One old man who was about a hundred shakes my hand and kisses both cheeks and he tells us this is the first time he's been able to walk around town for nine months. Capt. Dale Cheeseman, the assault troop leader, pulled in to secure the town and we sent out Coyotes to observe. Because there had been so much fighting in the area, the place was littered with mines and UXOs. The people were so overjoyed they forgot. They wanted to go and see what was left of their houses. And then they started stepping on land mines. You could hear it every hour, one would go off. You'd be thinking, "God, that could have been a five-year-old kid." And then it happened again.

It was around 2200 and I was eating a Hungarian goulash IMP and we heard BANG! Within thirty minutes the poor SOB shows up and his buddies have him in the back of a tractor. They dropped him off at the CP and his right leg is missing from about six inches from the knee down. It's completely gone, and the front half of his left foot is missing, he has burns on the underside of his arms and his neck. We didn't have any medics with us, but the guys did a phenomenal job. They wrapped him up. I'll never forget this: he was not screaming and he starts to fade out, so we kept talking to him. There were UCK soldiers around and then they all just broke out into hysterical laughter when the wounded guy said something to them. I asked them what was so funny. Remember, the guy is lying there with his legs blown off and his buddy is holding his head and he looked down and asked him "Jesus, Joe, where's your legs?" And the wounded guy looks up and says, "Fuck off, I'll pick them up in the morning!" And these guys erupted in hysterical laughter and I'm sitting there going "My God, this isn't funny!" They finally got him to a hospital and he lived.[29]

Command and Control: Working with the British

The Strathcona's recce squadron established its headquarters alongside 4 (UK) Brigade HQ at the nearly demolished VJ base just west of Priština. After the VJ and MUP withdrew from Kosovo, the concept of operations shifted to handle the power vacuum and preparations to deter any aggression by the VJ in the border areas. Working with a British brigade was a new experience for recce squadron members, but it carried considerable historical baggage at the higher levels. Hong Kong in 1941 and Dieppe in 1942 were pathbreaking events that are popularly portrayed in Canada as the catastrophic misuse of Canadian troops by arrogant British commanders.[30] Despite the close professional working relationship between 4 CMBG and the British Army of the Rhine during the first twenty years of the Cold War, relations were strained during the UNPROFOR period, particularly in 1994.[31] Working closely with the British brigades in Kosovo went a long way toward rebuilding the Anglo-Canadian military relationship.

In MNB (Center)'s ISTAR matrix, the recce squadron was responsible for collecting and reporting on:

- MUP, special forces, or stay-behind presence, structures, leaders, and intent
- Serb paramilitary presence, leaders, and intent
- UÇK orders of battle and boundaries
- Noncompliance of UÇK regarding weapons caches
- UÇK attitudes toward the undertaking and KFOR
- Combat indicators for a UÇK attack on KFOR
- Future intentions for individual members of the UÇK regarding K plus ninety
- Any other Albanian paramilitary structures or presence
- Local government activities administered by the UÇK
- Political parties, size, leaders, aims, funding, and relationship to UÇK
- Organized crime groups, leaders, and intent

- Local attitudes toward different political parties
- Any nonattributable terrorist attacks and trends
- Isolated Serb populations and threat against them
- Trends in Kosovar Albanian violence against the Serb population
- War crimes sites
- Village profiles, amenities, infrastructures, religious sites, key personalities[32]

An error in the original command arrangements established by the CDS earlier in 1999 caused some confusion for both rotations. Some thought that the recce squadron was supposed to revert to the command of the Canadian battle group once it deployed into Kosovo. This made no doctrinal sense: the Canadian AOR was far too small for the employment of an entire squadron of Coyotes, and recce squadrons are normally a brigade-level resource. Such arrangements may have been fine in Bosnia, where the Canadian AOR was sixty-three hundred square kilometers, but not for an AOR of twelve hundred square kilometers.[33]

The National Command Element in Macedonia, led by Col. Mike Ward and then Col. Ivan Fenton, retained operational command (OPCOM) of the recce squadron, but operational control (OPCON) was given to the British brigade HQ. The recce squadron commanders, Major Fleury and then Major Datchko, were expected to observe the employment parameters imposed by NDHQ in Ottawa. If at any time they felt they were being forced to violate those parameters, they could inform the NCE, which would then discuss matters with the brigade HQ. There were consultations, however, when politically sensitive operations were proposed that would have Canadian participation, particularly the Mitrovica operation.[34]

Similarly if Canadian units were asked to conduct operations outside of the MNB (Center) area, they had to consult through the NCE with the DCDS. For example, the operations conducted by the RCD recce squadron in the MNB (East) area required Ottawa's consent. The recce squadron had liaison officers in the brigade HQ at all times so they could see what was going on in terms of upcoming operations or fulfill logistics requirements. Indeed there were a number of Canadians, like Capt. Andrew Atherton from the RCD squadron, who served as exchange officers with British armored regiments, specifically ones that had been on previous Balkans operations.[35]

Kosovo: The Operational Environment

Recce squadron operations in Kosovo were conducted in a complex geographical and ethnic environment. The power vacuum and dysfunctional infrastructure posed many challenges. Living conditions for the Strathconas, according to Warrant Officer Joseph Ramsay, amounted to "living in four-man tents and eating IMPs for almost three weeks. It was a big thing when they finally got the flying kitchen set up." With thousands of NATO soldiers in Kosovo, human waste management was also a serious challenge: "We had portable toilets, but there was no chemicals for them. So I drove around trying to solve the problem. I met a German major who gave me a number of a guy in Germany who had the contract to fill them. So it took twelve hours to get hold of the guy and everybody but the old Dixie Man showed up to put the chemicals in."[36]

Working the areas of operation was fraught with uncertainty. Capt. Mark Connolly:

> You don't know what you're getting into. You don't know what's out there or what the reception is going to be like. You quickly got a certain feeling when traveling through an Albanian community and then when you were going through a Serb community. The Serbs would look at you rather stoically, but the Albanians would line the road and wave. . . . One of my policies quite clearly was to speak English to everybody and not try to speak their language at all. There were guys with the UN, guys who had worked in Bosnia, who were shot because they said "Dober dan" (good day) in Serbo-Croat to an Albanian. The Albanians didn't want to hear Serbo-Croat. The Serbs were belligerent in their own way: they gave us the three-finger salute. When they were withdrawing, they'd drive their tanks over the center line and try to make you go off the road.[37]

Driving in Kosovo was itself a highly dangerous activity, particularly in winter. Sgt. Gary Reid, RCD:

> I was scared to death. I would never show it to anybody, and anybody that knows me or that works for me knows what kind of person I am. I was in Somalia and elsewhere, but every day I was scared shitless on the roads in Kosovo. They were a freaking *nightmare*. Both driving on them and the surfaces themselves. We would get ice all the time: no sand trucks, no salt, nothing. So we're driving Coyotes around and it's like a hockey puck. I saw a Coyote spin out on a road with an eighty-foot cliff on it. She was hanging on like that, over the edge. We had to get two American ARVs [armored recovery vehicles] to winch it off. That would have been an expensive wreck. Hardest recce I've ever done.[38]

Capt. Mark Connolly: "There were cars passing with excess speed and narrow sight distances, no lights at night on the roads because the power was off. There were these small tractors with trailers all the time, carrying wood or you name it on the back, no lights, no nothing, traveling at slow speeds. I saw a car come careening in and slam into one: everybody was drunk. That was not uncommon."[39]

A car accident in Kosovo was very different from one in Canada: it could escalate into violence. Master Warrant Officer Pierre Whelan, RCD:

> There were a number of incidents. I think the worst one was when we were at an accident site, me and my driver, and there were cars all over the roads. The Kosovars don't handle accidents like we do; they don't clear the road. You get a huge group of people standing in the middle of the road and you can't get out. I went up to sort this out and I got caught in the middle of the fight. I had to get my driver to come out of the hatch with his rifle. They were very aggressive and we had to push them off, very in your face.[40]

Aggression extended to almost all situations, and all ages. Capt. Chris Hunt, of the Strathconas:

> There was a Serbian lady in her mid-twenties [whose] family [was] killed, and she comes up to me and she wanted us to go over to the

next Albanian village and burn it. She was serious. It was brutal. We met another one, we called her the "Serbian Anne Frank" because she kept a diary through the NATO air campaign. I got into a serious conversation with her about ethnic tensions. She looks back and cites 1352, when a group of Albanians went into a Serbian village and burned it, and then thirty years later, it happened again. Their whole perception of history is different. I mean, North America wasn't even discovered yet. It is bred into them. I met an Albanian kid who was four: he wanted to grow up to become a soldier and kill Serbs. It is just brutal to see how deep the hatred goes.[41]

Warrant Officer Joseph Ramsay, of the Strathconas:

The adaptability of mankind is unreal. It just floored me again; of course I'm on my fourth tour in the Balkans. I thought there would be nothing new. I thought it would be like every other place I've been (except Cambodia with UNTAC). The Kosovars got right back to farming, right out in the fields all summer once we got there. The fields probably had mines in them, but the people still knew they had to put food on the table, so they're out there cleaning it up, as if "It's happened, move on. We've got to get on with it." I always find it's the farmers and laborers who don't benefit from the Miloševićes and the Pol Pots. They suffer the most and, in the long run, end up benefiting the least from it all.[42]

Canadian NCOs also had to keep a close watch on their own people, since intense events in Kosovo could trigger past memories. Master Warrant Officer Pierre Whelan, of the RCD:

Bosnia with SFOR was more relaxed than Kosovo, but there were people in our unit, and other units for that matter, that had been in Bosnia with the UN, Bosnia with NATO, Somalia, and even Rwanda, sometimes all four. Some people had problems and had to go home and that's fine. The important thing is that a soldier is capable of doing his job later on down the road. I can replace equipment, but I can't replace soldiers. I would rather have an individual get sorted out so he becomes a better soldier. There were a lot of emotional issues for people who had seen things. For example, I had family involved in those operations and stories they tell are just incredible, but you learn how to deal with it in your own way and you figure out how to relate to certain soldiers who were also there at that time. There's a lot hidden in the background, so as a leader I have to know what's going on and deal with it solider to soldier. I've experienced these things and I know what they are going through and they respect that. You can't make it a collective thing. And we're still adapting as an army to handle [PTSD].[43]

For experienced soldiers, Kosovo was very different from Bosnia. Cpl. Kevin Malost of the RCD:

Kosovo was pretty laid back. When we were with UNPROFOR, there was a lot more action going on, you heard tank fire, you heard artillery. In Kosovo you heard the odd shotrep [shot report]. It was still pretty busy, though. I was more busy on this tour than I was with UNPROFOR. It was a constant go, go, go. We also had a better idea of what was going, there were better directives. There was no internet with UNPROFOR! Instead of a booked fifteen-minute phone call, you get half an hour on the internet. Welfare was better set up, leave was better.[44]

Operations and Missions

The departure of the VJ did not mean an end to Serb activities in Kosovo: intelligence sources indicated that the MUP was still operating but that its infiltrators were in civilian clothes.[45] Likewise, not all factions of the UÇK were compliant with the MTA and "UCK splinter groups remain as the largest threat to NATO Forces."[46] Lingering suspicion produced a situation that during KFOR's early days could have ignited and jeopardized the NATO-led mission. The bulk of operations conducted by the recce squadron related to stamping out the brushfires before they could get out of control. Priština, along with its immediate environs, was a priority task. Information suggested that extremists were monitoring KFOR communications. The Coyote's secure radio system was put to good use in support of British security operations in the city. Maj. Paul Fleury:

Our squadron was totally secure. Even the manpack radios. Unlike a UN mission, where all communications are in the open, we used secure particularly when we were doing sensitive ops. We worked with the Royal Green Jackets, who were going to blitz all the roads, shut them down, and search everything to see what we could get. We provided the comms umbrella for that whole operation so that the whole game wouldn't be given away. Downtown Priština was like that, with the UCK guys on their Motorolas trying to listen in. The Paras would go in unexpectedly and take them down. When we went into an area where there were problems, we seemed to be rid of those problems quickly. We went up to the university there after several people had been tied up and shot, the rest of the town was burning down around us, but our area was nice and quiet because we put a big hammer over everything. We detained forty people the first two nights we were there.[47]

Capt. Trevor Gosselin:

Priština quickly turned into a center of gravity. [Gen. Sir Mike] Jackson was concerned that if he lost Priština, the headlong withdrawal of every Serb in Kosovo would start. We had to demonstrate that the Serbs would be protected so that they could live harmoniously with the Albanians. Priština was a city of mayhem, like Northern Ireland. There were some UCK groups who were very professional, soldierlike, we got along with them, and then there were others. There was looting going on, rampant, uncontrolled looting, people are being evicted, people are being shot. Drive-by shootings. The UCK was reasserting itself in Priština, kicking out the Serbs. It was ugly: at the university a professor, a security guard, and a cafeteria worker were bound with electrical wire and shot execution style in the head. We had seventeen murders going on over a three-day period. We took over the university. There were the Paras, augmented by AS-90 artillery crews acting as infantry, and anybody that could walk, and us, plus assault troop. This is where the Coyote surveillance gear started to earn its reputation. We could deploy the mast and intimidate people. We didn't even have to be looking at anything. It would force them to behave. Hey, the UCK are probably a good bunch of guys in their own right, but technologically they can't match us or understand what we are up to. So we'd turn the radar on and have it swinging around and they would think they were under observation. They wouldn't say "Boo!" to us. So we put up a presence right on the corner of the streets with the mast. Park, put up some concertina wire. It was deception, but it worked. You know, people see this thing and they see this stuff vibrating around on top of the mast and all of a sudden they're law-abiding citizens of Priština![48]

Cpl. David Horne was with the assault troop during operations in Priština:

We patrolled Priština working in half-sections of four with the Paras. There was a problem at a former Serb government building, and they went over to sort it out. It turned out there was armed UCK in there who shot somebody in the street, so we went in. Our first two guys caught five and put them on the floor, yelling at them. When questioned, they told us there was another guy running around the building armed and they had just stolen a car to get there and so forth, then another guy comes in screaming that there is a shooter with a pistol running around. He's losing his mind. Another comes down, so scared he can't even say anything. Then the guy with the pistol comes down and we get him. It was quite scary, especially at night. We had NVGs, but you can't see jack shit. We wandered around these alleys with our flashlights. The locals didn't give a shit. Then we caught up with these UCK guys who were evicting Serbian civilians. Some girl would come up, telling the interpreter that they're taking her parents away and yittering and yattering. The Albanians complain about the Serbs, and the Serbs complain about the Albanians, but shut the fuck up, tell us what's happening! We ran down the road on the sidewalk, up the stairs, and these big fucking thugs were hanging around with guns in their pockets, roaming around just picking up shit. We bust in the door and ask them what the fuck they're doing, and they just look at each other and we just screamed at them for maximum intimidation. You have to show these bastards that you're not scared (even though you are), and you have to be the one in control. The scariest thing would be to rush into some building and some guy would be there smoking a joint and holding a shotgun. He could have shot us all. It was a fucking rush. I'm not a very violent person in that way, and you have to watch it. A lot of guys can get scared and overcompensate with force.[49]

Coyotes were also used to covertly observe the UÇK in Priština. For about two weeks the Strathconas were involved in observing the comings and goings at the "Munster House" (which looked like the set from the 1960s TV show). In this case "Herman" was not home, but the building was used by the UÇK as a meeting point and held by a platoon. All the platoon seemed to do was PT in the morning: running a hundred meters one way, then a hundred meters another, and then inspection. All incoming and outgoing vehicles were filmed and the license plates recorded. This assisted KFOR intelligence in building a picture of the UÇK structure in case they chose to escalate the situation for their purposes and had to be shut down.[50]

In other areas of the MNB (Center) AOR, low-level violence continued. The Coyotes were then used on "lurk" operations. Capt. Trevor Gosselin:

> We were getting grenadings in the houses. Serbs were leaving, and then Albanians were showing up, but we didn't make the link at first that this was done to generate funds. The INTERPOL statistics on drug trafficking were pretty heavy: heroin was the happening thing. So the line starts to blur between what is a political objective and what is a criminal objective. Lurks were when we pulled our vehicles into an alley or somewhere, using the shadows and darkness for concealment, and sit there quiet-like till something bad happens in front of you. You reach out and pounce on it. We did that with vehicles and patrols, wait until something looked suspicious, like someone reaching into their jacket for a gun, then we'd pop out and snap them up. We did all kinds of that sort of stuff. And vehicle checkpoints, or VCPs. We could turn a vehicle inside out. Confiscate UCK ID cards and weapons. They were supposed to be transforming into the Kosovo Protection Corps and they didn't want to give up their guns.[51]

MNB (Center) initiated Operation Hawk, which was the code name for a series of surprise vehicle checkpoints (VCPs) established along Route Hawk by the Second Battalion, Royal Green Jackets, supported by Coyotes from the recce squadron. In addition to searching thirteen hundred vehicles, the operation was used as a means to distribute pro-KFOR psychological operations material to the citizenry.[52] VCP operations could be profitable if one were so inclined: a British VCP team stopped a car with three people in it and found an illegal handgun. A bribe of 50,000 Deutsche Marks was offered but not accepted.[53]

By early July the recce squadron could report that "UCK demilitarization continues with only minor incidents. . . . The UCK we have encountered have readily turned over weapons upon request. The Serb exodus has diminished, largely because those Serbs who have opted to leave have done so."[54]

And then there was the Gracko massacre on 23 July 1999. Gracko is less than ten miles from Račak, and the significance was not lost on KFOR. Capt. Chris Hunt:

> At 0200 I was woken up and we were told to go down to Gracko. Thirteen Serbs had just been massacred. I was kind of in shock and I realized the political implications of this. Within an hour and half, we were rolling down into the village. We were going down to relieve the Royal Irish platoon that was in the village. The town had about two hundred people living in it. All the men were in one house mourning and basically getting drunk and all the women were in another house crying and consoling each other. Within an hour the first media showed up and it became a circus. At least fifty media people showed up. It was crazy. Very quickly our task shifted from just providing security for the town to preventing Albanians from coming in and then preventing the Serbs from going out to exact revenge. We protected the crime scene too. Some of our guys contributed to the investigation: they found the shell casings and empty magazines. The scene was spooky. There was a tractor still running twelve hours after the incident. A team of Albanians, probably three or four, with two on overwatch and the others as a snatch team, [had] rounded up the farmers, got

THE COYOTE HOWLS

them in a circle, and gunned them down. They were found in a bit of a bowl, hard to see. One guy made a run for it, got in the tractor, and then was shot. It was very eerie.[55]

The brigade and the recce squadron became "tactical firemen. Fire starts up, we go there, do the business, but the damage is done, the fire is set. The assailants were gone. We worked with the Royal Green Jackets, who set up an observation and patrolling plan."[56] It was almost like closing the barn door after the horse dashed off. Gracko, a small village of about twenty-five houses, was just southwest of Lipljan. Lipljan is a town of several thousand people located just off Route Hawk, the main KFOR service route from the Kačanik defile to Priština. Outside of Priština the Lipljan *opština* (municipality) held the largest number of Kosovar Serbs in the MNB (Center) area.[57] Lipljan was "a weird city. It's divided into Serb, Albanian, and Roma or Gypsy populations. We never had a problem with the Roma, but the Kosovar Albanians hated Kosovar Serbs, the Serbs hate the Albanians, and everybody hates the Roma."[58] The situation in Lipljan had to be controlled to prevent the fire from spreading, and Operations Othello, Salome, and Market Day were the result:

On market days in Lipljan, Albanians would wander into Serb crowds with grenades, drop the pin, let it slide down, move out into the crowd, which gives them five or six seconds, whatever the detonation period was, to walk away. We had several grenadings. So we would go in market day with the Coyotes and pull up to the center of the crowd and put the mast up. We had Sony Handicams and we would put troopers on top of the turret and he'd film everything. We could film everything, edit it, and send it up to brigade. As soon as the battle group CO caught onto that, they wanted everything filmed and it became a great source. So then everybody became upstanding citizens of Lipljan. It was very, very effective. There are no more grenadings, everybody is accommodating. Then the Albanians went into Serb neighborhoods, operating in two pairs, two couples. Couple number one in the lead would act as scouts and check for KFOR troops, while couple number two would go around to a Serb house and the woman would lob her grenade in and it would detonate. The Serb family would become scared, leave, and then they would take over the house and rent it out as part of a crime racket.[59]

The recce squadron shifted observation tasks to watch over the town to deter this activity. Then the Kosovar leadership decided to stage a demonstration in Lipljan to protest Kosovar Albanian detainees still being held in Serbia.[60] This complicated the situation further. Cpl. Jason Parteger:

> They had a large area where the Kosovars used to band together, and they said about two hundred to six hundred people would show up and ride through the city. We were to make sure that none of the people were carrying weapons, and we were to prevent the Serbs from taking shots at them. Our whole troop would go. The troop leader would meet them before arrival and make sure none were openly carrying weapons. They were carrying banners and signs. We'd use the thermal [imagery] on them because you can tell if a rifle is being carried under a jacket. You could see the heat differentiation between the two. The mast systems could see the whole area. We weren't hiding, and we wanted them to know we were there. I'd raise the mast to the highest point and then scan the whole thing.[61]

Infantry teams provided by the British units would discreetly apprehend anybody carrying a concealed weapon. The Strathconas developed a creative method to deter violence:

> We used Coyotes as fake OPs. We'd set up Coyote surveillance in the middle of the marketplace, but they couldn't see anything; it was all in dead ground [immediately around the vehicle]. The locals had no clue what Coyote was or what it could do, and they thought they were under observation. I found that the Sony Handicams that the squadron had were more useful than the Coyotes' day cameras in some cases. It is color, you have as good a zoom, it's digital and portable, and you can use it in covert OPs. We wanted to slap it on the mast. We'd take those on some operations, and if we had kids throwing rocks at our convoy or if we were in town and someone looked dodgy, you whip out that video camera and get

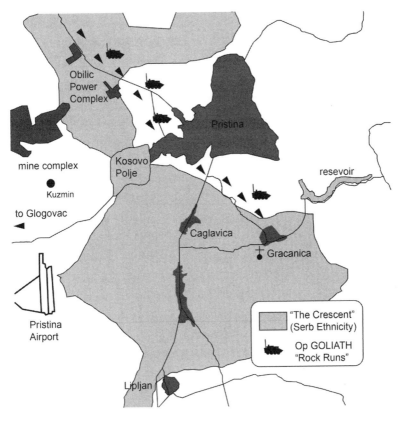

FIG. 11. The Crescent, 1999–2000.

their face on a picture: they know they've been recorded and after that they tend to slink off and find somewhere else to hang out.[62]

The Lipljan situation remained volatile and continued to be closely monitored during the RCD rotation.[63]

The other primary area of concern vis-à-vis ethnic tension was an area dubbed "the Crescent." Predominantly Kosovar Serb, the Crescent extended in an arc from the community of Obilić adjacent to the power stations, through the city of Kosovo Polje, which straddled the main east-west road across Kosovo, across Route Hawk to Kačanik, and around to the town of Gračanica. Gračanica was important for several reasons. It controlled the Gračaničko Jezero reservoir, which provided fresh water for Priština. It was also the home of the Serbian Orthodox Gračanica monastery, one of the primary holy sites in Kosovo in addition to Peć and the fields of Kosovo Polje. The Obilić and Kosovo Polje *opštinas* had the highest percentage of Kosovar Serbs in the MNB (Center) area.[64]

Tensions in the Crescent could clearly pose serious problems for KFOR. Interference with electrical power, water, and the two main road axes could shut down Priština, not to mention the whole province. Leaving the Kosovar Serbian population unprotected in the face of UÇK or local retaliation could provide Belgrade with enough propaganda fodder to justify an intervention in Kosovo from the outside, or to support extremist measures on the inside, which in turn would escalate the cycle of violence to unacceptable levels. Indeed the Gračanica Serb National Council's cooperation and participation in the multinational Interim Administrative Council (IAC) was seen as critical to the long-term prospects for peace in Kosovo since it retained some political influence over other Serb enclaves. Gračanica became a political center of gravity that demanded increased KFOR attention.[65] As with Lipljan, the recce squadron operations for both rotations were conducted throughout the Crescent and in concert with border and escort operations to stave off these problems.

The problems for KFOR in the Gračanica area initially involved the so-called Mystery Mortar Man:

> You know when something happens a couple of times, soldiers name it? Well, we had the Mystery Mortar Man. He would set up on a hill, drop five or six mortar bombs, splash them down in the area of the monastery, and then disappear. Of course we can't be everywhere and we don't have eyes on the whole province. And then somebody fired a 75mm recoilless rifle at a Norwegian camp nearby. We chased him in a helicopter. There were all kinds of random acts of violence. The monastery was very important. Archbishop Artemje is there and he is seen as the cornerstone. If he falls, then what is left of the Serb community will take off. They're pretty rattled. Serbs are getting knocked off. The Albanians know the ground, they know how people live. They're adapting to KFOR's presence, and then there's whole political hullabaloo when mor-

tar rounds land in Gračanica. Belgrade is leveling a propaganda campaign against Commander KFOR. The VJ had a couple of armored brigades over the border.[66]

It was never clear who exactly the Mystery Mortar Man was working for, but he didn't cause any serious damage to the monastery or its inhabitants. In time the recce squadron was selected to escort the archbishop from Gračanica to the border gates and back when necessary. Canadians handled this task without incident until January 2000, when the provision of this service was ended.[67]

The best means to handle the Crescent problem was a combination of presence and surveillance: these were called Operation Trojan and Operation Vandal. In some cases the Coyotes worked with the Canadian Griffon helicopters from the Kosovo Rotary Wing Aviation Unit (KRWAU) based at Donja Koretica. Cpls. Randy Payne and Troy Cleveland of the RCD:

[The locals] were afraid to go out and plow the fields because of nighttime mining. We set up in three points with the Coyotes, masts, and remotes to cover these fields and report everything in. They're not stupid and this wasn't a covert operation. We also had choppers there all the time and sensors going. We'd see a car pull off the highway and it would just stop and you'd see people get out, mill about, have a smoke, get back in the car, and stay there. If we lost contact with them, we'd call in the helicopter with the Nightsun and they'd put that on them to see what the hell's going on. The helicopter would get within twenty feet over this car, flash the Nightsun, and find out they're in the backseat screwing their brains out! It wasn't always boring: one night we saw this tractor trailer pulling up with no lights on, nothing and we followed this car and a vanload of people. We were using IR on them and FLIR in the chopper, maybe two to three kilometers away on the ground. The people got out and started to run down the road, and then another tractor trailer backed up to the building. We called in the Norwegians and they found a small cache of mines, an RPG rocket launcher with a few rockets, and grenades. Our guys later found a mine that was a mortar round set up like a booby trap. Right in the field. It would have killed a farmer in the morning.[68]

Warrant Officer Mike Brabant of the RCD:

We did some work with 430 [tactical helicopter squadron] with its Griffons. We had to watch the fields, and we'd send the Griffons over at random, change the timing, just to keep the locals off balance. We'd report someone with our systems from the Coyote, and the Griffons would be on the ground ready to react, staying hot and ready to roll. In ten minutes, we'd see cars stopping, a guy would get out, put something in the field, so we'd react. Sometimes he would be taking a leak. We also put some of the guys aboard the helicopters to explain to the crews what the Coyote was capable of so we could coordinate operations. The locals even had a nickname for the Coyote. I forgot what it was in Albanian, but it meant "Sees at Night." They knew when we put the mast up, this thing can see at night and it does magic.[69]

The recce squadron also provided overwatch for Kosovar Serb families returning to villages in the Crescent around Gračanica. Cpl. Kevin Malost, RCD:

We set up with the Brits, and the local people were moving back into these small towns. This was the first attempt to bring the Serbs back to their towns. The towns were cleared [of mines and UXO], but they really didn't want to go back. We lived in the houses to show they were safe and not booby-trapped. We overwatched the farming as well. Convoys of Serbs were driven past us so we could demonstrate that it was okay to come back. We spent a lot of time doing these tasks. There were no shotreps or burnings when we were there: it wasn't like UNPROFOR, where we always saw clashes and demonstrations. We did have one demonstration in Gračanica, but we were backup in the shadows for the Swedish troops there.[70]

The recce squadron also had the opportunity to work with the Gurkhas. Cpl. Jason Parteger of the Strathconas:

The greatest gang to me was the Gurkhas. I even traded with them for a Kukri [knife], which I gave to my father as a gift. We had a lot of fun with them. We did a lot of ops. They actually built a tower for us so we could put a remote sensor up there in place of a mast.

We could see all. We would support the Gurkhas in their weapons sweeps through the villages. We were parked on a hill and were watching one [Gurkha]. He was sitting in the ditch. It was raining like crazy. He had a smile on his face in the rain with all of his gear on and we watched the rest of these guys come in. Two of them took point and covered the rest, who then went into the building, and fifteen minutes later they came out with five weapons and ID cards. They put the stuff on their trucks and moved on. The guy in the puddle is a sniper; he gets up and moves to another position. We were amazed by these guys: if you took the average soldier and put him in a puddle in the rain, he's not too happy about that. We were there just to make sure nothing went wrong: if the Gurkhas had to shoot at somebody, they could show they were in the right [by using the film].[71]

To supplement operations in the Crescent, MNB (Center) extended operations to several small villages northeast of Gračanica throughout the spring of 2000. Capt. Brian Power, RCD:

We provided security for [Kosovar Serbs] returning to Kosovo. Serbia didn't treat them very well. These people went back to the motherland looking for support and friendship and they weren't wanted. [Belgrade] wanted to keep the Serbian population in Kosovo. The returnees didn't have access to health care and weren't receiving their monthly stipend from the government, which they were supposed to be getting for staying in place. These operations went hand in hand with Op Trojan. Assault troop went down there with a troop of Coyote: the Coyotes did surveillance on the area while assault troop patrolled. We had to determine what shape the housing was in, what threats there were, and provide a presence to discourage aggressive acts against the people. There were daytime presence patrols and nighttime dismounted OPs. Our guys were in place for nearly a month.[72]

Protracted surveillance and presence tasks could be trying, according to Warrant Officer Carl Cox, RCD:

I think our guys enjoyed being on the tours. You have the equipment you need, you have one mission, and a job that these guys have trained all their careers to do, and we were actually doing it. Morale was pretty high, but there was some pretty mundane taskings and the guys didn't always see the big picture. One example was watching Serbian farmers' fields in predominantly [Albanian] areas for mining. At nighttime the guys were seeing nothing except for rabbits. It was like watching paint dry. Everybody knew we were there and word gets out quick about your technology. . . . They knew how good this technology was and that it was able to see at night and in all types of weather, so they wouldn't bother to try anything. Our presence alone was a deterrent and nothing happened. The guys were a little pissed off because they were sitting around doing the square root of nothing for a couple of months on end. One time, though, we chased a vehicle down into a field. It was 0200 or so and they were coming from a bar in the next village, so we chased them in a Bison, and he was trying to run so we thought he was trying to hide something, so we finally overtake with the Bison. I mean, it's a big vehicle, but we could get 120 kilometers per hour out of it and it handles well, so he couldn't lose us and pulled over. We didn't find anything, but they invited us in for a drink, but they were very, very scared. In retrospect, we should have taken them up on the drink, but . . .[73]

Ultimately surveillance operations in the Crescent provided entertainment for the recce squadron because in time most of the action amounted to "a lot of people having sex in their cars"—making love, not war.[74]

Operation Goliath, also known as the "Rock Run," was connected to the need to provide security to Kosovar Serbs in the Crescent and in other areas, specifically Mitrovica. This routine operation started during the Strathconas' tenure and escalated in importance once the Dragoons got on the ground in December 1999. Capt. Andrew Atherton:

It was in December when we were taking over. Initially we had the Train Run. The train track was blown up [between Zvečan and Kosovo Polje] and they started using buses. There were Serb workers in Mitrovica who worked down in Gračanica. So we would send a troop at some incredibly unsociable time in the morning to

THE COYOTE HOWLS

escort the commuter bus. And someone else took it home, usually the French. We'd been there a week or two by the time we started taking over the Rock Run. We stopped the buses at Gate 3, searched all of the people on them, and escorted them through Priština to the Serb enclave at Gračanica. Then we'd take 'em back up and drop them off at the border. Coming through Priština wasn't too bad, but around Obilić was the worst problems. The problems started out small and we only had a Coyote escort, but then we got assault troop, and then helicopters, and it wound up being a three-hundred-man operation to run this freaking thing. Every Tuesday and Friday.[75]

Capt. Brian Power:

It was getting bigger and bigger. It nearly included an entire battalion. It eventually was three buses leaving Niš to Gračanica. The people either had family or worked there, or the people from Gračanica shopped in Niš. Three bright red buses. Kids would throw stones at them. KFOR was in a no-win situation: Kosovo is still part of Serbia and the Serb government wanted freedom of movement for Serbs within Kosovo. This was a big political thing, far beyond three buses driving down the road. Belgrade would not change the times, the routes, or even the color of the buses. There were reports that Serbs on the buses were instigating the Albanians as they drove by, that sort of thing. The Rock Run evolved from a troop escort to a troop plus assault troop. Assault troop would be located at key points of the route, with the battle group stationing other personnel securing whole sections of road, helicopters flying top cover. What sounded the wake-up call for us on the Rock Run was a rocket attack against a bus which was escorted by the French on its way to Mitrovica. This was the second attack and it coincided with the escalation of the situation in Mitrovica. Brigade reexamined the whole thing: lots of troops were tied up with it, which is what Belgrade wanted. There was no way to stop a child from throwing a rock at the buses. What are we going to do, shoot them? We put assault troop on the ground to try and grab the kids and turn them over to the UNMIK police. Well, a fourteen-year-old who's scared wearing sneakers is gonna run a lot faster than a guy wearing boots and carrying a rifle and ammunition! We tried to dust them off using the helicopters, but it reached the point where it got ludicrous. We eventually changed the route and brought it through the Russian sector in [American-led] MNB (East).

It was a frustrating experience for the members of assault troop. Cpl. Kevin Malost:

We tried to put people at different spots along the road, where the children were throwing rocks. And that didn't really work. We followed the buses, and then when the rocks would be thrown, we'd dismount and try to catch the kids. Capt. Ash Fleming was calling the shots and he changed tactics. At different hot spots, particularly where there is a schoolyard, we'd put a whole section in to watch out for the children. They would get a couple of rocks off at the bus. How do you control fifty or sixty schoolchildren with a section of ten men? We got the British to monitor the schoolyards and we followed. We also had a helicopter and we'd tell him, "There's a thrower, that guy's going to throw a rock," and we'd dismount and hand them over to UNMIK. They were probably released that day and back doing it the next time. It finally mellowed out a bit. Sometimes there would be injuries on the bus, people would get cut. At the beginning, the job was hilarious and then it got monotonous.[76]

The political significance of Operation Goliath was not lost on Maj. Tim Datchko:

We were overtasked and it took away resources I had tied up elsewhere. We had to demonstrate that we were committed to ensuring the safety of both the Serbs and the Albanians. If we were not there, they would not have made it. All these guys had to do was block the road and there would be a slaughter. We also had to make sure the Serbs didn't put protective guys like the MUP undercover on the bus with weapons. Or even a plain old Serb with a gun. All we needed was these guys firing at kids [with KFOR protecting them]. The teachers were out cheering the kids on, throwing rocks. But what were we supposed to do? Have some big assault trooper run down a ten-year-old kid? Rough them up? No way.[77]

There were never any terrorist attacks on the Niš Express buses while they were under Canadian escort. Once the recce squadron became involved in the Train Run bus escort mission, lethal attacks on it suddenly stopped.[78]

MNB (Center) was also concerned about the border regions. UÇK activity in the GSZ near Podujevo resulted in a burned MUP border post and a wounded Kosovar Albanian.[79] As discussed in the previous chapter, the VJ was supposed to observe strict guidelines, established in the MTA, that related to their activities in or around the ground safety zone. This in turn was related to KFOR contingency planning to repel a VJ mechanized incursion that could be triggered by violent events against the Kosovar Serb population inside Kosovo, whether contrived or not. Serb extremists or special forces infiltrating Kosovo would obviously pose problems. GSZ monitoring was linked to operations like Constant Resolve, which sought to provide a deterrent posture and to exercise contingency planning. For the recce squadron during the Strathconas' tour, the priority was the GSZ adjacent to the Podujevo bowl: the Dragoons took up this task and then were involved in observing the GSZ in the American-led MNB (East) sector in the spring of 2000 (see below).

Coverage of the border gates, called Operation Spectator, was important for KFOR because of the terrain. Capt. Chris Hunt:

> When we did our initial recces we found we couldn't establish OPs right on the border because the way it was laid out put the boundary right on a ridge line. We would have to cross into Serbia to get observation. So we pulled back but couldn't see anything. Helicopters could see in [but they had limited endurance]. A few weeks later the boundary was adjusted so it was four hundred meters past the ridge line. You could see all the way to Kuršumlija, which was important because it was a VJ battle group assembly area at the road junction. At the time, it wasn't our highest priority because brigade had other strategic indicators. We took the Coyotes to places where I don't think General Motors thought it could go. Because of the GSZ, the Serbs were not allowed to have any forces in there, but they had "farmers." We set up OPs to watch

the activity there. We had one right on the border and we had British UAVs flying over us. They thought the VJ had an electronic warfare-equipped BMP vehicle sending targeting information back to Belgrade somewhere in the area. It was actually a Coyote [that was camouflaged] with its mast up. We had pretty good surveillance. If the Serbs were sending special forces across, they were coming across as farmers or whatever. My gut opinion was that they had intelligence agencies in Kosovo but no active sabotage or armed raiding. You'd hear stories from the locals, but half the time it was something they made up or somebody was having a party and firing off a few AK rounds in celebratory fire.[80]

Covert OPS also were conducted, and it could get dicey. Cpl. Jason Parteger:

My most exciting one was our first covert [OP]. We did it because there was this Serbian house that acted as a barracks. We're right at the border. We had our gear two meters over the border; it was the tripod sensors. Both of them are sitting there, and three gentlemen decide to go for a walk up the hill. Our warrant [officer] decided that they were a threat because they were carrying weapons; all of them had AK-47s. So we loaded up and we had our flak jackets and helmets on, geared up. We wanted to make sure that three million dollars' worth of gear was safe. Something came over the air. I ran up front and all of a sudden the [three Serbs] came up to the top of the hill. The warrant jumped up, rifle up. "Please drop your arms," "Please be nice: we're just here to watch," all in Serbo-Croat. And then one decides to run, and he was carrying something heavier than an AK-47, like a GPMG. These guys, by the way, were not in uniform. We stopped the other two. Because of our time in Bosnia, one of our guys was able to speak to them. They were just curious and were not interested in causing any problems. The guy who ran came back and everything settled down.[81]

Not all of the Serbs were so cordial. Master Warrant Officer Pierre Whelan:

I was resupplying our troops at Gate 3, and they were in the middle of a confrontation with the MUP on the other side of the bridge.

The MUP always liked to do that, cause a bit of shit, fire rounds over people's heads. Our soldiers deployed and we backed them up. The guard commander conducted negotiations. The MUP just walked away. Then some of our other guys on patrol came up on a MUP patrol in the exclusion zone and forced them to leave. It's not like Cyprus: confrontation was the nature of the job. These situations could escalate if not handled correctly. The hatred runs so deep, it's nothing to kill each other. That's the bottom line.[82]

There were other violations of the GSZ as well as the ASZ. Capt. Brian Power:

We were assisting the Swedes when we observed Serb helicopters and Serb aircraft flying around in the no-fly zone. And we were pretty sure we saw a Mi-8 HIP fly into Kosovo, not directly, but using the terrain on the border as cover. The VJ also had an electronic warfare site up there too. That got really big. The guys got videotape of the helicopter. We watched him with the thermal and he was violating the ASZ by at least nineteen and a half klicks. He flew to the north, around a mountain, and disappeared. We took the tape back to the int[el] guys at Brigade and then right to KFOR. The patrol was debriefed at KFOR HQ the next day. A sternly worded letter of protest went to Belgrade. There were plans that if it happened again, to bring in an AH-1 Cobra or an AH-64 Apache and we were going to shoot it down.[83]

Maj. Tim Datchko noted that "we really had to be careful with the helicopter issue. The Swedes may have reported some lost Russian from Kosovo flying around there. The Russians used to fly all over the place with their Mi-24 HINDs. The Swedes even reported in a Griffon who made a navigational error. Luckily no one was shot."[84]

The VJ electronic warfare position and its defenses were of interest to KFOR HQ. Capt. Jonathan DeSwert of the RCD:

There was a place we called Sugar Top Mountain. It had antennas, sensors, everything. It was a Serb listening post. All the buildings seemed to resemble a weather station. They were deployed there and listening to us. And we deployed a covert [OP]. It was the best [operation] we had. We went to the border and deployed to a covert OP near what we called "the Alamo." It was an old German air defense position [from World War II] laid out like a ring. From that position you could see the entire valley. We moved in the remote EO sensor and put the vehicles behind the hill so they were not technically inside Serbia. We were able to record everything. It was sneak and peek: they were trying to find us and we were trying to find them. [We even filmed] the Russians dealing with the Serbs coming across the border.[85]

For more serious contingencies the recce squadron was integral to Conplan Thunder, the KFOR plan to repel a VJ mechanized incursion. Maj. Paul Fleury:

The main threat assessment was that the objective would be Mitrovica, where there was a large Serb population, but there was always the possibility of some sort of subsidiary action around Podujevo, so the original task had me going to work with the [PPCLI battle group], tack onto the them, sort of looking towards Mitrovica acting as a blocking force. I didn't like that plan. The PPCLI had seven of their own Coyotes to act as a screen and I'm a brigade resource. The Assault Troop have been trained to dig in and act as lay-back OPs. The Coyote guys were perfectly equipped; the Brits only had three ground radars. Well, I had a dozen radars, so my suggestion was to make us part of the Offensive Support Group, which is like ISTAR where you combine all of your targeting capability with the [artillery]. So we had the surveillance task on the border north of Podujevo and from the high features [in the area]. The Swedes were at Gate 4 doing the same thing, providing overwatch and targeting capability, but they only had six guns. We had to be prepared to do these tasks in addition to all of the other ones we were doing.[86]

Contingency planning went hand in hand with overt demonstrations of capability to provide a deterrent effect. One such demonstration was Operation Constant Resolve, held in November 1999. Capt. Chris Hunt:

The idea here was a show of force to impress the local population and also demonstrate resolve [to the VJ]. It was a good exercise to work on traffic control [a recce task] and see how we could do it. A whole German armored battle group from MNB (South) was going to go up through to Podujevo. I was expecting fifty Panzers. After they fiddled with it, it was down to a troop of Leopard 2s and a couple of companies of mechanized infantry, some mortars, and a reconnaissance company. The Turks and the Dutch were also involved. It was less impressive than I imagined. Our squadron was spread out in traffic control points from Stimlje to Podujevo. We did this because our squadron [radio] net was secure, one of the few secure nets in KFOR actually, and we could easily report the progress. It went smoothly.[87]

Another aspect of Constant Resolve and similar exercises was getting the VJ to reveal their surveillance and other capabilities. MNB (Center) helicopters, including Canadian Griffons, operating with ground forces that included the Coyotes and even the Canadian Leopards from the 1 PPCLI battle group, would coordinate an action designed to elicit a response. British electronic warfare and intelligence-gathering assets, as well as the recce squadron's Coyotes, would measure and record the response. Capt. Jonathan DeSwert of the RCD:

We wanted to see the Serbs' reaction. You know what they teach us in ITC about demonstrative attacks to see what the enemy will do to defend himself? Well, in comes Lt. Ray Miksa with his Leopards on the ground. Then in come Griffons from 430 Squadron, backed up with Pumas; they drop off airmobile infantry and secure a line of departure [LOD]. We had Mike Duggan with his Coyotes and remotes looking into the next valley at the Serbs' known outposts. I was stationed near a big grain silo and we have Coyotes everywhere. There's a mobile electronic warfare team [MEWT] scattered around. The LOD is secured, and then they crossed. The tanks took up positions. The Serbs didn't react, they didn't do anything. We came back and did it all over again. Someone over there must have woken up or got off their drunk and they all stood to, the VJ. On the third time we did this, they moved their tanks into positions and dropped off guys by helicopters. We found out they had a whole bunch of repeaters in the area: if one guy talked over here, it went through these repeaters, and if another guy talked over there, it went through another series of them. We even had an unmanned aerial vehicle [UAV] overhead watching: we caught it on radar.[88]

Capt. Brian Power:

Seven Brigade conducted Operation Calliope, I believe it was called, and it involved a battle group which had a company of Warrior from the Royal Green Jackets, a squadron of Challenger 2s out of Podujevo, with some recce vehicles and some aviation. Two days prior, we put in OPs all along the boundary. We had one on the huge grain elevator in Podujevo looking into Serbia. There was EW everywhere, DF [direction finding] teams. I set up with the EW command post and we got a pretty good idea of the electromagnetic activity [coming out of Serbia]. The exercise goes down, they turn everything on. [Initially] it didn't stir up as much activity as we wanted. The DF guys could only get within a grid square, so that's where Coyote came in [because we could observe more closely]. A couple of Scimitars moved up to this Serb OP to look like they were marking a line of departure. A combat team starts moving up the road, some aviation comes in and drops off some soldiers. We put the recce and the EW together. It got better later in the year. The British used a UAV called Phoenix and did the same operation again. So suddenly a UAV would be looking straight down on the Serbs. It was quite something and [served to test ISTAR].[89]

Taken together, these activities are reminiscent of those undertaken by Canada and its NATO allies in West Germany during the Cold War. The difference was the ISTAR component. During Operation Kinetic there were several challenges to the recce squadron with regard to interoperability and experience. For example, MNB (Center) had British unmanned aerial vehicles, British electronic warfare units, a Swedish electronic warfare unit, Canadian Griffon helicopters with ERSTA, and Canadian Coyotes. Each system had its unique capabilities but had never worked together. Coyote was completely unlike anything ever employed before. MNB (Center) learned early on that, for example, using EW to gather information on certain UÇK elements was difficult. On one Canadian-British operation designed to deter and then prevent UÇK weapons smuggling, the only thing that was intercepted was, "Don't use your radios." It took time to merge the capabilities. Coyote's mast sensor was digital, but it recorded on an analog videotape. Tapes had to be driven to the assessors. Canadian crews improvised and used a digital camera to take pictures of the video feed, clean it up, and then print it or transmit it (using other means) to the end users. UAVs could not remain aloft forever but had range and flexibility: Coyote could handle some areas, while UAVs could supplement coverage at longer ranges. In the Mitrovica operation, for example, Swedish and British EW units co-located with Canadian Coyotes worked together to identify and locate snipers.[90]

It took time, but the fusion paid off. Coyote employment in MNB (Center) also highlighted the need to supplement mast-mounted vehicles with a lighter recce vehicle. Coyote could cover a large area, and it was sometimes excessive to deploy another one to check out a specific point of interest. The British deployed a squadron of 30mm-equipped Scimitar tracked recce vehicles in Kosovo. Some exercises were conducted using Scimitar with Coyote operating together, and many recce squadron members thought that a troop or detachment from 2 (EW) Squadron should have been integrated into the squadron.[91]

The Dragoons and Operations in Multinational Brigade (East)

In addition to the KFOR operation in Mitrovica the Royal Canadian Dragoons conducted a series of important observation tasks in the American-led MNB (East) area of operations while they were moving from the former VJ base at Priština to the Canadian camp at Donja Koretica. Problems in the MNB (East) area were on the rise throughout the winter of 1999–2000 and escalated to near unacceptable proportions in the spring. The rise in tension was believed by some to be related to the drawing away of KFOR

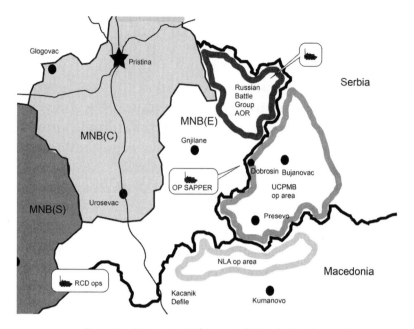

FIG. 12. Operation Spectator: Multinational Brigade (East) operations.

resources to handle Mitrovica. Numerous factions, Serbian and Albanian, and even a KFOR "ally" required increased scrutiny.

Four separate murders of Kosovar Serbs in MNB(E) followed by a radar-observed mortar attack from across the border in mid-December were the harbingers. Arms smuggling along the Macedonian and Albanian borders increased to the point where Commander KFOR mounted Operation Consistent Effort to assert more KFOR presence in these mountainous regions. Then an American liaison officer to the Russian contingent was killed by a mine strike. This action was followed by another mine strike on a Russian BMD vehicle, which wounded two Russians. The situation was further compounded with the assault and murder of a twelve-year-old girl by an American NCO and then the murder of three Serbs right on the interprovincial boundary. The murder of the child notably increased the tension in the area, and there was serious concern that the incident would be used by local factions as a lever with which to interfere with American operations to curtail movement on the border, particularly to and from the Preševo

Valley in Serbia, where Albanians were conducting an insurgency against Belgrade's forces.[92] Even recce squadron patrols had to be careful in MNB (East). As Cpl. Ray Power recalled, "After the American raped the little girl, they were a bit hostile to Americans, so when we drove around we made sure our Canadian flags [painted on the vehicle] were well washed and had the mud off them. We didn't want any mistakes to happen."[93]

Even the Polish contingent in MNB (East) was having problems. The former UÇK commander of the Nerodime region, Shukiri Buja, was resisting the Poles' attempts to exert KFOR authority. Shots were fired over Polish vehicles and at their compound.[94] Although the American contingent in MNB (East) had surveillance capabilities, there was nothing like Coyote nor were there any UAVs available at this time. There were the exceptional AH-64 Apache attack helicopters, which were equipped with FLIR, but like any aircraft they could not remain on task indefinitely. American legislation prohibited American personnel from operating in close proximity to the interprovincial boundary: this was still in effect and was directly related to the seizure of American soldiers by Serb special forces from Macedonia during hostilities in 1999.

Simply put, there were places in MNB (East) where Americans could not go. To make matters even worse, MNB (East) had one of the larger Russian KFOR sectors. Relationships with the Russians were obviously quite strained. Shots fired at Russian vehicles by Kosovar Albanians were returned in disproportionate fashion, particularly when the targeted vehicle was a BMD-2, which mounted a 30mm rapid-fire cannon.

One of the disconnects noticed by Canadian officers operating in MNB (East) was between force posture and information operations:

It was a national force protection issue down in the American brigade area. They had to wear their helmets and flak vests and always carried their weapons everywhere they went. [M-]203 grenade launchers, M-72 machine guns, the whole thing. They had to go places in groups of four, and no less than two vehicles. Normally they went in threes. They had guys behind the guns at all times [on the Hummers]. It didn't matter what the threat level was.

KFOR's message, however, at the force level was that Kosovo is a safer place, NATO's accomplishing its mission of establishing a safe and secure environment for the people of Kosovo, you know, the whole party line. The whole [information operations] plan in the American brigade area had to change. There was a contradiction here: Kosovo's a safer and more secure place, it's happy, why are all you guys walking around in groups of twelve wearing helmets, carrying weapons, the whole thing?[95]

Introducing the Coyotes into MNB (East) was easier said than done. The Americans were reluctant, even when the KFOR commander, by this time Gen. Klaus Reinhardt, who took over from Sir Mike Jackson on 8 October 1999, insisted. Permission also had to be sought by Col. Ivan Fenton at the NCE from Ottawa.[96] Colonel Fenton:

When Canada gives operational control of a unit to a multinational organization, that control is spelled out in terms of the size of the unit and what it can do. So when the brigade commander turns to Major Datchko and says, "I want your recce squadron to do this," if it's within the envelope of the agreement from Canada, he just says "yes sir" and does it. If it's outside the agreement, he can, in a small way, use his judgment and say that it's close enough to meet the intent. If not, he calls me at the National Command Element. I have a certain amount of judgment. If it takes him out of the geographical area Canada agreed to, or if he is asked to do a task which is different, I have to call [the DCDS]. For example, the recce squadron was asked to escort some fuel trucks to the German sector, which was twenty kilometers outside MNB (Center). I had to get permission from Ottawa every single time. I got tired of it and asked them to give us some slack. [MNB (East)] was different. It was outside our area, it was an American commander, it was a very high-profile mission in a very volatile area. I had to explain the tactical support if anything happened, the logistics, the chain of command, what my assessment of the risk was from land mines to getting into firefights. Unlike Mitrovica, there were no problems in getting approval.[97]

In the case of Operation Spectator, for surveillance operations in MNB (East) the recce squadron could go to work in the area, but only if the troops were made fully aware of the mine threat and only if an appropriate plan was established with HQ MNB (East) that permitted the crews to be fully capable of self-defense and to have the ability to bring in MNB (East) assets for immediate assistance in all areas: medical, fire support, and so on.[98]

Initial surveillance tasks in MNB (East) involved Russian activity:

We worked the area at nighttime. The Russians were working with the Serbians in different areas. We used to see a Mi-24 Hind helicopter come up from this area and go over to the border area. They were kidnapping Albanians from one area, bringing them back to their sector, and holding them for ransom. That went on for quite a while. We'd send the tapes in and right after that Apaches would come up and do a fly-by looking for this Hind. The Americans were waiting to take it out. We could see the people from the Hind running back and forth and getting money [for the kidnapped people].[99]

In another case RCD Coyotes monitored more than one hundred vehicles in the GSZ drive from Serbia into Kosovo at night through the Russian area of operations, all without challenge. It was unclear what was inside the trucks.[100] There was extensive contact between the non-Kosovar Serbs and the Russians, in the MNB (Center) as well as the MNB (East) border areas. Cpl. Troy Cleveland:

The Russians can fuck themselves as far as I'm concerned. They would have a BMP-2 at the border gate. Remember, KFOR vehicles don't have to be checked on the way in and no other KFOR vehicle could go into Serbia. These guys would go and talk to the MUP. It was goddamn obvious they had stuff in their vehicle since they were immune to searches. At this one checkpoint the MUPs were known to stand right on the line, ask a Kosovar Albanian for a light or something, and then grab him, rough him up, and then throw the guy onto their side. Russian BRDMs would come down to do business at this checkpoint. I went with Corporal Miller and Trooper Snider with the digital video camera to get a shot of the

Russians and the MUP. We used the low ground so they couldn't see us and took some pictures from under the bridge. I was busy taking pictures and I was spotted. Snider and Miller had their weapons at the ready in case the MUP were around, not of course to offend the Russians because they were our "friends." Once I lowered the camera, one of the Russians pointed his rifle at me and he got me in his sights. I told my guys that if any Russian did that again, they were to counteract their move. So I thought, "All right, you prick, I'm going to get you on video now." So I put the video camera back up and I pressed record. He wasn't going to get sucked in. So I reported it and the British lodged a protest and made a big hullabaloo about it. I mean, why would the Russians raise their weapons, just because they've been caught?[101]

Cpl. Steven Haynes:

We had the Russians come pay us a visit. They came up in a truck while we were doing our OP stuff. They wanted to know what we were doing there and how long we were going to be [at the site]. It was the American part of the sector and they were not supposed to be there. So we said, "No, we can't answer that." It reached the point where we had to lock everything up in the Coyote. Technically they were not allowed to see what was inside our vehicle. We didn't trust them: we observed them later talking to the MUP and even supplying them. We even had tape and pictures of it.[102]

The primary problem in MNB (East), however, was the activities of what ultimately became known as the UÇPMB or the Liberation Army of the Preševo, Medvedja, and Bujanovac.[103] The Preševo Valley is an ethnically Albanian area that lies outside Kosovo in Serbia proper. The state of affairs in Preševo was the result of Tito-era manipulations in the region. Northern Kosovo around Mitrovica was originally part of Serbia and the Preševo Valley was part of Kosovo. Control over each was swapped in an effort to break down the influence of ethnic politics and exert Yugoslav control. Under the agreements made to end the air campaign and introduce KFOR into Kosovo, no attention had been given to the Preševo Valley. The VJ and the MUP had conducted operations there but had not carried out ethnic cleansing measures to the same degree or effectiveness as they had in Kosovo proper. Indeed it is debatable as to whether the UÇK had any units or influence in the Preševo Valley in the run-up to or during the war. Preševo doesn't show up as a geographical command for any of the UÇK headquarters in southern Kosovo, and no UÇK personalities appear to have been assigned to handle insurgent activity there.[104]

The situation was very sensitive, in part because of the proximity of the Russians and their own involvement in cross-border activity with the Serbs:

> There was a lot of activity going on [in the border area], and you could tell there were somebody's checkpoints there because every time a car would come over the hill, you could track its heat signature. These vehicles came over the top of the mountain range, stop on the road, you'd see another heat source, one heat source would dissipate and then the first heat source would carry on down to the next checkpoint, go through the town and off to the west. Three Troop thought they were refugees. There was nothing but a steady stream of heat signatures coming over that hill every two or three nights. There were coming from the Serbian side to the [Kosovo] side into the Russian sector. I didn't buy the refugee thing. There was no way that there was this amount of refugees that has that many cars to use to escape this late in the game. The Americans called them refugees, we kept calling them refugees, but [we used the term as a code word for what was happening]. The signature was too large, especially at ranges of fifteen and twenty kilometers. It had to be vehicles. The Americans tried to stop us from moving OPs north [so we could watch this]. It went all the way up into the chain of command and [Ottawa] originally said no. We then went in with the understanding that it would be for no more than twenty-four hours. Then the Russians went ballistic and threatened to pull out of KFOR or move to another sector because they were miffed at us doing their job. It was pissing everybody the fuck off. We were saying, "Come on, man, we're all professionals here, let us do the goddamn job." We then pulled out and it's all a big mystery.[105]

At the end of January 2000 the cross-border movement in and out of the Preševo Valley from Kosovo was believed to consist of smugglers protected by former UÇK members.[106] By mid-February this had changed, as the chief of staff for KFOR, Major General Milne of the UK army, "expressed grave concerns about the Preševo Valley and the potential for Albanian extremists to undermine KFOR, as well as to destabilize Macedonia." He was distressed to hear news that Canada would be pulling out of KFOR by the summer, but "he did stress that we would be missing out if we did not keep 10–20 staff in KFOR HQ. He stressed that every one of our present staff is respected and that we would earn considerable credit at minimal cost."[107] The Macedonian situation related to reports about "the presence of a branch of the UCK in northwestern Macedonia, including the Skopje region."[108]

One month later there was information suggesting that "several hundred ethnic Albanians have fled the Presevo Valley for Kosovo due to the escalating tension there. UNHCR . . . is now doing contingency planning [and] estimates that if there is a flare up of fighting in Presevo, up to 70 000 ethnic Albanians might flee to Kosovo or [Macedonia]." Consequently the Macedonian government "is gravely concerned about a refugee wave from Presevo, due to the anticipated de-stabilization of the domestic situation and the financial costs that it would incur."[109] Six days later Commander KFOR issued orders to MNB (East) and its flanking brigades to increase security at the interprovincial boundary and to close secondary border crossing points. Commanders were also to substantially step up surveillance and patrolling on the border.

There were several schools of thought about what was going on. The Serbian view was that the UÇK in Kosovo was controlling the UÇPMB in Preševo, as well as the as yet unnamed group in Macedonia, with the ultimate aim of creating a "Greater Albania." Certainly this was being used as an excuse by the Serbs to resist Kosovar Albanian encroachment in Mitrovica, which contributed to the tension in that city that occurred simultaneously with the operations in the Preševo Valley. (Incidentally Mitrovica tied up substantial KFOR assets). Çeku and Thaçi were considered to be the prime suspects. Some elements in the Macedonian government went along with this thinking.[110]

Still others believed that the UÇPMB operations in the Preševo Valley were designed by the Kosovar Albanian leadership to distract KFOR from handling the Mitrovica problem effectively so that the Kosovar Albanians could push the Kosovar Serbs out of Mitrovica and, not coincidentally, the valuable mines in the region. A flip side of this was the possibility that the UÇPMB was taking advantage of unrest in Mitrovica to pursue its objectives and that Mitrovica was siphoning off KFOR resources. It was entirely possible that the UÇPMB was merely protecting the Albanian population from VJ and MUP harassment.[111]

A more considered view, which emerged in KFOR HQ and the more rational elements of the Macedonian government, was that the UÇPMB was a true splinter group of the UÇK, like the Irish National Liberation Army was from the IRA in Northern Ireland. The UÇPMB was not controlled by the UÇK, even though some UÇPMB members were former UÇK members and the UÇPMB used similar insignia. Indeed the unnamed Albanian group in Macedonia (identified in 2001 as the National Liberation Army, or NLA) appears to have had some former UÇK people in it, but it had more foreigners, particularly mudjahhedin trained in Afghanistan, and they were the ones running the show.[112]

All of this was not understood in the spring of 2000. Indeed it was critical at the time that KFOR get assets down to the border region to determine just what was going on before any action could be taken. That was where recce squadron and its Coyotes came in. If something was not done, the whole Kosovo enterprise could be endangered by the same forces that were set in motion in 1998. It was even possible that Belgrade might launch a mechanized incursion prompting the implementation of Contingency Plan Thunder or one of its variants.

Canadian activity centered on the town of Dobrosin, which was right on the interprovincial boundary in the American sector and in very hilly country. Maj. Tim Datchko:

The border was dotted with MUP bunkers and we'd watch the firefights between the UCPMB and the MUP. You could watch a UCPMB patrol go out, every night, at 2200, a six-man fighting patrol. Two hours later we'd hear an exchange of gunfire and rockets. The Yanks sat there. There were busy with hearts and minds in Gnjilane, where their big bases were, Bonsteel and Monteith. They wanted to deploy an engineer troop commander, a young captain to watch the gate, and that was all. The Americans could not go near the gate and had to stay a kilometer or two off the border. It was like in West Germany during the Cold War. The reason for this was the possible seizure of Americans by the Serbs. The British brigade commander reminded Commander KFOR: "I've got this nice bit of kit and I've got those nice Canadians that are authorized to go park their tires on the border." The Americans, he says, are making all this noise about what's going down on the border, and he said he was going to shame them into dropping that policy. The Brits were just overloaded with work and were being asked to do more and couldn't.

This U.S. Army engineer captain: all he wanted was a quiet little tour and he got stuck out in this little valley near Dobrosin. Nothing was happening until we drove through and they were wondering, "Shit, what's going on up there?" We set up the masts, we've got movement on the border . . . we even brought the engineer captain up for a look: they could come in our vehicles, but not in theirs. We did see some U.S. Special Forces at Monteith, and it looked like they were there in case anybody got snatched. I think they were also working the border, but that's just Datchko talking.[113]

The geography around Dobrosin requires some explanation. This town is located in a bowl surrounded by hills on three sides. Unless one is directly overhead or looking at it from the west, it is completely concealed. Even if an observer moves one hundred meters on the ground from west to the south, the entire town appears to vanish from most vantage points. A winding dirt road from the main Gnjilane road snakes through the hills to Dobrosin and then into the Preševo Valley to the village of Bujanovac, the target of several UÇPMB operations. It was clearly an observation challenge. Capt. Andrew Atherton:

> There were houses being burned, and a lot of it was on the other side of the border down in Preševo. The Albanians were on the wrong side of the border. They were dominating a town and were building themselves up into sort of splinter group of the [UÇK]. They ethnically cleansed this town, Dobrosin. Warrant Olsen kept a close watch on all of that. He would bring in tapes of people being expelled. These were Albanians from Dobrosin who were sent on to Gnjilane. The [UÇPMB] orchestrated the thing: there would be a group of ten, and ten minutes later, another group of ten moving in. We had to deploy a section of assault troop because we were worried about the security of the Coyote OPs; a couple of them were pretty remote out there in bandit country. There were American M-1 tanks at the main bases, but reaction would have taken time. The assault troop gave us a footborne presence to enhance the OPs. We even used snowmobiles because there was so much snow.[114]

Sgt. Gary Reid:

> We were watching Dobrosin just inside the border and there were a couple of firefights in there. Serb [MUP] would bump the [UÇPMB] trenches at night. Then the [UÇPMB] would bump into them and shoot back, then the Serbs would withdraw and we'd catch everything on video. One night Major Datchko was visiting the OP when there was a big rocket attack from the Albanian side into the Preševo Valley. We just happened to pan over there to watch the firefight when all of a sudden an RPG went off right in front of us. We couldn't follow the trajectory of the rocket, though, and left it up to the American Predator UAVs, which have a digitized feed. Our guys were all pumped up. It really hit the fan that time. It went on for at least seven minutes. The Serbs would then come in and shoot into the town of Dobrosin. It was pitch dark, but we had thermal [imaging] so we could see everything; the [UÇPMB] soldiers would pour out of the huts and form an extended line in

the darkness and they would have two dogs, one on either end, and just go across country in the pitch black. They had no night sights. The dogs acted as their sensors. We think the Serbs were in concealed positions firing and then they'd stop and the [UÇPMB] would advance. By then the Serbs were gone.[115]

Cpl. Ray Power:

The [UÇPMB] would go in and start a racket, they'd shoot wherever they could unexpectedly and then the next thing you know, the Serbs got a grip on what was going on and then fire back. We watched the [UÇPMB] withdraw. We got it on tape so nobody could deny it. RPGs were fired all over the place, especially at night. You could pick up the HEAT rounds: it was like red lasers all over the valley. The Serbs had a bunker and they'd approach it from different directions, different routes. There were a lot of little groups of people doing their own thing, you know what I mean?[116]

It was clear that the UÇPMB was taking advantage of the Serbs' reluctance to introduce the VJ and air support into the GSZ and ASZ. Capt. Brian Power:

The American force protection measures that were imposed prevented them from flying their AH-64 Apaches within five kilometers of the provincial boundary. On the ground they were not allowed to go within one kilometer. This gave the [UÇPMB] plenty of room to maneuver. One of the assessments was that the people in the Preševo Valley were going to attempt to gain freedom via NATO intervention. Nobody could confirm or deny that. Dobrosin sat right on the provincial boundary. In addition to the smuggling on the tracks and trails, the Serb special police and the MUP were conducting patrols where they shouldn't be, like within the five-kilometer boundary exclusion zone. We put in observation to watch it all. One of our OPs was even lased from Serbia: the Coyote's alarm went off and they were watching. We tried to find him: you just can't launch a burst of 25mm in the general direction, [but he shut down before we could retaliate]. Then Dobrosin was cleaned out.

Cpl. Steven Haynes:

We used the masts and the remotes. We were watching the training that was going on in Dobrosin, the [UÇPMB]. That was where they did their boot camp, like Cornwallis. They really can't do it in Serbia and they really can't do it in Kosovo, so they did it in what amounted to a six-kilometer no-go zone. They couldn't go into Kosovo any deeper: the Americans had M-1s there and they had AH-64s patrolling with their FLIR. Our FLIR is better than their FLIR, by the way. We knew the Serbs had their tanks close by; we could hear them in the distance, with their engines. The [UÇPMB] were training in there and they had RPGs, mortars, recoilless rifles, but mostly AKs. They didn't have any night vision, nothing high tech. They had a range off in the distance, but we didn't have "eyes on" that one. They did a stand-to at dawn and dusk. They mostly operated at night, over the hill. We'd hear rounds fired. We couldn't always tell who was doing what to whom. They would fire off and run back to the safety of Dobrosin. Having the OPs and the American position there essentially protected them, because if the Serbs attack, rounds are going to fly over and hit the Americans and then they might react.[117]

Capt. Jonathan DeSwert:

We taped quite a bit of training in the area. We deployed a mast sensor and caught them by surprise. You could stick it just over the trees and we could see into this low area and we caught them training. They saw our other cameras elsewhere and moved their training here, then we got them with another sensor. They knew what we had, they knew it was a sensor, but they didn't know it could tape. We watched them build a trench system in between the buildings. Warrant Olsen developed a technique to get the big picture rather than look at one thing. We started seeing helicopters, we recorded them, we recorded fast-moving aircraft, lights flashing in certain areas: on a clear night it was kind of silly for them to do that. We worked out a good relationship with the [military intelligence] platoon, and we started to coordinate with their mobile electronic warfare teams like we had in Mitrovica. . . . "Are you seeing this? Yeah. Record." The Americans brought in a UAV, and we saw them bring in Kiowa Warrior helicopters just to confirm what we were seeing. We were able to catch Serbs moving into positions to gain observation onto the village. The MUP could go in because they were lightly armed [but the VJ could not]. They were wearing . . . weird purple cam uniforms, which were pretty effective at night.

Maj. Tim Datchko:

There were still a lot of firefights along the border. Andrew Atherton and I actually watched one. We showed up there and were about to leave, and I said, "You know, every time I leave, the shit hits the fan." So I said, "Let's go back to the American fire base there." They called it Op Sapper: engineers were in it, it was loaded with M-1s and Bradleys and everything. It was a typical Vietnam-looking firebase. We hooked up with Warrant Olsen for coffee and sure enough, *Ka-rumph! Ka-rumph! Ka-rumph!* "What the hell was *that*?" and someone said, "Oh, they're blowing duds." And I said, "No way." Dobrosin was occupied by [UÇPMB] forces in a great big trench system. The MUP was doing a probe on them (they were always probing). The Americans had their spy planes, the Predator and all that, operating, trying to watch what was going on. They were hard to pick up, they fly really high up, but we got that on film too. You can hear it but not see it. The guys would have competitions: first guy to spot it wins, that kind of thing.[118]

UAV activity was the norm over the Preševo Valley:

We didn't usually see the American Predator: we saw the other one, the great big white one. The Hunter. There were two of them and they used them all the time. It was up eight or ten kilometers. We used to see some of the pictures, but they would intentionally blur them or black out the spots they didn't want us to see. It's dirty pool, you know: come up here and tell us what you see, here's some maps, here's what we want you to look at, and just ignore that blacked-out spot there and that blur. So I got to know one of the photographic analysts up there really well. Her name isn't important, but we set up kind of an "appointment," so to speak. . . . When I went back to the OP, I burned her name in the grass on the side of the hill. So I told her that when she had her bird fly over this area, take pictures of us so we could compare "capabilities." . . . I never got in to see if she got the pictures of it, but I'm sure she did. I hope she has the picture hanging in her office.[119]

Capt. Brian Power:

We observed the goings on in Dobrosin. We picked out some guys we think were U.S. Special Forces in the town doing some patrolling. The U.S. engineers manning Sapper were just as frustrated as us. Then the Americans did a big cordon and search operation in a neighboring town and found quite a large number of guns, lots of ammunition. Were the UCPMB just hauling it up to Dobrosin? Perhaps. They had a three-week training cycle. The intake would come into Dobrosin to be trained and disappear again. They would go back into Kosovo. We brainstormed about this for some time. They couldn't conduct training in Kosovo, since it was illegal to possess weapons. You can conduct all you want inside Serbia: what are the Serbs going to do about it when the U.S. Army is sitting right there [in Op Sapper]? It was the perfect little sanctuary. They fed themselves off the farming. The training cadres had their families there. I thought the Serbs would try to do something about it. The UCPMB started to use Dobrosin as a training base and then got more and more aggressive and sent out patrols. They got larger and larger, fighting patrols. It became a battle school. For the UCK as well as the UCPMB, sending their guys back into Kosovo for later? There was nobody that could provide the kind of coverage we were giving: night, day surveillance, with video-tape. You could see what they were wearing, what stage of their training cycle they were in. They used machine guns and RPGs, basic small arms. Their mortars were grabbed in the cordon and search. It never came together for us at our level. Perhaps it's not supposed to. But one of our PSYOPS initiatives was to discourage support for the UCPMB in Kosovo, particularly through the media, and reduce their popular support. NATO could have gone into Dobrosin and cleared it out. That would send a strong message to Belgrade. But Dobrosin was allowed to develop. I think we missed an opportunity. If we just packed up and went home, their protection was gone and they would go too.[120]

What was going on in Dobrosin and how did it fit into the larger picture? Canadian suspicions were aroused at several levels when Coyote surveillance tapes were sent back to HQ MNB (East) but not passed on to KFOR HQ. This was not done because the material was stamped "US Eyes Only." The commanders of MNB (Center) and Commander KFOR were not happy about this, but the Canadians were able to ensure that information collected by Canadian platforms held by Canadian soldiers deployed to Kosovo for the KFOR mission was passed to the appropriate KFOR authorities and that the information was not considered strictly an American resource for U.S. purposes. Some of this material involved observations of non-Albanians conducting training in Dobrosin.[121] Whether these foreign personnel were mujaheddin or not, or related to the NLA operations in Macedonia or not, remains open to speculation, as do their actual allegiances and paymasters.

The role of the Canadian recce squadron indicates that U.S. military forces in MNB (East) were not fully informed about what was going on in Dobrosin or the Preševo Valley and that their systems were incapable of providing the coverage they needed. For some reason the U.S. Special Forces detachment at Camp Monteith was also incapable of providing such information. As one recce soldier put it, "They couldn't see what they wanted with the systems they had. The Predators had limited capability: it was like flying over an area and looking through a straw."[122] Maybe someone wanted an unbiased second opinion and Canadian Coyotes were the means.

As with any Balkans intrigue, there are numerous explanations, some of which operate at several levels simultaneously. It is possible that the UÇPMB had some level of American covert support in order to apply pressure to the Milošević regime, maybe as payback for Serb infiltration in Mitrovica and the problems there. Perhaps that support was not properly coordinated with MNB (East) or KFOR. It is also possible that someone was interested in keeping track of former UÇK personnel who previously worked with or were equipped by NATO-member special operations forces during the air campaign. Perhaps guerrilla operations in the Preševo Valley were designed to draw off and pin down MUP and VJ resources that could have been used elsewhere, perhaps in Mitrovica or an armed incursion. It is equally plausible that American or other national infiltration of the UÇPMB with offers of aid and training could have been used to gather intelligence on the organization and its capabilities, perhaps with an eye toward disrupting it later. Clearly, having an understanding of the UÇPMB-NLA relationship, and the role of the mujaheddin in their operations, would have been useful in stabilizing Macedonia. As for the UÇPMB, perhaps it was designed to demonstrate to the UÇK money men in the Albanian diaspora that the money and support they provided was still needed and was being put to good use.[123]

The Preševo Valley situation would eventually escalate after the recce squadron redeployed to Canada in May 2000. It would be resolved only with the coerced disbandment of the UÇPMB by KFOR with the assistance of the European Union in the summer of 2001, months after the Milošević regime had collapsed. This operation, called Juno, was followed two months later in Macedonia by NATO Operation Essential Harvest, which was mounted to disarm the National Liberation Army. That operation including the RCD's recce squadron, this time led by Maj. Roger Cotton, which had redeployed from SFOR in Bosnia to Macedonia.

Warrant Officer Joseph Ramsay of the Strathconas summed it up best:

> One thing that was nice was there was a lot of new soldiers who didn't realize how good it was in Kosovo for us. Having been to Bosnia and Cambodia and been around people who really didn't like us and were sick of seeing us around. The younger guys all thought this was neat, but it was a shock for those that had been in Bosnia, where nobody smiled at us. I was really impressed with our soldiers, with their professionalism. You hear the old guys say "the new army, the new army." Well, I've been in the new and the old army, and there's no way that you would have got the old army

to move as quickly and adapt as quickly as these soldiers did in Kosovo. In the past we did our job well, but the adaptability wasn't there. [Mechanized operations in Germany] were immensely different from this, and [unlike UN missions] we had a mission and a goal for everyone. We bonded quickly to get it done and it was impressive. It made me feel good to see it.[124]

EIGHT

As the KRWAU Flies

Canadian Griffons over Kosovo

There's no Hell like Tac Hel!

—ANONYMOUS

Just then flew down a monstrous crow
As black as a tar-barrel;
Which frightened both the heroes so,
They quite forgot their quarrel.

—LEWIS CARROLL, *Through the Looking Glass*

The deployment of the Kosovo Rotary Wing Air Unit (KRWAU, pronounced "crow") with its CH-146 Griffon helicopters occurred during a period of great change in how the Canadian Forces (CF) handled airmobile operations. The Griffon machines were themselves suspect: they were the product of political and operational compromise. Technical problems with the aircraft were well publicized. Yet the statement of requirement (SOR) put out by NATO asked for a tactical helicopter contribution, and the Air Staff decided to step up to the plate and send Griffons. The KRWAU story is similar to the Coyote story in that the employment of the Griffons illustrated the changing nature of how information is collected, processed, and used in the operational environment. Conceptually the Coyote and Griffon were complementary systems in the ISTAR world, yet they had never been employed before in the same theater of operations, especially one as information intensive as Kosovo. When properly employed, the Griffon demonstrated that it could provide a salient and effective Canadian contribution to coalition operations.

This chapter examines the development of Griffon and its use in Kosovo by the men and women of the KRWAU. Two squadrons provided the bulk of personnel assigned to KRWAU: 408 Tactical Helicopter Squadron (408 Squadron or 408 THS), commanded by Lt. Col. Bruce McQuade from June to December 1999, and then 430 Escadron Tactique d'Hélicoptères (430 ETAH), commanded by Lt. Col. Serge Lavallée from December 1999 to May 2000. There was significant overlap in the roles and missions carried out by the KRWAU during both deployments. Consequently the description of operations conducted by 408 THS and 430 ETAH are blended together here to avoid repetition.

Canadian Tactical Helicopter Development before Kosovo

Throughout the last half of the Cold War, helicopter support for the Canadian Army was provided by three types of aircraft. There were seven huge CH-147 Chinook medium transports, each capable of carrying forty-four troops, plus forty-six CH-135 Twin Huey light transports, similar to the UH-1 used by American forces in Vietnam, which could each carry an infantry section of ten soldiers. Reconnaissance missions were undertaken by the sixty-eight CH-136 Kiowas, machines resembling the civilian Jet Rangers. There were no gunships carrying guided antitank missiles and cannon like the American AH-1 Cobra or AH-64 Apache: the Kiowa mounted a 7.62mm Gatling gun for self-defense and some spotting rockets, while the Twin Hueys could take two C-6 medium machine guns. By the start of the 1990s stabilization campaigns these machines were all approximately two decades old, and in the era of vast budget cuts the NDHQ bureaucracy decided to replace them all with one helicopter type to save money. A planned Canadian Forces light helicopter project to replace Kiowa and a new transport helicopter to replace the Chinook were both killed in 1989.[1]

In November 1991 the commander of Mobile Command, Lt. Gen. Kent Foster, and Brig. Gen. Lew Cuppens from Air Command developed a requirement for the ability to simultaneously lift three light infantry companies: this amounted to one hundred aircraft and assumed ten persons carried per machine. There was no specific machine in mind, just the requirement. The existing Twin Huey fleet would be supplemented by fifty-four new aircraft, and the Kiowas and Chinooks would be dropped. At this point there was no perceived need for a recce helicopter, given the demise of the NATO Central Region commitment: the new machine would be prioritized to handle utility tasks like lift, with light observation coming a distant second. Ten Tactical Air Group accepted that both were valid missions, but there wasn't enough money to handle both.[2] Before any further discussion could occur, Marcel Masse, the defence minister, announced in April 1992 that the CF would purchase one hundred Bell 412 helicopters. The fact that these were built in Quebec ensured that the primary driving factor in Griffon acquisition was domestic politics. The contract had already been awarded by September 1992.[3]

The problem was that the statement of operational requirement was still being formulated by Mobile Command and Air Command when the announcement was made. What *exactly* was the new machine supposed to do and how was it to be equipped to do it? One just does not take a machine off the shelf, give it to a military unit, and tell them to use it. Given the unfolding operational environment of the 1990s, the Canadian Forces needed a machine to respond to "the increasing demand for United Nations intervention in Third World disputes. . . . The [Canadian Forces utility tactical transport helicopter, or CFUTTH] should be equipped to survive in these environments." Another important factor was the need for a helicopter equipped for special operations missions: these machines would need state-of-the art navigation and night operations capability. Consequently the SOR called for a helicopter that could handle the tactical airlift of troops and equipment, logistic airlift, casualty evacuation, reconnaissance and surveillance, direction and control of fire, and command and liaison. It also had to be capable of operating in a high-threat environment and thus be equipped with threat detection equipment, countermeasures, ballistic protection, and a reduced infrared signature.[4]

Note that the Kiowa, Twin Huey, and Chinook were unarmored and retained no passive defensive capabilities: they were the aerial equivalent of jeeps and trucks. The CFUTTH program essentially called for a slightly more sophisticated and better protected "truck" that could also be used as a recce "jeep" in a pinch: a (very) small number of the "trucks" would be modified with more sophisticated sensors for special operations.

Indeed the overseas employment of Canadian helicopters in the 1990s, coupled with the loss of the Kiowas, produced a decline in recce skills to the point where they were almost extinct after the Cold War. There were five such deployments: Op Calumet supplied nine Twin Hueys to the Multinational Force and Observers (MFO) in the Sinai, where they acted as transports for verification observers in a classic interpositionary peacekeeping environment. Op Saladin included four Jet Rangers and four Twin Hueys to support UN observation missions in Central America.[5] Again, these machines were generally used for command and liaison functions.[6] Helicopter operations in Somalia (Op Deliverance) included the use of three Sea Kings and five Twin Hueys to support the airborne regiment in airmobile operations. Indeed the lack of joint doctrine was telling: the Sea King pilots joked that they didn't need any since they'd seen *Apocalypse Now* six times.[7] The first CH-146 Griffons deployed to Op Stable Haiti in April 1997, to replace the eight Twin Hueys operating there. This was followed by the first Balkans deployment of four Griffons to SFOR in Bosnia in early 1998.[8]

Several paths then converged in 1997 and ultimately affected Griffon employment in Kosovo. First, there was a growing recognition within the tactical helicopter community that these machines could be more than aerial trucks or jeeps.[9] Maj. Scott Davidson, who was on exchange in the UK with a Lynx squadron, brought back some good ideas along these lines. Second, there were doctrinal developments in the army (there also were air force officers in the Directorate of Army Doctrine) pertaining to ISTAR and Coyote that potentially applied to the future use of helicopters. Both services were by early to mid-1997 able to gain the support of the chief of the Land Staff, who was at that time Lt. Gen. Maurice Baril, soon to become CDS.[10] Like the Coyote team, the tactical helicopter community was about to make lemonade out of a lemon.

Out of all this emerged an expansion of Griffon's operational roles and capabilities. The statement of requirements that included sensors and navigation for a limited number of special operations was part of the basis: Why not use these capabilities in all of the machines? Again, Davidson's experiences in the UK were brought to bear: he wrote a paper recommending that the helicopters be equipped for "reconnaissance, intelligence, surveillance, target acquisition," dubbed RISTA, a concept that was developed in parallel by elements within the Directorate of Army Doctrine. In an environment where the belligerent forces were equipped with shoulder-launched surface-to-air missiles and other sophisticated air defense weapons, the only way a helicopter could survive was if its crew could detect the threat first and then evade it. Thus, improved infrared and thermal imaging sensors and passive defensive measures like flares and chaff were critical. These sensors, however, could also be used in a dual role: they could provide surveillance and, if necessary, acquire targets for other friendly systems: artillery or antitank weapons, for example. Indeed it was not much of a stretch to arm Griffon with a precision-guided antitank weapon, since it might have to fire back at a system that threatened it, so the helicopter could go about its work safely.[11]

Instead of lobbying for another aircraft, for which the CF was unlikely to get funding, the army and air force pushed for add-on capabilities for Griffon. Part of this was driven by the need to keep pace with allies and retain saliency in future operations, while the need to protect the aircraft and its crew in an increasingly lethal environment was as critical.[12] Debates between the army and air force then broke out over the division of labor between a Griffon with RISTA capability and Coyote, probably generated by concern for competition over scarce resources. In time RISTA was redesignated electro-optical reconnaissance, surveillance, and target acquisition, or ERSTA. ERSTA components include a sensor package consisting of a third-generation FLIR, low-light day TV, a laser rangefinder/designator; an airborne control station mounted in the back of the helicopter to process data, images, recordings, and streaming video; and a ground station in a truck where information is passed to and from the helicopters and into the ISTAR system. The objective is to be able to move from the ability to merely detect a target to identifying it and then passing data on to a weapons system that can kill the target, or in the case of a stabilization operation, provide situational awareness to commanders so that they can plan and execute operations.[13]

The ERSTA project was only partially under way when the crisis in Kosovo reared up in 1998–99. Consequently the Griffon as deployed with the KRWAU was not yet equipped to the projected ERSTA standard and wound up performing a variety of tasks.

The Griffon and Its Capabilities: Walk Around

The CH-146 Griffon is essentially a militarized commercial medium passenger helicopter based on the Bell 412 executive transport. It was acquired by those in NDHQ who believed that Canada would participate only in no-casualty peacekeeping operations. Consequently the basic airframe had no armor, was not hardened to resist electromagnetic pulse, and had performance problems related to its power and weight. Specifically the rotor and engine were designed for executive transport speed, not military lift or endurance. The one hundred aircraft were only useful to move unarmed passengers around in a North American environment. To make the Griffon a useful operational machine, several modifications were required.

It is best to view Griffon as a living system, a platform, as opposed to a flying truck. Several add-on kits were developed by the air force to make Griffon extremely flexible. In various combinations, these add-on kits could tailor a basic airframe for a specific mission in under two hours. First, there was ballistic protection. An armor package consisting of composite materials was developed. The Griffon could carry two C-6 medium machine guns. It could mount a complete missile attack warning system (MAWS), which would provide directional tones to the crew if an air defense system locked on to the aircraft and would automatically fire chaff and flares to confuse missiles. Reduction of the infrared signature of the exhaust was a permanent modification. In terms of sensors the Griffon can carry a variety of forward-looking infrared (FLIR) systems, which are connected to a VHS recorder. For example, the first Griffon SFOR rotation and subsequent Op Kinetic deployment was equipped with the AAQ 501, a second-generation thermal imaging system (as opposed to the ERSTA's third generation). In addition, a Nightsun 3.8 million candlepower focusable spotlight was also available, as well as global positioning system (GPS) navigation. Night vision goggles (NVGs) are standard equipment for the crew.[14]

The differing combinations of add-on kits produced differing levels of compromise in the performance of the helicopter. For example, if a Griffon was tasked to conduct a patrol insertion and was armored and carrying FLIR, it might be able to carry only four or six fully equipped soldiers instead of the advertised ten or eleven because of the weight of the add-on kits and the additional crew. This had to be carefully monitored by the crew and maintenance staff, which increased the number of people needed to support Griffon operations. Cutting back in this area produced increased strain on the staff and increased the level of risk.

The Griffon's crew depended on the mission. In addition to the pilot and copilot there were flight engineers, like Cpl. Aaron Nickerson of 408 Squadron: "We control the back of the helicopter, we run the machine gun, load and unload the troops, and handle any emergencies or situations that back up the pilots. I take care of the plane from sun up to sundown, inspect it, and take care of any damage."[15] If the FLIR or other sensor was attached, a mission specialist, like Sgt. Robert Wheatley (408 Squadron), becomes a crew member: "A mission specialist comes from the combat arms (I'm with the infantry) and is responsible for the field craft in the squadron and machine gun training. We handle the FLIR, Nightsun, and any specialty equipment for observation. We also man a machine gun and bring our ground operations expertise to bear when required for the pilots."[16]

There were concepts to arm the Griffons with CRV-7 rocket pods, a GAU-19 .50-cal Gatling gun, and AGM-114 Hellfire antitank missiles, but these plans remained in development long after the KRWAU returned home in 2000.[17]

Squadron Organization for KRWAU Operations

Planners in Ottawa, in conjunction with 1 CMBG in Edmonton, determined that the KRWAU would be built around eight Griffons. This number was based on British requirements in the same NATO SOR process that produced the Coyote requirement in early 1999. Normally a tactical helicopter squadron has between eighteen and twenty-four helicopters, so the KRWAU was essentially a third of a squadron. The CO, Lt. Col. Bruce McQuade, along with the DCO, Maj. Jim MacAlese, and his staff were confronted with the task of figuring out what slice of 408 Squadron would go to Kosovo: "I manned it with one and [a] half air crews per aircraft, so we had ten crews of three: two pilots and an FE [flight engineer]. We needed a command element and it had to have a fairly big signals detachment. We would be in the field, so we had additional rad[io] techs. We had to be self-sustaining in all areas. The total organization ended up being 170 or 180, plus the 43 military police [the Airfield Security Force] which caused some concern."[18]

Everything had to be pared down. Ultimately the KRWAU consisted of a headquarters (operations, intelligence, signals), the UTTH flight (the utility tactical transport helicopter crews and the Griffons themselves), the ground support flight (logistics, maintenance, flight surgeon, chaplain, and administration) and the Airfield Security Force (ASF).[19]

According to Capt. Denis Boucher (430 Squadron), the KRWAU also had about seventy ground vehicles, about half as many as a full squadron. These included four fuel bowsers, fire trucks, tool trucks, auxiliary power units, communications trucks, and a command post vehicle: almost every class of Canadian Forces vehicle, from ten-ton HLVWs to LSVW. There also had to be a separate maintenance section to keep all of them running. "When a tactical helicopter squadron is working with a brigade in the field, it's an entirely portable and self-supporting organization—kitchens and everything, spares, water, and rations."[20]

The juggling of numbers and positions appears mundane, but it was integral to how efficiently the KRWAU functioned, which in turn affected operational capabilities. Not having enough people in one area and too many in another could place too much strain on one part of the organization. For example, Capt. Barbara Palmer, the senior aircraft maintenance engineering officer (SAMEO) of 408 Squadron, was responsible for "all the technicians that fix the aircraft, anything that is aircraft related that isn't flying. I'm responsible for any modifications, performance parameters, and maintenance issues because the cycle for the Griffon is very strict. We narrowed the usual structure quite a bit. We dropped from 120 to 36 [technicians]. It is quite a drop. Especially in determining the number of people and requirements. It's difficult for maintenance because I can't tell you what's going to break, and when something breaks on a helicopter badly, it doesn't go anywhere."[21]

The original organization established by 408 Squadron carried over to 430 ETAH when the rotation occurred in December 1999. It was so effective that Captain Palmer's replacement, Capt. Andrea Andrachuk from 430 ETAH, used the same structure, "and in the course of our six-month tour none of our missions were missed because of maintenance. It went pretty well. The fact that we didn't have all sorts of secondary duties like we do in Canada helped too, since there was nothing else to do than work."[22]

The ASF deserves some mention. Essentially the ASF was the product of empire-building by some within the air force and military police community who wanted an organization similar to the RAF Regiment, an RAF organization trained and equipped like an infantry battalion and employed in the airfield defense role. The ASF was hastily cobbled together from individual military police (not from formed sub-units) across Canada, provided with heavy weapons, and given rudimentary infantry platoon training. The justification for its deployment was the terrorist threat. There was great debate as to whether the battle group could perform the defense role just as well, but vicious turf wars tend to be fought over such things and the forty-three-member ASF deployed with 408 Squadron in the summer of 1999. The positive aspects of the ASF deployment meant that the ground crew did not have to rotate onto guard duty tasks and could focus on their aircraft.[23]

Deployment to the Balkans: 408 Squadron

As we have seen earlier, the Canadians were not welcome in Thessaloniki, and it took some time to get the Griffons ready to go. As Capt. Erik O'Connor, a pilot with 408 Squadron, recalled, "We flew from Edmonton into Thessaloniki, Greece, but the reception wasn't too warm and we ended up staying in some sort of military prison for our safety. There was a lot of graffiti all over the place saying they didn't want us there. We did everything at night. Sleeping during the day with 40-degree [104 Fahrenheit] heat was quite uncomfortable. We didn't have diplomatic clearances and then they didn't want us to go."[24]

Cpl. Aaron Nickerson, flight engineer:

> We went down to the port and helped the technicians build up the planes. They take the basic parts, rotor blades, and the masts off so it will fit on a ship. We started in the morning and took sixteen hours to get eight helicopters going. We did a quick test flight over the Greek harbor [at night], signed that it was tested, and then off to Petrovec, Macedonia. The bombing was still going on; it was a good air show. You could see them launching missiles at night, KC-135s were circling around refueling F-15s, A-10s would pop up for fuel and scoot back.[25]

There were continuing problems for 408 Squadron's ground crew once they drove up from Thessaloniki. Cpl. Terry Merritt was driving a truck through Skopje looking for the rest of the squadron: "We left the NSE [National Support Element] and we were driving through downtown Skopje and suddenly I lost my windshield as a huge rock came through it. We started losing windows like crazy. One of our guys got nailed with a rock near Prelip. Helmets and goggles became mandatory. We were traveling at 70 kilometers per hour, and the thing just comes through. Then a car bomb blew up right outside the NSE. We then moved on to the airport, which was more secure."[26]

From Capt. Barb Palmer's perspective, Skopje's Petrovec airport was "prime real estate for every air force that was in theater. It was chaos. It rained, there were huge ruts the size of vehicles, and then

[it] would be baking hot the next day, all the tents were packed together. We were fifty feet from the runway where they had C-5A Galaxies taking off all hours of the night. There were Brit helicopters. There were Italian helicopters; almost all of them were armed. The safety implications were severe [if anything went wrong]."[27]

With the helicopters at Petrovec and the support personnel at Prilep, 408 Squadron prepared for operations. Capt. Erik O'Connor flew the first Griffon mission into Kosovo:

A tasking came in. They wanted the Canadians. We quickly mounted the door guns, loaded the bullets, and took off. It was right after one of the last NATO bombing runs in Kosovo. It was critical that we support an RRB [remote rebroadcast site]. Since it's so hilly, the only way to communicate long range was with HF. We then flew the Kačanik defile. It's this beautiful valley. It was overwhelming, your heart's pumping three times its normal speed because you don't know what's happening in Kosovo, and you don't know how the people are going to react to your presence. We flew to Uroševac and then Priština and then we came back.

It was a very, very simple mission, but being the first it was uncomfortable. We had to make sure our rules of engagement were all understood. We get back and the guys wanted to know what it was like; you're a guinea pig, eh? We saw multiple houses burning, 20–30 percent burning in Uroševac, a roof missing. We were flying tactical all the way. Fifteen feet. There's no limits there. It was amazingly intense to see the houses burning. People were jammed into refugee camps. The damage was extensive, especially around Priština.[28]

Soon after, Cpl. Aaron Nickerson and his crew flew their first mission out of Petrovec:

The Serbs were withdrawing. We were trying to spot their T-72 tanks and other armored vehicles and escort them out. And they were trying to hide, too. They were trying to hide in the tree line from the British Challengers which were advancing down the road. We spotted them. Then the Challengers would stop and traverse the gun barrels right onto the T-72s and get ready to blow them away if they didn't leave. The Serbs were deliberately delaying and we'd catch them. The Albanians would run up the side of the hill firing RPGs at the tanks and the Serbs would fire down the hill at them. It went on like that for awhile. The UCK wanted payback and at every chance they would take potshots at them. We watched it all using our systems. [The UÇK] was getting pretty blatant about it, but they backed off when the American and German tanks rolled down the road. Then some idiot in a Lada fired an AK at a British Warrior, which then opened up with its [30mm] and the next day we found vehicle pieces all over the road.[29]

Operating from the austere Petrovec environment was getting increasingly difficult due to the spatial limitations, so Lieutenant Colonel McQuade sent his people out to look for alternative basing arrangements. Capt. Erik O'Connor:

[The CO] sent us up to Podujevo and we flew over an old airfield near there, but there were many, many cluster bombs covering the place. We then had to divert to Priština and pick up some Gurkha officers. They had two guys get blown up trying to clear a school that was full of mines, somewhere to the west of Glogovac. These guys were just pulverized. As we were flying into Glogovac, we flew over a little asphalt runway. So we banked and went and looked. It was damaged, but it was an old abandoned airfield. Once the situation with the Gurkhas was secure, we got hold of the boss. Once everything was first come, first served, we decided to move in. We thought about operating out of the smashed-up VJ camp near Priština, but the air was too shitty [because of the Obilić 1 and 2 power stations that were upwind]. They didn't want us to go onto Priština airport because that was Russian territory. There was this underground hangar right under the hill and they didn't want anybody else to see it. We wanted to go see, but we were told no. So that's how we came to set up our base at Poklek.[30]

Combat engineers from the Gurkhas came in and cleared the place of UXO (unexploded ordnance). An advance party on wheels from the squadron drove up as soon as possible to grab the airfield before anybody else could move in.[31] Coincidentally, what became known as Camp DK was located in what would become the Canadian battle group area of operations.

KRWAU: Command, Control, and Working with the British

Like the Coyote squadron, the KRWAU was a Multinational Brigade (Center) brigade asset. As the CO of 430 ETAH, Lt. Col. Serge Lavallée explains:

> My Canadian commander was Col. Ivan Fenton, the Canadian contingent commander of [Task Force Kosovo, who replaced Col. Mike Ward]. So I got my orders with a capital "O" from him. From an operations point of view the brigade commander was my boss for day-to-day operations. Within his area of operations, MNB(C), I was responsive to him for any tasks which were in my capacity to do within his area. However, to use the Griffon in the size of the [brigade AOR] was a waste. We could have done a lot more, we could easily have gone into the other multinational brigade areas; it just would have taken liaison. I could not, however, do this without approval from the Canadian contingent commander. This came from the chief of Defence Staff.[32]

The CDS's intent of course was to prevent the possible misuse of Canadian forces and to ensure that Canadian command was exercised at all times.[33]

The KRWAU developed its relationship with the British brigade HQ through liaison officers:

> We actually had a good relationship with them. They had already been on the ground for four months, so when we arrived just after the bombing campaign ended and 4 (UK) Armoured Brigade was moving into Kosovo, it took us a few days to get it all sorted out. They quickly realized we were there to support them . . . We put an LO [liaison officer] into the headquarters, Captain Clat; he went into the headquarters and lived with them. We also sent one of our intelligence sergeants to work with him and [Capt. Dave Travers]. Initially the British weren't sure what they wanted us to do

because they weren't sure what we could do. They never worked with the Griffon before. They had Lynx and Puma, which had very different capabilities.[34]

The British Gazelles, which also operated in the area, were too small and carried only four personnel. The Pumas were larger and could lift more but were less maneuverable and didn't have enough room or enough windows for recce. Griffon ultimately had a better visual capacity and had sensor systems.[35] The RAF pilots were risk averse, as Corporal Nickerson noted: "The [RAF] wouldn't go play, like, they wouldn't allow them to go downtown [in Priština]. We'd go in there, it was a small area, but thought it was safe, it was within limits, but the Brits were like 'Oh no, we're not going anywhere near that.'"[36] MNB(C) came to rely more and more on the KRWAU's Griffons. Maj. Steve Charpentier of 430 ETAH: "We went to the brigade commander's O [Orders] Group and there was this guy hammering on the tables, saying they loved doing business with the Canadians, they're really professional, 'that's what we want, we don't want to fly with those god damn shitty Puma pilots.' This was one of the Brit company commanders who we'd done an insertion with. The British air guy just wanted to crawl into a hole."[37]

In terms of numbers there were only three Pumas: one was dedicated to casualty evacuation, and one was usually always in maintenance. There were also three Gazelles, but they had a limited capability compared to the Griffons. Most of the Lynx were redeployed with 5 (UK) Airborne Brigade back home early on in the operation.[38]

In time the system for tasking the Canadian helicopters was a well-oiled machine, as described by Maj. Jim MacAlese of 408 Squadron:

> The brigade HQ would get a request from a ground unit, and then it was handed to the brigade aviation representative, who just happened to be our LO (since we provided most of the helicopters), then he and the operations officer would put together the plan, deconflict it with other ongoing operations and air movements, figure out what we could do or not do, turn down missions we couldn't

do, and then pass us the plan. Normally the LO would just send it all to us and we'd carry it all out. . . . We never had to have the Canadian Task Force Kosovo intervene: if we said we couldn't do something, the British accepted that.[39]

The Operational Environment

Although its problems were not unique to the Balkans, the flying environment in Kosovo had its own peculiarities. It was hazardous, and given that there were no crashes or serious accidents involving the KRWAU's Griffons, it is worth describing.[40] Major Charpentier of 430 Squadron:

> I've been to the Sinai with MFO, worked in the NATO environment in Norway during Brave Lion with Kiowas, but this theater in Kosovo was challenging. All your life you train and exercise, and you always talk in the cockpit about what it would really be like if we were at war—we'd fly much lower, that we'd be flying at twenty feet off the ground, and so on. I heard that for twenty years. Then we get to Kosovo and we're flying fifteen feet, nap-of-the-earth. I was concerned that some of our younger guys would operate with a wartime mentality, that no rules applied any more. Then we learned about the wire threat, the old rusty power transmission towers, so rusty you can't see them. They're all over Kosovo because of the power plants, like a big spider web.[41]

And it happened. A Griffon from 408 Squadron, with Capt. Pete Lyon as copilot, got caught:

> We were doing a border recce and ducked down into this little valley. We were coming back to the main route and we were supposed to turn into Priština to drop off our troops. We made a wrong turn, and I asked the pilot if he knew where he was going and he said, "Yeah, just up ahead is a valley we can turn around in." I was still looking at my map and the next thing I know I hear this loud BANG and I looked up and I see all these marks all up the windscreen. I was, like, "Okay, what the hell just happened?" and then I hear him say, "Wire strike!" and then I saw the outside air temp gauge dangling in front of my face. We actually hit three wires

and they got caught in the cutter and broke. They all impacted the nose of the aircraft. One right under the pitot tubes and it snapped them off, the second hit the screen and went into the upper wire cutter, and the third slid down and got the lower cutter. So we got the aircraft onto the ground and there were several scorch marks along the side. The windshield wipers were all bent, the window was scarred, the FLIR ball on the left-hand side had been hit so you could see arcing of the wires on it. The wires were charged; they were live and we went through them. Our flight engineer had a good close-up view of the live wires flying by his face.[42]

According to Lyon, the flight engineer recalled, "Thank God for cheap communist wire or we'd be all dead!"[43]

The sheer randomness of how armed individuals on the ground react to helicopters was noticed by Sgt. Bob Wheatley and his crew from 408 Squadron:

There were various threats, many of them which could not be anticipated. You take a squadron and drop it in the middle of some place that you've just been bombing. So these guys are flying all over in the middle of the night, the people on the ground get pissed off, and everybody has guns. You're going to pay the price sooner or later, and we got shot at a fair amount over there. Yeah, they're not overly accurate and a lot of guys still have the idea that this aircraft is moving too fast for anybody to hit. However, the guys down the road [Serb extremists and UÇK] are practicing aircraft drills and they know the drills to shoot one of these things down. So if they really wanted to do it, all they had to do was sit and wait. We took a few rounds. Thank God I didn't get shot at.[44]

Lt. Col. Serge Lavallée of 430 ETAH emphasized the mine threat, which also affected tactical helicopter operations:

Mine warfare was a big thing, so the crews had to reorient their thinking when they left the base for any reason. If you had to land in a hurry somewhere, you couldn't just land anywhere. It happened once with Major Charpentier, when he had an engine failure outside of Priština. They were working the aircraft hard doing something at low level and an engine flamed out, so he reacted quickly: he had to land because he wasn't sure if the cause was fuel contamination, which meant the other engine could go too. So he headed for the brigade HQ pad, which was several kilometers away instead of just putting down in a field: we developed specific areas to land to avoid the mines.[45]

The weather was as usual a major issue, but flying in that region was made more difficult by the decayed communist-era infrastructure, especially the five giant smokestacks and the cooling towers of the Obilić power plants. Capt. Erick Simoneau, of 430 ETAH: "And then there was the smog. It amazed me. It was in every valley, though less so in the Drenica at Poklek because the Obilić stations were on the other side of the ridge. It wasn't a very healthy smell either. It was all coal and dust. That combined with the corrosion and rust on the transmission towers and drab gray colors of the buildings made flying difficult since everything was sort of camouflaged."[46]

Capt. Pierre Lalancette, 430 ETAH: "We'd have to fly using [global positioning system] because every morning the valleys would be fogged up with big-time pollution. Obilić particularly. We'd fly over the clouds and then have to descend into Obilić's smoke plumes. Fortunately the brigade AOR was relatively small. We could be anywhere in twenty minutes. It got to the point where we didn't even need to use the map anymore; [we] knew the reporting points by heart. We could use the ridges like a railway track if the valleys were too fogged in."[47]

Mother Nature and decayed communist industry, however, were the most benign aspects of the operating environment. There was still a threat posed by air defense systems and lasers. The damage caused by missiles and guns is well understood by those who have studied the air campaigns of World War II and the Gulf War. Lasers are another thing altogether, since they can damage the eyes and cause a crew to crash their aircraft.

In briefings KRWAU crews were told that the UÇK had SA-7 and SA-14 man-portable air defense missiles (some looted from Albanian storage sites) and that mujahhedin personnel operating with them might even have Stinger missiles. In addition, it was probable that Serb extremist groups, in Macedonia as well as in Kosovo, would have access to SA-7, SA-14, and SA-16 missiles. The Belgrade regime was also considered capable of moving air defense systems into or near the air safety zone to interfere with NATO aircraft.[48] For comparative purposes SA-7 Grail is an infrared homing missile with a speed of Mach 1.7 and a range of six kilometers. SA-14 Gremlin and its SA-16 variant are improved versions of SA-7: the SA-16 uses a laser beam to guide the missile instead of IR homing.[49]

The Griffons were equipped with a missile attack warning system (MAWS). Capt. Les Beothy of 408 Squadron explains:

> The MAWS would pick up any infrared emissions, like from a missile launch, and would indicate to us which direction a suspected missile is coming from. There are four little eyeball-like sensors mounted on the aircraft. MAWS was connected to the countermeasures dispensing system, and it would pop out flares. It could be set to manual or automatic. On automatic, several would pop out and divert the missile. It's extremely sensitive: the hot glare from glass buildings could set it off. This happened daily. It got the adrenalin going. When we got an indication, you quickly look at the indicator to see which direction and get the crew to spot. They we turn towards the missile and get the hottest part of the aircraft, the tail exhaust, away from it, then drop the flares. We could also use buildings to mask ourselves from the missile.[50]

The flaw with MAWS was the good old "garbage in, garbage out" phenomenon, as Warrant Officer Robert Boucher of 430 ETAH noted: "MAWS is all pre-programmed for a specific theater: it has a software package which has the threat missile types in it. Only so much information can be put in that database so that the system doesn't get overloaded. The intelligence people have to be on the ball to ensure that the right types are loaded for the area."[51] In a hypothetical situation, if the intelligence system doesn't have accurate information on an "allied" system like Stinger, the Griffon's crew might not be able to react to the threat in time and would be in danger of being shot down.

MAWS was not set for nontraditional heat signatures, so the ground crews had to sort that out as well. Corporal Nickerson noted that "some kid with a Zippo lighter on the ground would set it off, it was so sensitive. One day we punched out thirty-two flares. We had more chance of lighting up somebody's house than actually getting hit."[52]

Capt. Pierre Lalancette of 430 ETAH: "We were never hit with a SAM, but we got a lot of MAWS warnings of a missile approach. The software was old. It was stressful and it was taking a toll, but we still had to react as if it was real, 'MAWS warning, front left!' and then maneuver. We changed the software and it was less annoying. There was one incident when a Griffon was on the ground dropping off troops and a truck with a hot exhaust drove by and set off the MAWS, which was on automatic. It was kind of scary."[53]

There was also a threat emanating from Serbia proper. VJ air defense forces, which included SA-3 missiles in fixed sites and SA-6 Gainfuls on mobile launchers accompanied by Straight Flush mobile radar systems, caused problems in the air safety zone: the mobile systems could move into the ASZ and then out of it. Griffons on patrol along the border detected the VJ radar systems shift from "search" to "track." Shifting to "track" contravened the military technical agreement, and if a shift was made to "fire control," such a move permitted NATO forces to take lethal retaliatory action as they saw fit. In the first case the "track" was deemed to be an error, but the second time it happened it was considered harassment. Two American AH-64 Apache gunships accompanied a Griffon on a flight that was designed specifically to determine VJ intentions. This mission was also covered by U.S. Air Force "Wild Weasel" aircraft equipped with an AGM-88, which was a high-speed antiradiation missile that was used against surface-to-air missiles. The VJ air defense radars remained silent and posed no further problem for Canadian aircraft.[54]

As far as can be determined, there were no SAMs fired at Canadian Griffons during Operation Kinetic, though man-portable SAMs were recovered during weapons raids against the UÇK.[55] The laser threat, however, was a different story: in some cases there was clearly malevolent intent.

The air force wanted the SPS-65 rearward laser warning receiver (RLWR) for the Griffon, but due to bureaucratic wrangling there were not enough to send to Kosovo. Indeed some air force planners thought that Kosovo was going to be a peacekeeping observer mission like the MFO in the Sinai, were dismissive about the threat, and didn't want to spend money.[56]

At 2200 hours on 12 July the copilot of a Griffon assisting ground forces in overwatching the town of Lipljan noticed that a laser was trying to acquire the aircraft. Capt. Les Beothy maneuvered so that the flight engineer and the mission specialist could see where it was located. The FE saw the target in an unlit house: the beam was a thousand meters long and narrow: it flicked on and off.[57] Then two 7.62mm tracer rounds (and thus six to ten ball rounds) passed two hundred meters from the rear of the helicopter. The pilot banked hard left, dropped his altitude by a hundred feet, and circled around so that they could cue the Gurkha quick reaction force. Fortunately the Griffon's crew suffered no eye damage.[58] The Gurkhas were unable to catch the perpetrators: the shooters were sophisticated enough to fire from a position located on an inter–battle group boundary, which complicated the coordination of the pursuit.

Capt. Erik O'Connor noted that "in July and August, while flying at night, we got lased so many times it became a normal thing. Sometimes it was difficult to tell if it was aggressive or not. Some guys went to the hospital. A friend of mine was lased with a range finder. That really hurts. He was grounded. The lasing thing was considered a threat: we could have used the ROEs if we wanted to retaliate."[59]

The complication was that the lasing came from a number of sources. Corporal Nickerson: "We got lased by kids who had those pen lasers: sometimes thirty times a night, so we had the British army guys in a Land Rover who'd pull up and they just kick the crap out of the kids with the laser pointers. Another time it was the French troops in an APC. The idiots lased us. We got on the radio and told them if they lased us again, we were allowed to shoot at them. They stopped."[60]

The Kačanik defile, as seen from an abandoned Serb position. With multiple
bridges and tunnels, the Kačanik defile was the only main service route into
Kosovo for NATO troops building up in Macedonia. A combined Gurkha/
parachute regiment force air assaulted in to seize the vital ground. Author's
collection.

The Coyote reconnaissance vehicle, with its mast-mounted sensor system, had no counterpart in NATO forces deployed with KFOR in Kosovo. Radar, thermal imaging, and camera systems were used to full effect on every operation the Lord Strathcona's Horse (Royal Canadians) and the Royal Canadian Dragoons participated in, from border surveillance to tracking illicit shipments throughout the province. DND/CAF.

TOW under armor vehicles had a dual role in Kosovo. Their sensor systems assured protracted observation at night, while the antitank missile capability contributed to the defensive plan in case Serbia intervened again. DND/CAF.

A wide variety of illicit nocturnal activities were conducted by various local ethnic groups throughout the province. Substantial numbers of image intensification equipment were deployed down to the lowest level in KFOR to improve coverage. DND/CAF.

The decision to deploy tanks as part of the KFOR entry plan paid dividends once KFOR downshifted to stabilization operations. The Leopard C2 had good night vision equipment and like the TUA became part of the Contingency Plan Thunder defensive plan. They also made intimidating vehicle checkpoints. DND/CAF.

Contingency Plan Thunder, designed to slow a potential Serbian mechanized incursion before airpower could be brought to bear, relied on British tanks like these Challenger 2s, as well as Canadian and German Leopards. Author's collection.

The CH-146 Griffon proved adept at weaving in and out of Priština's urban canyons. Having a modular attachment system, some Griffons were equipped with Nightsun searchlights. DND/CAF.

The vast Obilić power complex, fueled with coal from mines around Mitrovica, supplied electrical power to surrounding countries, including Macedonia, Albania, Bulgaria, and Greece. Possession of these facilities was a crucial objective for any entity asserting control over Kosovo. Author's collection.

Russian troops unexpectedly deployed from Bosnia to Kosovo, which led to a crisis between Russia and NATO. Eventually they were integrated into KFOR next to areas dominated by the Kosovar Serb population, but there was still friction with Western forces. Author's collection.

The deliberate targeting of Kosovar Albanian houses for burning by Serb paramilitary, police, and military units led to a humanitarian crisis beyond the expulsion of the population. These houses had to be reroofed and made habitable before winter set in. Engineers and Pioneers worked alongside Kosovar Albanians to complete this task as quickly as possible. DND/CAF.

The movement of people between the Kosovar Serb enclaves and Serbia proper by bus had to be protected by KFOR convoys from revanchist elements in the Kosovar Albanian population. This became known as the "Rock Run" because people threw rocks at the convoy. After a time they began to harass the convoy with IEDs instead of rocks. Author's collection.

The decision by the Kosovar Albanian leadership to escalate the situation in 2000 led to a mass march of thousands of people from Priština to the northern city of Mitrovica that had as its objective the occupation of the Serb communities north of the Ibar River. DND/CAF.

1 RCR's Pioneer platoon became the object of international media scrutiny when the bearded Pioneers lined up their M-113A2 vehicles across the bridge separating the Serb and Albanian communities in Mitrovica and then held the crowd back without the use of lethal force. M.Cpl. Brendan Massey's image was on the front page of newspapers around the world. A Canadian admiral in Ottawa, not understanding army tradition, later demanded that Pioneers be investigated for wearing beards. After being treated like criminals, the Pioneers eventually received CDS Commendations for their actions. DND/CAF.

There were indications that the pen lasers were given to the children from some entity to deliberately disrupt or interfere with KFOR air operations. The possibility also existed that this entity wanted KFOR to overreact and shoot children for propaganda purposes and thus discredit NATO.[61]

The dismissive attitude was no longer apparent to the Air Staff in Ottawa. Steps were taken to supply the KRWAU with laser visors. These had a greenish-yellowish tint, but they could not be worn at night: they interfered with the use of night vision goggles. NVGs even amplified laser light and could cause even worse laser damage to eyes: this occurred in September, when a Griffon flying with no exterior lights on was tracked five times in ten minutes with a red dot that was moved directly into the crew's NVGs: the pilot and FE developed discomfort in their eyes and had to be treated.[62]

The RLWR systems were deployed to Kosovo, but it took four months for them to be acquired and delivered. Fortunately the RLWR system was installed when a more serious situation developed.

German CH-53 transport helicopters flying around Priština and in the border areas were receiving an abnormal number of RLWR hits. Soon Canadian Griffons were getting lased more and more. In-theater technical analysis completed at the KRWAU determined that this was not children with pen lasers: it was definitely some sort of rangefinding and tracking system because of the light frequencies it employed. Once again planners in Ottawa were dismissive and claimed it was pen lasers, despite the information sent back. Then American UH-60 Blackhawks and AH-64 Apaches were lased. Operating out of the KFOR loop, the Canadians, Americans, British, and Germans quietly got together to assess the situation. A joint operation was mounted to determine what was going on. The Americans formed a hunter-killer team of UH-60 Blackhawks and AH-64 Apaches to respond to the provocation, while the Canadians and Germans provided support. Analysis determined that the laser was a Russian air defense tracking system based in their zone at Priština airport near the aircraft bunker. Another was based just outside the ASZ in Serbia proper. American and German diplomacy was used to get the Russians to cease and desist (which they did) while Canadians in Ottawa kept insisting that it was a pen laser.[63]

The motives remain obscure but relate to an "enemy within" scenario. Informed speculation suggests two: Russian industry wanted to test the effectiveness of its new systems against NATO aircraft and at the same time Russian intelligence could observe how NATO forces reacted to this threat. This information could be sold to other nations (e.g., Iraq) to improve their air defense systems. This activity could have overlapped with another possible motive: that this was a test of a Russian contingency plan to disrupt KFOR operations from the inside if the VJ intervened in northern Kosovo. The sudden appearance of hundreds of laser pens in children's hands throughout the Priština area was probably not coincidental to this activity.[64]

Indeed Canadian pilots had been victimized by Russians wielding lasers before, most notably off British Columbia in April 1997, when a Canadian Sea King was lased while observing the Russian intelligence vessel *Kapitan Man*. Two men received serious eye injuries. That incident was hushed up by the Clinton administration with the help of the Canadian Department of Foreign Affairs to avoid aggravating relations with Russia.[65]

Roles, Missions, and Operations

Lt. Col. Bruce McQuade's initial assessment of the mission, based on his May 1999 recce visit to 4 (UK) Armoured Brigade, was blunt and realistic and formed the basis of what the KRWAU would do in Kosovo over the next year.

> [The] use of aviation in the surveillance role has not been well thought through by the Brigade staff and therefore the types/frequency of aviation tasks are difficult to quantify. I suspect [the commander of] 4 Bde will use his [aviation assets] principally in the [utility] role while initially training and experimenting with the surveillance mission. . . . [With regard to] recce and surveillance the unit will focus on rear area, verification and economy of force operations. Much has been made by the [Canadian] staff and orders have reflected the surveillance and recce capability of

the FLIR-equipped Griffon and its complementary role with the [Strathconas'] Coyote systems. However, the low quality of the present FLIR recording system and experience with its very poor reliability and the limited magnification (read: stand-off capability) have led me to conservatively guide the Bde staff expectations. . . . There is no doubt that we would be a far more valuable [resource] if we were equipped with [RISTA]. . . . ERSTA level capabilities should be pursued with vigor.[66]

Indeed the SAMEO, Capt. Barbara Palmer, accelerated training for her mission kit technicians and provided for more spares to try and counter the FLIR's unreliability. Lieutenant Colonel McQuade determined that there would be plenty of command and liaison as well as resupply missions that the KRWAU could handle.[67] Essentially these roles and missions carried over to the 430 ETAH rotation under Lieutenant Colonel Lavallée.

Maj. Jim MacAlese noted that there was some expansion once the brigade and the KRWAU were comfortable with each other: "They weren't expecting us to come over and do troop lifts and that sort of thing, which of course is what we had been practicing for the last year [in Edmonton with 1 CMBG]. We'd sort of gotten away from the reconnaissance stuff when we jettisoned the Kiowa, but we slowly moved back into it."[68]

It was necessary for 408 Squadron and later 430 ETAH to comb through their roster of pilots and find personnel who had served in Kiowa units in the past (this tended to be the older members).[69] Their expertise with low-level recce was brought to bear, as Maj. Christian Drouin of 430 ETAH recalled: "There were still some guys from the last Kiowa squadron, like Captain Belanger. They had a good amount of knowledge about recce. So we set up scenarios in the simulator, one day and one night with NVGs, and we went back through old recce task briefings and procedures."[70]

In some cases the former Kiowa pilots were pulling pamphlets and notebooks out of old footlockers and flight bags from their basements at home.

The KRWAU was expected to contribute the ISTAR information matrix while it was going about its other activities. For example, areas of interest for the KRWAU included identifying MUP activity, stay-behind Serb special forces' presence, leadership, capabilities, and intentions; reporting any VJ activity in the ground and air safety zones; reporting any indications of UÇK noncompliance with specific reference to weapons caches; and to collect any information on the UÇK attitudes toward the undertaking and KFOR's enforcement of it. The KRWAU was also to identify any actions that posed a threat to the security of KFOR troops, as well as to report theft of equipment or sabotage. Information priorities also included the identification of isolated Serb populations and what their attitude toward KFOR was; collection of evidence of war crimes; and identification of local attitudes regarding the Kosovar Albanian political situation with reference to Thaçi and Rugova. Data on any nonattributable terrorist attack or trends were also to be sent in. Note that all members of the KRWAU, both ground and air crew, were expected to contribute information. If, for example, the ground staff sent a mobile repair team to a remote location, they were to prick up their ears and keep their eyes peeled on the way. Information collected in this way could add to the ISTAR picture and perhaps fill out areas that technological means could penetrate.[71]

The first KRWAU operations from Camp DK (which had acquired the moniker Crow's Nest) focused on supporting British units in Priština. Priština was for all intents and purposes a series of concrete obstacles built in a valley, with the downtown to the south and suburbs flowing north. It was an urban canyon. The downtown was dominated by a sports facility, which featured a peaked roof with eight spires: it looks like a series of churches folded up and stacked together next to a football stadium. The heights to the southeast overlooking downtown featured University City, with rows of dorms and the electrical engineering school across the street. Priština was relatively untouched by bombing: only the PTT (Yugoslav phone company) communications building and MUP headquarters were completely devastated by highly accurate strikes with precision-guided weapons. Smokestacks abound, and most of the lights were off. It was eerie flying over

Priština, according to Warrant Officer Robert Boucher of 430 ETAH: "When we first arrived you could see that only part of the city had lights. They didn't want to overload the power, so they were switching the lights off in several neighborhoods and leaving them on in one or two. Then they'd switch it to the next and it would go dark. This one was going black, this one was lighting up, all to share the electricity. At the end of the tour when we left it was all lit up at night."[72]

The Nightsun was a useful tool, according to many KRWAU personnel. Maj. Jim MacAlese:

> We worked with the parachute battalion, and they were quite imaginative with their use of helicopters, based on their experiences in Northern Ireland. . . . In Priština, for example, we came in equipped with three or four FLIR, figuring that's what they would want. And we also had Nightsun, which is a huge spotlight. It tuned out the Brits weren't interested in FLIR because they didn't want us not being seen: they wanted the people on the ground to see us [operate]. They wanted maximum visibility. So they liked the spotlight. The shock effect of all of a sudden having five million candlepower light appear over top when you were concealed by the darkness [was unnerving]. Guys just froze, so the troops could move in and grab people that were causing problems. The British had observation posts on top of old buildings that had some bomb damage, so we resupplied them. . . . We came in with generators: the rest of the valley was black, there was no electricity. There was no running water, phone service didn't exist. Surveillance and presence were our biggest thing, out there making noise so people on the ground knew we were there.[73]

Sgt. Robert Wheatley: "We did overwatch at night. We'd run with the FLIR and watch things with the NVG. We'd have a section of Paras with us. If their friends on patrol on the ground got hit, we could intervene. And not just pick up the wounded. We'd help out. They could hear us at night, but they couldn't see us. We'd fly around blacked out. Other times we used Nightsun and it was all overt: it's like a big candle in the sky. The message was, we were like God, who's watching everything."[74]

Capt. Erik O'Connor:

At night we did surveillance over Priština. Just the fact that we flew with the Nightsun kind of calmed things down. We saw an increase in criminal activity when we stopped or reduced the amount of flying. It was exciting in the beginning because I had no limits and I could fly tactical all over the ground. I was flying in between buildings, doing approaches on buildings, resupply on top of high-rises, so you're not landing, you're hovering and off-loading water onto a twenty-story building. We worked with 1 Para [1st Battalion, Parachute Regiment], an outstanding unit. They were very, very keen on doing things. They were more interested in working with us than with their own people. Our attitude was, "We don't know if it'll work, but we'll try," unlike their pilots. [Mines were a problem] so we used an Olympic swimming pool to land in. We also worked with some of our people who one day would be wearing an MP uniform, and then Strathcona's, then something else next. We just supported them and they went about their business.[75]

The KRWAU also worked closely with the cream of British light infantry units while in Priština. Cpl. Aaron Nickerson:

We took care of the entire British AOR, but we worked downtown constantly. We did a lot of work with the SAS [Special Air Service, UK] who were working the rooftops. I remember landing on a fourteen-story building in a very small area. We got right downtown. These British airborne guys just didn't screw around. One time there was a riot and somebody was taking potshots at them and they wanted us right downtown to put the door gun right above them and keep the [shooters'] heads down. They didn't care. It's like, "Oh yeah, come on." Machine guns open up downtown. The problem was that there were one or two gunmen and there were thirty or forty women and children in the street. [We didn't have to fire and the gunmen took off]. We also worked with the Gurkhas, these short chubby little guys, but my God they were wired tight. We were jumping from rooftop to rooftop, and somebody with an AK started shooting at them. One helicopter had risen four feet and prepared to leave, so this fat Gurkha just jumped into the air and caught the helicopter. We would also move sniper teams around: they'd overwatch the riots and track anybody with guns.[76]

Maj. Steve Charpentier at times had to deal with problems generated by the routine:

We did a lot of jobs with the British [in Priština], but some of our guys didn't understand, the younger ones. They wondered "What are we doing here?" I was starting to have a little rebellion from one of my senior pilots who was saying, "What the heck are we doing spending all of these hours, we do nothing," blah blah blah. We were doing a great thing. The mere fact that we had two choppers above the town making a lot of noise, spotlight and everything, it deterred criminal activity. And that's what the Brits wanted from us, but sometimes the pilots could not understand that. You couldn't touch it, the results of your actions. It's like the Cold War. Exactly how do you quantify it? The intelligence guys were keeping track of incidents in the town, and they told us incidents dropped off. . . . The biggest problem [during our tour] was not terrorism: it was Albanian against Albanian, criminals trying to rape or steal young girls and put them into prostitution. I have four kids, so I was satisfied we were doing a good job.[77]

Maj. Christian Drouin came to similar conclusions:

It was tough on the guys to do surveillance at night every night for four or five nights a week. They thought nothing was going on, which is what we wanted: nothing going on. After a while the crime rate was really low, so the brigade said, "Okay, we'll do a test here during the transition [from 408 Squadron to 430 ETAH]: we won't use choppers at night." So for about a month choppers stopped flying over Priština and the crime level soared. So we said, "Okay, we'll see if it's really linked to the helicopter surveillance or not," so they started the Eagle VCP [vehicle checkpoint] task where we worked with the [British] battle group in Priština. We would take their officers on board, and they would put in roadblocks and control points at night almost randomly. Within one week the crime level went down drastically.[78]

The Eagle VCPs involved two types of Griffon operations. Cpl. Aaron Nickerson's crew was a frequent participant:

We'd be out with the British: they got out a lot at night. Somebody would run one of their roadblocks, so we'd put on the goggles and black out the helicopter. We'd take off down the road and pull ahead of the car and then just hover fifteen feet off the ground, put the spotlight on, and put the machine guns on them. They'd just stop or go into the ditch. We'd disembark the troops and they'd conduct the search. We did a variation. The troops would be in the back, we'd fly along the main highways around Priština, wait until there was a break in the cars, land, block the road, conduct a search, get the troops in, and take off. This was so they knew we could be any-where at any time. The problem was, everything could be going just fine, but you could get in a firefight in seconds, so you're all wired tight the whole time. It was exciting! This was the first time Canada did anything like this. Bosnia and Haiti weren't even close.

Capt. Erick Simoneau was involved in the search for a Koso-var Albanian radical:

The Swedish battalion had eight VCPs out, and they were looking for this guy, stopping cars, checking under the hood, looking for weapons. From the air we saw some vehicles that were in the line turning around, so we started to covertly follow them. We stayed above him so he couldn't see us in his mirrors. We saw where he was heading: he dropped by one house, switched cars, drove to another house, and we started to think something was going on so we called in an assault on the house. The ground troops came in on APCs, so we dropped the Swedish commander off at his CP. They did an assault and found lots and lots of weapons. We did five more of those, and in every case we found weapons, mines, and equipment. In another case they used an ambulance to transport weapons, since the ambulances would just run through the check-points. Then we saw one have a collision and weapons dumped out into the ditch. They told us later that these operations were effective because the UCK weren't moving stuff around as much.[79]

Griffons were also used to provide surveillance of suspected UÇK personnel. First Battalion, Parachute Regiment, would shut down the cell phone system in a given area. The UÇK was dependent on cell phones, so when they would go down during UÇK operations, there would be a lot of activity on the ground as they tried to sort out their communications. The Griffons would be watching and recording reactions to see who was who.[80]

The importance of having a low crime rate in Priština is self-evident. Until the UN could get into Kosovo and set up the UNMIK police force, the situation would deteriorate and internecine Kosovar Albanian violence would break out. A spillover effect of that would result in the targeting of Kosovar Serbs, with attendant political ramifications. The KRWAU's role in this effort was significant since it was effective in supporting MNB (Center) in its efforts to control Priština and contain the violence in that politically critical city.

There were few direct fire incidents involving the Griffons while working over Priština. When something did happen, there would be no end of bureaucratic problems with Ottawa, as Lieutenant Colonel McQuade noted: "The possible engagement over Priština is being investigated. Crew debriefs were completed late last night as they were a night crew and require rest. The situation is not clear cut. Info/action/event passed up the Op chain and probably picked up by media in Pristina and released there. NDOC already calling the unit. Minute-by-minute management by Ottawa frustrating—call it the tyranny of real time—but they also feel the need for additional paper every time a tracer is fired over Priština. This will slowly paralyse the units Ops and command staff."[81]

On 30 June 1999 a Canadian Griffon was involved in an incident in which the crew was forced to fire its door-mounted machine gun. Sgt. Robert Wheatley:

We were on track from Glogovac and heading east to Priština. We were redirected by the liaison officer in the headquarters to go southwest. The British troops down there were taking sniper fire from a spot near Gračanica. The aircraft commander, Captain Cameron, asked what the basic distance of a sniper rifle was and I told him twelve hundred to thirteen hundred meters for a really good one. So we stood back a klick of the target area and looked for the sniper. We spotted him: he was fiddling around in the trees up on top of the hill. White shirt, black vest, black pants, really good camouflage. . . . We circled him for about ten minutes and he was doing nothing. You'd see him stand up every once in a while and look around, get back down, fiddle around some more. But we couldn't tell exactly what he was doing, and we could not pick up any weapons in his hands either.

We came in closer and at one point he actually stood up and put up his hands. The only problem is that the aircraft cannot take the surrender of anybody: we weren't allowed to land [because of the mine threat]. So we watched him for another hour. Then he went over the ridge and back down to an old MUP barracks. At that point he had a jacket which stood stiff, about four feet, so we knew he had something but we couldn't see it. We had contact with the British troops by this time and they were trying to get a patrol up there. We followed the guys, and he was getting upset with us. Then we got an MAWS warning which triggered the flares.

He looked at us, saw two Land Rovers coming at him, and he ran about six hundred meters. We were circling and guiding the British onto his position: we came around with the unarmed side of the aircraft, so he decided to take a shot at us, but we swung around, so he planted both feet and started firing at the British. At that point we decided to open fire on him [and I had the permission of the aircraft commander]. He was moving around the trees and his weapon was functioning because we could see the smoke, but we were too high to get an angle on him: the first six rounds were about six feet short of the target. The FE let me know I was short, so I brought the gun up and fired another seventeen into the tree line. We saw no movement after that. We came into a hover and the British troops surrounded and then captured him. We were low on fuel, so we left. They found a small arsenal in the trees there.

It caused some questions with some of the guys about what we were doing, moral dilemmas. My first inclination was that eighteen years of training paid off. I've been in too many situations in

1992 and 1993 [during UNPROFOR] where the rules of engagement don't allow you to shoot back unless someone's bleeding.
Some people had a problem with it, but when it comes to self-
defense, don't question what I did. It's my life or his: we have four
guys and a multimillion-dollar helicopter. I'd rather be judged by
twelve than carried by six. There's a lot of people in Canada that
just don't understand that.[82]

Keeping an eye on the UÇK's activities became more and more
important. The Griffons were part of a larger operation to track
smuggling from Albania. It was difficult, according to Maj. Jim
MacAlese:

> Intelligence had a number of specific vehicles that were going to
> be going to Albania, pick up weapons, and come back. We tried to
> covertly follow them, but it didn't work out that well. They'd pull
> into somebody's yard to have a coffee and wait us out, so they knew
> what we were doing and made it difficult for us. It was an inter-
> esting mission, fast paced. We started in Podujevo and they came
> through Priština. I am not sure if they set us up or if they knew
> they were being watched, but they went into Priština (you know
> what that place is like), slipped into an underground garage, waited
> for half an hour, and slipped out again. They were crafty about it.[83]

These operations continued throughout both KRWAU tours.
Capt. Pierre Lalancette and his crew had their share of them:

> I was the mission commander for a night insertion we did with
> the British forces. We had four Griffons and one Puma transport-
> ing troops up north from Podujevo and drop them into Lipljan
> to reinforce the Finns. There was word that illegal weapons were
> cached in these houses, so the plan was to basically shut down the
> town and search the suspect houses and vehicles, so it had to be
> quick. We did it with full NVGs: it was the first night formation
> with NVGs we did. We trained for it, but this was our first. The
> Finns closed the town down, blocked all the roads. Our job was
> to act as a show of force and drop in so we could demonstrate that
> we could show up at any time with a lot of people. We learned that
> there were some limitations to Griffon when you put all the armor

on; we were quite heavy with the troops on board. Number Two aircraft had to pull 100 percent just to slow down and land. We did two insertions that night, one east of the town, came back and picked them up and dropped them to the west. It looked like there were more troops than there actually were the locals.[84]

According to Maj. Steve Charpentier, a "carrot-and-stick" approach was used in some of the more remote villages east of Priština, particularly those closer to the border. Intelligence knew weapons were cached in these areas, but the locals were in bad shape because of the winter:

> We had five Griffons involved, two waves for the insertion. The mission was to do a tactical insertion of troops and seize some weapons. There was snow up on top and you have to be careful to avoid a white-out. You don't want to overtorque your engine on top of a mountain. . . . I dropped a flare to check wind direction, then I went past the village to see if anybody would engage. We were expecting retaliation and trouble on this one. It went off pretty well. We landed and all of the people came out of their houses and they all had big smiles. The Brits seized some old weapons, so I'm pretty sure the real stuff was spirited away. The second part was humanitarian; we then flew in flour and beans and stuff like that to calm everything down after all of the excitement of guys jumping off helicopters with weapons.[85]

Not all operations were successful, as when MNB (Center) tried to catch the UÇK while they were training. Cpl. Aaron Nickerson recalled, "We were with the Royal Green Jackets. We spent three days camping up near Podujevo, waiting for the big arms bust. And we had them too. We had like three hundred troops involved, Special Forces, everything and everybody's trying to catch these guys. And then the fog came in. We couldn't launch the helicopters. That one sucked."[86]

It was, in the end, a useful exercise for the KRWAU's forward arming and refueling point party.

Keeping an eye on Kosovar Serb–Kosovar Albanian violence was another important task, and the Griffons played a supporting role. For example, on the night of 20 August 1999 there was a drive-by shooting in the Serb village of Crkvena Vodica: weapons were fired and a grenade lobbed at a café. Four men were wounded. Right afterward the perpetrators threw a grenade into a playground, but nobody was injured. A demonstration followed, with the local Serbs demanding that the Russian KFOR contingent protect them. A QRF platoon from 1 PPCLI responded, as did a Griffon that provided top cover "to help calm the populace through the use of the Nightsun to illuminate the surrounding area." The crowd dispersed, and there was no further agitation at that time.[87]

The most sobering missions flown by the KRWAU involved mass grave reconnaissance. Capt. Pete Lyon flew some of the first:

> The biggest thing that sticks out in my mind was the early stages of our entry into Kosovo and the search for mass graves. It was one of our big missions early on. KFOR wanted to find as many as possible and get the investigations going. We would get satellite photos that would indicate that there might be a mass grave in a given area, so we would fly in and check. There were a lot of them around. On one mission, I was handed a stack of papers with several locations highlighted. They'd interviewed the refugees to get witness statements saying this person was killed, that person was killed, these were the circumstances. The investigators had to photograph the sites to confirm. For example, an entire family was lined up against the wall and shot and their bodies dumped. It was kind of spooky really. I couldn't believe that people could do these things. I couldn't believe that you could line them up against the wall, especially somebody you don't even know, and shoot them. Especially the children. Whole families were killed just because of who they were. In Canada we have racism, we have hatred, but we don't go around killing people. I couldn't believe it. It was different from Haiti: we saw a mass grave there full of unburied skeletons, but in Kosovo they tried to disguise how it was done and where. Like, the Serbs would bury them in a cemetery so it would look a normal burial. . . .
>
> North of Kosovo Polje right along the railway track there was a field with a grave dug diagonally across one corner, and there were

eight or ten holes dug up with two or three bodies per hole. We had to keep a close eye on that site because the Albanians would dig them up and rebury them properly. We heard that the refinery near Glogovac had been used to dispose of bodies in the smelters. There was no evidence left.[88]

Cpl. Aaron Nickerson:

We went from surveillance work to locating and digging up mass graves. Oh yeah, that was always a fun job. I was pissed off. One was by the power plant and another near Kosovo Polje. There were about 90 to 110 women and children. Albanians. The Serbs just lined them up and shot them. They'd make them hold the kids and just shoot through the kids and kill the women. It saves ammo. We would fly over and the wild dogs who were starving would tear pieces off. So you've got these corpses, kids and women, and the wild dogs are pulling the bodies out and munching on them. This was even before the investigators got on the ground. The locals would call the Brits, they'd call us, and we'd send out a helicopter and find it. We had to be careful: there were mines everywhere. The Serbs would lay the bodies down and mine the whole area because they knew people would be looking for bodies.[89]

Border surveillance operations were critical in maintaining situational awareness vis-à-vis the VJ. Warning was needed to conduct deterrence operations and then to take on the VJ if they mounted an attack against MNB (Center). The primary area of interest for the KRWAU was the provincial boundary sector northeast of Podujevo, from the boundary with MNB (North) to the boundary with MNB (East). The activity in this area differed significantly from the Priština operations.

The KRWAU was involved in a nightly mission that "[we] flew across the Kosovo-Serbia border and [did] the power presence missions there, every night."[90] The lack of a stand-off ERSTA system inhibited such missions: "We would fly as close as we could to the border so [we] could look over into it, but it was difficult terrain and we couldn't see very far. It's just all hills and trees and pretty difficult to get in."[91] On occasion AH-64 Apaches would augment Griffon presence.[92]

There were serious concerns about VJ special forces infiltration and connections to MUP activity:

> We were called in by the British unit in Podujevo. This was one of our bad areas. The Coyotes were involved; they weren't shy about asking for overhead watch because they knew they couldn't see everything. That thermal imaging unit they have is very nice. But trees don't let you see through them. We flew in and used our NVGs to supplement what they were doing. So [the Serbs] are bringing in guys at night. We reacted to these border incursions, and sometimes it was a MUP patrol: technically they were allowed to patrol [under the military technical agreement]. The Serbs had a "self-defense force" [in their Kosovo enclaves], a nice political term for it, but they were using it to intimidate Albanians. They had a very nice clean short haircut, and they'd walk around in long black jackets on a hot day. They were coming though east of Podujevo, through these small villages. It was easy to penetrate and they'd make their way to Priština. We would track the incursions blacked out, with the FLIR, and then sit back and watch while the British dealt with them. One time the British paratroops told these guys to drop their weapons: one guy decided not to, so he was shot. We used the videotape system: the intelligence people could pick out all sorts of little things which helped them out.[93]

VJ activity on the border continued throughout both tours, and the Griffons were continuously employed there:

> One of the most exciting ops was a mission on the border. The British had to go across the border and take pictures of some tracks which were within the five-kilometer GSZ [to prove there was noncompliance with the MTA]. They [the British] had tanks and everything lined up at the border, and we were to take the troop leader on a recce and then were to work with the quick reaction force. Tensions were high: the Serbs told their people in the area that NATO was going to come across and invade Serbia. Anything

could happen. The column approached the border, and the commander crossed in his jeep with the tanks in overwatch. They came back with the information, but the situation remained tense. This was a bit of a show of force operation. Our adrenalin was going big time. . . . If we had had to fly across the border, something had really gone wrong.[94]

Another recalled that "the guys in the battalion covering the border reported that they were seeing Mi-8 HIP helicopters in the border area. We started to do more and more observation on the border and those HIPs were sling loading equipment back and forth."[95]

Maj. Steve Charpentier:

I was flying up near Checkpoint Four, right along the border. I saw four guys in green uniforms and a military vehicle right below me. I reported it in. We were flying really low, with the door guns aimed, we had the antimissile system on, we were taking pictures. Then we heard that there was some sort of helicopter from Serbia entering the zone. Call sign Magic, the AWACS, picked it up. He reported that he was seeing some traffic, so we scrambled the copter and we went in sneaky-like to try and take a picture of them. So our guys were hiding here near Gate Four, the Griffon was sneaking around just waiting for the Serbs. This went on for hours. I then saw a chopper, but this one was German. I don't know what the heck he was doing there, since this was not his sector, but here they were, yee haw, a thousand feet on the other side of the border at fifteen feet. We realized these guys were part of the game, trying to find these Mi-8s we were looking for. There was at least one Mi-8 [seen], but the rest were false reports.[96]

The KRWAU's role in defending against a mechanized VJ incursion and its predecessors was limited by the aircraft's capabilities. The Griffons initially

didn't have a specific role. We obviously would support anything, and it could have been anything from moving small elements of troops up to a hill with some antiarmor weapons, or a casevac, the normal routine-type tactical helicopter missions. We weren't going to get involved in any battle. There may have been some reconnaissance required, to sit on top of a hill, but the Griffon wasn't equipped with the optics [we needed] and we would have to get close: we would prefer to be able to stand off ten or fifteen kilometers, but that capability wasn't ready at the time.[97]

When Conplan Thunder and its successors replaced the earlier plans, the Griffons had an expanded role. The KRWAU would support the brigade units with normal utility taskings, but the brigade plan was to move closer, right on to the border, and there was a series of options to deter and also preempt VJ operations. The vulnerability of the Griffons operating in the open Podujevo bowl was negated. The Griffons became part of the recce and surveillance phase over the border since they had demonstrated their capability of working in the close terrain of the hills east of Podujevo on previous operations.[98]

There were ongoing problems with the Russians. Griffons were scrambled on a number of occasions to maintain observation of Russian activities and to record them in case they got out of hand. In one incident some drunken Russians "drew down" with a machine gun on a Canadian checkpoint, were tracked by the Griffons, and pulled over by the Finns. The Russians were then beaten up by a Finnish captain who wanted revenge for the Soviet invasion of Finland in 1940 and told them that "if you don't want us to do what we did to your grandfather, stay in your camp."[99]

By the time 430 ETAH had replaced 408 Squadron at the KRWAU, the Russians were operating an Mi-24 HIND gunship unit out of the Priština airport. Keeping track of what they were up to became a MNB (Center) task. The Coyote surveillance operators needed to familiarize themselves with the IR signatures and emissions of various aircraft so they could provide accurate identification. Coincidentally Lt. Col. Serge Lavallée arranged to have a "fly-in" barbecue at the Camp DK airfield for all KFOR members operating helicopters: the United States, Netherlands, Germany, Ukraine, Belgium, United Kingdom, Italy, and the United Arab Emirates. The Russians were also invited with their HINDs.

Squadron Ground Operations

Supporting Griffon operations from the ground in Kosovo was quite different from the routine back at Canadian Forces Base Edmonton or Valcartier, though in many ways the processes remained the same. As Cpl. Nathalie Castonguay (430 Squadron) put it, "I'm a trucker, and I'm there to refuel helicopters. That's the only thing we have to do, but we do it professionally."[100]

The ground environment outside of Camp DK, however, served to remind all KRWAU members of the nature of their mission. Capt. Andrea Andrachuk (430 ETAH):

Poklek is a small community and it's all Albanian; there are no Serbians whatsoever. It was attacked during the war and lot of people were killed, as well as some of the children. There was a mass grave nearby down a muddy road. There's not much there. It's a little farming community, there were cows and kids running all over the place, but you could tell these kids didn't have a family anymore. They'd come up to you and talk, sometimes for twenty minutes and I couldn't understand them without a translator. When I had one, some of the kids talked about how they hated Serbs and things like that. You know, from a seven- or eight-year-old that's a bit strange and sad to hear. Lt. Lynne Gerard, who worked in Ops, taught some kids to dance, so one day we went to see the school open and the kids did a Britney Spears dance. It was so cute and Lynne was crying in the back she was so happy.[101]

Chief Warrant Officer Mike Guay (430 ETAH) noted that the Poklek school project was an important activity for KRWAU personnel:

We started with a very good, strong morale base and we maintained it. It surprised me because you always expect it to dip a couple of months in. The quality of the camp was a factor, but we also did a school project locally. The majority of the people in the squadron partook in that and got involved. It gave them pride and I think it contributed to morale because it gave people something to do outside their job. It also contributed to stabilizing the environment. It got us out of the camp (where we were restricted most of the time) and into the local area. We were able to contribute to rebuilding. It was satisfying and it made people feel good about themselves.[102]

Sgt. Sylvain St-Gelais (430 ETAH) took over from his 408 Squadron counterpart, who was involved in starting and running a Scout troop that had increased its roster to twenty kids from the local area. Working with the Dragoons, St-Gelais set up soccer games and cookouts.[103]

Although these efforts may appear to be minor or insignificant given the scale of violent activity in Kosovo and the operational mission priorities, they were part of a larger effort within the Canadian area of operations to achieve the objectives of the NATO presence: a stable and secure environment throughout Kosovo.

KRWAU ground crew were subjected to the same environment as the ground forces. Cpl. Terry Merritt (408 Squadron):

> We had to go to downtown Priština to get LPOs [local purchase orders]. Once a week they were killing people. It was a normal city and then things would go crazy. One night we got caught in a scuffle. Zim [the Albanian interpreter] and I were in the front and we took a civilian van. We started to use rented vehicles to lower our profile. But we were still in uniform. Kosovo Polje was a Serbian town and a hot spot. Someone shot two RPGs into this neighborhood. This happened once a week. We didn't know until we pulled up that there were a couple of hundred protesters in the middle of the road protesting. We were the first vehicle on the scene and then there were about ten Brits and two armored vehicles. We thought they'd let us through because we're Canadian. Then the crowd went nuts and chased after a civilian and started hitting him with sticks. So Master Corporal Jericho ran out to give the Brits some help, because they were outnumbered. A big fight broke out, and I saw his little [air force] blue beret popping in and out of the crowd, and there was this fist pumping up and down. Then some lady pointed at Zim and screamed and then they came at the van, threw a rock through the windshield, and shattered it. So I threw it into reverse and I was going to smash our way out and the crowd is getting closer with their sticks and rocks and then Jericho arrived and jumped in. The Brits' Albanian interpreter was

all bloody, so we said, "Hey, can we help you out?" And he said, in perfect British English, "No, I'm okay, mate." The crowd pulled a guy out of his eighteen-wheeler cab and beat him up. Zim was ducked down and almost in tears. He thought he was dead, he'd seen so many people get killed before. The British pointed the weapons from the armored carriers into the crowd and prepared to shoot. They finally suppressed this thing by talking the crowd down. It was scary as hell.[104]

As Chief Warrant Officer Mike Guay summed up his experience,

It was quite something; it gave me an opportunity to see what damage occurred in-theater, how widespread it was, and the conditions of the people. That was quite an eye opener. It makes you reflect back home how lucky we are, especially when you hear people complain and you think back and say, "Boy, we have it good." Certainly we have reason to complain sometimes, but when you take it into perspective as to what these people have gone through and how they suffer, and see how they pick themselves up and go on with life, it's quite amazing.[105]

NINE

Finger on the Pulse
Battle Group Operations, Part I

The main characteristic which distinguishes campaigns of insurgency
from other forms of war is that they are primarily concerned with the
struggle for men's minds, since only by succeeding in such a struggle with
a large enough number of people can the rule of law be undermined and
constitutional institutions overthrown. Violence may play a greater or
lesser part in the campaign, but it should be used very largely in support
of ideas. In a conventional war the reverse is more usually the case and
propaganda is normally deployed in support of armed might.

—FRANK KITSON, *Bunch of Five* (1977)

The Coyote and Griffon helicopter squadrons operated all over
the Multinational Brigade (Center): these units functioned as the
"eyes and ears" of the brigade as well as in a rapid reaction capacity. The third Canadian unit deployed to operate in MNB (Center)
was a mechanized infantry battle group. The battle group, which
brought a whole host of unique capabilities to the table, occupied a specific area of operations and in the process became intimately familiar with its inhabitants. In this way the battle group
also provided "eyes and ears," albeit in a different way. The battle
group became responsible for coordinating humanitarian assistance
and reconstruction in addition to its ongoing armed stabilization
and deterrence roles. In doing so, it also demonstrated that forces
trained and equipped for medium-intensity warfare were flexible enough to handle operations across the spectrum of conflict.

The next two chapters detail battle group operations for two
rotations. The first battle group, deployed from June to November

1999, was based on 1st Battalion, Princess Patricia's Canadian Light Infantry and included sub-units from the Lord Strathcona's Horse (Royal Canadians) and 1 Combat Engineer Regiment (1 CER). It was commanded by Lt. Col. Steven Bryan, who was subsequently replaced by Lt. Col. Shane Brennan. The Operation Kinetic Roto 1 battle group, which arrived in December 1999, was based on 1st Battalion, the Royal Canadian Regiment (1 RCR), commanded by Lt. Col. Bruce Pennington. It included armored support provided by the Royal Canadian Dragoons. Chapter 9 addresses the organization of the battle group in Operation Kinetic and the nature of the Drenica Valley and its inhabitants, as well as the stabilization operations conducted by the 1 PPCLI battle group in the Drenica Valley and its vicinity throughout 1999. Chapter 10 covers operations by the 1 RCR battle group, particularly those conducted in Mitrovica in the spring of 2000.

Anatomy of a Battle Group

In Canadian doctrine a battle group consists of a mechanized infantry battalion of eight hundred to nine hundred troops and more than sixty armored personnel carriers, a tank squadron of eighteen tanks, and combat engineering support. During a conventional war the battle group usually works within the framework of a brigade group: a brigade group has the equivalent of three battle groups, plus a recce squadron, an artillery regiment, a combat engineer squadron, a tactical helicopter squadron, and a service battalion. In conventional war the three infantry companies in a battle group take and hold ground by closing with and destroying enemy forces. To support this action the battle group retains a variety of supporting sub-units: some of these capabilities, like the tanks, for example, are attached to the battle group temporarily from their parent units by the brigade group, while other capabilities are integral to the battle group (that is, "organic") to help keep the battle group as self-sufficient as possible at the lowest level of command.

The fluctuating missions for Kosovo and the fact that the battle group was working under the control of a British brigade group meant that Canadian planners had to craft a unit that could handle combat tasks as well as stabilization tasks, while at the same time allowing the unit to be somewhat self-sustaining. This was no mean feat. In the case of Operation Kinetic (+), we have seen that a modified battle group was generated in National Defence headquarters under political duress. Consequently the structure of the Op Kinetic (+) battle group was unique to the Kosovo operation, and its constituent parts require some explanation.

The fundamental organization of an infantry battalion includes a battalion headquarters, three rifle companies, a combat support company, and an administration company. A rifle company usually consists of three platoons and a company headquarters for a total of 120 troops and fourteen armored personnel carriers (APCs). For Operation Kinetic (+) there were two rifle companies, each with three platoons. The platoons, which usually had three sections of ten soldiers, were reduced to three eight-person sections.

The infantry platoons for Kosovo were equipped with C-7 5.56mm assault rifles, C-9 light machine guns (also 5.56mm), C-6 medium machine guns (7.62mm), M-72 light antitank weapons, and 84mm Carl Gustav short-range antitank rockets. Night vision equipment was generally available. Just before deployment 1 PPCLI received the 40mm M-203 grenade launcher attachment for a number of C-7 assault rifles.

The platoons in Kosovo were equipped with an uparmored Grizzly armored vehicle general purpose (AVGP), which was a training vehicle acquired in the late 1970s. The Grizzly is a six-wheeled chassis that has .50-cal and 7.62mm machine guns mounted in the turret. The commander and driver, section leader (a sergeant), and five riflemen make up one of three sections in the platoon: the platoon leader (a lieutenant) has a dedicated vehicle in which his or her platoon headquarters is mounted. The company commander (a major) has two Grizzly vehicles, a Bison APC ambulance, their crews, and a company staff, plus a number of medium and light wheeled logistics vehicles (2.5-ton MLVW and 5/4-ton LSVW). The Bison is an eight-wheeled APC: its ambulance variant has a medical detachment.

A combat support company generally contains four capabilities: in Kosovo, the tank troop was added to form what Lt. Col.

Steve Bryan called his "Porcupine" company. The combat support company, however, was cut back to 169 people despite the addition of 18 Strathconas from the tank troop.

Normally a battle group would retain an eighteen-tank squadron to provide maneuver and shock capabilities. The tank troop deployed on Kinetic (+) consisted of five Leopard C1 main battle tanks, each with a four-person crew and equipped with a 105mm L-7 gun plus two C-6 machine guns. These vehicles were originally purchased in 1979, but the demise of several tank replacement programs over the course of fifteen years forced the army to continue using the Leopard C1. The Leopard Life Extension (LLE) project consisted of four modules: a thermal sight, improved ordnance, appliqué armor, and an electric turret control system. David Collenette, then minister of national defence, visited the Strathconas on an exercise at CFB Suffield while they were preparing to deploy for Operation Cobra, a NATO forced-entry plan for Bosnia in 1995. When asked, the troopers told Collenette that they needed better armor. In one of his last acts as minister he approved the LLE. The LLE modules gave the C1 appliqué (add-on) armor and improved ammunition for the main armament but did not include a thermal imaging sight. Leopard C1s did, however, retain their original but aging Belgian SABCA laser fire control system and a low-light television (LLTV) night fighting system.[1] Warrant Officer Steve Brown of the Royal Canadian Dragoons noted that even NATO allies in Kosovo "didn't recognize the vehicles as Leopards because of the add-on armor," which was useful for deception purposes.[2]

The battle group included a reconnaissance platoon that had six Coyote recce vehicles. Unlike the vehicles in the recce squadron, the battle group's Coyotes were not equipped with the sensor mast system, though they retained the tripod sensors. The recce platoon, like its brigade-level counterparts, screens the battle group's movements, provides traffic control, and reports on enemy movements.

The mortar platoon provides indirect fire support to the battle group out to five kilometers and works intimately with the longer-range artillery, which is usually a brigade group resource.

In Kosovo the mortar platoon consisted of forty people (vice fifty-five) and had six L-16 81mm mortars and their crews, each with a Bison APC, plus two fire control parties. The Bisons were to have a fixed firing point in the back so that the mortars could be fired from the vehicle. This variant, called the Wolf, was supposed to be made available for Op Kinetic (+) but ultimately was not deployed. The mortars had to be dismounted from the vehicle to fire, which limited their ability to "shoot and scoot."[3]

The anti-armor platoon was equipped with the TOW under armor (TUA) vehicle, equipment that was acquired in the late 1980s. TOW, which stands for tube-launched, optically tracked, wire-guided, fires an antitank missile. In Canadian service TOW missiles came in two variants: the B and the F. TOW is the top-attack variant, which allows the warhead to detonate above an enemy tank, above a point where the tank armor is thinner. The launcher itself is mounted in a turret that is also equipped with a C-6 machine gun and a thermal imaging sight. The chassis was a standard M-113A2 tracked APC. The anti-armor platoon in Kosovo was initially equipped with six TUA vehicles or three two-vehicle sections; Roto 1 equipped it with eight TUA vehicles. Although not integral to anti-armor platoon, the battle group also had between eighteen and twenty-four ERYX antitank missiles, which had a range of six hundred meters. In theory TOW engages at long range, ERYX in the middle, and the Carl Gustav in close, to form a layered antitank defense for the battle group.[4]

Two organizations provided the battle group with mobility, countermobility, and construction capabilities: Pioneers and combat engineers. The Pioneer platoon is a part of the combat support company, while combat engineers are usually a brigade resource temporarily tasked to support the battle group. In the case of Op Kinetic (+) the battle group retained its Pioneer platoon and was augmented with an enlarged combat engineer troop.

Pioneers, according to Warrant Officer Rick Duncan of the Royal Canadian Regiment, are generally "larger, more mature soldiers because of the intensity of the physical labor necessary. If something needs to be humped, size is a factor." Pioneers are capable of entrenching; doing demolitions, obstacle construction, and mine warfare; and assessing nuclear, biological, and chemical warfare threats. Warrant Officer Drago Ranisavljevic of 1 PPCLI explains that "the engineers have heavy equipment which we don't have: they do heavy bridging, large obstacle construction, and major defensive digging."[5] In effect combat engineers have more extensive training in depth in all areas, while the Pioneers have a specialized skills set. Pioneer platoon consisted of twenty-nine personnel, in three sections of eight plus a platoon officer. It was mounted in four M-113A2 tracked APCs that had been modified with a dozer blade and an HP-1 hydraulic system capable of powering augers, chainsaws, jackhammers, and impact wrenches.[6]

Instead of a field squadron 1 CER augmented the first battle group with what amounted to a robust combat engineer troop. It included an engineer planning cell embedded in the battle group headquarters, one field troop consisting of four combat engineer sections, and an armored engineer section. This forty-eight-person sub-unit was equipped with four M-113A2 tracked APC engineering variants (similar to the Pioneers' M-113A2s in terms of capabilities), a Beaver armored vehicle launched bridge (AVLB) based on a Leopard tank chassis, and two Badger armored engineer vehicles, also based on the Leopard hull. The Badgers were equipped with a hydraulic scoop and dozer blade. Bulldozers, dump trucks, and bridging equipment were all left back in Canada and supplied as necessary by the British brigade group. The combat engineer troop also retained the services of two mine countermeasures vehicles. Maj. Chris Stec of 1 CER: "There is the Nyala, which is South African and has a high chassis and very large tires. You do the Hail Mary and drive it into a mined area: the chassis absorbs the shock. Three months into the mission we got the Aardvark half-track mini-flail, something like the Sherman Crab from World War II. It's mainly for antipersonnel mines."[7]

The battle group also included an expanded intelligence section, as well as a sniper section: both organizations were augmented from time to time by other specialized personnel. The sniper section, according to one member, was prepared for "dismounted close reconnaissance, intimate direct fire in a general war setting by selective destruction of key targets. When it became a more internal security type operation, our role was more covert. This is just semantics—we were not covert: we were simply there and no one noticed. Our role was direct and close surveillance in both rural and urban settings. Most of the time we worked for the battle group, which had specific questions about specific areas. We're an information-gathering asset." The sniper section carried the C-7 assault rifle and the C-3 7.62mm sniper rifle. Night vision, laser binoculars, encrypted communications, digital video cameras, and GPS were some of the other equipment carried during Op Kinetic (+). Eventually a single Barrett .50-cal sniper rifle was deployed well into the first tour: the Barrett could engage targets out to two kilometers.[8]

Finally, the brains and sinews. The battle group headquarters included some sixty-eight people divided into traditional G-staff positions: personnel, intelligence, operations, logistics, civil-military cooperation (CIMIC), and signals. It also included the engineer advisor from 1 CER and an armored advisor (who acted as a senior liaison officer) from the Lord Strathcona's Horse. There was also a military police section for discipline, criminal investigations, and movement control. The headquarters itself was mobile and was mounted in Grizzlies, Bisons, and M-113A2s. The support company included a maintenance platoon with a Taurus armored recovery vehicle (ARV); a transport platoon with ten-ton HLVW trucks, including pods for moving fuel; a medical platoon with Bison ambulances; and several flying (that is, mobile, not airborne) kitchens.[9]

In essence, a battle group is an extremely versatile organization, even when it is cut down from nine hundred to six hundred personnel. The employment of the Canadian 1 PPCLI and 1 RCR battle groups in Kosovo demonstrated this repeatedly.

Deploying A Company, 1 PPCLI

1 PPCLI's A Company, led by Maj. Stu Sharpe, deployed to Kosovo at the end of June 1999, well ahead of the rest of the battle group. There were several reasons for this phased deployment. Lt. Col. Steve Bryan:

Priština was just eating up soldiers. Rollo's brigade plus 5 (UK) Airmobile Brigade were all in there. The British wanted to get 5 (UK) Brigade out; they had done their job getting us through the Kačanic defile and had other tasks. There was increased pressure to try and get Canadian troops into the MNB (Center) [area of operations] as quickly as possible. We were in a position to airlift one of our companies and the Grizzly was airportable, so we said we could do it in fourteen days. I went over on a reconnaissance and met with Rollo and Ward. Rollo determined that his main problem areas were Priština and then the Crescent, the areas with the ethnic mix. The Drenica Valley was a special case because it was 100 percent [Kosovar] Albanian and it needed to be covered off with forces that were more mobile than the dismounted light infantry from 5 (UK) Brigade. I was anxious about getting the Drenica AOR. As I learned in Bosnia, if you deal with only one ethnic group you only get one picture of the problem. You need a balanced picture of the problem and [to] be forced to think about the complexities of it. It was helpful in my mind to provide the unit with a broader experience as opposed to the more narrow Drenica Valley. So I was anxious to preserve part of the AOR which was multiethnic.[10]

Maj. Jerry Walsh was the battle group operations officer:

There was a real push by the British to get the company on the ground immediately. Part of it was that the British wanted the force to be built up rapidly, but Canada also wanted a flag on the map, on the multinational map. [Canada] wasn't going to get it until there was a force that occupied a piece of ground. Recce Squadron, let's face it, did a fantastic job. They were a very mobile force, they were pushed into different areas to fill the gaps, they had the technology. But until Canada had something firmly in place, occupying the ground, they weren't going to get the flag. DFAIT was giving a push, Colonel Ward was giving a push, and Lieutenant Colonel Bryan concurred and said we had the capability to push in a lead company. There were different pressures at different levels. I spoke personally to Colonel Ward and he said, "Jerry, this is something we need to do. We have to get this one on the road." [The Drenica Valley] was a nice piece of ground. Glogovac wasn't as big as

Priština or Mitrovica, but Glogovac was the heartland. Glogovac is where they needed somebody with the eyes and ears to be, to be sending accurate and detailed information on the movements of not only the people but [the UÇK]. It's a big crossroads. There was also a bit of "flash" involved at [the Priština airport], one of the most high-profile pieces of ground in Kosovo: the first forces that a visitor would see in addition to the [RAF Regiment] stationed at the airport would be the Canadians, actively patrolling and dominating the heights. We didn't want to be in sleepy hollow. The Drenica Valley, where we were assigned in the end, was the key to understanding the entire Kosovo issue. That was evident to the commander of 4 (UK) Brigade and the commander of KFOR, who came out to visit us on numerous occasions. . . . [If the situation was going to get out of control] the first indicators would show themselves in the Drenica Valley.[11]

Maj. Stu Sharpe had been preparing for weeks and the operation was finally on:

We did a lot of live fire getting ready to deploy. It was comparable, in my experience, to my Germany days [with 4 Canadian Mechanized Brigade Group]. We were ready. We had a long weekend, and I was called by the duty officer and told to turn on CBC *Newsworld*, so I turn it on and there's the minister announcing that 1 PPCLI will be flown into Kosovo within sixty days. Then we were told we would be going in in fourteen days, so Lieutenant Colonel Bryan brought us into the loop and told us that the Brits needed infantry. After two days it was on. The whole company went, all the vehicles, all of the Grizzlies went by Antonov [rented transport aircraft]. I think it was five to seven chalks of Antonovs to take all the vehicles and the sea containers for the company. We zeroed our weapons, did a last confirmatory live fire, and uparmored the vehicles. We then got the troops on an Airbus and flew out of Edmonton to [CFB] Trenton, where the Airbus promptly broke down. We spent the night sleeping on the floor. Then we flew to Zagreb for refueling. The anxiety level in the aircraft as we flew over was high, you could see it, you could almost cut the air with a knife. We landed in Skopje and [were] met on the tarmac by Colonel Ward and then staged through Sveti Nikole. A Company deployed north on 4 July and I went into Magura to link up with the CO of the Gurkhas. The problem that the British had was that they had a very large area, and they had to fill the [power] vacuum quickly to prevent the UCK from taking over. They also had to rotate troops out; the Paras were leaving and they were trying to get the Royal Irish Regiment in, and in all the adjustments they couldn't lose coverage of the MNB (Center) AOR. The British were overextended and needed infantry now. The situation was changing on an hourly basis. We had at least one civilian mine strike per day, right when the area was handed over to me. That dropped off significantly as the people became more aware and educated. The UCK soldiers were out there disarming the mines and probably stockpiling them too: they never turned them in to NATO. Then there were two Gurkha engineers killed, down in the area we called "Cluster Alley," where lots of cluster bombs had been dropped. Now by this point the Serbs are gone. Our job was to implement the undertaking and demilitarize the UCK. I learned that the [Drenica Valley] was the heartland of the UCK and that their headquarters was up there. We got some maps of the old UCK and VJ positions: we used them to identify the high mine-threat areas. I didn't realize how little I knew. I thought what I had was what everybody else had. Meanwhile, down in Lipljan and Priština, everybody had all sorts of gory details about where they were operating and what was going on, but the Drenica Valley was one big black hole.[12]

And not only for A Company: on 14 July three Albanian men crawled out from a cave nearly dead from starvation, not realizing the war was over.[13]

Battle Group Area of Operations

The Canadian battle group AOR covered two distinct areas: the Drenica Valley and the critical areas surrounding the Priština airport to the north and south. The Drenica Valley is shaped like a V: it is one kilometer wide in the south and opens up to seven kilometers wide halfway up, at Glogovac. The top of the V, near

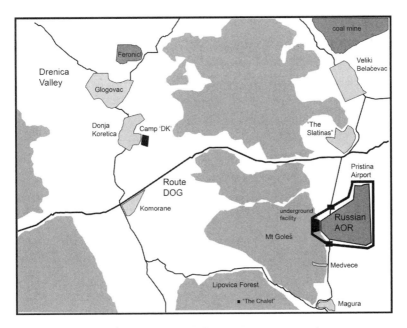

FIG. 13. The southern Drenica Valley, Priština airport, and environs.

Delice, is about twelve kilometers wide. The main east-west road across Kosovo, Route Dog, bisects the Drenica Valley about one-third of the way up. The bottom third is rugged, hilly, and can be accessed only by dirt roads, which quickly become washboardlike with rain. The northern two-thirds are open farming land, while the hills are heavily wooded. The north-south road extends from the town of Komorane on Route Dog to the town of Glogovac, to Delice, Srbica, and ultimately Mitrovica. Glogovac is the economic center of the Drenica Valley and is dominated by the massive Feronikl plant. There are numerous small settlements in the hills west of Glogovac. To the east there are smaller numbers of more isolated villages, and then over the hills is the mining complex servicing the Obilić power stations. This area, between Obilić and Kosovo Polje, is volatile: the towns of Crkvena Vodice, Ade, and Grabovac seethe with ethnic hatred, as do Veliki Belaćevac and the Slatinas: Velika Slatina and Mala Slatina, which are next to the all-important Route Dog.

Going south from the Slatinas along the base of Mount Goleš is the Priština airport, the underground complex occupied by the Russians, and the fish farm near Radavo, which is on the other side of the runways. The road runs past Medvece, a mixed Roma-Albanian village, and then Magura, which hosts another mine nestled in the southwest corner of Mount Goleš. Deep in the countryside beyond Magura is the Lipovica Forest, which brings us back to the base of the Drenica Valley.

Ethnically, the Drenica Valley is nearly 100 percent Kosovar Albanian. Lt. Col. Steve Bryan noted that "there were many layers of clans and families within the valley. So on the surface it was very quiet and simple, but you kind of scratch away the veneer and it was an interesting piece of ground. It was complex."[14] The Jashari family, massacred back in 1998, was from the north of the valley, and the first armed resistance against the VJ and MUP started in that locale.

In many ways the Drenica Valley is considered by many to be the heartland of the UÇK, and consequently there was substantial fighting in the area in 1998–99. Maj. Jerry Walsh was the operations officer for the Patricia's battle group: "The VJ pushed down [from the north of the valley] and the people retreated to the hills, not to the refugee camps. These camps in the hills were very austere, but some held between seven and ten thousand people. The families would live in the hills and the men would come down into the valley at night to fight. The VJ just wreaked havoc in the villages, firing at everything. The UCK would also lift the VJ's land mines and then re-lay them, draw the VJ onto them, and then fire."[15]

The use of land mines was extensive in the Drenica Valley, which in part shaped the nature of operations there for the UÇK and then KFOR. Capt. Don Senft, the Strathcona's armored advisor to the battle group: "The VJ was a mechanized force and stuck to the roads and stayed down in the valleys with their tanks and APCs. The UCK ran the mountaintops and laid mines all along the bases of the hills. Then the VJ laid mines along the UCK mines to stop the UCK from coming down at night and pissing them off, then the UCK laid mines on the hillsides to deter VJ from coming up to get them. If you took a mine map of the AOR, 90 percent of the mines are in two neat ribbons north to south."[16]

Capt. Mason Stalker was a platoon commander with A Company: "[The AOR] was an interesting area, especially in the south. We were able to get a tour [from former UÇK members] because this is where most of the battles were fought. You go through the valleys in helicopters and you can see homes built [deep] in the valleys, and there are caves to provide protection from air attack. The mines were just brutal. One area we called 'Cluster Alley.' VJ vehicles were moving through there [and got hit]. There was even a Serb [MiG 29] that was shot down into the forest. There was a lot of destroyed equipment."[17]

Warrant Officer Lee Humphrey, from the mortar platoon, was based out of Komorane:

This was the area where the UCK and the locals went into the mountains to hide. There was a great deal of indirect fire devastation, but the VJ didn't really make it south past Komorane. The VJ just sat back and bombed the crap out of them: they knew that if they went south [below Route Dog] they were going to lose. You can't take mounted forces down there. We later saw the UCK trench line, and it would have been devastating to the forces conducting a dismounted assault. They had done everything we had been taught about laying out a defensive position. It was well documented, it was well concealed, all interlocking fields of fire. There were withdrawal routes, there were rally points. A lot of people that got involved with the UCK after the war were the people that didn't do the fighting. They were like the old French Resistance, you know, *everybody* was in the French Resistance at the *end* of the war. . . . We saw it as the tour went on. Well-respected war heroes were pushed aside by the bureaucrats and the popular guys who didn't do a lot of fighting but did a lot of hiding. They had some solid fighters, they were brave, but a lot of them died during the war. The less brave rear echelon types came forward to lead the UCK after the bombing and the withdrawals. This was the origin of the splinter groups: you could see the infighting beginning, the power struggles.[18]

The area to the east of the Drenica Valley was the edge of what KFOR called the Crescent, which was an arc of Kosovar Serb–dominated villages and towns, some of which were of mixed ethnicity and some of which were 100 percent Kosovar Serb. Maj. David Corbould, B Company commander: "[The Obilić and Kosovo Polje *opštinas*] were very politically sensitive and had Albanians and Serbians in there. The British had a tank squadron in Obilić, and the headquarters of the Irish Guards battle group in Kosovo Polje, which was politically sensitive and of historical significance. There was a lot of tension between the communities there. There was a large Serb enclave in the town, similarly with Obilić, a large mix of Kosovar Serbians and Kosovar Albanians. Same with Cuculjaga, southeast of Magura. Kuzmin was Serbian with some Roma."[19]

B Company also had to deal with the complexities of the Priština airport, better known as the APOD (aerial point of debarkation). The B Company AOR was split by the presence of the Russian AOR. The Russians occupied the underground facilities beneath Mount Goleš and controlled the north-south road from Magura to Route Dog. Given the continuing political problems of having Russian forces operating as part of KFOR and their resistance to KFOR HQ direction, it was left up to the Canadian contingent and the RAF regiment squadron to observe their "allies" and contain any problems that might trigger rash behavior.[20]

The UÇK in the Drenica Valley and Environs

When the Patricia's battle group established itself in the assigned area of operations, there were several UÇK groups still in place throughout the area. As discussed in previous chapters, the UÇK's structure and nature varied considerably and were the subject of some speculation. Some NATO members had deployed special operations forces to advise UÇK groups during the air campaign, and these personnel were able to act as liaison officers when KFOR arrived. It is important to understand that the UÇK itself was not KFOR's enemy. As with any postwar end game, however, the KFOR leadership anticipated that not all UÇK fighters would want to go along with the undertaking and understood that not all groups were under effective central command, as they would have been in a traditional army. Consequently specialist personnel in MNB (Center) HQ and at the battle group worked quickly to build up a picture of the UÇK groups in the Canadian AOR and determine their intentions. The groundwork developed early on was critical to the successful efforts of both the Patricia's battle group and the Royal Canadian Regiment battle group to implement UÇK demilitarization and transformation, which in turn reduced the level of potential violence that could be directed at the Kosovar Serbs, Kosovar Albanians, and KFOR.

When the Patricia's battle group deployed to the Drenica Valley in July and August 1999, the UÇK was in the process of turning over its weapons to the secure weapons storage sites and proceeding to the designated assembly areas for registration. This was to be completed by 20 August. By K + 90, or 19 September, the UÇK was supposed to be transformed into the TMK, the Kosovo Protection Corps. No UÇK insignia, uniforms, or military training were permitted by the undertaking, which had been signed by Hašim Thaçi, the commander in chief of the UÇK.

The battle group was confronted with several overlapping problems, only one of which was UÇK compliance. The consolidation of power by competing Kosovar Albanian political entities had the potential to turn into a civil war. In the process of this consolidation, political elements would most likely use a variety of methods to get public support: intimidation would predominate, not speeches. Such moves posed a challenge to the authority vested in KFOR to maintain a secure and stable environment. KFOR and the UN Mission in Kosovo (UNMIK) could not carry out their mandate if KFOR had its power undermined by a parallel power or powers.

The primary political divisions had many names and even more acronyms, but the two competing leaders were Ibrahim Rugova and Hašim Thaçi. Rugova led the so-called shadow government of Kosovo, which essentially was the LDK or Democratic League of Kosovo. The armed elements of the LDK, the Freedom Army of Kosovo (FARK), had been incorporated into the UÇK in the past. The opposing faction was the Thaçi-led provisional government of Kosovo (PGOK), which later became the Democratic Party of Kosovo (the PDK). At the same time, however, Thaçi was the commander in chief of the UÇK, and Agim Çeku was the chief of staff: this gave PGOK an edge over Rugova if he tried to consolidate power, since the FARK had been subsumed into the UÇK and the UÇK leadership loyal to Thaçi would keep it that way. A proposed interim government would ultimately, in theory, combine the PGOK/PDK and the shadow government/LDK into one entity with two coalitions of political parties. The Kosovar Serbs and the Roma would also be included, again in theory. To the Kosovar Albanian leaders the UÇK logically was the Army of Kosovo in waiting. The problem of course was that Kosovo was not an independent country and remained a province of Serbia.[21]

The UÇK's Drenica Operational Zone (OZ) was Thaçi territory, pure and simple, and thus contained a number of units or entities that were part of the political drama being played out in the fall of 1999. The battle group was in fact dealing with UÇK forces from three different UÇK operational zones: Drenica, Nerodime, and Paštrik, mostly because of the nature of the terrain and the KFOR brigade area boundaries. There were no secure weapons storage sites in the Canadian AOR: the closest was WN-1, located in Srbica in the MNB (North). There was one designated assembly area in the Canadian AOR to handle two of the UÇK brigades in the region: 114 Brigade and 113 Brigade. Keep in mind that for the UÇK forces, a brigade is more like a small light infantry battalion of fewer than a thousand men.

The 114 (Fehmi Ladrovci) Brigade had its headquarters in Srbica, just outside the Canadian AOR. It was considered to be the largest and best organized brigade in the Drenica OZ and was under tight control by the postwar OZ commanders, Shaban Shalla and Sami Lushtaku. There were three battalions (really companies), which were located in Glogovac, in an area west of Obilić, and in Srbica. There were four companies per battalion (platoon-strength each). The 114 Brigade lost two respected commanders during the war, Fehmi Lladrovci and Ilaz Kodra. When the battle group took over, Nuredin Lushtaku was the commander: he was the cousin of the OZ commander and is believed to have been one of the founders of the UÇK, which included three members of the Jashari family

(Tahip, Adem, and Hamze), Sylejman Selimi, and the Lushtaku family.[22] Sami Lushtaku was considered to be "absolutely friggin' whacko, a complete psycho" by those who studied him.[23]

The 113 (Muje Krasniqui) Brigade also belonged to the Drenica OZ. Its headquarters was in Glogovac after the ceasefire, and it commanded three "battalions": one was in the northern part of the Drenica Valley, another just outside Glogovac to the southwest, and a third was deployed well to the west, outside of the Canadian AOR. The 113 Brigade was led by a former physics professor, Hysni Shabani, who took command when the original commander, Muje Krasniqui, was killed in the fighting.[24]

During the war, the entire Drenica OZ was commanded by twenty-eight-year-old Sylejman "Sultan" Selimi, a geology student closely connected with the Jashari clan. A hard man, the "Sultan" was believed to have executed the mayor of Kosovo Polje in 1998. Apparently he politely introduced himself before shooting the man through the head. Sami Lushtaku took over the OZ when Selimi was promoted to command the (as yet unformed) National Guard.

The most mysterious unit in the Canadian AOR was 121 Brigade. It belonged to the Prizren-based Paštrik OZ, which lay in the German-commanded MNB (South) area of operations. The 121 Brigade was located at a site called the "Chalet," a nearly unmolested wartime sanctuary base that lay four or five kilometers west of Magura in the Lipovica Forest. It was commanded by Haxhi "Toppi" Shala. After extensive Canadian collection efforts, 121 Brigade was found to contain "the hardcore cats, not the basic UCK GI Joe, hardcore through and through, hardliners who saw some of the heaviest fighting and very nationalistic in their beliefs."[25] Indeed many members of the UÇK's higher command structure were former members of 121 Brigade. It was a favored formation in terms of equipment and training: 121 Brigade exclusively wore surplus Swiss army "Alpenflage" uniforms and climbing boots.

The 121 Brigade had a link to another mysterious unit, 60 Special Forces Brigade, which was based south of the Priština airport and was commanded by the Nerodime OZ in Uroševac. Each OZ had a special unit. Sixty (SF) Brigade was "called Special Forces," recalled one person, who "wouldn't equate them to being anything like our version of special forces. These were the hardcores with a nut case for a commanding officer. They probably watched too many movies, but they could look professional with flak jackets and berets. There was some fixation at brigade on this unit because its colonel would blab and it would stir the pot."[26]

The UÇK also maintained an intelligence-counterintelligence command called the ZKZ: it had sections in every brigade. Each brigade also had a military police unit, called the PU. During the transformation process ZKZ and PU personnel were used to form the (illegal) civil police force, the MRP.

To further complicate matters, word filtered through that there was a Hezbollah group moving around Kosovo, plus elements of an organization with connections to Osama bin Laden. Reports also came in that Chechen mujaheddin had a presence in the region. What their capabilities were and what they hoped to achieve no one knew, but the potential for serious trouble was very real if KFOR did not get a grip on the situation quickly.[27]

The Rest of the Battle Group Arrives

Between 21 July 1999 and 4 August the balance of the Patricia's battle group arrived in Kosovo: a tactical headquarters flew in earlier to take command of A Company and prepare for operations, while the others deployed by air and sea. Company Sgt.M. Ed Haines, B Company, who had previously served multiple tours in Cyprus, Bosnia, and Somalia:

> I thought the deployment was put together in a real rush given the fact that the Canadian Forces doesn't control its own strategic lift in most cases. The ship was hired and loaded up. We were supposed to train ship-loading parties. The ship went away and the air flow started. That was put together as best we could given the circumstances. We flew over on Tower Air, you know, the CF rented from the cheapest bidder as opposed to the standard and the flight over was basically terrible, one of the worst I've ever had. The troops, a lot of the younger guys, didn't know what to expect. Some of the older guys had an "Okay, here we go again" attitude.

As soon as they heard Tower Air, a lot of the older guys who had been on UN missions before knew exactly what was going to take place. The top down guaranteed that we would get fed on this flight, and NDHQ assured us the flight would be up to standard, but it was a rickety old 747 with a bunch of U.S. airline steward-esses from Atlanta, Georgia. Just getting a drink of water in some cases was impossible. And the meal was nonexistent. We flew over without even eating. We stopped in Gander and couldn't leave the aircraft, and then on to Paris. People were burned out. By the time we got to Skopje, people were tired, hungry, dehydrated, and then we hit the heat there of course. We couldn't even get cold water. After several hours, we got on the buses for Sveti Nikole and the ship-unloading party took off. They were just bagged.[28]

Several days later the vehicles arrived and the battle group deployed to Krivolak training area to shoot the weapons. Three days later it was off to the area of operations. A number of serious problems surfaced during this time. Capt. Don Senft:

The Leopards went over by ship, a terrible Ukrainian ship. It was an absolute nightmare. When the guys opened up the tanks for the first time in Greece, they found a lighter with Russian writing on it on the floor of one of the turrets. Clearly the crew or who-ever had been poking around in all of the vehicles, because some of the locks were cut off, like on the Coyotes. Recce platoon leader Clint Dawson had sealed his vehicles from the inside and they were cut. So whoever was doing it was poking around our latest, great-est vehicles. They had them for a month so they could do anything they wanted with them.[29]

The Strathcona's tank troop leader, Lt. Mike Onieu, was not impressed: "The tanks were really in disarray. The troops did an excellent job of sorting it out, but it was not a great way to start the tour. When they popped the hatches open, all the tools, gear, and everything was overturned. Why this was so, I don't know, but I'd like to hang somebody for it. There was a lot of essential gear missing: guns and tools."[30]

Cpl. Scott Marshall, a driver with the Strathcona's tank troop:

We didn't even believe we'd be going. Five tanks? That's insane. At least a squadron. So we worked up for three weeks: we didn't even have the add-on armor. It was welded on at Long Point in Montreal before putting the tanks on the ship. The entire battle group then went over on one airplane! We were shoulder to shoulder. Tower Air: not exactly a luxury airline. We got a sandwich, maybe. It was eighteen hours. They were nice enough to open the doors on the tarmac in Paris: Nobody get off! Wave! Hi! Landed in Skopje and just died from the heat. We were on a bus for Greece, Thessaloniki. It was all a blur. We got in at midnight. It was 50 [degrees Celsius, 120 degrees Fahrenheit] and humid and couldn't sleep. Then we unloaded the tanks during the day and it was even hotter! We got British low-bed trucks from a combined NATO tank delivery unit to get them up to Macedonia. At least we didn't have any rioting. Just graffiti: Death to NATO. The Royal Canadian Dragoons sent five tanks top of the line from Petawawa to Montreal for us and something happened at Long Point. Not all of the RCD tanks that were sent were loaded for us. The tanks, we found, had no machine guns: no coax[ial machine guns], no small arms, no radios, nothing. Then we had a navigation problem: there were no maps to get us to the camp in Macedonia. So one of the guys downloaded a map on his personal computer and we used that. We unloaded the tanks at KTA, but nobody was there! The TOW under armor guys were in the same boat. I was the highest-ranking corporal there: everybody else were troopers and privates. No crew commanders and one maintainer with the ARV [armored recovery vehicle]. A Patricia captain showed up the next day to let us know what was going on. We then got our rifles and bullets, finally. Then the battle group left and we waited for the low beds. This time it was Italians, who spoke about five words of English. Nobody spoke Italian. So we don't know if they're here for us or if they're lost. No clue. I watched the guys try to do communication with porno mags and apples. It was hilarious. We were trying to show the Italians where we were on this map: they had no clue. They just nodded. We followed Canadian logistics trucks, but the low beds kept breaking down. But we made the border. By a quirk of fate we met another Canadian column. They took off; the Italians missed it and drove right through Priština! We ended up missing a turn out in the middle of nowhere near Serbia, with the Leopards on Italian transports driven by these weird Italians. Then a tire blew. We had to get the Leopard off the truck to change the tire. We got that done and then we met a Canadian Iltis [jeep]: "Where the hell are we and how do we find the camp?" We finally made it in.[31]

The anti-armor platoon was not faring well. Warrant Officer Hubert Kenny:

> We didn't take our own TUAs. Four came from 2 RCR in Gagetown and the others from the Van Doos in Valcartier. I didn't take my own TUAs, which was a bit of a pain. They had no weapons, there were no C-6 machine guns. Parts of the launcher system were not even in the vehicles! All we had was a carrier with a whole bunch of kit that couldn't be used. We had plenty of ammo, more than we'd seen in Canada, but no way to fire it. I had ninety missiles backloaded, and each vehicle had twelve. We were supposed to have the F version of the TOW [top attack], but we weren't even sure if those arrived. The troops' morale was not exactly the highest. The missile guidance system, the heart of the system: we had none. We had to deploy to the camp in Kosovo without being able to fire missiles. It was very, very embarrassing.[32]

To make matters worse, only four of the six TUAs even arrived on the ship: two were still back at the base in Valcartier. Across the board the battle group was missing or unable to use any of its C-6 machine guns: the bolts were at CFB Trenton. They had been removed from all the weapons provided by logisticians from 3 Canadian Support Group at Long Point. Close protection weapons for the armored vehicles had to be scrounged, and not enough could be found to protect all of them.[33] Despite all of the challenges encountered by the men and women of the battle group in the Kosovo operational environment, Operation Kinetic demonstrated that improvements had been made in the Canadian Army in the 1990s. Maj. Jerry Walsh:

Let's compare Kosovo to Somalia, which I was on too. Start from the soldier. What did the individual soldier have on the ground in Somalia? The bare minimum. We were bare ass in the desert and it was hot and dry. We didn't have Tilley hats [initially]. We didn't have tents. We were on foot for most of it. When I look at Kosovo, we had what we needed at the individual soldier level in short order before we deployed. Soldiers had Kevlar [frag vests], they had frags [grenades], they had night vision goggles, they had 203s. We had new C-9s. And we had up-armored vehicles. Ballistic goggles. I was getting calls from Ottawa to see what else we needed. I said we could use some laser designators for the weapons and bang! We had them off the shelf and they showed up. We were fortunate to have a group of officers that were educated, that understood a multinational environment based on their experiences in Bosnia, Croatia, Somalia, and other places. They understood where the whole Kosovo thing fit into the big picture. You had to understand the Montenegro issues, the Albanian issues, Greece, Turkey. You had to understand it all, in order to understand the Drenica Valley.[34]

Operating Environment

Once on the ground, the men and women of the Patricia's battle group were confronted with a unique environment, unique even to those who had served in the Balkans before. Capt. Mason Stalker:

We got into Glogovac and [patrolled up near the Feronikl plant]. It had been bombed. Six days before we got there, there had been a mine strike right there: the car and debris were still there. There was a hole in the ground. The British explained they were patrolling this route and a Lada was following them. They went over the mine, and then the Lada blew up. Can you imagine that? This is the first story you hear when you get to your town, your AOR? All we could do was say "okay" and take notes so that we could brief the soldiers and ensure they were prepared for what they needed to do.[35]

Sgt. Richard Walsh, battle group headquarters:

There was at least six generations of hatred there. These people beat to death a seventy-year-old man at a rally because he is a Serb.

When questioned about it at a press conference, some Albanian reporter goes, "He's a Serb, he deserved it." We found during our deployment that by the time the kids are five, they're tainted. You talk to them, they talk about Serbs and then motion as though they are cutting their throats. Kids are born and taught "Serbs are bad" or "Albanians are bad" instead of the boogeyman. You could see it in some of the schools where we were trying to get the Romas and the Albanian students [together]. The kids didn't like each other. It didn't matter that they were kids and they all like soccer and everything else. Just the simple fact that the kids was Roma or Albanian meant they couldn't get along.[36]

It took some time to sort out support. Cpl. Barb Hays was a company clerk with A Company and was a crucial contributor to the smooth operation of the CIMIC cell:

We had 110 guys [in Glogovac], and for a month and a half there was no mail. It didn't come until a week before the battle group got here, and half of that was for the other companies which hadn't arrived. There was no phone for four weeks, and we weren't allowed to use 408 Squadron's. We finally got satellite phones, but we spent more time going "Are you there? Did I lose you?" It was very frustrating. I had to beg, borrow, and promise favors to get a barber kit with a set of clippers from the National Support Element [NSE] so our guys could cut their hair. We were even in the dark about the NSE . . . we almost were working independently. The Strats did a great job: they knew they would have to work on their own. I loaded my truck up with the idea I may not get resupply for three months, which was good because we didn't—not the things I need. Like paper.[37]

Cpl. Brent Richards, B Company:

We went in with nearly nothing and for the first bit we were sleeping in four-man tents on rocks. The engineers made a parking lot, but the rocks were like boulders, fist size, and that's under the tents. We didn't have showers for the longest time, so we did bird baths. It was a hard go: 40 degrees [104 Fahrenheit] and no shower. There were incidents. One night in Magura there was a fight between the people downtown: one of them threw a grenade and we got the quick reaction force [QRF] in there. The grenade drops right in front of them and everyone was scrambling to get down. It turns out that buddy was so drunk he didn't pull the pin. He just threw the grenade, but there was a mad panic to call in the explosives ordnance disposal [EOD]. It was crazy. We cordoned off pretty much the whole town that night and detained people. The center of our camp had an empty pool in it, so we put them in there. It was just booze, nothing political. Then the [Romas] had their house burned. The locals threatened to do this and then they actually did it. This was right after we arrived; we didn't know what was going on yet. [Fortunately] there were no firefights.[38]

Trooper Melissa Dubbs, a Leopard gunner from the Strathconas' tank troop:

What sticks out in my mind was the lifestyle these people have over there. I definitely have a greater appreciation for living in Canada and being Canadian. I was very proud to start with. But then you go over there and it really bothered me. Kids running around with no shoes on and stuff like that, people were sick. I remember this one little boy had a huge gash across his head because he got bit by a dog and it was all infected and gross. He had a sort of bandage, but it was awful. It was dirty, the electricity was bad, there were outhouses. There's nothing for them in the country. There was no welfare and poor health care.[39]

Capt. Jeff Gill, administration officer for A Company, was on his first tour ever: "There was nothing in place, no administrative structure. There was no electricity, no running water. The people's basic needs were provided by the humanitarian agencies that were just dumping loads of flour, wheat, or whatever in central locations. The transportation system was off the rails, they had nothing, no source of income. It was a society that had collapsed. About 75 percent of the structures were either damaged or totally destroyed. Living conditions were poor."[40]

There were environmental hazards as well. Maj. David Corbould:

The air quality was shit. There was coal dust, there was the power plant, just puking out crap into the air to the point where there was smog everywhere. We were breathing it in. Initially there was no monitoring, but we identified right away that it was a problem. All we had, though, was a pre-med tech come out [to Magura] and say, "Yeah, you know, you guys should get checked out." Well, we knew that. Then another pre-med tech comes from the rear party, the NSE, and said, "You know, this air is really bad. You should get it checked." I said, "Up your butt." Then a team from *Ottawa* comes out to check whether or not we are complying environmentally, you know, have the oil drip pans under the vehicles and so on. And we're still waiting for word on air quality tests, but these guys are more concerned about drip pans. And they tell us, "You know, you guys should get that air checked out." Thanks for letting us know! We were waiting four months later.[41]

Warrant Officer Lee Humphrey from the mortar platoon had served in the Balkans with UNPROFOR, and the contrast was notable:

The soldiers were really proud of what they were doing. They could see the difference as time progressed. I think the part that made that easier was that the people we were dealing with were very different from Bosnians, Serbs, and Croatians. These people worked their asses off. All they seemed to want when we first got there was material, and they didn't expect us to do anything for them. They were the hardest working people I've ever come across. They were rebuilding their houses, one at a time. They'd all get together in their town and rebuild a house. And then move on. The animosity we'd seen in Croatia wasn't there. Every day we'd drive down the roads around Komorane and the kids would swarm up. For four straight months they were still waving like mad and screaming "NATO, NATO, NATO!" It was a really different atmosphere, and that kept morale up a lot.[42]

Down in Magura, Company Sgt.M. Ed Haines had another perspective:

Morale was an issue, and it was a difficult one. It wasn't like we were getting bombs dropped on us or we were engaged in firefights or anything, so it wasn't to that level. Past missions and times where soldiers had additional stress levels put on them, we didn't have to face that. It was the anticipation of that all the time, but it never materialized. So there was no emotional release. We were trying to stay up and prepared for it, and that was the line that was being pushed. Maybe the [situation] was misread at a higher level and [they should have dropped it down a notch]. We didn't have to be at that heightened level all of the time, to have soldiers on the edge. I mean, a soldier has to be able to react to a situation, but it seemed that every patrol, every mission we were going out on was "Beware of this, beware of that" and when it didn't materialize, the disappointment came in. . . . From the soldier's point of view, he would see orders coming in from battalion. He couldn't see past those [levels]. There was a lack of sleep and long hours [because of the leave situation]. Fourteen days off in four and half months is grinding and grueling, and it wore people down.[43]

The situation in the portion of the AOR that lay outside the Drenica Valley and had mixed communities was smoldering. Capt. Don Senft:

The moment the [Kosovar] Albanians came back it was payback time. [We had to] protect the limited number of [Kosovar] Serbs that were dumb enough to stick around when all these pissed off people came roaring back from their one-hundred-kilometer walks through the mountains. I went in there thinking it was going to be a Bosnia scenario, where there would be Moslems on the short end of the stick with no equipment, no weapons, and the big bad Serb guys pushing them around. But the [Kosovar] Albanians came back. It was the Balkans mentality: the fact that their house had been burned to the ground and grandpa put down the well to make the place unlivable, and the [Kosovar] Serb house next door just recently vacated because the [Kosovar] Serb saw the [Kosovar] Albanian coming back and took off; it still has a roof on it and it hasn't been burnt and the well is still serviceable. Instead of moving into that [Kosovar] Serb house, they light it on fire and then poison the damn well! So now they have nowhere to live. We ended up trying to stop them from burning down the houses and poisoning wells and from conducting grenade attacks and RPG attacks and drive-by shootings.[44]

Lt. Col. Shane Brennan: "There were no large-scale operations conducted [by the UÇK] against anyone, but individual acts of revenge and violence continued. That was always disturbing. Our assessment was that the people that were involved in any potential war crimes were not the people staying [behind in Kosovo]. They were the people that had no relatives in Serbia proper. They were too old or too young to leave. There was no retreat for them; that was their home. They were the real victims, as much as the Kosovar Albanians were victims earlier on, particularly the ones in the rural areas."[45]

Road hazards remained a problem. On one occasion members of the battle group had to report that a "local cow ran into the side of moving Grizzly. Cow injured. MPs investigated and determined that we are not at fault."[46]

1 PPCLI Battle Group Operations

Drawing on the undertaking and taking into account the MNB (Center) concepts of operations as expressed by Brigadiers Bill Rollo and Peter Pearson, Lt. Col. Steve Bryan developed with his staff the best means to accomplish the battle group's objectives in its area of operations:

My intent with the UCK was one of constructive engagement. They were not our enemy, but early on it was unclear as to what status they would have, particularly when you have different areas like the Drenica Valley and Kosovo Polje. The attitudes that the locals held towards the UCK differed in these two portions of the AOR. The only way you find out who they are and what they are interested in was by being engaged as opposed to being belligerent with them. You need to know who the players are. We also didn't know what the role of the [transformed UÇK] would be early on. It wasn't a matter of confrontation with them. There was, however, a set of KFOR rules and guidelines which the UCK had to conform to, and we sought to apply them strictly and consistently. On a number of occasions, this annoyed the local UCK leadership, but in the long run I think it served the unit well. As a result, I think we were able to extrapolate this [into other areas].

The challenge of the first two and half months was the establishment of a secure environment that would allow for institution building. There was a complete vacuum of law and order. There were no civic governments. In some cases there were shadow municipal governments that were operating with Serb acquiescence and then there were truly underground shadow governments [which didn't]. The most obvious area was education. There was a decade-old shadow education system. There were no [Kosovar] Albanian civil servants or civil governments. In other places there was, but it was suspected of organized crime infiltration: local groups of thugs dressing in police uniforms and behaving as police, demanding that you pay 50 deutsche marks to set up a stall in a local market, for example.[47]

In one case a sixty-nine-year-old woman was evicted for not paying her "rent" on a stall. MPs were brought in to confront the thugs and reinstall the vendor at the market.[48]

KFOR could secure the environment, but somebody had to apply resources to rebuild those structures so that they would remain in place over the long term:

> KFOR for the first two months had to fill the void. There was no effective UN civilian police force and no effective UN civil administration. The UN provided a [representative] to Glogovac municipality by October, but he was only one guy. My A Company commander, Maj. Stu Sharpe, essentially became the mayor of Glogovac. His job was to put in place fair and equitable solutions to local problems in order to reduce tensions but without presupposing a long-term solution. [We could not] undercut the long-term end state where there is a proper UN administration first, followed by a local administration. So we dominated the AOR through presence to discourage illegal activities. In the eastern part, we also headed off interethnic violence as well. There were instances of grenade attacks and shootings, most of which were ethnically driven instead of criminally driven.[49]

An example of problems that could arise from a lack of coordination in civil administration matters between KFOR and the UN related to who controlled what records in Glogovac, as a situation report noted:

> Representatives of UNMIK Claudia Cesare and Lawrence Truman conducted a liaison visit with A Company. . . . The purpose of the visit was to ascertain the state of the municipal archives, specifically land titles, for Glogovac. Over the course of the visit, the UNMIK personnel indicated their intention to hire locals to sort and catalog the remaining records beginning next week. This is of some concern as it will allow the local UCK to position itself as a power broker by influencing who is hired. It is recommended that UNMIK employ civilians from outside the Drenica OZ who will be less susceptible to pressure tactics by locals.[50]

In essence Lieutenant Colonel Bryan's objective was "to establish the conditions for success of the UN administration when it arrived." If the shadow government got too tight a grip in Glogovac, this would be jeopardized, "so we needed to buy the UN time. We organized garbage collection, getting fresh drinking water, adjudicating accommodations issues."[51]

Not all battle group activity was as systematic as it appears in retrospect. In many cases it was a matter of "no one's doing this, somebody has to do it, we're going to have to do something." There was substantial confusion in the AOR when nongovernmental relief organizations (NGOs) arrived and started up projects without any coordination: "Some NGOs were supportive of having us act in a coordinating role, others were not and wanted nothing to do with us. [After previous experience on other operations] we determined that we would truly dominate the NGOs."[52]

Maj. Jerry Walsh, the battle group operations officer, was involved in establishing the dispositions of the troops to assure presence:

> We had three ground holders. A Company was in the north. B Company was in the southeast and northeast and helped with keeping control of the mining areas, which was key because . . . [of Kosovar] Serb workers there and it provided power to the whole

region. Because of the division of the ground [Mount Goleš] we used mortar platoon as a mini-company to cover [Route Dog]. They were equipped with eleven Bison, were mobile, and had very experienced NCOs. It wasn't ideal, but it was workable. There was an incredible amount of traffic on that road, and we confiscated a large number of weapons. It was the underground's MSR [main service route].[53]

Major Walsh's staff determined that the initial main and supporting efforts were to develop detailed information on the UÇK and to establish as many effective civil-military cooperation (CIMIC) activities as possible to stabilize the Drenica Valley:

Our focus for the initial month was based on the time crunch. [The bulk of the battle group] came in a little late and not enough intelligence work had been done on the Drenica Valley by [KFOR]. The K + 90 deadline was approaching. We had to tell people to take off their uniforms, but we had to identify them all first. We wanted to be able to identify those leaders who we thought might not give up, the ones that might melt away and become ghosts or gang leaders. So we put a big push on for information gathering to put into [the] ISTAR [matrix]. Fortunately, Lieutenant Colonel Bryan and I had been on the ground for several weeks and we had a solid plan. By the second week in August we were functioning at 75 percent and the troops were keen. We had a good foundations to go on. 4 (UK) Brigade HQ said it was the most comprehensive package they'd seen: other battle groups came to our staff, our CIMIC staff and intelligence staff, and said, "How do you guys do it?" It was reflection of the troops on the ground and that they understood what we had to do. I could walk over to 408 Squadron and ask, "Say, can you support us with this or if you can't with a dedicated mission, could you get us some thermal imagery on the way back from another mission?" It was great.[54]

ISTAR collection priorities for the battle group were slightly different from the Coyote and Griffon squadrons. The battle group was to identify and report on

- MUP, special forces, or stay behind presence, structures, leaders, and intent
- Serb paramilitary presence, leaders, and intent
- UÇK orders of battle and boundaries
- numbers of weapons in storage sites
- noncompliance of UÇK regarding weapons caches
- UÇK attitudes toward the undertaking and KFOR
- combat indicators for a UÇK attack on KFOR
- future intentions for individual members of the UÇK regarding K + 90
- any other Albanian paramilitary structures or presence
- local government activities administered by the UÇK
- political parties, size, leaders, aims, funding, and relationship to UÇK
- organized crime groups, leaders, and intent
- local attitudes toward different political parties
- any nonattributable terrorist attacks and trends
- isolated Serb populations and threats against them
- trends in Kosovar Albanian violence against Serb population
- war crimes sites
- village profiles, amenities, infrastructures, religious sites, key personalities[55]

On the CIMIC side, Major Walsh saw efforts in this area as part of the battle for legitimacy:

> We could not have anyone exercising any type of authority over the civilian population. None whatsoever, whether it be a local politician or local party or former police force. We even had people in the community who [had] served in some capacity with the VJ and the MUP. Believe it or not, these people still existed [particularly around Kosovo Polje]. They were still around. In the [Drenica Valley] the people were coming back and things like municipal

records had to be secured, who owned what. We had to listen to one side, then the other; somebody had to make a decision because people needed somewhere to live. Major Sharpe and his people were deeply involved in that. Guys like Maj. Doug Delaney and the CIMIC guys, they were making it up as they went along. There's no doctrine. He was inventing operating procedures for international aid organizations. Fortunately Doug and I [had been] in Somalia, where we had done something similar.[56]

Capt. Todd Hisey worked in battle group operations:

Back in Canada we were getting information about Kosovo from the internet and our own intelligence sources. We also put together biographies on all of the key players, and we found out they were all linked back to the Drenica Valley. We figured out early on that the valley was a key area. Whatever happened in Kosovo emanated out of this area, and there were all sorts of family ties. It was a shock when we got there and [KFOR HQ and MNB (Center) HQ] did not grasp what was going on in there or what the significance of the valley was. So the entire battle group really became an intelligence battalion. Every soldier was a collector on the ground, gathering as much information as possible about the UCK, its leaders and capabilities. We were on the MSRs all the time. We set up vehicle checkpoints and tracked their movements as best we could. We pushed the companies into their areas, and they got to know the local people and main players. We made our presence known. CIMIC started to work on the "hearts and minds" aspects. These capabilities all overlapped: CIMIC, psychological operations, public affairs and [other capabilities].[57]

Psychological operations or PSYOPS is a term that has negative connotations of secrecy and manipulation dating back to the Vietnam era. Since then, a more inclusive and accurate term, information operations, has succeeded PSYOPS. Civil-military cooperation, or CIMIC, is a similar instance in which the definition of CIMIC is based entirely on how the user of the term wants to define it. During Kosovo, however, Canadian doctrine and its terminology were in flux, so older terms were sometimes mixed with new ones.

Information operations are designed to prevent adversaries or potential adversaries from manipulating information inputs and thus deceiving friendly forces in order to prevent them from achieving their objectives. They are also designed to prevent adversaries from interfering with the provision of information to a population that friendly forces want to influence. Information operations are also intended to prevent hostile media from manipulating Canadian policy makers with information or images that do not provide context for an event and thus prevent friendly forces from achieving their objectives.

CIMIC operations, on the other hand, are designed to develop a relationship between the friendly forces and a civilian population. This relationship has several uses. First, it is beneficial to both parties in that living conditions for the population are improved and the population is less inclined to be immediately hostile or oppose operations in its area. Second, it is a source of information that assists the friendly force in achieving its objectives. Third, CIMIC operations build a bridge between the force and the people and will have long-term positive effects economically, politically, and militarily.

Information operations, information collection through ISTAR, and CIMIC all overlapped to produce a synergy that permitted the ground forces (e.g., the battle group's sub-units) to be employed more efficiently and effectively in pursuit of KFOR objectives. The basic battle group concept of operations did not radically change when Lt. Col. Shane Brennan later took over as battle group commander.[58]

In the case of the Patricia's battle group, operations planners were confronted with a series of problems brought on by the hasty entry into Kosovo and the fluid and tense situation. Capt. Todd Hisey:

> Our primary concern was getting our message out: stability and a secure environment. This is where the British missed it big time. The initial PSYOPS product was produced in two languages in the same media: Serbo-Croatian and Albanian. When the Albanians saw anything with Serbo-Croatian on it, they'd just throw it away. So I go to brigade and tell them I'm in a predominantly

Albanian AOR, but I have some Serbs too. Do not give me stuff in both languages. Well, we had to go and produce our own stuff using PowerPoint and graphics packages. For example, when we read patrol reports we found out that the various age groups liked different things. The little kids liked *Tom and Jerry*, while the teenagers liked the Spice Girls. So we pulled these pictures off the internet and added them to our topics. We started a mine and UXO campaign where the message was "Don't touch mines of explosives!" Tom and Jerry were used to say these things in Albanian. Then, for example, we needed to tell everyone that the power was going to be off for some time while repairs were made. Same thing. When we started to take down illegal MRP [police] stations, we put up posters and handed out flyers with a big NATO flag stating that this was an unauthorized station and that NATO and the UN were the only authorities in Kosovo. Our patrols would hand out leaflets and we would tell everybody exactly what was going on. It was totally coordinated. I had some experience in Bosnia [with SFOR] and I drew on that. It wasn't black propaganda. It was legitimate means of communicating. We had incidents where a twelve-year-old girl had her legs blown off because her parents sent her to gather wood in an area loaded with cluster bombs. While they stood on the road! Kids even were making homemade bombs because that's what they learned in school. We also had an anti–plastic gun campaign [because they looked too real].[59]

All information operations had to be carefully coordinated so that military operations did not inadvertently disprove the messages sent out in the information operations campaigns. There were problems coordinating with other agencies, however:

We started our own newspaper in Albanian. The stuff that the OSCE and the UN [were] producing that was distributed in our area was not helping us. Their headlines were full of negative information. They [the UN] were unable to see themselves in a good light. So we took the positive stuff from the UN, mixed it with our information on what was going on in our area and then distributed it, after input from the company commanders in Magura and Glogovac so we could make it even more area-specific. We were able to measure the effects. My understanding was that the reception was positive by the general populace. In Bosnia the locals used it as toilet paper. In Kosovo some people came from far away every week just to get the paper and read it. A Company in Glogovac put up a local message board near the HQ. We could see people reading it and nodding their heads. We gave them facts, where their own Kosovar Albanian newspapers were misleading them: whatever the slant of the paper's owner was. We would put up an unbiased information product to [counteract that].[60]

The battle group information operations personnel were able to provide feedback to KFOR efforts in Priština. For example, the locals would not tune in to NATO/UN radio stations because everything was in both languages. The Kosovar Albanian media thought it was a joke. The listeners were mostly the KFOR soldiers, not the locals.[61]

CIMIC operations were critical to the battle group's efforts to exert control over the Drenica Valley. A Company reported early on that "the UCK appear to be maintaining the appearance of compliance and cooperation while working behind the scenes to challenge our authority indirectly through special interest groups, businessmen, etc."[62] The battle group CIMIC cell was, however, completely ad hoc in that all of its personnel were "double hatted" from other critical jobs. The combat support company commander was the battle group CIMIC officer, and the CIMIC clerk was the A Company clerk. The projects cell was the battle group combat engineer advisor, while the CIMIC warrant officer was the operations warrant officer. The two CIMIC teams, Team 1 (Stimlje/Lipljan) and Team 2 (Glogovac/Kosovo Polje), were the battle group forward observation officer/forward air controller (FOO/FAC) teams.[63] Maj. Doug Delaney, of the combat support company:

I got over there and the CO said, "You're going to handle CIMIC." So I put together an estimate. I needed space, a phone, internet access, and a clerk. My first operations estimate put together what had to be done in terms of rebuilding, civil infrastructure, municipal government, all of the stuff to make things run. Beyond that, I had no guidance. It was all implicit. I was asked by the chief of the

Land Staff, "What did you think of the standard operating procedures [SOPs] and doctrine?" and I told him, "I don't know, I didn't read them." I had some experience with this before [in Somalia]. I gave myself a month to figure out what needed to be done, the end of August. We needed things that could win the hearts and minds, things that you know had to be done so people could make it through the winter: shelter, food, medical supplies. Nobody had a grip on what the humanitarian organizations were doing, the least of which was UNHCR or ECHO, which was supposed to be the central coordinating agency for all this stuff. We had to gather information on them too; we didn't know how those organizations worked. We were skeptical about the [NGOs], particularly what you see in the news when there's a crisis.[64]

Brigitte Deschenes was with the Canadian International Development Agency (CIDA): "My gosh, in Kosovo there were so many NGOs. I remember when I first arrived there were only a few of the internationals that went in right behind KFOR. Within a week and half we already had 50 NGOs, and within three weeks there were about 200. It was a free-for-all, I mean, Kosovo has two million people in it and is the size of Algonquin Park, and then there [were] 350 NGOs. It was scary. And all of them wanted to work in Priština because it's more visible."[65]

Maj. Doug Delaney: "I needed money. UNHCR was dependent on contributing governments and I couldn't control them. The British had DFID, and the Americans had USAID, but we had no connections to them. I remembered we had CIDA. I called a number in Ottawa and asked them if they had anybody in Kosovo. And they told me, "Yeah, Steve Salewicz is there," and they gave me a number. Of course, there were no phones working, no cell coverage. I knew Care Canada was located downtown in Priština, so I went downtown a couple of times to look for him."[66]

Steven Salewicz from CIDA: "I went in with a knapsack and a checkbook. It was a bizarre situation. I saw USAID go by, I saw DFID with their big four-by-fours and I'm like, 'Hey, stop! Canada's here!' I felt like a poor cousin. Not in terms of resources: I had my checkbook and it was bigger than theirs in many cases, but I had no resources. I was using a CARE vehicle to get around. I was tapping into everybody else's resources."[67]

While he was walking down the street in Priština, a jeep drove up. Major Delaney emerged and asked Salewicz if he was from CIDA. When he replied in the affirmative, Delaney threw him in the back and lit out immediately for Glogovac: "I knew he had to be Canadian when I saw him wearing the Mountain Equipment Co-op stuff."[68]

"Doug was frustrated by the lack of UNMIK presence in the Drenica Valley," according to Salewicz, "and he had to fill that vacuum."[69] Delaney was convinced that "the UNHCR was very ineffective in organizing things," and there were problems that could affect battle group operations:

> UNHCR subcontracted everything: they were big and had a pile of money. So, they needed a food distributor for Glogovac and they had Action against Hunger do it, who were quite good really. They had a comprehensive program for delivery using the Mother Teresa Society. The problem was that every aid organization just rushed into the area and everybody picked a little town, and then you'd have the Swiss Disaster Committee, and then you'd have Islamic Relief, and then Canada's Center for International Studies and Cooperation [CECI], and on and on. They had no boundaries like we do in the military. Then they'd try and deliver it to all of the villages without a central distribution point. The Swiss developed their plan without consulting anybody and wouldn't change. Then CECI came in with a reroofing plan, but then the Swiss Agency for Development and Cooperation [SDC] rebuilt the roofs they wanted to, while CECI and Islamic Relief had emergency shelters. This caused dissension: "Why is *he* getting a new roof and I'm not?" UNHCR did not coordinate any of this. Then there were the locals who were not getting fuel, so they were cutting down trees. We were looking at another Bosnia deforestation problem, so we had to regulate woodcutting since there was no municipal government to do that. Plenty of wood from the NGOs for roofs, none for fuel.[70]

Then the UÇK shadow government attempted to assert control and interfered with relief and reconstruction activity. Most NGOs were unsure as to how to handle this. Brigitte Deschenes:

> It's very hard, especially if you are from Canada and you go in with a big heart and really want to help, and if you don't look at the situation carefully you get manipulated, and if you don't understand the politics and the powers behind them, at the very least the [local] power struggles, you know, you can get used. A lot of NGOs go in with the greatest of intentions but get used. Having somebody like Doug Delaney and [his CIMIC cell] could help stop that. We were in contact on a daily basis. [Steve Salewicz] would phone him up and say, "I've got this report from an NGO: what's the real story?" and he'd call back and say, "They're pulling your leg," and give me an assessment about what was going on. He would get into heated discussions with [NGOs] when they weren't performing well or giving enough attention to the [Drenica Valley area].[71]

In essence the battle group CIMIC cell would tell NGOs that if they didn't want to coordinate with the Canadians, then find another area. This approach worked very well, but it included some British aid organizations, which caused some consternation at brigade level. Major Delaney:

> They were, to their credit, right there at the beginning, and they had the tap running full bore. I never asked them for money, [but] they funded a couple of things. There was a difference between immediate emergency relief and long-term development. The British wanted to control everything and wanted us to submit everything to the G-5 at brigade. But I told them that this was a national issue, particularly when we're dealing with Canadian agencies. We're not going to do anything that is incongruous with what the KFOR commander is looking for, but you should bear in mind that these are nationally funded projects and we will not be seeking your approval for anything. And it worked. They threw a dinner for me when I left, and all I had basically done was tell them the whole time to fuck off.[72]

That led to unrealized ambitions:

It worked out well—we saw that things were working in our area. We knew we were on to something between Steve, myself, [Wendy] Gilmour, and a few of the other Canadians. We gave priority to CECI and the other Canadian NGOs when we were using battle group resources to move things. We almost took UNHCR out of the picture. We didn't get sucked into their bureaucracy. From a national perspective we loved the idea of having CECI or CARE Canada deliver stuff with their maple leafs on their vehicles because the people identified with this. They don't see the difference between a Canadian soldier and a Canadian NGO: they see the same thing. There were so many maple leafs around. Then Steve and me bumped into an RCMP guy downtown. He had a Cyprus ribbon on, and it turned out he had been in the airborne regiment there in 1974. The RCMP were complaining about their Inmarsat phone not working, so we worked on that and we were short on cops, so they were ready to send me some RCMP guys in exchange. It was shut down at the last second and they were sent to Mitrovica because they spoke French and that was the French Brigade AOR. It's too bad: Canadian cops, Canadian air workers, Canadian soldiers. It would have been great![73]

The centerpiece for the battle group CIMIC effort was the ability to bring together information. Cpl. Barb Hays:

Databases were the solution, keeping track of everybody. The information we were getting from the patrols alone was huge, but there was no setup. [When A Company arrived] the Brits had set up patrol files. But there was no real way to keep a running watch on activity unless you pulled them out all the time. The hardest part was putting together the database without knowing exactly what the battalion would want. So Corporal Leeward, Major Sharpe, and myself got a pretty good system going and we added a digital camera. We taught the platoons how to use it and what we wanted. We were lucky these guys were computer literate and understand how it works. The purpose of the database was to sort reports on what towns in the AOR had the most urgent requirements and then we prioritized them. Some had electricity but no water. Some had water but no electricity. We were able to give an integrated report to battle group about what needed to be done and where. It was updated daily. It would flow from us to CIMIC. Major Delaney did the CIMIC mass coordination of the NGOs. We gave our database to the other NGOs as a basis to expand because we might move out of a particular area. Just keeping track of the NGOs was difficult. There were certain NGOs who were working some towns but would not visit other towns, so we kept track of that too. We kept a list of the head men of all the little towns. We needed to know which head man got along with which head man so we could make sure there was enough coverage. If we didn't, there would be problems; the inputs to the database came from the guys patrolling, they would talk to the locals. They were there every day. The intelligence and recce guys were doing their own things. We could pick up information on, say, UCK activities and they would pick up information on CIMIC needs and we exchanged it.[74]

In some cases CIDA money was used to subcontract construction assistance, which in turn had a dual purpose:

When the [UÇK] was demobilized and the TMK was coming into existence, Doug Delaney started engaging TMK members at twenty deutsche marks a day, which was more than they had been getting. They weren't showing up on time, but once they were getting twenty DM, by God they showed up. It may not have been five hundred guys, but there were twenty-five or so local people. I'd rather have them working instead of being stagnant somewhere, plotting, working on their weapons caches. It was extra manpower and they had skills. [This was bending the DFAIT rules regarding impartiality,] but it kept the TMK guys out of this whole brooding mode. The pressures that DFAIT put on CIDA make sense maybe in a global [scheme of things.] You can't do a huge project that is seen as political and not think about repercussions for Canada, [but this was small and useful].[75]

The Pioneer platoon was the CIMIC cell's "muscle." Warrant Officer Drago Ranisavljevic was involved in Operation Comfort.[76] Ranisavljevic commented that

for the first two weeks we were in the country, we were kept close to the camp, with the priority being local defense. After that, we went to Magura. That was our first project introduction to the population. B Company was occupying the old police station and community center. We had to set that up for them so they could live there. We had to remove part of the playground and a bunch of destroyed stuff, but we didn't want to cut the kids off from playing. This could cause local problems and relations were going down the tubes pretty quickly. So we built a playground for them and things improved. CIMIC then took more priority. We also helped out the former UCK as employers and teachers. We taught the local militia engineering skills: how to use hydraulic equipment, construction techniques. So we were all over the place. We had ex-UCK [now TMK] teams and we had them compete: the guys from Komorane would go to the north of the AOR to work and the guys from up there came south. They rebuilt infrastructure or improved it. We worked alongside them. This was important. We just didn't want to show up and occupy the buildings the MUP had and start running patrols and so on: they'd associate us with an occupation force. It balanced out the vehicle checkpoints and those activities.

An example was a school we worked on. It was near Trpeza, an area that was totally devastated. There had been fighting back and forth. Mortar platoon found it. We did a recce with the engineers. We asked the locals how long it was going to take to reroof the school: "Well, probably forever." We went over and we started the roof. We had three-quarters of it almost done in about three days and then due to lack of resources we had to come back and finish it two weeks later. Put in seventeen hundred square meters of roof. A news organization out of Toronto came by, and one guy was a civil engineer by trade. He shook his head. "I wish I had a work crew like you guys back in Canada." A lot of houses needed reroofing because winter was coming. We took our local builders and had our platoon rotate through the priority houses. We got all these guys who normally put the roofs up in Kosovo to teach the whole platoon how to do it. The structures are different in the Balkans, the materials are different. We had to adapt to the Balkans architectural environment. Six of our guys and four locals could put a roof on, shingles and everything, in two days. We nearly reroofed the entire AOR. Power: there was another challenge. The main water supply pumping station needs power, but in order to crank up the water, you had to juice the power lines. They were in the woods and overgrown. We would end up getting airlifted out there with chainsaws to clear the lines. That's several kilometers. The locals saw us everywhere: it paid in spades. They would even talk to us after a while. I had an advantage: I was born in Croatia. I never had problems. The translators at times were a bit miffed, I think, because the locals would try to get something across to us when we were doing construction jobs, and the translators didn't have the technical background or basic understanding of how things worked so the locals would start cursing in one language. I'd shake my head and I'd answer them back and they'd look at me. The translators would throw their hands up in exasperation, and we'd have it out one on one and get the job done.[77]

Cpl. Barb Hays:

It was really interesting watching the change. When we rolled into Glogovac, the place was deserted. It was a mess. It was a slum. Then people started feeling comfortable about coming back. Within two months, you could see the difference. The market just exploded. Before, there was nothing, you had one or two stalls with farmers or people bringing in some goods and within two months it boomed to over forty. And another month after that it got bigger. You could see it once we got the schools fixed up. The way people dress. It was the smaller places further out we were worried about because of the spotty NGO coverage. It was frustrating. Our patrols out there were getting pretty emotional when "their" town was ignored. Even our medic, Corporal Brown, got out and patrolled with his Bison ambulance. They did amazing work.[78]

In time Major Delaney was concerned about developing a culture of dependency with aid. Indeed Major Corbould's B Company noted that the towns of Veliko Bare and Krajiste in his area "are relatively well off compared to the villages in the north. My concern with these villages is the likelihood of crime and extortion. . . . There is evidence of it now and it will only increase as businesses and families become more financially secure. Will continue to monitor these villages. . . . As a note, patrol reports indicate that cars entering the villages have new TV's, VCR's and satellite dishes. Any requests for aid should be closely reviewed."[79]

Demining was an issue that required attention. Maj. Chris Stec, Royal Canadian Engineers:

> Canadian policy in itself does not allow us to do general mining clearance. We can only do it in support of the operation where it is essential and whenever it assists in saving lives. If there was a mine incident, that would be okay, but general clearance, no. There was a disconnect, there was a need to give the battle group CO his boundaries. We had a problem before in Rwanda where the CO of the field ambulance wanted us to do a lot of stuff, but we didn't have the resources and he didn't understand. In Kosovo NDHQ told us to use the British parameters, but that didn't work because we were field engineers and the Brits had specialist EOD people. Who handles belligerent mines and who handles NATO UXO from the air campaign? The cluster bombs, for example. Within two weeks two British engineers were killed. They were Gurkhas who picked up cluster munitions, and they didn't know what they were doing. It could have been our people. We needed to know the specs on NATO ordnance and where it was dropped. Nobody would answer those questions. We couldn't get that information. The CO tried to get it, but somebody told him it was UK eyes only and couldn't be released to him! The irony was that the officer commanding the EOD squadron had been an exchange officer at our engineering school. We got the information from his second in command when he was on leave, and we gave it to our mapping and charting establishment people who made maps, which we then distributed to the battle group. I also developed a

relationship with the embryonic UN Mine Action Coordination Center: there was a Canadian lieutenant colonel from KFOR HQ who knew the people there, so I forged a relationship and got information from them. We found out that the UN would not recognize military mine clearance! They go over the ground inch by inch, we blow a lane and have different procedures. So we would task the UN mine clearance teams: one of them was even Canadian sponsored. So they could cover off areas that we didn't have the resources to get to.[80]

Another important task that the battle group had to deal with immediately involved support to the International Criminal Tribunal for the Former Yugoslavia (ICTY) and its ongoing investigations into war crimes. The Drenica Valley was a focal point for ICTY activity throughout the Patricia's battle group deployment. Initial attentions were directed at the Feronikl plant. Lt. Col. Steve Bryan:

> There was this big smelter outside of Glogovac. We had heard rumors from the locals about what it was used for by the MUP, but we had no idea if these stories were true or not. It was used as an assembly area for the MUP and VJ. The locals will tell you that they left a couple of days before the NATO bombing campaign and were not there when NATO bombed [the plant]. [We heard] it had been used to incinerate dead bodies. Yet there were a series of mass graves two or three kilometers away. We provided logistic support for the exhumations. Some of these folks had been in the ground for two or three months. It was hot, nasty work for soldiers. [But I wanted presence] in that area. The fellow who ran the place told us people were looting and he wanted to use his own armed guards. We couldn't allow that: informal policing. So we set up Coyotes nearby with all the radars and thermal imagery with a section on standby, and sure enough we caught a bunch of looters. This got around in town that we were watching and it increased our credibility.[81]

Capt. Don Senft, in his role as liaison officer, observed ICTY proceedings related to Feronikl and vicinity:

The Serbs were smart enough to hide all of their stuff in power stations, factories, and mines: NATO [airpower] sought them out wherever they were, and this damaged the infrastructure. I learned from the locals that NATO's targeting was three days slow. The Serbs hid all their artillery pieces and some of their tanks in the Feronikl plant. They [apparently] used it as a torture center and used the big ovens for melting coke to actually dispose of the bodies. We then had the [ICTY] come through. . . . We had all-Albanian villages in the AOR, so the Serbs focused their slaughter in the area. There were mass graves in the hills. [We think] they were used as human shields while the bombing was going on, and when they left they just murdered them in a bunch of irrigation ditches up there. There were eleven mass grave sites in our AOR, and while we were there the FBI and RCMP recovered twenty-seven hundred bodies. [The ICTY] only looked at the ones that had forty or more people buried in them. Every time you went to a village, however, they could lead you to a spot where five or six people from that village had been killed and dumped into a hole, but [the ICTY] didn't have the manpower to deal with all that stuff. There were hundreds of those graves. We didn't have enough engineer coverage to prove the ground [because of mines], so we couldn't dig all the people up.

We put patrols into the back country area to hopefully find more graves. [The ICTY] Belgians and FBI showed up and we provided security. They had their own tents. The engineers would clear the site using the Badger AEV, plow the site, the tents would get set up. It was a pretty clinical process. It stunk to high heaven. They had a thing called a body bucket, like a big steel stretcher. They would take the body and the goop out of the ditch and put it in that, split the skull or the chest to get the bullets, take the clothes off and put them in a clear plastic bag and put the clothes on display, so that somebody might be able to recognize them. The bag and the pile of goo that used to be buddy had a number on it. But the Serbs were smart and about 70 percent of the graves that we visited, they actually had the people switch clothes. The locals would say, "That's my husband's shirt, but those aren't his pants, and his shoes are over there." Only seven hundred were positively identified;

the rest were miscellaneous piles of goop: the Serbs put the guy in a black bag, stuck him in the hole, poured lime on him, and engineers would pile dirt over them. They even booby-trapped all the mass grave sites. There were mines found in every one of them.[82]

The troops in Maj. Stu Sharpe's company were dealing with war crimes scenes from the start of their deployment. The push was on from the local population because they were concerned that decomposition would render the bodies unrecognizable for identification and reburial purposes.[83] Major Sharpe:

A Company had most of the mass grave sites: there were about fifty different sites that the ICTY investigated. Some of course had only one or two bodies. The first one we did was up in St[aro] Cikatovo, right under the power pylon. It had about seventy-odd bodies, individual graves, fairly shallow. These were people who had been killed throughout that area and then brought in and buried there. The company task was usually at the section level. It was access control. Get the media to the proper public affairs people, keep the locals from walking around. It was treated like a crime scene site. The stench was just horrific. You could smell it downwind. [At this site] these were all soldiers. The investigators took witness statements. The toughest thing for the troops was the stench. Some of them didn't like the emotional side of all this, families coming through, ladies passing out, women wailing and so on. The stench, you never get used to it. It's in your clothes and you have to get rid of it. The forensic guys were very proud of their craft and wanted to show it off, but nobody wanted to go see the gory details. Our soldiers stayed on the perimeter.

We buried one young lad up there we nicknamed "double tap." We saw that the body hadn't been claimed and nobody knew if he was Serb or Albanian. Nobody was going to touch him. The dogs were getting him, and in the end 3 Platoon volunteers, myself, and the CSM [company sergeant major] dug a hole and buried him. By the time we did that, his head was gone.

I was concerned about the welfare of the troops. I had to make a tough call up at a big massacre site in Vrboche. The Serbs came in from three different directions, the V J from one and the M U P from another. They got in there and killed a lot of people. The locals buried the bodies, and then got away: they'd come back at night and then leave in the morning. One of our interpreters lost family members in this one: his father, brother, and most of his cousins. There were twenty-three bodies here, nineteen there. As soon as the I C T Y broke the soil, the locals wanted the bodies back. They didn't want the U N playing around. They knew who was in each hole, they wanted to bury them properly. There was one individual in the town who was quite vocal and it concerned the I C T Y. They wanted a sentry: it's night, no lights, wild dogs everywhere. Again, the stench was overwhelming. I got a section up there. This went on for weeks. There were bodies in a drainage ditch: many were not claimed. What did all this mean? It was part of stability, closure for the locals. It helped in our relationship with them. We collected information from them and passed it to the I C T Y and they would go out with engineers or pioneers.

Regarding Feronikl, we heard that ten people from Poklek were taken there and then thrown in the smelter. The problem with that theory was that the smelter was turned off. There were no workers to run it and it would take several days to get it running. We had no physical evidence that would support claims that people were tortured, buried, or disposed of there. However, similar things may have happened elsewhere and the story got around. Or it may have happened a while back. I don't want to play down any of the torture, but proving it was not easy. Clearly there were a lot of people killed and there was a lot of destruction.[84]

Capt. Mason Stalker:

We found a trench system and it was full of bodies. They were civilians, shot in the head and pushed in and covered with sand. We didn't know it was there at first because of the bushes. We were fifty meters away and didn't even know. The Serbs had pushed old dead cows and debris on top. Our senses were heightened after that. They even tried to hide what they'd done by putting [massacred civilians] within an existing cemetery. The I C T Y guys would show up and do the autopsy in the tents. The disturbing thing was the number of people who stopped to watch all of this. They'd sit down at the side like it was T V.[85]

Cpl. Barb Hays:

3 Platoon worked very closely with the gravesite manning and providing overnight security. It was eerie. Anybody will tell you about the smell. I did go out there. The guys that had done tours before knew what to expect and it was no problem. Me, I was involved with the Lockerbie terrorist attack cleanup in Scotland when I was on exchange. It didn't bother me at first. The only time it actually bothered me is while I was typing out the British patrol reports: they were the first ones to control the area. They were gathering lists of names of families that had been killed. I spent days typing out lists of names, ages, and that. It finally got to me. There were hundreds, hundreds. But it was whole family lists, mothers, fathers, kids right down to two years old. After a day or two of doing that it was even more difficult. As a mother, it was hard to imagine all of this.[86]

A Company personnel were even approached by a man who "came by the camp with a skull in a box, stating that he wanted to confirm if it was the head of his brother. [The] man was directed to the ICTY."[87]

The battle group was involved on many occasions in crime prevention through presence. Maj. Jerry Walsh: "Both rifle companies had instances where kidnapping was deterred. I remember three teenage girls in particular who came in for full protection, and they kept a very close eye on them. In Magura I recall vividly the abduction of a girl. They went out looking for her. We increased patrols in the vicinity of the schools, set up VCPs looking for suspicious vehicles, that type of thing."[88]

Operation Grasshopper was also put into play to discourage evildoers. Capt. Todd Hisey:

We worked a lot with the Griffons from 408 Squadron and the British Pumas from 33 Squadron: strangely enough, we were Canadians flying in British helicopters flown by a Canadian on exchange, Capt. Dave Belanger. We would do everything from reconnaissance, covert insertions, VIP protection, extractions. In Op Grasshopper, you take a section of soldiers (usually Anti-Armor Platoon), throw them in a Puma, and take off around suppertime. Imagine you're driving down the road in a red Lada and all of a sudden you see a helicopter land in front of you and all of these soldiers pour out and start searching cars. And fifteen minutes later, the helicopter comes back, picks the guys up, and away you go. A helicopter VCP. It was great. Totally random. We used Op Grasshopper on all of the MSRs, dirt roads, everywhere. We found out that the randomness of it bothered smugglers, and it forced them to find alternative means of transporting weapons.[89]

Dealing with illegal policing issues was absolutely critical. Early on in the tour A Company was confronted with a situation in which "the PU refuse to abandon the old MUP building and allow [UN civilian police] to establish an office at the site. . . . This is a direct challenge to [UN Mission in Kosovo] authority and represents a significant shift in attitude."[90] Reports flowed in from local residents "that the PU are operating in the Glogovac area [and an] unconfirmed report states that two PU personnel entered the home of two men suspected of stealing a tractor and stated that if the men did not report to the local PU station, the PU would return the following day."[91]

Lt. Col. Shane Brennan:

There was no UN administration on the ground and no local civilian administration: a lot of it was Serb-dominated while it was there. Some of [the illegal police] were connected to the UCK, many were not. They set up their own parallel municipal government and police force. They were trying to fill a void and probably intimidate people as well. They obviously wanted to give a greater Albanian flavor to Kosovo immediately. They didn't achieve what they wanted to achieve. There was a [KFOR] crackdown on the illegal police: we put out a variety of different directives. It was a threat to the UN police force that was setting up. If people were detained by people imitating police, dressed in black, this was a problem. They did have uniforms, but they dressed in black to pretend they were police. When the heat was on, they wore normal clothes. These people didn't carry weapons largely, but they were using intimidation tactics, roughing people up, threatening them. This had an influence on the people. It did terrorize a lot of people.[92]

Maj. Stu Sharpe:

We had contingency plans to take down the illegal police stations. There were a number of them that we were always ready to raid and shut down. Komorane was one. We knew where the "police" were. We observed them, we had OPs that watched them, we videotaped them, we knew who was who, what cars they used. We also knew that if we took them down they would find another place to hide and we'd have to find them again. They were trying to police their population; it was very much thuglike activity, grab somebody, beat them up. They were also cleaning up collaborators, or anybody that worked with the Serbs or people that weren't liked. The term "collaborator" was used loosely, but people were abducted, people did go missing. The relatives of some of our civilian employees went missing: there was an electrician who was forced to work for the Serbs. These people just disappeared: got picked up one night and off they went. When we left, young girls were being kidnapped, probably for prostitution. The criminal element was growing. The links were there between the UCK and organized crime; [we were told] that the UCK was involved in running gas stations and collecting illegal taxes from people. You know, you want a gas station here, you can have it. How much money you got? We actually stopped a van for some reason and while he was being interrogated by the police I rifled through his logbook and receipts: all sorts of UCK receipts came out as well as scrip. When the guy goes to a gas station he hands over this piece of paper and he gets gas: it's all illegally taxed. [Instituting a clampdown undermines the legitimacy] of the structure.[93]

Inconsistent implementation of KFOR policy caused some problems. Capt. Don Senft:

The PU was the normal Eastern bloc seedy underground intimi-
dation-type police force. Once we found out where the illegal police
station or underground information posts were, we put . . . a cordon and search [operation] in and shut the place down. We made
a very visible [display] of moving in to arrest people, shut the
damn thing down, and let them know that the only police here is
NATO KFOR, none of these people have authority, their ID cards
are bogus, blah blah blah. The tanks were actively involved in that
stuff: they were the inner cordon, they would establish the traffic
cut-off and sometimes roll on to the objective with the infantry
that were going in. It was a show of force. The PU even established
a station in the Glogovac municipal building, right over top of the
civil administrator's office, directly adjacent to 113 Brigade. There
was an illegitimate self-appointed [Kosovar] Albanian civil administrator, with an illegal police force right next to the UCK HQ. We
let this stuff go to K + 90, but after that it wasn't supposed to exist.
When Gen. Klaus Reinhardt took over as KFOR commander, he
ordered theater-wide raids to shut all this illegitimate crap down.
That happened KFOR-wide, except in the French sector. The French
ignored his order and didn't raid the PU. The French were actually using uniformed PU members: they wore black coveralls,
they wore a white PU armband like our MPs wear. They called
them the Black Tigers and used them to guard their headquarters
up in Mitrovica. We don't know why they were doing this. They
thought this was a legitimate organization helping to restore them
to self-government. It caused problems because we bordered on
the French [AOR]. . . . A guy from Glogovac would be driving to
work in Mitrovica wearing his PU uniform, we'd arrest him, take
his weapon, impound his car, whereas the French would let the
guy show up and go to work guarding the French HQ![94]

Illegal policing and civil administration activities continued to
build throughout September 1999. A Company personnel noted
that "local authorities are actively gathering information on business, hotels and craftsmen" for the purposes of unauthorized tax-
ation. The local Kosovar Albanian administration continued "to
challenge KFOR authority" and retained senior administrators

who were, in fact, UÇK and MRP personnel. Indeed Izet Ibrahimi, the senior administrator, was "openly critical of international efforts" and "viewed the international community as an obstacle to his efforts." As the month wore on "the local administration is becoming increasingly militant. Town administrators are issuing eviction notices [and] in some cases are threatening to destroy buildings that were constructed without a permit." Most of this activity was supported by illegal police organizations.[95]

Other challenges, according to Warrant Officer Rick Oliver, from the battle group headquarters, flowed from this state of affairs: "There was a grenading incident in Glogovac. In a related case this person showed up at the HQ. He'd been beaten up, thumped pretty badly by the 'police.' We gave him medical treatment and got the story out of him. There was political intimidation going on. Another political party wanted to start up in Glogovac. You just don't do that in the heartland of the UCK. You just don't. These guys, they just don't have a concept of a multiparty state; they're very authoritarian. They wanted independence, but they didn't want Kosovo joining Albania."[96]

Operation Wolverine, conducted in October, was designed to secure the Glogovac MRP station and curtail illegal policing activity. Led by Capt. Erik Liebert (the A Company commander, Major Sharpe, was on leave), the operation was considered a success. A covert survey team, which included members of the sniper section, was inserted at 0100 hours to observe the target building; the outer cordon was established three minutes later. The entry was scheduled for 0640 hours. Within nine minutes the building had been secured: locked doors were forced and two MRP personnel plus two kitchen staff were detained. Although no weapons or explosives were found, there was a substantial amount of paperwork and other documents that were then examined by intelligence personnel. Follow-up measures included an information operations campaign directed at the Glogovac population, which was intended to notify them as to the purpose of the operation.[97]

Data collected during Op Wolverine was used to establish the nature and extent of other illegal policing operations in the battle group AOR. Operation Quarterback, the contingency plan from which Op Wolverine was derived, also targeted a suspected MRP "station" in Veliki Belaćevac, which was in the B Company AOR. Sgt. Richard Walsh: "We had an operation where we took down the police stations in Glogovac and Veliki Belaćevac. We knew where all the police forces were and we had photos of their hierarchy. We did that through various means. . . . The word came down from KFOR HQ: shut down the police stations. It was a well run and coordinated operation."[98]

One participant in the operation recalled that

the station in Veliki Belaćevac was different. It was a cordon and search at first. We had been observing this place for a long time. There was this guy, we called him "Speckles" because he wore this shirt with little gobs on it and reconnaissance of the place saw him there all the time: every picture I saw, he was wearing that shirt, always dressed the same way. Well, we waited. A Company took the station down [in Glogovac] early in the morning when it was still foggy. In our valley we waited for the fog to lift, and we waited until there were some people actually on the ground. We got one guy who was working for the city of Veliki Belaćevac: he was collecting information on aid and helping out the NGOs in the area. He wound up guilty by association and was busted with the rest of them. He was working the area, itemizing everything, because the Kosovar Albanians wanted restitution from the Serbs, so the aid agencies were paying people money to replace a lot of stuff. We went in: we found the town archives dating back to the 1940s or 1950s. We boxed them up. We didn't figure out at the time what the UCK wanted with them. It was a legitimacy issue, ultimately. How do you prove you were born there? How do you prove anybody died there? How do you prove your roots, your heritage? What about property ownership? Well, they have to prove that: remember, the Serbs decimated the area, and if somebody comes back from overseas and he's an ethnic Albanian who lived in Kosovo years ago and all of his family is dead, he can go to the archives and sort out what he owns. Veliki Belaćevac covered a large area.

Not to mention mineral resources: it's next to the biggest open pit coal mine in Europe.

So while we were there, we grabbed people as they showed up for work and then whisked them off. I videotaped everything, and said, "I want this, and this, and that." There was stuff tacked up all over the place. There were books and books with names, doodling, memos. As soon as I had the translator start going through it, we determined that the MRP or PU had all sorts of stuff: grenade collection from ex-UCK, a guy complaining about his missing tractor, a report of a body in a river underneath a bridge. They were actually doing low-level policing stuff. We knew they were out there doing it, we knew they were trying to subvert the system. We weren't sure if they were running a protection racket, but it sometimes looked like they were running a numbers thing. People were showing up with pieces of paper: it was like a lottery. Two guys would come in, and we had our teams watching them. They'd stand by the door, shoot the shit for a while, and wander off. It was like they were getting orders for the next shift. There was one guy who seemed to be the boss; there were others who were the muscle for the building. Nobody had a uniform. Some wore blue shirts and dark pants. They had identity cards. They were signed off by the chief of the MRP for the UCK.

The locals didn't necessarily accept the legitimacy of the MRP and PU, but a lot were farmers in the middle of nowhere and have no education and see a lot of guys dressed a little smarter, a little more cash going around, so well, okay, these guys must be in authority. So we got the guys, took the pictures, brought the documents out, and ended it. The OC was disappointed because there were no weapons. But I noticed during the surveillance that there was another bunch of guys down the street, about 250 meters away from the MRP station. It looked like they were bunking and eating there. So we went and looked and we saw this kid with a big seed bag, running away. One of the boys from B Company yells at the kid to stop: the kid drops the bag. We went into the compound and started a search. We found two AP mines, two AT fuses. Two AK-47s plus magazines, one RPG, one roll of time fuse, a box of non-electric detonators, 311 rounds of ammo, three license plates, and various UCK uniforms, posters, and personal documents. It was a family affair: four brothers, grandma, the whole bit. We found pictures of guys holding weapons with Albanian eagles carved on the butts.[99]

The materials collected during Op Quarterback provided significant insight into the provisional government structure and personalities, and KFOR was later able to exploit that information and thereby rein in extremist elements in the former UÇK. It was considered to be an intelligence coup by KFOR HQ and resulted in dramatically increased respect within the multinational force for the Canadian contingent.[100]

B Company operations had a different flavor from those conducted by A Company. Maj. David Corbould had a uniquely shaped and populated company area, which required creative use of the resources at his disposal:

> We were going to replace the British company operating south of the airport. 2 Squadron of the RAF Regiment was tasked with perimeter security and they were occupying the former MUP building in Magura: they occupied that so that the [MRP or the PU] didn't occupy it. They denied access to it. It's a perception thing with the locals. If I'm the UCK and I occupy the building, I have the authority. 2 Squadron was actively patrolling the perimeter, and they didn't have enough manpower to do anything else. The Royal Green Jackets were tied up with Lipljan, where there were grenade tossings and drive-by stuff. [Our area] was critical for anybody who wants to control all the mixed communities. . . . I had the tank troop attached. The area we had was large. I wanted to sit on the high ground outside Magura for contact and security. Magura was a key town for the regions. We took over the rec center there and based B Company from it. I had to put a permanent presence in Kuzmin, plus patrol the whole area. I also had to occupy former MUP buildings, and I also had to secure a Serb Orthodox church in Krajiste way in the south.[101]

The Gracko massacre became a factor in Major Corbould's planning:

KFOR was certainly sensitive about the criticism that was coming from Milošević and the international press after Gracko: "Now wait a second, the Serbs aren't being protected here. Serbs are on the losing end. They're the ones being attacked, so it's your problem." In addition to Gracko, there were various bombings at churches. Like the church at Veliki Belaćevac was destroyed. One corner was rubble. The church at Krajiste had been bombed: the whole steel dome was upside down and there was a lot of internal damage. We had to occupy those twenty-four and seven. We stretched people pretty thin, and communications were a problem. We had to set up an RRB just for the company net. There were problems with slag and large mines, which produced atmospheric problems. There [were] also problems with coal particles in the air.[102]

B Company's reporting shared an example of the level of distrust among the inhabitants in its AOR:

As of 01 Sep 99, problems in Plementina over schooling for Serb and Albanian children has increased the perception of fear amongst residents. The fire, started on the bridge on the morning of 02 Sep 99[,] has made the bridge non-serviceable to vehicles. . . . B Company nightly patrols in the area have indicated little activity after dark. I suspect that most incidents are instigated by the mixed residents of Plementina as that has historically been a hot spot. The residents of Hamidja simply fear the Serbs of Plementina and are afraid to go to Obilic because of its proximity. Patrols have indicated that Hamidja is essentially blacked-out during the evening and residents use dogs (tied-up) as their early warning system.[103]

The patrolling routine was exhausting for B Company personnel. Cpl. Brent Richards: "There wasn't a lot of sleep for the whole tour, particularly in the sections, you know. People weren't getting eight hours of sleep a day or anything along that line. So you come in, work from say midnight to eight out patrolling, then have breakfast, sleep for a couple of hours, get up, help build the camp, have supper, go to bed for a couple of hours, and go back out on patrol. Forty degrees plus [100+ Fahrenheit] of heat didn't help."[104]

Company Sgt.M. Ed Haines:

We were spread right out. If there is anything I could comment on it was the manpower requirements. There was a lot demanded of the platoons. Everything was sliced and cut and chopped to meet the headquarters requirements. But from the rifle company sergeant point of view when you see a headquarters that's beefed right up to the maximum with all kinds of extra people that don't do anything put push paper and you don't have enough bayonets on the ground to do the job. . . . Soldiers were working that tour, on patrol, standing vehicle checkpoints, conducting maintenance on their weapons or vehicles, feeding. By the time there was any time for rest, five to six hours within twenty-four he was out doing the same thing again. The schedule was brutal. And then the leave plan kicked in, which cut back the number of people even more. We conducted mounted and dismounted patrols every day throughout the [company] AOR.[105]

Sgt. John Devine:

It became a long tour. We were going out patrolling all the time but not experiencing anything. As commander, you have to keep your troops up in case something does happen. And the troops are getting tired because we didn't have enough manpower, really. Especially during leave. Like at the vehicle checkpoints: it was literally twelve hours on, twelve hours off. And that was your eat, shave, shower and kit, then back again for twelve hours. Sleeping was a problem: it was too hot. Even just laying on your air mattress, you'd be pouring in sweat. Patrolling around Magura: the thorn bushes were so hard they actually blew the tires right off a Grizzly. There were some incidents, though. I had an encounter with a UCK leader when the UCK was disbanded. He came into Magura for a little celebration. He was down at the bar with all of his troops and they were in uniform. I was the patrol commander at the time and told him he was being escorted out. I wanted to take his picture, and he got quite upset about that. Later I heard that there was this list that went around: apparently my name was going down on this UCK list of people never to be allowed to return to Albania! Myself and Master Corporal MacDonald made the list. So this guy is upset because I made him stand in front of the whole town of Magura while I took his picture like a criminal. He was escorted out without incident and his twenty-five to thirty soldiers complied. It was a lot different from Croatia, where they would have pulled out RPGs, or they'd lay a mine on your patrol route. We never had that problem with these people. I mean, they'd have their Slivo [plum brandy] and they get crazy and drunk, but it was different. They'd kill each other in a heartbeat. Those blood feuds apparently carry on forever until one of your generations has revenge for your family. That's very difficult to keep out. It would usually happen at night or between two or three people; there was no big firefight.[106]

Presence taskings became somewhat macabre. Company Sgt.M. Ed Haines:

We did have ops primarily in the vacated Serb churches. We manned two of them just about the entire tour. Krajiste was one, Pomazatin was the other. Both had been blown up already, and so it was just a concern that they were going to be completely destroyed. So having a soldier stand on guard on a shell of a building twenty-four hours a day was pretty difficult for the men to understand. We just kept reinforcing to them that if the Serbs were going to come back, they needed their areas, too, and were entitled to it. That was the main line, so we followed orders. It was stretching it. Especially at one church. It was quite comical. Pomazatin was in a mixed community, but the Serbs were chased out of there. It was near Kuzmin, where the Strathcona tank troop was. The locals were all Muslims. The concern was that homemade bombs made from old propane cylinders were found and there might be more. There had been some pre-clearing by the Gurkhas, but the engineers hadn't gone in yet. We didn't let our guys sleep in the building itself, [so they slept in the graveyard]. The gravestones in this orchard were immediately behind the door, and they had carvings and paintings of the people who died. There was one with an old lady, and everywhere you went the eyes followed you around. And the soldiers set up their four-man tent. We had a couple of tough old guys who didn't sleep very much at all because every time they moved around, heard a noise, or whatever, they'd turn on their flashlights to check and the old eyeballs of the lady would follow them around. There were a couple of soldiers that were bothered by it—to say the least.[107]

Then there was the Crkvena Vodica problem. Situated astride the main road between the Kosovar Albanian–dominated communities of Ade and the town of Obilić, patrols in Crkvena Vodica noted the presence of "four or five men who carry themselves with confidence. They appear fit and possess a military bearing. Suspect this may be linked to a Serbian incursion." Indeed the Crkvena Vodica "self-imposed town leader Boban Stankovic is listed on the suspected MUP/VJ list."[108] Maj. David Corbould:

We had Kosovar Albanian traffic driving between Obilić and Ade. You have guys, civilian workers or people, just driving around, down through this mixed community, with the Albanians on the high ground and the Serbs on the low ground. There was this corner store where they sold beer and stayed out on this patio to shoot the shit and have fun: talk about the old days, I guess. This vehicle drove by and tossed a grenade at the store and then tossed a second grenade about fifty meters away. There were kids playing [at] the playground nearby. Now, none of the kids were injured, but there were four minor injuries at the café. They were taken to hospital by the locals. We sent a patrol into town as part of the quick reaction, and they were faced with a very angry crowd, between fifty and hundred, max. It was now nighttime and they were telling us they wanted the road closed and they didn't want traffic coming through the town. They started putting barriers up, rocks and all that stuff. So Lt. Steve Charchuk had a crowd control problem on his hands. We sent in a translator, who was Albanian but spoke Serbian, but as soon as she showed up the crowd got very angry: some of the old ladies with sticks tried to get at the translator. The tank squadron in Obilić had one and we got him. This community was highly agitated. Everything calmed down by the morning. Petty Officer Robert Estey, one of our MPs, did an investigation, pictures, everything to show that we were doing a really good job. We told them we would handle vehicle movement and that they could take down the barriers. We didn't want this escalating into an armed barricade situation. We were in control, we will decide, not them. We make the rules.

What came out later was [that there were strangers in town]. MUP doing the policing. Steve and I had a couple of meetings with the head man: I'll provide weapons search, traffic control. What incited them, though, was when Kosovar Albanians would drive through and make the throat-cutting motion. So that afternoon Steve and I are sitting across from these people on the street. They're being good, they're talking, no problem. I have traffic control. Then an Albanian drives by, honks his horn, and does the victory sign. We thought, "Oh, great!" So I close the road. Guess what, I say, anybody leaves and they don't have ID that they live here, they're not coming back in. I want a list of all the people who live here right now and if they go out and don't have ID, they're not coming back in. I don't care what your ethnic background is. We caught somebody. We found out later it was a guy who was the brother of somebody who was part of the Obilić regional council, a Serb, who was trying to agitate things a bit. We had to contain it right away. I also had recce platoon Coyotes to overwatch the town. PO Estey and I thought this reeked of Serbs doing the [grenading]. The grenades weren't right, and AK rounds had been fired high. There was no metal from a fragmentation grenade. It could have been a stun grenade, just a boom with no damage.[109]

A challenge to KFOR authority in a critical area was therefore successfully defused. Then Hašim Thaçi visited the coal mine near Crkvena Vodica, which caught B Company by surprise:

The visit was intended to be a quiet tour of the mine, [but] the workers and the bused-in participants quickly became belligerent when my soldiers requested personnel with weapons to show their WACs [weapon authorization certificates]. . . . The crowd of four to five hundred illustrated their frustration with KFOR. As we blocked the exit routes for weapons searches, we were viewed as interfering and therefore something to be abused or hated. It is only when KFOR are doing as the crowd wishes will they show signs of goodwill. Essentially they cannot be trusted when formed in groups and their mood can change in a matter of seconds. Mr. Thaçi's bodyguards: three individuals looked and performed professionally, the remainder (eight) appeared very nervous when confronting KFOR soldiers. The effects of no crowd control training: understandably the soldiers and leaders involved in the incident experienced frustration. Actions required to control the crowd were not commonly known or understood. We have not conducted crowd control training as directed by NDHQ. If we run into a similar incident in the future, we will take a more stand-off approach [to] gathering intelligence and photographs. We must remember to conduct our [weapons] enforcement away from a crowd which may be provoked.[110]

This event highlighted a number of problems that would come back to challenge the 1 RCR battle group in the rotation that followed.

The battle group's tanks were based in B Company's area of operations. Lt. Col. Steve Bryan thought the Leopards "were, early on, extremely useful tools," though the operations officer, Maj. Jerry Walsh, explained that "we wanted a full squadron, we accepted a half-squadron, and then it was only four. We were disappointed, but the threat from the north, we believed that was real. Tanks gave us a higher standing within the brigade and within the force. It wasn't a peacekeeping operation and there was an external threat."[111] The Leopard troop "sent a message," Lieutenant Colonel Bryan said. "They patrolled the whole AOR and not just their little piece of ground, because I wanted everyone to see the tanks. That's part of credibility, and the [Leopards] run well on roads. The drivers were very experienced and squared away. If we had to move them quickly, they knew all the routes."[112]

Major Corbould's employment of the Strathcona's tank troop in his company area involved presence as well as patrolling:

I needed a permanent presence in Kuzmin because of the Serb schools. There was a nice hardstand there, a basketball court, which we put the tanks on, perfect for maintenance and changing tracks.

The Leopards were on stand-by to support the battle group, but their maintainers were always present, so that took care of Kuzmin. The tanks were on a moment's notice to move and were used to set up vehicle control points or other missions anywhere in the AOR. For example, when a political date arrived, they would increase their patrolling. Remember, we had four tanks out. Well, 121 Brigade weren't sure if we had twelve tanks or twenty tanks. The tanks worked in patrols of two, which were random in their movements. We'd also taken all identifier markings off—no call sign numbers: they couldn't tell one tank from another. It worked pretty well.[113]

Capt. Don Senft:

The tanks were used as a show of force. The tanks rolling around was a sign, a symbol of peace. The noise it makes, seeing that thing around, and knowing that a big Canadian flag is flying from it, we were a deterrent through sheer presence. They were fast, mobile, and light compared to the M-1, Challenger, or Leclerc. We could get into places that no other NATO tank could. We succeeded in deluding the UCK into how many tanks we had: I met with their key commanders on a weekly basis, and they were under the impression we had twenty-five to thirty Leopards in-theater. We clearly achieved the aim: constant presence and we were able to deter large-scale attacks and retaliation. We used them right off the bat so that people got used to seeing them around so that if they showed up at an incident and not [sic] held back, it would not be seen as an escalation of force.[114]

Lt. Mike Onieu, troop leader:

Lieutenant Colonel Bryan was a very armor-oriented kind of guy, and he was big on integrating us into all of his planning. If there was going to be an uprising somewhere, or it looked like a mass funeral was going to get out of hand with a lot of weapons involved, he'd be right there in the planning phase: "Yeah, you send the tanks, ready to go." We'd send the tanks in. After the change of command, there was more of a feeling that we were a backup contingency force. There were occasional events on Route Dog: some criminal elements somewhere on the route and then we'd go and set up vehicle checkpoints [VCPs] and wait. Sometimes we'd catch them, sometimes we wouldn't. It would always be a red Lada that was responsible for all kinds of things. There were so many red Ladas that it became symbolic of all the criminals. It was impossible: it was like looking for a red tractor. When there was ethnic tension in Kosovo Polje or Priština, we'd put out VCPs, sometimes randomly. There were some really mundane tasks like harvest over-watch: we'd park a tank in some field and watch the farmer. That was after [the Gracko massacre]. My impression was that there were problems in Kosovo Polje, but in the outlying areas there was not a lot of tension. We would show up for meetings between [the belligerents]. In theory the delegates were there to rationally talk about things and they'd go right to hell. They would pound the table: "You killed so and so," and the other guy would go, "You're a moron," and it would go right to hell.[115]

Basing the troop in Kuzmin had its advantages:

It was close to the main routes, and it was a [Kosovar] Serb town close to Kosovo Polje, and there was some concern that the [Kosovar] Serbs would be attacked, and this was a good way to eliminate that. We were also close to the church at Pomazatin. Unfortunately for us, it was us guarding the thing for a couple of weeks. We were looking at a bombed-out church. It was odd. I'm not sure how it was rationalized. It came down to fear of an Albanian attack. There was also concern that maybe the [Kosovar] Serbs would attack their own church, giving them an excuse. Commander KFOR directed that it be done. It was from high up. It stopped for a while and then we had to do it again. It went back and forth. Kuzmin was a sleepy little village of about two hundred [Kosovar] Serbs. We never saw any problem in there. The concern was that if Kosovo Polje was attacked, they would drive through Kuzmin. There were protests or riots in Kosovo Polje all the time. Warrant Mackenzie, our troop warrant, got involved in one when I was away on leave. This car came though and the crowd rocked it and hit the driver with a piece of lumber. The locals were always afraid that they would be attacked by [Kosovar Albanian] snipers from the mine's slag heaps. We would hear "They're coming tonight for sure," then we didn't buy it anymore. "Hey, you're safe with five tanks parked here; call us if things get ugly." And nothing ever did. Until the Norwegians took over from us and one of them was shot.[116]

Trooper Melissa Dubbs:

Most of the time we did foot patrols through the town. The warrant [officer] and the troops spoke to a few people regularly, went in and had coffee. There was a [Roma] family at the back of the town we checked in on. A local family kept inviting me over for dinner. The coffee, I love it. It's nice and very strong. They like our presence of the tanks, even though they made a lot of noise. Some guy had a little shop, and his stuff would rattle if we drove by too fast so he asked us to be careful. We drove by slowly and that was it. They told us they felt more secure with the tanks there. We found out that the locals liked us better than the Norwegians: we were friendly and they were not. We patrolled with the tanks all the time. We had to get used to the add-on armor: there were a few bumps in the rails and the odd bus or two, but otherwise it was okay. At night we used the NSCS [thermal imaging system], when it was working. There were two towns we were observing, [Kosovar] Serb towns. We'd switch the NSCS on and we could see pretty good, watch all the vehicles moving. Sometimes when there were negotiations we would send a call sign for overwatch as an intimidation factor.[117]

Lt. Mike Onieu:

If the [belligerents] thought we had more than we did, that was good. It definitely kept crime down around us. People really behaved themselves when we were in any given area. Nobody took pot-shots at us or anything at all. The main point of comparison was the German contingent. They had all sorts of problems. Whenever they worked an area with heavy mech, there were all sorts of problems. Priština was bad, but when we rolled the Coyotes in there and put up a mast, they back off. We had a whole bunch of cases like that: it was weird. We talked to all sorts of people [to get feedback] like, "Do you have any problem with tanks rolling around your village?" One response we got was that it was a whole lot better than the Serb tanks rolling through! I know I would be pretty upset if heavy armor had rolled across my front lawn and the smoke, dust, loudness, and road damage followed. None of these people had any problem with that. They got concerned if we *didn't* roll past them. There were people who said, "I haven't seen you in a week! Where have you been?" We never talked to anyone who said, "You guys are really pissing us off." Now, when you're talking to someone who's got tanks and weapons, you're going to say whatever they want to hear, right? I think I would.[118]

The Russian contingent based at the Mount Goleš bunker complex and the western part of Priština airport posed some special challenges to B Company. Two Squadron of the RAF Regiment could only do so much since the primary local north-south road from Magura to Velika Slatina ran through the Russian sector: B Company ran the checkpoints into this sector. Maj. David Corbould:

> The Russians came out to visit this Serb area around twelve o'clock at night. There was one of our sections returning from the Can Con Show [entertainment], and suddenly a couple of shots were fired. Sergeant Menard's section was there and had to confront [the Russians]. One Russian was at the barrier and put his weapon down and lay down on the ground right away. The other one ran off in the dark, about a hundred meters away and kept firing his weapon. Sergeant Menard got to the scene. The [Russians] were really getting out of control. They did fire blindly into the darkness. Menard yells, "Put the weapon down, put the weapon down," but the guy fired off another round, so then Menard fires a warning shot. The Russian finally put his weapon down, but he still had something in his hand. We weren't sure what it was. Sergeant Menard had the C-9 gunner cover him, moved in, and found it was a magazine. The Russian was drunk. I showed up and linked up with the MPs, and we turned these guys over to the Russian camp. Reports were that they were publicly flogged the next day in front of the Russian battalion and sent back to Russia.[119]

The situation with the Russians was disconcerting for Cpl. Brent Richards: "Every time you'd drive up to one of their checkpoints

they'd always cock their weapons even though we were KFOR."
Company Sgt.M. Ed Haines:

> We were watching the Russians as much as we were watching the
> UCK or criminal activity. Nobody really knew what was going
> on in there. There were concerns amongst the soldiers and NCO,
> along the lines of "What do we do next." [We had] to be aware of
> when the Russians got paid. They may have some loose soldiers
> running around, getting liquored up, that sort of stuff. We had a
> concern one night when a couple of Russian soldiers came in and
> our people that handled the security of a Serb enclave had seen
> these guys before. They were intoxicated and they identified a
> female in a farmhouse and they wanted to get together with her,
> so to speak. I guess the husband or father chased them away. They
> got upset and fired off some rounds. Our guys had to fire a warning
> shot to calm that situation down. There was this fish farm near the
> airfield, and we always had confrontations with them: "What are
> you doing? You're not supposed to be fishing." Fortunately none
> of that escalated.[120]

Another Russian contingent based outside of the Canadian
AOR south of Mitrovica encountered problems with former UÇK
members operating from the northern part of A Company's area.
Capt. Jeffrey Gill:

> The Russians to our north presented problems. They conducted
> patrols in our area without invitation. We made a point of get-
> ting them out of there and establishing lines between the units.
> We had to tell the locals not to be hostile towards the Russians:
> for the most part they listened. But the UCK were sniping at the
> Russians. The Russians were holding some celebration: it was for
> one of their saints or something and [they took some fire]. So we
> deployed our reconnaissance detachments to watch this hot spot.
> There was the odd shot going in there. Then one night there was
> heavy machine gun rounds going into the Russian camp and the
> same amount of fire going out. The next day, "nobody saw noth-
> ing" and the Russians weren't saying anything. We found out later
> that some ex-UCK members were still conducting training and

they had their own little range back there. We had other sources of information that confirmed this, but they were just firing on a range. It was like two separate cases. We didn't actively go in to pursue them, we didn't want to flush them out: we wanted to find out what their plans were and what their next step was. So we investigated and had other assets assist us [including TOW and Coyote] and then everything that was going on up there stopped. The local villages were Kosovar Albanian, but not all went along with the UCK: there was disproportionate distribution of humanitarian aid, depending on loyalties: it was a Hatfield-McCoy situation. The Russians only returned fire when fired upon. But then a couple of RPG rounds were fired at a Russian BTR. That raised our eyebrows.[121]

Maj. Stu Sharpe was concerned that matters could get out of hand:

The Russians were claiming they were being shot at by Albanians and recce platoon was brought in to observe, working in my area but looking into the Russian area just north of our boundary. Then I heard from UNMIK that after we left, a Russian soldier went missing for ten days and then they found him in the Glogovac area, strangled and with ten bullet holes in him. In another incident a Russian BTR-80 ran over an Albanian man, clearly a traffic accident, but the locals were just ready to [take them apart]. We almost had to start peacekeeping between the Albanians and the Russians. Nobody knew in the early days what the Russians were doing. We knew they had interests in our AOR, so we kept an eye on them.[122]

It was difficult to discern what was going on or why, but there were odd things afoot in the French-led Multinational Brigade (North):

The Russians in the French AOR had an electronic warfare [EW] collector of some kind in the camp. We had recce units watching it. Could it have been collecting on the UCK and NATO forces for the Serbs? Who knows. There were firefights all the time up there. Somebody, probably the UCK or ex-UCK was pumping rounds at the Russians. The French, of course, love those guys [the UCK], and they denied that this shooting was going on, and if it was, it was our fault. Why can't the Canadians control the UCK [on the edge of the interbrigade boundary]? So we showed them some Coyote footage of the fire going back and forth in their area of operations, and then they claimed there was no firefight![123]

The matter of UÇK transformation dominated the battle group agenda in the fall of 1999 as K + 90 day approached. The UÇK was supposed to disband, and a new, smaller, and unarmed organization called the TMK or Kosovo Protection Corps was to emerge. In the run-up to K + 90 and after, key UÇK leaders continued to build political support under the cover of elaborate remembrance rallies and funerals in which UÇK fighters were reburied en masse. These events came under close KFOR scrutiny. Capt. Jeffrey Gill:

> It was quiet after K + 90, when most of the uniforms were gone. But there were these large funerals when they would wear UCK insignia, where you'd have up to ten thousand people attending. These funerals were for their war heroes, the fallen. Suddenly you'd get ten thousand people descending on Krajkovo. We'd attend. Now this is where it got touchy, because the rules and regulations set by KFOR included the stipulation that they weren't allowed to wear uniforms. But this changed. The main points were, no uniforms, no weapons, no firing. During the Krajkovo funeral, they had special permission to wear uniforms and special permission to carry arms, but they weren't allowed to fire. But sure enough, when you have ten thousand people, what were we supposed to do? Wade in and arrest them? Do we send in a section of ten men? So we wound up videotaping the whole thing and approaching them after. We never ran into any seriously hostile encounters; there were a couple of verbal exchanges. But in this situation we were helpless to enforce our policy. How far did we really want to go? It wasn't an intimidation issue or that we didn't want to fight. It was cause and effect. What would this do? Risk our troops for what? This situation wasn't going to escalate. They'd fire off a few rounds, which was unsafe. But to escalate a situation with ten thousand people present wasn't worth it. I'd be on the radio: so and so has fired ten

rounds in the air. Okay. Continue observation. Then talk to the guy, blah blah blah. NATO direction was wishy-washy. And then there were the rallies. They were huge, too, usually five thousand people. They'd carpool and have convoys, and sure enough out of the windows they'd start firing. So what do you do? Pull over the convoy? This was frustrating. We were more than willing to arrest people. The problem was that we'd busted people before for carrying weapons without a WAC [exemption] card and they'd be out the next day because some high-up politician would demand their release. It would even happen at weddings. The underground would surface at funerals and weddings. They're a very passionate people.[124]

It was clear to Canadian personnel that the reburials were extremely important to the people of the Drenica Valley. People killed elsewhere were relocated to their home village in as many cases as possible. If the deceased was UÇK, the families wanted people in uniform present and salutes fired into the air. Even though it was in violation of the undertaking, Gen. Sir Mike Jackson authorized these activities. It probably would have caused KFOR more problems in the long run. KFOR troops kept a respectful distance, but the battle group's Coyotes and TOW under armor vehicles were used to provide observation. An additional benefit was that relationships between former UÇK leaders and the emergent Kosovar Albanian political and criminal leaderships could be ascertained by such close observation. Capt. Don Senft:

[As a liaison officer] I was invited to a lot of UCK functions because they were allowed parades with Commander KFOR's approval. I dealt with key people like General Çeku. Two of the UCK founders had been killed during the war: Izmet and Adem Jashari. When you see UCK posters with all the bearded guys with rocket launchers and little white hats, those are the Jashari brothers. They were going to have this parade, but it was kept quiet. It was going to be on top of one of the mountains, where their general staff HQ was during the war. I caught wind about this by playing everybody off against each other and I did some digging. Remember, they weren't supposed to be a military force any more, but they were having parade practice. I got the location and I drove up with a couple of our snipers and a couple of engineers in case there were mines up there. It was an amazing facility: World War I–type trench system, bunkers, small hospitals underground. There were wells: it was a small city. But it was empty and I thought I'd been had. Then I started hearing about the number of people that were going to show up: ten to fifteen thousand. Brigade just dismissed this out of hand: no, you're a sucker, they got you hook, line, and sinker. Sure enough, on 29 August, there were PU guys in uniform doing traffic control on all the major highways. Then we learned that they laid the equivalent of a four-lane highway with a gravel surface to the site in a week and a half. They had parking control. We estimated that there were twenty-eight thousand people there, in this natural amphitheater, they had a stage, an 80,000 watt sound system. This thing was so huge it would have taken the entire KFOR to shut it down. We sat there in our Grizzlies completely surrounded by twenty-eight thousand Kosovar Albanians and watched a four-and-half-hour memorial service for the Jashari brothers. They had folk singers, they had bands, they had dancers, they had political speeches. The entire underground movement, the LDK, was up there speaking. It was a great chance: I had a digital camera and recorded the whole thing. All of the zone commanders were up on the stage and introduced one by one. Everybody was chanting UCK! UCK! UCK! And I just looked around and thought, "There is no fucking way we are demilitarizing anything." Not in four months. People just kept pouring in like bugs. They treated us great, though. They didn't see us as the oppressor; we were there helping them. All of their speeches were clear: without the help of NATO, the UCK would have been unable to defeat the Serb army and so one. People were throwing us beer, wine, bread, chocolates. Our Grizzly filled up with this stuff.[125]

The honeymoon period eventually ended, however.

The people who caused the battle group HQ some concern (and this may have reflected brigade and KFOR HQ concern) were the hardliners from 121 Brigade and its affiliates in Maj. Dave Corbould's area of operations. There was another disturbing development:

We got rid of the illegal police stations, and when we did that we inserted a sniper OP, covertly, into adjacent buildings. When we were doing that we realized from them that the companies were under observation. It was a mix of illegal police, criminals, and locals. They were following our patrols, using cars from their own networks. They were gathering on our guys. The covert OPs were able to confirm the fact that this was going on. We inserted more covert OPs to get confirmation, and we discovered that [121 Brigade] was involved. The companies did a great job at getting information [generally], but the snipers were needed for the close-in detailed stuff. We built up quite a dossier [on 121 Brigade]. We had evidence of noncompliance [with the undertaking]. . . . They were in uniform, with UCK badges at the Chalet, their headquarters. There were some people, very high-level people, who showed up. We were surprised. They were members of the UCK and other organizations that were vying for political power. Why would they be showing up at this location? We were, however, concerned about information leakage: we didn't want these people to know we had them under observation. We found out that Çeku was provided with information we gathered on 121 Brigade, and he drove right down to 121 Brigade and gave them the same information. It turned out that someone in KFOR HQ handed someone in Çeku's headquarters. It nearly shut us down. It took a long time for our LOs to build up a rapport with 121 Brigade. We just stopped sending stuff to [formations higher] than the battle group. In another case, the information we sent in on the Russians made it into an intsum [intelligence summary] and the Germans gave it to the Russians [in another sector], so we had Russians showing up at our camp going, "Hey! What's going on here?" We were told [from some of our sources] that 121 Brigade was going to gun down some Russians at one point. Russian vehicles had been seen in that area: they also had a bad habit of sending a supply convoy through our AOR [on Route Dog] every day. We were afraid that the boys in Komorane were going to take a shot at it. Radio traffic from 121 Brigade suddenly increased tenfold and there was movement on the ground, so we had to put a clampdown on it. That's when we raided the compound at Komorane with mortar platoon. What that did was generate more UCK radio traffic times four. Which was quite useful.[126]

The Russian problem, according to Sgt. Richard Walsh,

was that the [Kosovar] Albanians wanted nothing to do with the Russians: it was a Slav thing. The [Kosovar] Albanians hated them because they supported the Serbs. They didn't trust the Russians because they would not work within KFOR's chain of command. Some Russians were trying to maintain a presence. Some were just sitting on their butts in camps. We had one unit which was professional: it was an airborne unit. They all spoke Russian and English, which meant they were pretty well trained. They could have been Spetsnaz [special forces]. But they were under German control. They put on the usual demonstration for the CO, you know, breaking boards and eating glass. There was massive hatred for the Russians in our area. We were always getting reports from people claiming that the Russians were crossing into our AOR. We did have evidence of this, especially down near the airport.[127]

Other suspicions were raised:

The British were not initially convinced that there was a problem in the battle group AOR. Their resources were really focused else-where. Jackson was suspicious, but when the evidence started to mount, he told the brigades that "we believe the Canadians." We swayed them with our information, and the final clincher was at a Joint Implementation Committee meeting when we showed them a picture of Çeku wearing a new Kosovo army uniform: instead of UCK on the badge it had UK. Suddenly, the British realized that the Canadians weren't just blowing wind through their sail. A lot of people wanted to believe that the UCK was toeing the line. Most of them probably were, except the hardcore guys. If anything was going to go down, it was going to be in our AOR. Our sources were at the secure weapons storage sites. The UCK declared they turned in 100 percent of their declared weapons. The weapons they were turning in were shit: old AKs, rusted Mausers, stuff like that. No RPGs. Our guys said to the UCK guy, "You guys couldn't win a war with this!" and the UCK guy looked up and smiled, "You don't really think we fought the Serbs with those weapons, do you?" They had RPGs, ATGMs. We had photographs of UCK with SA-7 guided missiles. None of these were turned in.[128]

The battle group put the pressure on. The next time Çeku came through, a Canadian VCP attempted to detain his bodyguard and confiscate their weapons, a risky undertaking since UÇK bodyguards had a habit of loading an armor-piercing round in the chamber and keeping the safety off.[129] This resulted in a temporary standoff. Even though the bodyguard's weapons were exempt from the terms of the undertaking, it sent a message: "Nobody really cared that the Canadians were over there until we started busting high-level figures. And suddenly everybody and their dog wanted to know what the Canadians were doing. We had credibility." The Drenica OZ commander privately told his staff (and this made it back to the battle group) that the Canadian contingent interfered the most with his activities, far more than the French, Italians, or Russians.[130]

The mortar platoon was tasked to conduct a cordon and search operation along the critical Route Dog. Warrant Officer Lee Humphrey:

> We did a large raid on a compound in Komorane. It was the largest NATO haul by that point. The troops were getting bored with the area because it got very, very quiet. There were a couple of grenadings chucked through windows: a local businessman had his brother accused of being a collaborator, so they wanted him out of town. He packed up. We put in patrols trying to catch them. We finally got permission for this raid. We had several other raids turned off at the last minute but this one was coordinated with the British and the Finns at the brigade level. It was designed to send a message, a big message. We had mortar platoon with its Bisons, we had a section of TOW, a section of engineers, an ambulance, and two recce dets [detachments] with Coyotes, plus snipers. I'd say we had sixty people in this raid. After having observation in place on the compound for forty-eight hours, we hit the place at 0900. The guards that were there briefly resisted. They threatened

us, they were quickly overwhelmed and flexi-cuffed. One guard put up a struggle, but that was very quickly sorted out. We had some very large people as part of the entry team. So they went in, there was no panic. Our guys started to haul out equipment. There was everything from RPGs to a Sagger antitank missile, tons of grenades, AKs. There was a mortar. There was a recoilless rifle. There were mines, a lot of mines. We had six truckloads of the stuff. Six ten-tons! They had been stockpiling this stuff: it wasn't just being transshipped along the [Route Dog] MSR.[131]

It was evident from intelligence sources that the effectiveness of the Canadian battle group in controlling its area of responsibility forced the noncompliant elements of the former UÇK to remove other weapons caches and shift them to the French sector, where they were not subject to the same level of scrutiny. This was confirmed time and again by belligerent TMK and MRP personnel passing through Glogovac and being upset about the difference in the two sectors; they were vocal about it to Canadian personnel.[132]

When information arrived indicating that members of 121 Brigade were planning to kill members of the Russian contingent, a decision was made to put pressure on 121 Brigade. A contingency plan, Operation Thunderbolt, had previously been established by Lt. Col. Shane Brennan and his staff to take down all noncompliant UÇK activity simultaneously throughout the Canadian AOR.

Major Corbould had already established a robust patrol routine in the Lipovica Forest, ostensibly to monitor illegal logging but also to watch the Chalet and look for weapons caches. His patrols visited the 121 Brigade HQ at the Chalet both randomly and regularly: for example, they might search one of the three buildings or all three. There might be more than one search a day. This activity laid the groundwork for a battle group–mandated cordon and search operation.[133]

The snipers went in first:

We inserted in and rotated teams a couple of times. We produced our own reports, complete with graphics, which were used in the briefing packages. We nickname the target personnel and produce a dossier on each, with the images. In this operation, we were in position six days. There were the people and the vehicles, including the ubiquitous red Ladas. Intelligence added this to their data base. We also had aerial photos. We had to be able to tell our guys, "We will be here." Remember, we're dressed funny and we don't carry normal weapons. We produced a complete report, including our own graphics packages. This was given to the low-level commanders, so they could target their items of interest. With laser binos and GPS, we could say, "Okay, boys, you're going to get out of the vehicle here, run eighteen meters to the gate, it's fifty-two meters to that building, which has its lights on day and night, that building is occupied." A high level of detail. Using digital cameras and being able to print stuff off and produce a picture of the operating area, they had a better idea of what the place was like. It was a hoot—it's why I stay in. I talked to guys who had a horrible tour over there: they hated it. But we had a ball. This was as much fun as Somalia was.

We were a force protection capability, overwatching B Company when they raided the place. We provided commentary [on] the action, advising directly to the commander of the ground forces. For example, on one operation the target was adjacent to an aid center, and it had a lot of children moving about. It was our call when that operation went down, when to launch because of the intimate knowledge of the area and our ability to place a single bullet where it had to be. "Surgical" is a neat word, because that's the bottom line. It is more politically acceptable to kill one armed agitator than it is to spray the crowd with a machine gun, and there are times when that choice has to be made.[134]

The Chalet had some interesting transient guests:

The Black Tigers were part of the Guards Rapid Reaction Group from 121 Brigade. The commander was twenty-nine years old, physically fit, and has a reputation as a ruthless murderer who got his position by deeds, not words. They got $8 million from a private donor in Germany. They had third-generation night vision goggles. Instead of AK-47s, they had H&K 93s, and MP-5s. They were pretty well equipped. The donor gave money exclusively to that unit. Sometimes there were mercenaries there. They were the Storm Troopers; they actually wore dogtags that said "Storm Troopers" in German on them! They didn't try to hide it. "We are Storm Troopers, we are from Albania, we come here, we train units to platoon size on infiltrations, survival escape evasion resistance, . . ." and so on. And then there was a group from Germany that called themselves the Waffen SS and openly wore two lightning bolts on the left arm. When we tracked them, they changed clothing. They were Germans who didn't speak Albanian. There were other ones who said they were working for the US government, but they had fake IDs. And then there were guys from Agricultural Enterprise of Kosovo. They were all completely skinhead and they were in incredible shape, built like Arnold Schwarzenegger. We ran into them on a regular basis at 121 Brigade. The SAS were watching these guys before we got there and handed over their surveillance to us.[135]

Another view:

The Tigers interested us. Even though they were in Zone 1, that zone had interests throughout the country because of the way it was aligned with the other OZ boundaries. So these guys were hard to keep track of. They could turn up in the German area, the American area, the French area. Whenever something nasty happened, some massacre or drive-by shooting, where there was a mass execution or a school bombing. Usually you could link it to somebody from that unit. You couldn't link them to the actual crime; they weren't that dumb. But you could do it circumstantially. "You were in Prizren last week and that's when the Serb school there was completely bombed and eleven kids were killed. Is that a coincidence, Tiger?" Big smile on his face—they know how to play the game. They knew we had to get evidence. It was like playing chess.[136]

And if that wasn't bad enough, 121 Brigade was receiving logistics support from an NGO. The Mother Teresa Society aid distribution center in Magura provided food to brigade personnel on demand, and it was thought that the food was a form of payment from the UÇK.[137]

Maj. David Corbould:

After K + 90 we were constantly checking up on [121 Brigade] to make sure they were in accordance with the agreement. Up until K + 90, the battle group liaison officer dealt with them. Once K + 90 hit, it was my role to make sure the assembly area was secure. I sent a patrol down every day, and I went and talked to them and explained what I was doing. 121 Brigade was authorized three weapons, and I wanted my people to see the weapons and make sure their serial numbers were the correct ones. [Brigade] was putting pressure on the UCK. We did a big cordon and search of the area. The reality was that we were doing nothing more than what we had been doing on a daily basis. It was frustrating from that respect because battle group headquarters didn't seem to acknowledge that. They threw all sorts of assets at me. There was recce with Coyotes, TOW under armor, night vision. So we did it, but I kept everybody else out on the outer cordon and did not show our presence. I sent in the section to do its normal thing with the LO. All the other resources were used to control access to the area.[138]

There was nothing to be found in the Chalet or its surrounding buildings, and the operation appeared anticlimactic to its participants. At another level, however, Op Thunderbolt coincided with a brigade-wide plan designed to send a message to noncompliant elements and extremists in the Kosovar Albanian community: further noncompliant activity was unacceptable and KFOR would act to maintain stability. It is probable that there was an information operations aspect to this plan and that it amounted to a massive display of NATO resolve that had effects elsewhere. Indeed the constant scrutiny placed on 121 Brigade and its associates by B Company over time may have convinced extremist elements not to use the area and may have led UÇK elements to centralize in Komorane weapons that were then seized by the mortar platoon. In any event, no Russians were killed by members of 121 Brigade in the vital APOD sector.

Ongoing problems in MNB (North), however, increased in intensity throughout the fall of 1999. The Patricia's battle group was nearly called upon to intervene by the new KFOR commander,

General Reinhardt. Although the battle group was ultimately not employed in this operation, the debate surrounding its participation laid the groundwork for operations conducted by the 1 RCR battle group in the spring of 2000. At the end of October 1999 improper staffing of a contingency plan that involved the Canadian battle group really irritated Lt. Col. Shane Brennan. The plan involved the possible deployment of company-strength units from non-lead nations (nations not commanding multinational brigades) to conduct "security operations." Brennan and his staff realized this was coded language designed to "send 'other' nations' troops as crowd control parties to deal with a difficult situation in Mitrovica." He was willing to use the whole battle group, but only if KFOR established a new AOR, and he had no intention of sending "soldiers piecemeal into this situation that continues to develop due to a lack of strategy to overcome ethnic tensions there." The plan did not meet the criteria for the employment of Canadian forces and was in its language deceitful: "The crowd control aspect is again not stated but the intent is not to send [forces] to guard a battery factory. . . . Those other tasks are clearly the unsavoury work of continual crowd control-type operations which the French are tired of."[139]

Col. Mike Ward backed up Colonel Brennan and demonstrated that the command and control system designed to protect Canadian interests worked:

> The problems in Mitrovica in the north, where the French were under a fair amount of pressure, not according to the French brigadier, but according to Commander KFOR. His G-3 decided that what they would do was to rotate platoons in from all troop-contributing nations from the other areas of operations to familiarize themselves with [MNB (North)]. The command and control relationship was really dodgy. Logistics were dodgy and then the actions in event of hostilities were also very dodgy. We don't typically deploy platoons away from the company, but typically there should be a tether back to a battle group commander in case the going got rough. And none of that had been addressed in that particular plan. We said we weren't interested unless it was elevated to

a level where there was at least a company involved. . . . When you throw a mish-mash of troops together at the platoon level inside a foreign national command, with a foreign language, then . . . the potential for chaos, not to mention catastrophe, is there and we wanted to avoid that.[140]

Colonel Ward's successor, Col. Ivan Fenton, was eventually confronted with similar problems when he was forced by circumstances to reexamine the battle group's role in Mitrovica as the situation spun out of control in the spring of 2000.

TEN

Come On Feel the Noise
Battle Group Operations, Part II

Insurgents are bound to rely to a considerable extent on the people for
money, shelter, food and information. Insurgents therefore need to build
up a programme in which violence is carefully balanced by political,
psychological, and economic measures, if it is to be effective. . . . Often
insurgents do things which seem pointless or even damaging to their own
cause when viewed in the context of harming the government, but in fact
the actions in question may be solely concerned with achieving support
from the population by coercion or persuasion.

—FRANK KITSON, *Bunch of Five* (1977)

Operations conducted by the 1st Battalion, the Royal Canadian
Regiment (1 RCR) battle group built on the solid foundation provided by the Patricia's battle group. There were, however, a number
of differences that characterized the RCR battle group tour. The
area of operations shifted to remove the mixed communities north
of the Priština airport from Canadian control and pass them on
to British and Norwegian units. The CIMIC activities designed to
stabilize the community, particularly Operation Comfort, in addition were either well under way or completed before the rotation
of the units. This permitted the RCR battle group to improve on
other CIMIC projects that were of secondary importance in the
run-up to winter, as well as to provide important support to the
nascent UN political and policing administrations operating in the
Drenica Valley. The UÇK had by this point disbanded and a new
organization, the TMK, stood up with Canadian assistance during
the second tour. The 1 RCR battle group was, however, confronted

with other problems: the smoldering ethnic conflict in Mitrovica and an outbreak in violence between a Kosovar Albanian community and a Roma community located next to the vital APOD and its unpopular occupant, the Russian KFOR contingent.

Planes, Trains, and Automobiles: 1 RCR Battle Group Arrives

The hand-off from Roto 0 to Roto 1 in Kosovo in December 1999 was far from a seamless sequence of events. Indeed the 1 RCR battle group's odyssey from Petawawa to Kosovo nearly reached epic proportions. The alternate service delivery or ASD policy established within the DND in the mid-1990s to save money and staff time, coupled with Canada's critical lack of strategic airlift, resulted in the contracting of a civilian airline called Tower Air to fly Canadian personnel into the theater of operations. Cpl. Alan Spencer from 1 RCR was a participant in what the battle group members called "Planes, Trains, and Automobiles" (after a John Candy movie of the same title):

I was on Main 5-5. . . . We got on the plane at CFB Trenton, loaded up, started to fly over, got there, and went into a holding pattern around Macedonia. The airport in Macedonia is in the valley, in between two mountain ranges, and fog was heavy. There was cloud cover and they couldn't get a clear path to actually go in and land. So we were in this holding pattern for a while and then we flew to Greece and landed. It was a spur of the moment thing, and the Greeks didn't have a problem with that. We unloaded our kit ourselves and onto trucks. We then got permission from the Greeks to go into town and stay in a hotel. Then the buses showed up in the morning and we went to the border region in Macedonia; there were tunnels and mountains. There were vehicles lined up on the right-hand side of the road: nothing but vehicles, for miles. The border was closed. So we sat in traffic until there was enough room to turn around, and we headed back to stay for another night and then tried again the next day. We couldn't get through. On the fourth day they tried to fly some guys in by helicopter and then somebody came up with taking the train. We had a train that they got from somewhere; it was a shot-up Serb train with a stolen Italian engine. There was no heat, no lights in the cabins, there were bullet holes throughout, the windows were smashed . . . so we loaded up two cars' worth of kit and away we went. On the train, into Kosovo. As we were passing the border the train conductor blew the horn a couple of times at the border: we could see everyone still stuck there, lined up. So we got to Kosovo, dismounted, unloaded all of the kit, got on trucks, and went to the camp. Main 5-5. Planes, trains, and automobiles.[1]

A similar sequence of events occurred on Main 3 as well. The persistent efforts of the movement's staff notwithstanding, this episode had numerous ramifications. Situation reports bluntly and correctly stated that "the record of timelines of flights for this roto is not good and Main 3 especially is delaying handovers. As well as producing a hugely detrimental effect on morale of outgoing personnel."[2] Most of the battle group was restricted to static tasks and could not implement patrol coverage of the AOR. Reports noted that

the succession of delays with the individual flights . . . dangerously depleted the effective strength of units on the ground for a few days. Soldiers who have been frequent flyers with this contractor report that they have experienced delays every single time. I trust that we are rigorously measuring the quality of service, what it means to our mission effectiveness and our soldiers' morale. . . . Many soldiers made the obvious contrast between the imperative to "buy Canadian" (e.g., in buying LSVW trucks or tactical aviation helicopters) yet instead of giving business to a sinking airline like Canadian, we use a low-bid American firm for charter flights. The corrosive aspect of their observation was that they saw the soldiers' welfare and safety being sacrificed in order to use the lowest bidder.[3]

On arrival the battle group was confronted with a winter that was different from Canada's. Cpl. Alan Spencer of the recce platoon: "During the very early part of the tour, in December and January, and February when it was really cold, when we'd go out on patrols. It was the first time I've seen anything like this. It wasn't

COME ON FEEL THE NOISE

snowing all the time, but the frost was so heavy that it would actually grow across the chain link fence and almost close it over like a complete wall. Anything that was metal, things that were never touched and sitting around would have frost growing off it. It was pretty neat to see."[4]

Snow and ice control (SNIC) was a real problem: there were no spreaders to put grit on the roads, which limited vehicle movement and thus patrolling throughout the hilly areas in and around the Canadian AOR. Expedient measures were employed and some SNIC measures were implemented, but it took time to fly in the appropriate equipment and operators. It took the rest of December to deal with the matter.[5]

The 1 RCR battle group also arrived just in time to confront the "enemy within": Y2K. Now a blip in history, the "Year 2000" problem generated near–mass hysteria when the belief that the world's computers and the systems that depended on them would catastrophically collapse suddenly dominated the mediascape. A Canadian Forces–wide contingency plan, Operation Abacus, was designed to coordinate the protection of government computers and to restore social order in Canada if such a collapse occurred. Abacus occupied planners for months: massive military resources were dedicated to it. There was concern that if military computing systems went down, the resulting confusion might be exploited by hostile elements. Operation Kinetic was no exception: there was even a rumor making the rounds that the Coyote's computer system was not Y2K compliant.

Fortunately no catastrophe emerged, but MNB (Center) put together Op Millennium (the Canadian component was Op Lombardo) just in case there was some form of civil disorder over New Year's. Maj. Pat Koch (pronounced "co"), the company commander of 1 RCR's Duke of Edinburgh's Company, had a situation on his hands:

> We had upwards of two thousand people, maybe three thousand people on the main street of Glogovac. We understood that this was likely to happen so we surged on the towns. I had my patrols everywhere, on every corner, and [I had] 3 Platoon, that was my

platoon permanently stationed in the town because they knew the area, knew the people, and were more comfortable there. The other platoons had cordon and searches, more like VCPs, outward. There were a number for former UCK members, and those we knew still to be UCK members, who sort of strolled into this crowd and they started chanting. They were trying to get this group whipped up into a frenzy. There might have been eight or ten of them. The locals, however, had said, "Thank you very much, we supported you guys during the conflict and you guys were swell, but we don't need you anymore and you're becoming a part of the problem." So for the most part, except for some very young kids, everybody ignored them. They realized they were being ignored, so they had to escalate things. I happened to be walking down that street with my sergeant major and my signaler, and there was a patrol from 3 Platoon, led by Sergeant Earl. A guy from this UCK group raised a pistol above his head and shot off three or four rounds: this was designed to fly in our face, but we had the UNMIK police here basically saying, "Sorry, we're here and still in charge." So I rushed in there with Sergeant Earl, but they were very smart and passed the pistol off to someone else. We knew who it was, and there was concern that if we went in there too aggressively, things could escalate and we've got a mob of three thousand people who are now turning on us. . . . Sergeant Earl came in with his guys and he was very calm, none of us were excited, and the fact that we'd come in on these guys so quickly obviously surprised them and they were taken aback. Our guys made a little cordon in the middle of this jostling group of people; everything was quite civil and we talked to them through interpreters. The guy who had the pistol denied it (of course), but he was taken to the edge of the crowd, questioned, and searched. My guys, who are young guys, never had to deal with this type of thing before and one expected them to get a bit excited, but they were very calm, very professional, they knew what had to be done. They knew what the threat was and dealt with it.

We saw on numerous occasions that a solution to a problem would come from a sergeant or some young master corporal. I always told the guys that if they had a better idea than mine, I don't care, rank is irrelevant if your idea is better than mine, I'm using it and I told them they would get credit for it. If you've got it, throw it out. I was surprised and happily so.[6]

The problem of crowd control and how the RCR battle group handled this particularly dangerous type of operation was recognized by both the Task Force Kosovo commander, Col. Ivan Fenton, and the 1 RCR commanding officer, Lt. Col. Bruce Pennington, prior to the Roto 1 deployment. The operational-level aspects of the problems in MNB (North) notwithstanding, the tactical issues were difficult to address. Since the Oka standoff in 1990, governmental policy had stipulated that crowd control or riot control was a police responsibility in Canada, not the responsibility of the armed forces. The advent of numerous peacekeeping and stabilization operations in the 1990s, however, meant that Canadian troops would be confronted with these situations and there might be no police to deal with them in states that were destabilized. Such a situation occurred in April 1998 in Drvar, Bosnia, where an RCR company had to intervene to protect the lives of Bosnian Serb returnees from threats by local Bosnian Croat agitators: the Joint Staff, which at the time included Colonel Fenton, frantically had to come up with a solution since policy and reality did not match. A policy review was pending in 1999–2000. When the 1 RCR battle group deployed, it was not equipped with CS gas (tear gas), visors, shields, or batons nor had the battle group personnel received specific riot control training. Sometime after the New Year's Eve events, Commander TFK was able to secure approval from Ottawa for the deployment of pepper spray and CS gas grenades and training for their use, but it took several months.[7]

Adapting to this role posed few problems. The training program for 1 RCR battle group, as established by Lieutenant Colonel Pennington, recognized that

as an Army we need to train for war, so we need to train for combat operations, and then it's too easy to go from combat operations and step back and go to peacekeeping or peacemaking operations. If you train only for up to mission specific or peacekeeping operations, it's difficult to change your psychological bent, change your approach to business and get into warfighting. I think with training for combat operations, that's where you get the real discipline of a soldier, the skill levels of a soldier, the capability of working under duress, the capability of dealing with stress and much stronger team organization. When you do pure peacekeeping, what I interpret to be peacekeeping operations, where you train a person to stand at an OP and observe and report but not necessarily to do anything about you, you have a very different philosophy.[8]

The battle group concept of operations remained based on the four-pillar structure discussed previously, but it was refined on the ground by the battle group operations staff. Maj. Omer Lavoie:

> We did an exhaustive mission analysis once we got into theater. The concept of operations was for the twenty-four and seven domination of the area of operation. We achieved that through patrolling, checkpoints, and surveillance operations. The concept recognized that we had to decentralize down as much as we could, and that meant that we had to push sub-units out. We put a company in Glogovac, another in Magura, as the PPCLI did. The mission statement was different. Their role was to *establish* a secure and stable environment. We changed that to *maintain* a secure and stable environment in order to facilitate the United Nations Mission in Kosovo (UNMIK). UNMIK couldn't go in and the OSCE couldn't go in and conduct elections, train police and everything if there was no secure stable environment. Our concept of operations didn't change [since the two were compatible].[9]

1 RCR Battle Group Operations

Despite some boundary changes, the AOR occupied by 1 RCR battle group roughly corresponded to the 1 PPCLI AOR and was split into two: B Company, led by Maj. Rob MacIlroy, took Magura and the area near the Priština airport, while Duke's Company, under Maj. Pat Koch, was located in and around Glogovac. The combat support company and its unique resources roved and supported the two rifle companies.

The main effort in the early days was assistance to UNMIK, and that drove information gathering. Maj. Rob MacIlroy:

COME ON FEEL THE NOISE

We knew what we wanted to achieve here. We wanted to reestablish government as quickly as possible. We wanted to go in and prevent Serbs from deploying military forces into Kosovo. We also knew that we had an internal security issue. We had to adjust our areas to correspond with the municipal boundaries. We needed information on that. We needed to know who, exactly, we would be interfacing with: the UN was going to come in and establish government and we had to assist. We couldn't stick our heads in the sand, so what was the best way to get the information needed to support that? What was [the UN] organization going to look like? Were there budgetary issues? We shouldn't be vying for scraps of money. This drove my goals. I looked at the four pillars and I did my mission analysis. What does this mean for me? If UNMIK is successful, then I will be successful. Peace has been established. If the UNMIK administrator, and the administration, works, then security will work.[10]

Maj. Pat Koch:

The PPCLI had broken the area up and were rotating platoons from area to area every couple of months. I considered that, but I prefer to have the same faces showing up for six months because people are more likely to approach someone that they know or recognize. So I broke my portion of the AOR into three sectors. The PPCLI established themselves with a main camp in the center of town: it was a critical point for them when they first moved into the area because the company commander was essentially the mayor and he was the lynchpin for many things. When we got there, they were in two camps: the main company camp was in an abandoned shirt factory on the edge of town, with a platoon house in the center. This was important because it was on the edge of the market. And they shared a building with UNMIK police and the local mayor. This had a positive psychological effect on the population. I kept it that way.

Outside of Glogovac, I ensured that every village in our area would be visited at least once every three days, usually more often, but it may be passing through, waving at some kids, stopping and talking to someone in the market or the town elder, just to make sure everything was okay and that there was aid distribution. The locals were telling us things that hadn't been passed on before. A lot of it was relationships: who was doing what during the conflict. It gave us an idea of who we should be watching. Who was important, who was hanging out with who. We have five murders during our time there: two of them were people brought in from Priština and dragged into the woods. There were murdered Gypsies. Our information assisted with the investigations.[11]

When 1 RCR battle group arrived, it appeared as though the situation in Kosovo was relatively quiet. Maj. Pat Koch:

I think [at that time] that the PPCLI probably had the lion's share of the stabilizing work done and we were in the maintenance phase. It was wintertime and people were so much more focused on staying alive. I had one sergeant who worked his butt off, a very competent man, Sergeant LaBelle. He adopted this one family: there were twelve or fourteen people living in a tent with a small potbellied stove, and we were scavenging wood from pretty much everywhere, and it was the worst winter in a hundred years or whatever. I remember him driving out to this family to deliver some pallets we'd chopped up for firewood: the kids would run out and hug him, and the parents would say things like, "Thank God for the Canadians."[12]

The synergy between ISTAR, information operations, and CIMIC remained a key element of successful operations in the Canadian AOR. Picking up where the PPCLI battle group left off, Capt. Jon Herbert, a platoon commander from B Company, had his work cut out for him:

The Patricias had obviously done a good job, but they also did a good job in making us feel welcomed: in the first week all we got was "Hey, chicken fucker" from the kids. They knew the RCR were coming and the Patricias put out the welcome mat. We dominated the area with presence patrolling. There was a lot of underground stuff going on. For the most part I think the civilians wanted to live peacefully and didn't enjoy this blanket of blackness, crime, and fear of reprisal and death. I couldn't imagine living under that. I think midway through our tour the appreciation for the Canadians, especially B Company, changed. We had people in villages on our borders that would show up at the gate. These people would walk miles and miles and miles to come to our gate and say, "Can you come and give us aid?" They heard about the "Jug Head" aid truck, they heard about the patrols investigating every report. We would send out patrols if people reported individuals wearing ski masks. They also knew that the mortars and Duke's Company would do the same. The people knew we had good cooperation and they could depend on Canadians to do the job, help them out. Sgt. Mike Miller became the sheriff of Magura. The kids were drawing him on the sidewalk. The amount of information that Int[elligence] got from all of this was amazing. We'd send these patrol reports in and they were inches thick. And that's even when mid-tour guys were getting lazy. Battalion would come back and say, "We need more information." You want information? We'll give it to you. Photos and disks full of digital photos. One of my corporals, Moxom, wrote these awesome reports: four or five pages, sketches . . . it was amazing.[13]

Sgt. Kevin Earl, a section leader with Duke's Company, understood very early on that the remnants of the UÇK remained a factor and had to be watched:

We foot-patrolled the place from one end to the other. We'd do four-hour foot patrols and do two or three a day. This area was mostly ethnic Albanian. Initially we had to develop a picture of the current leadership of the [UÇK], so we had digital cameras and went around and got pictures of people, placed names to the pictures, figured out where they worked, and started to flesh out the structure: okay, that guy has this job, what did he do before the war? There were people in these communities that are ordinary citizens now that held positions before, but those positions were sponsored by Serb authority. They were ethnic Albanians, but the Serbs put them in charge. So of course these guys bailed the moment things started to look like the Serbs weren't going to maintain power anymore. Everybody and their dog was getting whacked. They were viewed as collaborators. I would try and find out because there were problems getting aid to certain areas and the aid is, believe it or not, controlled by locals. So that became an issue with me. Who are these guys? Who are they oriented with? We built a big database. We could type in license plate numbers and it would go back to this person and all their known links. Everything from fuel to people who owned fuel stations, where this coal is coming from. It was all linked together in a big, big clique of military-oriented people, and the people that were outside of it weren't getting anything. There was all this shuttling going on because the guy who controlled aid in Glogovac was a thug. But none of the aid agencies had bothered to figure that out. They just gave him stuff and he distributed it. Well, half of it was going to [UÇK] training camps. One of our interpreters had an uncle in the [TMK] and was an operations officer. She heard every conversation. I brought that forward and she was gone the next day. It all revolved around who was who before. The PPCLI came in and established control, and we got into the fine details.

The intelligence picture allowed us to address problems that weren't on the surface, like the drug trade, like graft. There were no cops at the start of our tour. We worked with the UNMIK police in our building when they showed up. It was a matter of "okay, you tell me what you want to know" and then we could reach out into the branches: Did you just buy this auto parts store? Who owned it before you? Has this always been an auto parts store? Where do you get your auto parts? Stuff like that builds the picture and these guys are all linked together or they are the same guy in six different forms or they all lead back to one guy. We'd get the intelligence. . . . We always ran tight patrols and at nighttime we'd run very black patrols, like NVGs mounted on everybody in the shadows, no noise, hand signals. It injected an air of uncertainty. They never knew where we were or what we were doing. It forces the [UÇK] to move their headquarters out of our AOR.[14]

While Duke's Company worked closely with UNMIK in Glogovac, Major MacIlroy's B Company liaised with UNMIK authorities in Lipljan:

COME ON FEEL THE NOISE

Our standing tasks were the two roadblocks north and south of Priština airfield [to keep the Russians in], we had our own camp security tasks, patrol tasks, and we did information gathering for humanitarian assistance and to help aid agencies decide where to put their assets. We would attend the meetings in Lipljan run by the Finn battalion. They held a weekly NGO meeting and we would pass information on. We also had to make sure that the aid agencies were actually putting the aid in the right spot. Understand that you might talk to a western European at the meeting but that they've hired locals to deliver. Their concept of verification is somewhat different from ours. The fact that the driver came back with no aid on the truck is sometimes a really good thing. Where that aid went was another issue, so we would verify with our patrolling. There were different ethnicities in the towns we were involved in: Serbs, Albanians, two types of Roma. We found that aid going to certain towns was not being distributed fairly and we would confirm that. This was a huge dissatisfier if you're not getting aid and everyone else is.[15]

Maj. Pat Koch:

I think we overwhelmed the Int[el] staff at the battle group level with all the information that was coming in, possibly at the brigade level as well. We had the main routes going through here. I was very particular about patrol reports: they became a running commentary on what was going on. I wanted to make sure that soldiers realized that, yes, we're doing this a lot, but still every single soldier is important and you might come back with one little tidbit of information: this particular person there, for example, which to you doesn't really mean anything, but when we bring that in and we put them with a bigger picture, then all of a sudden it becomes very, very important. These are lessons I personally learned from Somalia. I won't take credit for all of this; it was basically sitting down with my sergeant major and my 2IC [second in command], and we determined that one of the biggest things we have to combat here is going to be complacency and boredom. We had to defeat that without using make-work projects, filling sandbags and so on. This was a serious mission. If you speak to the soldiers, some will say they were disappointed doing CIMIC-type activities because it wasn't our task and others would suggest that they enjoyed that side of things because it gave that feeling of having successfully accomplished something.[16]

B Company was confronted with new and different problems in the Lipljan area, some of which required the appropriate application of information operations. Maj. Rob MacIlroy:

I attended the Finn bat[talion] meetings with the UNMIK administrator, Henry Bolton. He would talk about the increased level of disinformation directed at UNMIK from various political groups. These were outright lies—that UNMIK was only supporting the Serbs, that Bolton had a Serb wife. He wasn't married, okay? That the UNMIK administrator was trying to do this, that, or the other thing. These political groups would also take credit for things that UNMIK was accomplishing in the community. This was a legitimacy battle between the shadow government and UNMIK. The only way you could fight that was by telling your story. There were two mechanisms we established to do that. One was called Operation Soap Box and the other was the newsletter. We connected with this fellow in the Brit brigade. He was fabulous: he did translation and reproduction. This was a big issue because Henry didn't have the mechanism or resources to do it. So we would meet at our camp for a sit-down shit session. I would provide supper and beer. We would have the UNMIK chief of police, our staff, and UNMIK people. What do you guys want to tell the people? It would be anything from a new traffic light provided by country X or whatever and we would write a story on it for our two-page paper. My idea was that you had to grab people's attention, so I wanted to put in a puzzle. And there was a section for NATO information. The first issue was about Canada, the second about Finland. The answer to the puzzle would be in the next issue, so people would want the following one and so one. We would outproduce the opposition by bombarding them with information. As for measuring effectiveness, that was up to Henry. People were coming up to him to confirm that his information in the newsletter was in fact correct.

Lt. Eleanor Taylor was the ramrod behind this. I always try to select the best person with the skills for the job. Eleanor was this. She's an English major, super keen. The success we had in the company was that the three platoon commanders were friends and they worked together. Same with the platoon warrants. They were very close. There was no competition, no animosity. These were three of the most capable officers I have ever met. They ended up doing all the work, not me. So Eleanor Taylor is the person behind the newsletter. She would drive to Lipljan, get the germ of the idea, write the story herself, come back to Tony Quinlan and have them vet it, translate it, and proof it. We did two thousand in Albanian, five hundred in English, five hundred in Serb and within forty-eight hours we had it delivered to every village in the sector. We'd give a stack to the patrol commander and they would hand them out at the impromptu checkpoints. We gave copies to the police in Lipljan, and to Finn bat. It was fabulous work.[17]

Operation Soap Box was also designed to counter undesirable political influences:

The code words were all based on an Elvis theme. Henry Bolton's code word was "Elvis" and the site for the speech was "Graceland" and we had different report lines, like "Blue Hawaii." I tasked Lt. Alex Haynes and he had a bit of fun with it. Again, one of the problems was disinformation from these political groups. The municipality is so large that Henry is like a figurehead that no one sees, and therefore if you are not seen, you are not trusted. You have to get out, put the lollipop in the baby's hand, kiss the girl. Good old politics. We picked market day in Magura. Now here's one of the problems that you have: if you give too much warning, the political groups could do a demonstration. It gives them legitimacy. It's very easy to talk down to someone who is being translated. But you also don't want to have an event where no one arrives, because that sends a message too. You also have to have sufficient security if something goes wrong. We put in snipers for overwatch. We also had [TOW under armor] anti-armor assets attached to us: they went out on patrol and were positioned outside the town so that if anything went wrong they can shut the place down in a heartbeat. We used a truck as the speech platform so if there was trouble he could just drive away. Then we laid out mine tape [to keep people back]. It was just as effective as barbed wire, psychologically. They won't go beyond that. So one hour before the speech we distributed flyers: these were translated that morning so that the interpreters couldn't tell anybody in advance. We stuffed them into the market about two hours ahead of time. Henry drove up, we walked him out the truck: there were about two hundred people and he got a standing ovation. He also took questions and talked for an additional forty minutes. For the next two days our patrols got feedback from the people: they believed him and thought he sounded like an honest man. This is telling the story. It was his way to combat negative information.[18]

These operations also employed snipers:

We'd been in the cement factory before and done some recces. We had the best spot which could cover where the dignitary was going to speak. Our job was early warning and observation. We inserted early in the morning and gave running commentary, which is vital to the rifle company. We gave numbers of people coming in on the roads, observed to see if anybody was gathering. We kept our eyes open for weapons and anything that looked wrong. We had eyes on the whole time. It was a nice quiet gathering. We were there for about eight hours. That sort of mission repeated itself throughout our tour. Bolton was unpopular in some of the towns. We had rules of engagement, and thank God it wasn't necessary. They were better, though, than the old UNPROFOR [rules of engagement in Bosnia and Croatia]. We had Clause 14: we could use deadly force to protect ourselves.[19]

Political credibility also rested in the effectiveness of the battle group CIMIC effort. Operation Comfort measures, implemented in the fall of 1999, went a long way toward boosting political credibility, but there was still work to be done. The 1 RCR Pioneer platoon was retained as the CIMIC cell "muscle," also known as the "Bob Vila Crew." Warrant Officer Eric Rolfe:

We did more roofing: that was good for the guys because it was good for morale. We were able to go out there and we could actually, physically help somebody, you know what I mean? I think about 90 percent of the population appreciated that. They were happy to see these guys come in. Some families had seven kids and no husband, or no other immediate family. They loved to see us coming. The kids would crowd around and just yell; they wanted to touch you and things like that. You didn't see a lot of facial hair on the men over there. [Our Pioneer beards] were unique. We got a reputation for doing the roofs; they made the link between the beards and home improvement. It was better than in Bosnia. Our guys could see a difference in the things they did.[20]

Warrant Officer Rick Duncan:

We did everything in the form of humanitarian aid. We put roofs on; I think by the end of it we did twenty-seven homes and a school. That was the big thing over there: "We'll fire you out of your house and then we'll burn it." And over there everything was brick, so it was the roof that would collapse in on itself. So the different aid agencies would drop off building supplies, but if all the men in the village had been killed, it just left the women and children. So we did the roofs. It was different for the soldiers because it was done differently there. We had to learn how to use their hatchet and their tools. It was a whole different world. Working with Japanese aid agencies and the French: each one wanted their presence known and for that village to be identified as a Japanese or French project. [We just] went in independently, fixed roofs, and helped people.[21]

Aid distribution was carefully monitored to avoid charges of discrimination. Capt. Jon Herbert:

We had a CIMIC section and one of our guys, Master Corporal Allan, did a bang-up job. This guy drove around in a stripped-down MLVW; it had the tarp off. We called it the "Jug Head truck." He spent days and days driving [around] this AOR, loaded with free stuff for the towns. We got tons of aid. He and his two guys delivered the stuff which came down from the main camp, just sea cans of it. He would clear it out in two days. He also cataloged all of it.

This German major showed up, a staff officer from KFOR HQ. [General] Rhinehart sent him personally to check it out because supposedly the Canadians were withholding aid. So we sat him down and hauled out the aid file. And this guy's jaw just dropped. We had this printout that was a matrix of everything that had been handed out. Everything! Toothbrushes, soap, mittens, boots, hats, those Legion hats from Canada, soccer balls, tools, saws. . . . He must have thought we were just going to gloss him over. Then we pulled out our village files. These were started by the British when the Gurkhas were in Magura, then the Patricias built them up and passed them to us. It was very dynamic, these village studies. Eleanor [Taylor] had it first, then Alex [Haynes] and they were constantly updated. "I will report," he said and drove straight back to the general and said that the accusations were false. They had been made by the Roma, who wrote a letter to the Red Cross. It was from a village that we did a cordon and search on. One of the Roma, either the headman or one of his flunkies, said, "The Canadians don't give us anything." We shooed the major into the aid tent and asked if wanted to go with the "Jug Head truck" run. He declined. We gave him photocopies made with our junky old photocopier with a big black toner line through it.[22]

The establishment of the UNMIK police force in Kosovo was instrumental in reducing the burden on KFOR when it came to routine law and order duties and to increasing the legitimacy of the international community in place of the shadow government. Given the multinational nature of UNMIK, combined with the fact that KFOR personnel were already intimately familiar with the circumstances on the ground, a premium was placed on cooperation in the Canadian AOR. Maj. Omer Lavoie:

We started up a weekly joint planning session with UNMIK, with police operations. We brought in the police detachment commander, who was an Austrian policeman, and we'd sit around with key personnel from the battle group. We would look out over the next week and see which operations would be joint police-military. And for the most part we considered almost every operation that we conducted to be a joint operation. This was necessary for legitimacy, and they also needed backup. We needed to know what they were doing, in any case, if they needed support. In terms of rations, the police station in Glogovac, which covered five hundred square kilometers, had an establishment of fifteen to eighteen constables: there were usually fewer when some were on leave. They were spread pretty thin. They had primary lead for police investigations, they had tactical primacy in the town of Glogovac itself. But beyond that, they had no such primacy outside of town. There was a case where in the western part of the AOR in the middle of the night shots were fired in a bar. Well, UNMIK police called me to say they were going down there and I immediately sent a platoon down to form an outer cordon, and the two cops went in. It was designed to show that it wasn't only two guys there and that there were APCs sitting outside also. And I think by doing that you can probably defuse a lot of situations and prevent a lot of things from escalating because they are immediately outnumbered.[23]

Examples of UNMIK-KFOR cooperation were commonplace. Essentially UNMIK police were saddled with serious deficiencies. Sgt. John MacDougall was in the military police with the 1 RCR battle group:

There were not enough vehicles, not enough equipment. They had some poorly trained officers. There were a lot of countries that sent people that were not police officers. In some of those countries, if your father was wealthy, you could buy your position. We did some training with them, showed them simple things like protection of a crime scene. They were a good bunch of fellas but no training. One guy was in charge of a basketball team. That was his job on the police force. You needed to be a trained police officer, like the British, Irish, and most of the US guys. There were language barriers. I had an office in their building in Glogovac. They didn't have proper radios, so I would have one of my guys with a jeep available. Once you were out in the boonies, unless you had access to an RRB site, you don't have contact. Eventually they got Toyota four-by-fours: Japan gave them a whole fleet; that was their contribution. They had no radar guns, no digital cameras. We went with them to every crime scene to help them out. Their crime lab was a nightmare. It got better when some RCMP, Ottawa police, and Peel Regional [Police] showed up and the British [Criminal Investigation Bureau].

Then there was the justice system. They were trying to get some judges, but there wasn't enough room for all the criminals so they hung on to the murderers. The UN took over from the British-run prison. Anyone who was criminally charged would intimidate the judges, so it took a lot of police just to guard the judges.[24]

Warrant Officer Steve Shirley from the mortar platoon:

We had pretty good relationships with the UNMIK police. Each guy had their own AOR and one guy was our liaison. We had an Irish guy and a couple of RCMP guys. There was a house almost right across the street from our complex, and there was an incident just down the road where buddy had threatened a guy with a gun. The UNMIK cops asked us to back them up. We surrounded the complex and kept observation on it: they went in to search the place for weapons. There was no problem. We went through the place. We found a few small things, but we didn't destroy the house. We were polite and courteous to the people. They were really scared when we came in. They were used to the MUP kicking down doors and they thought that was going to happen. You could tell by the look on their faces that the [jig] was up, but when we opened something, we put it back and made sure they were there to see we weren't stealing stuff. When we left, the whole attitude had changed and they were offering us coffee. When we went there all I saw was a woman with her child; she was holding her child on the floor and it was a sad, sad sight to see that. They were terrified. We reassured them everything was fine and asked them permission. We were going to do it anyway, but we asked through an interpreter, explained why we were there. Of course they denied everything. This sort of stuff gets through the town, within forty-eight hours. We had reports at the front gate that they were glad to have us there. Now it all seems pretty trivial for a war-torn country, but in that community it was a big deal. We really made giant leaps in gaining trust and cooperation that day. The guy in the house had UCK memorabilia and had been part of it, but we didn't take anything. A hat badge is not going to make a big difference.[25]

Even the TOW under armor vehicles were employed in assisting UNMIK and gave new meaning to the concept of the RIDE program [an anti–drunk driving campaign]. Anti-armor platoon's Sgt. Hayward Russell:

We could see people thermally at night, up to about eighteen hundred meters. You could see, and if something was happening you could identify certain things. For example, there was one person driving his car down the main road. He was really going fast and the UNMIK police wanted him stopped. He threw a beer bottle out the window at night, and our guys saw the beer bottle because of its thermal signature. We held it and guided the police on to the bottle, this is where he went through, keep going, going, going— Stop! Okay, there it is. And sure enough there it was.[26]

Crime in Kosovo sometimes took on bizarre proportions. Sgt. Kevin Earl:

There was prostitution—it was there big time. The drugs, the fuel grafting, extortion . . . there was a guy who was very violent, using grenades and stuff like that just before we got there. We determined who he was. This was a previously lawless area of operations for them. You know, there were minivans with Ontario license plates running around. Germany, Swiss, Finland. Serbia doesn't have any contact with Interpol, so you can't even run a plate. It's illegal for the cops to run the plate to see if it was stolen. They couldn't even run a VIN. The guys that were involved were big-time [ex-UÇK and TMK] guys. They owned two gas stations. I have pictures of them with this guy who was an Austrian neo-Nazi who caused a bunch of problems in Mitrovica. He owned a café; I think it was the Hitlerena Café. He dressed like Hitler and drove a stretch Volvo. We eventually got him and put him in jail when we were in Mitrovica. He operated in the French AOR with impunity. I caught this guy in Glogovac and he was dressed like Hitler. This piqued my interest and I found out about him. His brother was the [TMK] commander for a huge area and he raised funds in Austria and Germany. We tracked his car. So it was the guys who owned a certain café, and the guys with the Ontario minivan, and there were connections. We started out with "Wow! That's a really weird Volvo! Let's go talk to that guy." We caught him when we were running Operation Steel Gate trying to close off the northern part of the AOR because shit was going from our AOR to Mitrovica. So this guy was coming back and forth and he was just too weird. So we checked him out.[27]

Sgt. John MacDougall:

His real name was Yemen Xhinobci. He had a couple of different aliases. There was this house of ill repute located down in B Company's AOR, the Club International. He got himself into trouble down there. He was a restaurant owner and drove that stretched Volvo with his pennants flying, a Kosovo flag on the right front fender and an American flag on the other. He presented himself as "Herr Hitler." He looks the part, dresses the part. Even his photos are similar to the real ones of Hitler, you know, the ones with him playing with the dog. His brother-in-law owned a pizzeria in Glogovac. He was visiting all the time. He was a joke until he started to get himself into trouble and his friends were found with weapons and grenades. He was supposedly ex-UCK. He was considered dangerous, enough that the PU [Kosovar Albanian shadow police] had reason to stop him. This guy's oars were not necessarily in the water. He did have access to some fairly bad fellas, though. They were criminals and he was probably [among their] hangers-on. Even they called him "Herr Hitler." He was a bit of a village idiot and that's the way we liked to treat him, but he had connections.[28]

As with any posthostilities zone, Kosovo had a burgeoning black market with associated crime that crossed the boundary between political and criminal:

Everybody you dealt with over there, as far as I was concerned, had a hidden agenda, or something fishy going on in the background. There were no copyright laws or anything, so it was all black or gray market. Everybody's looking for a cut. Like the guy who set up his stall in Glogovac market. He's got to pay money to somebody to do that. Gas stations got burnt because they weren't buying gas from the people they should have been buying from. They were owned by some people high up in the UÇK. Down at Obilić A and B, the UN was hauling coal in and it was going out of there as fast. If they ran out of oil, it might take days to get the plant up and running. It would cost about $30,000. Somebody was making money every time it was shut down. At one point they were going to have KFOR guard the coal. People were being murdered for stealing wood to keep warm in the winter. You could never prove it. There was no way to find prewar criminal records, so we built on the database started by Petty Officer Estey in the fall of 1999. . . . There was a mistrust of the police and we worked hard to overcome it. They'd come and tell us something and then the next thing you knew somebody goes by and throws a Molotov cocktail at their house or drives by and shoots it up with an AK. We've had murders in the middle of a small town at 1200 in the daytime. Nobody sees anything.[29]

Transforming the UÇK, Containing the Russians, and Preventing Dirty Bombs

The transformation of the UÇK into the TMK occurred during 1 RCR battle group's tenure in Kosovo. Essentially, there were three TMK detachments in the Canadian AOR: they corresponded very generally to the original UÇK dispositions. In Glogovac 311 Detachment consisted of some two hundred personnel. Its superior headquarters, also designated the 311, was located in the French-commanded MNB (North) AOR. In Komorane 201 Detachment was a support and logistical unit. It had about sixty personnel and was considered inactive by the battle group. Finally, there was the 2 Detachment's Guard Rapid Reaction Group (GRRG). It was located west of Magura, at the infamous Chalet. The GRRG inherited the attitude and reputation of the previous occupants. It was the most active and well organized of the detachments in the Canadian AOR.[30]

What exactly was the TMK and what was the battle group's role in dealing with it? Maj. Rob MacIlroy:

One of the problems with dealing with the TMK was that they were an army unit. To meet the agreement, they had to drop arms except for ceremonial weapons and you want them to become a nonmilitary or a civil emergency organization, but at the same time you don't want to give them any tasks. The problem here is that if you don't give them something, you can't take anything away. You can't enforce discipline with these types of units unless you're willing to give them something and we weren't. We, NATO. All we were doing was promising them ID cards, which was taking forever. We promised to get them uniforms, which turned out to be undersized French junk, so they got their own. So your legitimacy with them is plummeting. What reason do they have for not going around our backs? What do they have to lose? Nothing. And what are we going to do to them? Nothing. What can you do? Say they don't exist? In their mind they won the war, not NATO; now, that was debatable. But in their mind they are the winners. Why are they being treated this way? Why are they not being treated like professionals?

One of my objectives was to assist them to become a professional, nonmilitary force. I believe that idle hands are the devil's playground, so you keep them busy. The commander there was keen on building an obstacle course. Now there are military overtones to that. Johnny Herbert and Sergeant Good, who was Ranger qualified, went down for a look around. They took the NATO-standard obstacle course and marked it out on the ground. The commander modified it to his specs and his men built it. It even had a rappel tower. Warrant Ryan, one of our parachute instructors, assisted. We also taught them first aid. Warrant Murphy and the medics did that. We taught methods of instruction. We had flip charts made and translated: no PowerPoint here! We were going to do this right or not at all. They were working until midnight doing lesson plans. They were floored. They had never seen anything like this before. I purposefully selected each of the warrant officers and the sergeant major to lead this: our NCOs are the best instructors in the world. When the TMK held a UN-sponsored first aid competition, these guys who were trained by my guys kicked ass.[31]

Master Warrant Officer Paul Mason:

We concentrated on search-and-rescue techniques. We also did map and compass navigation. One week we did training, we had our medics train them in basic first aid. Like how to construct a litter or how to do a scene survey. We worked on methods of instruction so that they would be able to teach their own people, which in turn would be passed on. I told them to go home and prepare a lesson plan. The next day I had an interpreter beside me and I saw this guy teaching, so I asked what he was teaching. He says, "He's teaching about the mortar." I thought I told them not to use military stuff for the MOI [methods of instruction] class, but he claimed that was all he knew and that's what he wanted to do: pass on what he learned in the war. So he's going on and on and he's holding a stick and then starts to bite it. I asked the interpreter, "What's he doing now? If he's teaching mortar, why is he chewing on the stick?" "Well, they didn't have any earplugs so they took the stick, put it in their mouth and when they fired the mortar, clamped down on the stick to save their eardrums.' That was interesting! So I cut them off there and told them to prepare lessons on first aid. . . .

They loved it. They were looking for something to do. The Patricias just had time to make contact and teach them a little bit. The TMK never had any weapons [at the Chalet]: we searched the place every two weeks just to make sure. We taught them leadership, how to form a group, and how to pass on information: we always used a rescue or forest fire scenario. The commander had a degree in engineering: overall they were pretty compliant.[32]

Rallies were still common when the RCR battle group took over. In many cases they were observed by the sniper teams:

There was a farmhouse that required observation. It was a suspected gathering point for UCK radicals or whatever: they found old flags and stuff in there. We were a two-man team dressed up in Ghillie suits, cammed right up, overwatching this farmhouse. Because of road restrictions and mines, we couldn't go too far off the hard pack. We were lucky there was this nice hedgerow that we tucked ourselves into and we had excellent observation. Tractors went back and forth behind us all the time, but that was okay. We noticed an increase in activity in the field over the course of twenty hours. There was five people, then eight, then twenty, groups of twenty people wandering by. We weren't detected. Then about forty people meandered through the hedge. They still didn't detect us. This was a UCK rally, two hundred meters from our left! There were guys with AK-47s, wearing uniforms, speeches were going on. Intelligence hadn't prepared us for this at all; there was no mention in the mission brief. There were hundreds of people. We freaked out one poor Albanian guy. He was yelling at his kids, because his kids were playing in the hedgerow. The kids hadn't seen us; they were about four feet away. He turned to yell at the kids and his eyes got really, really, wide. His kids took off, and he ran off at the high port yelling and screaming, so we radioed in for an extraction: they came in with a Grizzly and pulled us out. The duty officer originally told us to hold in place and continue, but he had appreciation for what was going on. There were three or four hundred people there! We got out of our Ghillie suits, wiped off the cam. We did, however, get nice close-ups of all the guys firing their weapons.[33]

There was, however, always lingering suspicion that the TMK could provide cover for UÇK people who wanted to continue the fight. Meanwhile the behavior of the Russian contingent down the road from the Chalet was just as likely to trigger incidents, not only with the local population but with other KFOR contingents. In many cases such incidents involved drunken Russians careening around Kosovo in armored vehicles. Cpl. Alan Spencer from the recce platoon watched the drama unfold from the back of his Coyote vehicle:

One night we were on patrol, watching the Priština airport. There were two Russians who were drunk [and] blowing through the farmer's fields and suddenly here we were chasing a frigging BTR [wheeled APC]. We kept the surveillance on it and they came up to Radevo, where we had a platoon house. The tankers kept a Leopard there. These stupid buggers come down on the black track with this BTR. The Dragoons had got the word, so there was this tank looking down at this little BTR, with the gun pointed at them. It was funny. The BTR was just looking at them and it was a stand-off for a few minutes and they retreated to the main road, where the Russians got a hold of them, beat the crap out of them, and took them away. That was the one bad thing we had to deal with there: the Russians were always getting drunk, selling stuff, trying to get booze. At the northern VCP two Russians stole a civilian car, put civilian clothes over their uniforms, and tried to get out to get booze. Some of the guys from Duke's Company even found a Russian who had been missing. They thought he was AWOL, but when they found him half of his clothes were ripped off. The dogs had [been] at him and there was a bullet hole in his head.[34]

Master Warrant Officer Paul Mason:

Our biggest problem with organized crime was basically the Russians. There was a store in Vrelo not too far from where their camp was. They would go in there, threaten the owner, steal all of his booze. They would then throw him to the floor and go away. So we put some overwatch in there and informed the Russian LO, who told his CO. They tried to shut it down, but they were right across the road [and didn't]. Once these guys got a bit of wobbly pop in them at night they would wander off. We had a VCP to the south to turn them around. Then we had a problem identifying them in civilian clothes: who was an officer and who wasn't. So we convinced them to come up with an ID card and give it to the officers. The Brits produced that for them. Then we had a bunch of Russians who hijacked the store owner's car, made the store owner drive it, and tried to get through a VCP. There was a grenade in the car, which we confiscated. There were twelve hundred of these guys in that camp and they had nothing to do except bother Bravo Company![35]

TOW under armor vehicles were brought in to supplement the 1 RCR Coyotes watching the Russian KFOR contingent. Sgt. Hayward Russell:

We were just about finished [with] our patrol and were coming down this road and these Russians which had too much to drink came driving around in a BTR-80 eight-wheeled APC. It had a turret with a 12.7mm machine gun mounted in it. He was just going crazy through this town, so we blocked him off. We put some more vehicles in there so he couldn't get away. He didn't like that much: we tried to get him out of his vehicle, but that didn't work. The tank troop then got involved, but the tanks couldn't maneuver very well in the town. Then the Russians didn't want to play, so they got in the turret and started to swing the gun around. We noticed, though, that the barrel was packed full of newspaper. The company commander then told us to back off. Then the Russian started causing more trouble and started going through the town like crazy again. The Russian bosses finally came up and got a hold of him. We had him pinned down, but nobody wanted to play. We had two Leopards and two TUA to get him. I mean, we would block the road and he would go off into the ditch, hit a house, skirted another house, and so on. This went on for six hours.[36]

Rough justice was meted out: the Russian perpetrators were publicly flogged.

Kosovo's decaying postcommunist infrastructure occasionally produced serious environmental hazards to the Canadian soldiers during Operation Kinetic. Several of these lurked inside the Feronikl plant east of Glogovac. Capt. Jay Harvey:

Our patrol was contacted by a local who worked the plant: it had been seriously damaged during the bombing campaign. The patrol received a report that there were radioactive containers. Our engineers attached to the battle group led by Capt. Chad Rizzato went to see if he could find these things in the plant. He talked to the technical director, and he was shown one or two of them still mounted on a conveyor belt. They were used in mining. Mounted on a conveyor belt, one of these radioactive spheres, as they were called, had a small aperture which sent a small beam of radiation across the belt to a receiver. As the ore travels down the belt, it gets dumped into a bin. When the bin backs up and is full, the ore stops this radioactive beam from hitting the receiver so there's no flow any more, the bin dumps and empties, and the process starts again. We're talking old Soviet technology.

Unfortunately some of these radioactive spheres were damaged during the bombing campaign. They were being held in a warehouse: it was bombed, caught fire, and melted the lead plugs out of some of the spheres. I was the battle group NBCD [nuclear, biological, chemical defense] officer and as such was tasked to investigate. I met with the technical director, who indicated he didn't know what was in these: he indicated that they weren't damaged to begin with, but I insisted that he show them to me. Cpl. Gerry Wicht went in with an ABM300, a radiation survey meter. We had personal dosimeters, all alarm capable. We went to the damaged warehouse. We then walked around a pile of scrap metal, which we later figured out was blocking some of the radiation. That was why our alarms didn't go off immediately. As we rounded the corner, all of the alarms on all of the equipment we had started sounding. All of them. Every single alarm we had, and we had four between us. We took a quick reading and left to limit the exposure. The turn-back limit for NATO was 2 Sv per hour. The fast reading I took was 500 Sv per hour. So 250 times the NATO turn-back limit. We turned back.[37]

Aside from the hazard posed to those unaware of the risk, the radioactive spheres had other lethal applications. With the correct amount of explosives strapped to them, they could have formed crude dirty bombs that could have been employed either against KFOR or against a population center to deny it to a particular ethnic group. NATO in fact rated this as a possibility back in 1999.[38] Lieutenant Colonel Pennington and Colonel Fenton asked for and got a technical assistance visit (TAV) to assess the problem.

The TAV was escorted through the cordon and quickly determined that the emitter was a Cs-137 gamma radiation emitter. When measured using the TAV's equipment, the reading was 13,000 Sv per hour. The battle group hung signage and maintained a cordon of the area. A civilian contractor arranged at the brigade level eventually removed the material for disposal.[39]

The Pioneers from 1 RCR battle group were also involved with assessing the effects of depleted uranium (DU). Sensationalistic media reports concerning the use of this material in ammunition fired by tank-busting aircraft like the A-10 during the conflict produced an uproar when a number of Italian soldiers returned from Kosovo and suffered various cancers and leukemias years later. It was alleged that these men had contracted their diseases after coming into contact with wrecked armored vehicles that had apparently been hit with DU rounds. Were Canadians so exposed? Capt. Jay Harvey, Pioneer platoon commander:

> I conducted surveys all over the Canadian AOR, as the NBCD officer, and I mean *all* over the Canadian AOR. I was in bombed-out vehicles looking for depleted uranium and found absolutely no sign or trace. DU is obviously an extremely valuable weapon. People said these vehicles were bombed out with them. There was a 2S1 [self-propelled gun] that was hit with depleted uranium rounds. I conducted a survey with a micro spec 2, which is a spectroscopy system. It will pick up any amount of depleted uranium. There was absolutely nothing. I am a fastidious records keeper, and I have all of the surveys I conducted.[40]

Indeed the campaign against DU was an attempt to bring pressure to limit NATO and Western military capabilities before the air campaign in Kosovo. It had as its origin an Iraqi disinformation campaign initiated back in 1990 during the first Gulf War and remains fodder to this day on anti-American and environmentalist websites.[41]

Cordon and Search at Medvece

In February 2000 the battle group's attentions were directed at Medvece. At first glance Medvece isn't much of a town. Its orange-roofed brick houses are off the beaten path and are nestled at the base of Mount Goleš, tucked away from the north-south road leading from Magura to the Russian-held bunker near the Priština airport. One could miss the entrance to the town if one was driving too fast along the route: shielding it from view are piles of rusting construction equipment and numerous deteriorating buildings that once served the trains passing by on the railway line to

Kosovo Polje. The town itself is split in half by a creek, which is small by Canadian standards.

There were reports that weapons were moving in and out of the town: night surveillance was initiated on 2 February and directed at a potential meeting place. The specific threat and potential target were unclear. The proximity of Medvece to the Russian KFOR contingent was cause for concern and had been as well during the 1 PPCLI's tenure. Despite the fact that the UÇK was disbanded and the current occupants of the Chalet had nowhere near the capability that they once possessed, no one could be sure: there was concern that "shortly after their swearing in, there are early indications that the leadership of the [TMK] will not be compliant with the intention of their charter. Most zone commanders will likely follow their own agendas that are not in harmony with the goals of the international community."[42]

The situation in Medvece suddenly destabilized on 4 February. Lt. Alex Haynes:

Somebody managed to get a grenade in under a car. It killed one guy and wounded another. That night there was already a section there: they were doing a VCP on the road. Master Corporal Crellin's section [was] 150 meters away. They were there with an UNMIK officer, "UNMIK Rick" from Seattle. He had a bomb-sniffing dog. So the grenade went off and Master Corporal Crellin started advancing towards where the explosion went off, showing quite a lot of courage in my opinion: UNMIK Rick and the dog took off. The section tried to save one guy: he died. They saved the other one. I showed up ten minutes later with the quick reaction force section led by Master Corporal Ravensdale. We immediately started searching some of the stores. We found nothing at that time.[43]

Lt. Eleanor Taylor was the duty officer:

Master Corporal Crellin was out doing a VCP and then a call came in on the radio: "Explosions heard in the background, send QRF." We had heard explosions all the time: civilians blowing up mines, firing a gun, blah blah blah. So every time we heard an explosion, it did not necessarily mean that we had to send the QRF. I told him to send a proper sitrep because I didn't know what was going on. The next transmission said there had been a grenade attack, that they heard small arms and were advancing to see what was going on. At this point I realized it was fairly serious, so I immediately sent the QRF and ambulances. I wasn't thinking of anything else at the time except I had better find out what was happening, advise higher, and send backup. You know, here I was sitting faithfully in the box [command post vehicle], and there were these guys out there facing God knows what. The next report was that there had been an explosion in a car, one dead who died in the section commander's hands, and there had been small arms fire. Battalion started screaming, and things just started to whirl up. They had a helicopter on standby, the commanding officer came zooming down . . . everybody was there except me, who was in the box, wishing I could be out there. It was really a section commander's ball game; he was the one dealing with it. I got to look at the faces of the people when they came back and they were pretty gray. I did nothing heroic, but it all became very real at that point.[44]

Maj. Rob MacIlroy: "It was too late for one guy, but our medics did an outstanding job; Master Corporal McInnis particularly. When we responded, one of the things we wanted to set was the tone: you search houses, but not willy-nilly because you don't know where the guy came from. We didn't know which house he was from, so you search the headman and every sort of group that the villages have appointed as their representative, usually one from each ethnic group. My standard procedure was that representatives from each group get searched, top to bottom, not just one."[45]

But nothing was found in this quick search.

The problems in Medvece were not necessarily related to aggression by former UÇK troops against the Russian contingent, though the town could have been used as a base or staging point for doing so. Lt. Alex Haynes: "That town had some serious issues. It's almost evenly divided between Gypsies and Albanians, and there had been a couple of grenade attacks before: one guy had one tossed into his yard. These were Gypsies who had been driven out of Magura."[46]

COME ON FEEL THE NOISE

Lt. Eleanor Taylor:

In Medvece we had problems with the Romas and the Albanians. The Serbs weren't even an issue. We had been warned about this by the Patricias that there were constant squabbles between the two groups, but they usually sorted it out on their own. This time, though, it was winter and they were not allowed to chop down trees. The people in Medvece were in a kind of Catch-22. A load of wood was dropped off by an aid organization, and it was supposed to be split up evenly. But there were two or three refugee families: they were not originally residents of the town. The village head-man wanted to give them wood, but the other people there didn't. I thought we could work this out with some low-level negotiations, talk to the headman, talk to the people. All of a sudden this big riot breaks out, pitchforks and bricks, not at us but at each other. We were in the middle of it, myself, two sergeants, and a driver, with thirty or forty belligerents. We were getting shoved around, but we pushed the people apart and jumped up on a ledge and told them that if they didn't get themselves sorted out the wood will be gone and no more aid would be dropped off. We said we would be back tomorrow. This placated them and the headman got upset and said, "I quit! I don't want to be the headman anymore!" And he started to cry. I told him that I sympathized with his position but that he would have to remain headman at least for a little while. I told him that the people we took over from told us that he did an excellent job and we were very happy with his work. The next day the wood was in all the appropriate places.[47]

Lt. Col. Bruce Pennington:

The Bravo Company commander said he would like to run a cordon and search operation, so I gave him snipers and TOW. They went in the night before [on 9 February], watched the village, and came up with a plan. This wasn't five houses: it was forty or fifty. We were also learning as we went: we know how to do cordon and searches, but we were also learning how to interpret the information we had. There were lessons to be learned from this specific case. Major MacIlroy made arrangements to get some British search dogs and their handlers. I was also very interested in the operation and made arrangements to have a Griffon helicopter available to watch the operation. I was able to listen and talk on all of the radio nets. You have a completely different perspective of what's going on from the air: you can see everything. I'm watching the village and the pilot says, "Do you see how all the villagers are interacting?" He was trying to pass on what he learned when he was working with the Finns or Swedes on another cordon and search operation. "I see a whole bunch of people down there." "Okay, reference the red brick building; see the people in the courtyard?" They were just standing around talking. "Do you see the people standing in a circle near the white building?" Yes. "Why are they standing in a circle?" So the pilot started to fly smaller circles, not too obvious. "I'm going to fly over them. If they disperse, then they have something to hide. If they just look up, they're probably just talking about what they had last night for supper." We flew over and they dispersed, running away. I called up the company commander and said, "I'm looking over building such and such, we saw people behaving in a strange manner, get a patrol up there." They searched them and found pistols and some grenades. I said to the company commander afterwards that he should think about getting a helicopter the next time he did an operation like this![48]

The snipers covertly crept in to observe:

Two teams deployed out of Bravo Company's AOR in Magura. They went up past the cement factory into the hills west of Medvece. There were four of us. We were in location for twenty-four hours plus. Our role was to overwatch, to see if any activity was happening prior to the search, if they'd been tipped off, if they were trying to cache weapons or anything unusual. A lot of the time the interpreters were not reliable, they had friends who would tell two friends, and so on and so on. We moved to a lay up [a] position near where our OPs [outposts] would be. We found an effective OP with optimum arcs. The second team would be farther back, with a better view than the first team. They were more like backup because their main focus was down on the hill; they couldn't see what was going on behind them. We had a very limited ability to travel off routes [because of the mines and UXO]. We had to request this covert OP, then we had to request engineer support. So when we went to do this covert OP, an M-113 with a dozer showed up with a Bison ambulance! They had two guys with metal detectors that wailed away when they came close, and every spot where they found metal was sprayed with orange paint! This was all done before we went in during the day, in full view of the town! We went in by foot, though the route had been proved by the Nyala vehicle before.

We had really good comms, and we kept a running commentary with Bravo Company and [the CO] of all significant events. That way they are apprised of the situation at all times. So we don't have any big surprises. Then Bravo Company started their cordon and search.[49]

Capt. Jon Herbert:

The north side of the town was Albanian; the south on the other side of the stream was Roma. The OC and I planned it out. The OC said he didn't want to shut the town down, so we weren't establishing a proper cordon. We basically did roving searches once we got in there. We had so many battalion assets: TOW, a helicopter, and snipers for observation. The snipers were dug in doing overwatch. We broke the platoons into three QRF sections that would move to the center of town with the other sections fanning out from there, with a regular QRF from Magura outside. We were all in Grizzlies. Once we started with the observation, the snipers were providing us with lots of information. If anybody tried to leave or move about the town, they would pass it on. We didn't have enough people to picket each house after we searched it. . . . The houses were all in close proximity: we would finish one house, have a section start moving, and then people would start coming out of the woodwork, so we would move into where they came from. We saw one person start moving around, so we stopped them. A family came out of another house, one we searched twenty minutes before. We stopped them and they all had grenades. We arrested them, turned them over to UNMIK and the military police, and confiscated their weapons. That happened throughout the day.

We would stop people in the streets and search them. Ah, here's a weapon. Our roving sections all had metal detectors to assist in this. We had the two British sniffer dogs. They were very good, but they got tired by the end of the day and ended up chasing some cats. We found a couple of pistols. They even hid one with a mentally retarded women, because they didn't think we would pay any attention to her. One of our sergeants said, "Something isn't right here!" He stopped her and found two pistols on her. These people were just losers. They were using kids to move weapons around. Later on one of the sergeants came up and said, "Sir, you have to see this." We went into this one house, and the owners, who were Roma, had their suitcases packed and on a shelf. Every Roma house had their things packed, ready to go. When we asked them, they told us they feared for their lives. If they had to leave they would just pick up their cases and go. There were a lot of arguments in this town: the Kosovars were getting all the food. During this cordon and search, we also checked the attics. We brought the owners in with us during the searches and watched them. If they got nervous, we'd intensify the search. We would find bags of wheat. One guy had three cows in a shed: they were blind because they had been in there three years. We brought them out into the sun and they were all screwed up. It turned into the Calgary Stampede. They were stockpiling and selling the food. Free food was given to them, and they sold it for hard cash.

The dog teams were an important asset. Master Warrant Officer Paul Mason:

We had one platoon for search, another on the cordon. We moved in straight from Magura at first light. We closed off all of the roads leading into town with an anti-armor detachment of two TUA and the other sections from 4 Platoon. 5 Platoon was responsible for the searches. We also had this dog team. There was this British corporal, and she had two dogs with her. They were fantastic. They could really sniff things out. They found a pistol in one of those big stacks of hay. The dogs were going crazy, and we dug in and found the pistol right in the middle of this sucker. I couldn't

COME ON FEEL THE NOISE

figure out for the life of me how the dogs could do it. That stack of hay was almost all frigging horseshit.

The situation in town was tense. The Roma were from Magura, and the people of Magura basically ousted them when the conflict was on. The Roma were living there in Medvece but wanted to go back to Magura, and we were trying to negotiate that but with no luck. The headman in Magura was stubborn and didn't want them back there. The Roma from Magura were originally pretty well off and owned the majority of the town. They weren't getting it back.[50]

The snipers remained behind to watch some more and then were withdrawn. Another potential flashpoint was headed off at the pass, but a much larger one was brewing.

Mitrovica

The image that is most associated with Kosovo is that of Cpl. Brendan Massey of the 1 RCR's Pioneer platoon in Mitrovica. Kitted out with C-7 assault rifle, body armor, and load-bearing vest attached to his massive torso and topped off with a shaven head covered by a boonie hat, with impassive sunglasses masking his eyes underneath and sporting a matted ZZ Top biker beard, Corporal Massey standing guard on the Austerlitz Bridge in Mitrovica became the ultimate symbol of NATO resolve in the Balkans. The picture was soon on the front pages of newspapers worldwide.

The men of 1 RCR's Pioneer platoon are quiet, intense people not used to public scrutiny. Indeed they would be the first to admit that operations in Mitrovica in February 2000 were not a solo show; they included elements from nearly the entire Canadian contingent: the 1 RCR battle group sent Pioneers, snipers, recce people, and an infantry company, while the RCD sent Coyotes and 430 ETAH deployed Griffon helicopters, all in support of one of the most critical KFOR operations since the entry into Kosovo in the summer of 1999. Yet the Pioneers' unique appearance and their stand on the bridge drew the attention of the world's media, and it was with great pride that Canadians saw their soldiers' professionalism displayed for all to see. But what went wrong in Mitrovica? Why were the Canadians sent to a city that lay far outside the Canadian sector?

As discussed in previous chapters, the northern region of Kosovo was rich in natural resources, and Mitrovica was the gateway to this area. It also possessed substantial mining-related industry and sufficient housing stock, something that was in short supply in other areas. Ethnically, the bulk of the population in Mitrovica was Kosovar Albanian, with a Kosovar Serb minority: the rural region to the north was almost exclusively Kosovar Serb. During the war many Kosovar Albanians had been run out of northern Mitrovica, and some Kosovar Serbs went north. In general terms there was a long-term problem, as well as a short-term problem. The long-term problem related to Kosovo and its desire for independence from Serbia. If this was achieved, with the Kosovar Albanians dominating a newly sovereign state, such a state would need a viable economy. It would therefore need access to the resources in the north. The inconvenient fact was that the north was dominated by Kosovar Serbs.

The short-term problem related to tactical moves by Kosovar Albanian elements to achieve more and more political control, with the ultimate objective of independence. The Mitrovica situation, as it developed, provided a number of stepping stones for laying the groundwork. At the same time, UÇPMB activity in the Preševo Valley kept Belgrade's forces occupied and KFOR distracted. Or was it the other way around? The danger was that if the situation in Mitrovica got too far out of control, the possibility of a mechanized VJ incursion to protect the Kosovar Serbs in the north was real. At the same time, there were Kosovar Serb and Serbian elements that sought to stimulate such a move. At many levels Mitrovica was test: Could the Kosovar Albanians who wanted independence push the Kosovar Serbs out using nontraditional methods? How would KFOR react and with what methods? What would Belgrade do? Could "salami tactics" be used to slice and whittle away at KFOR to wear it down?

The apparent catalyst, however, was an RPG attack executed against a French-escorted UN-sponsored refugee bus in the MNB (North) sector on 2 February 2000. Two were killed and thirty wounded: all were Kosovar Serbs. At first KFOR HQ interpreted this attack as Belgrade's effort to demonstrate to KFOR that the Serbs could or would not be protected. The next day violence erupted in Mitrovica when another victim from the bus attack died. The violence indicated that the Kosovar Serbs would not just stand by any longer; they would respond with force. Then someone threw a Molotov cocktail at a French VAB APC. Russian troops responding to an inter-Albanian confrontation in Kamenica in MNB (North) shot two people, and then a Russian soldier escorting Kosovar Serb children was shot in retaliation in Berivojce.[51]

Between 3 and 7 February ethnically motivated attacks occurred not only in Mitrovica but throughout MNB (North). KFOR HQ determined that it "was in reactive mode and was making plans to separate the Kosovar Serbs and Albanians." The Italian-led MNB (West) deployed VCPs to isolate the MNB (North) area, while MNB (Center) did the same. An American infantry company from MNB (South) was brought into Mitrovica to reinforce the French.[52]

The situation in Mitrovica had calmed down by 8 February, but that quiet didn't last long. Three Kosovar Albanian leaders— Thaçi, Rexhepi, and Mahmuti—stirred up crowds in their areas. The theme was one of defiance and accusations that French KFOR forces favored the Kosovar Serbs. One leader even used the term "UÇK" in the present tense. Information gathering in the Canadian AOR indicated that the population generally favored anti-French measures, and analysts predicted that there would be a confrontation with the French forces in the near future. The pressure was stepped up on 10 February: the first meeting of the Kosovo Transitional Council, a multiethnic component of the NATO/UN-led Joint Interim Administrative Structure (JIAS), was subjected to three large Kosovar Albanian demonstrations. The propaganda thread spun from these was that KFOR was permitting Serb violence. A three-hour protest in Djeneral Janković blocked the vital Kačanik defile MSR to Macedonia and thus demonstrated how vulnerable KFOR was to such action.[53]

The crisis escalated further on 13 February. There were several firefights in Mitrovica following the shooting of two French soldiers. Initial reports were that Kosovar Serbs had fired the shots, but the analysis pointed toward the Kosovar Albanians. French, Italian, and British forces in Mitrovica engaged armed individuals on both sides throughout the day, killing one. Concern at KFOR HQ revolved around the probability that any KFOR forces seen to be supporting the French would also be targeted by the Kosovar Albanians. Something had to be done to de-escalate the situation—and soon.[54]

In its winter 2000 iteration Mitrovica was in worse shape than the commanders of Op Kinetic Roto 0 had experienced during a similar situation encountered back in November. Col. Ivan Fenton, the Task Force Kosovo commander, was convinced that "the troubles there might have triggered [a Serb] military incursion."[55] Canadian involvement in Mitrovica, however, was not assured: there were numerous complicating factors.

To deploy units or sub-units outside the MNB (Center) AOR, permission had to be sought from the DCDS after the request was received by the task force commander from Commander KFOR and the commander of MNB (Center): this was similar to the process surrounding the employment of the RCD near the Preševo Valley, and it would take time. Second, the mission in Mitrovica might involve Canadian units conducting some form of crowd control. The Canadian policy in Ottawa was in flux, and the impact of unrealistic restrictions had already been demonstrated in the Drvar riots in Bosnia and in smaller operations undertaken by the battle group in Kosovo. Third, the more timid and skittish people in the Ottawa policy world might attempt to exert influence to keep the Canadian contingent out of harm's way for fear of media repercussions.

Broadly put, there were those who thought or argued that Canada was being used to do other people's dirty work in an environment where the French or KFOR or both had lost control of the situation. A variant on this argument was that the British in command of the multinational brigade were prepared to misemploy Canadian "colonials" instead of their own forces.

The arguments for a Canadian deployment to Mitrovica had two very strong points. First (eventually borne out by a British report) was that "the RCD/RCR recce capability is the most high

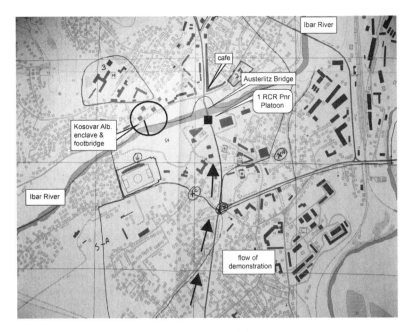

FIG. 14. Operations in Mitrovica.

value/high return [surveillance and target acquisition] asset to be deployed by KFOR in Mitrovica."[56] The second argument related to history.

During the UNPROFOR days in Bosnia in 1994 the relationship between the Canadian contingent and the British commander of the UN force was extremely poor. This related to misunderstandings between the two entities about who had operational command and control over the Canadian battle group. On a number of occasions the Canadian contingent refused to participate in what its commander viewed as needlessly risky situations with dubious benefits in a highly lethal environment. Consequently British officers referred to the contingent as "Can't Bat," a play on the UN term "Can Bat." Both Lieutenant Colonel Pennington and Colonel Fenton were sensitized to this. As Colonel Fenton put it, "We can't be seen as a country that does only the easy parts of the jobs in theater."[57] Similarly, the 1 RCR battle group CO was equally convinced: "I felt as a Canadian and a military officer that we had been committed to operations under NATO, that we should be doing everything that everyone else in NATO was doing. We're part of that team that was there at the time."[58] These arguments held sway, and Canada committed forces to Mitrovica.

The stage, or rather the chessboard, for the Mitrovica disturbances was for the most part centered on the Austerlitz Bridge, which was right downtown.

The Austerlitz span is one of two bridges over the Ibar River in the city proper. Three-quarters of Mitrovica lies to the south of the river: this area is mostly Kosovar Albanian. The other quarter of the city, on the high ground north of the river, is mixed Albanian Serb, with Kosovar Serb predominating in this mostly residential area. A bizarre communist-era sculpture that looks like a warped, conal *T* crowns one of the hills. To the west of the bridge on the north side is a grouping of three high-rise apartment buildings. Immediately south of the Austerlitz Bridge is a market street, the pale yellow cultural center, a concrete sports arena and gymnasium, the town council building, the library, and several high-rise office and residential buildings.

Led by Capt. Simon Parker, the 1 RCR's recce platoon and its Coyotes departed for Mitrovica on 15 February. The battle group snipers also deployed around this time:

> There was a two-day delay. I got a call in our quarters to get down to the CP immediately. Two French soldiers had just been shot on the eastern bridge. Nobody knew exactly who had shot them, but because they were French, they assumed it was the Albanians. We were told that we were deploying to Mitrovica to assist A Company of the Royal Green Jackets. The mission wasn't stated other than to provide sniper support. We packed and then we were stood down, pending national authority approval from Ottawa. This went on for two days. Then Colonel Fenton showed up and briefed us. It was unusual that the contingent commander would do that. I normally received my instructions from the [intelligence officer] or [operations officer] or sometimes even the CO. Then we got approval and we went in the same time as the recce platoon. We set up in the auditorium building.[59]

Cpl. Alan Spencer, a surveillance operator from the 1 RCR's recce platoon:

We had one sensor mounted on its tripod on the vehicle, and we used buildings [along the river] as cover for the Coyotes on the perimeter [of the no-go zone around the bridge]. We actually put a sensor on top of a building looking down. We were split up, on each side of the road. We were watching the Serb side of the river. You could pick out the key characters just from watching through the optics. We called them The Jackets. They wore the same type of jackets, just different colors. You'd see them start in the morning, sometimes at night. They'd gather in this one café right here on the corner [next to the north end of the bridge]. Basically everything happened out of this market area [next to the main road to the bridge]. There were a few trees, a concrete area, a sitting bench, a couple of newsstands, kiosks. They guys would be on their cell phones and another guy would come along and start talking. Then he'd take a message to somebody else. These guys were in charge of pushing all of the women forward in the demonstrations, moving them up to the front line, so it looked like it was all the women throwing rocks. Whenever something bad happened, these jacket guys were all around the outside perimeter, coordinating it. It was hard to say if they were armed. They most likely had pistols on them, but I don't know. We could see it all happening, but there was nothing we could do about it, because they were on the French side, under French jurisdiction. The French were friendly towards them too. They were friendly enough to be caught on tape. Now, that could have just been friendly talk, but it was almost like the French were letting them do this; that was the impression I got. The French also had snipers set up; their optics were the same as ours. They weren't Serb. The French higher-ups couldn't get over the information we were giving our people about their soldiers; they didn't know how we were doing it. The RCD guys showed up after us and deployed a Coyote with a mast.[60]

The RCD were sent up to augment a planned cordon and search operation that was scheduled for 20 February, the day after MNB

(North) had established a "no demonstration" zone around the Austerlitz Bridge.

Capt. Brian Power of the Dragoons:

> Not to slag off the French or anything, but they weren't having a lot of success in there. . . . We sent a troop of Coyotes to work with the Royal Green Jackets. The idea was that they were going to set up on the south side and then do a cordon and search on the north side. There were some beautiful spots on the north side for OPs: one was near this monument to what might have been the most productive tractor makers or something, but we weren't allowed to go up there. We ended up sitting on the south looking across the river. Everything [that was going on] in Mitrovica was happening along the river anyway. There was an OP to the west and another next to the bridge. The idea of the surveillance was to support the [Royal Green Jackets].[61]

Starting at dawn, the American infantry company moved into a Kosovar Serb neighborhood opposite the eastern bridge. A mob prompted the French commander to withdraw the Americans. A combined Canadian-British operation in the Kosovar Albanian sector, however, proceeded without incident. Poor coordination between MNB (North) and UNMIK resulted in UNMIK police not being informed about the cordon and searches until it was too late, which hampered the search effort. It was later revealed that UNMIK police were opposed to working with the French. Back in January 2000 UNMIK police had been abandoned by French troops and then beaten by a mob.[62]

The RCR snipers had a clear view of events as they unfolded:

> We were on top of a ten-story apartment building after we arrived on the ground. I was dispatched to link up with our British sniper counterparts. They were from the Royal Green Jackets. They had been up there for thirty-six hours. I didn't know the area or who was who. Their CO was busy directing the infantry company. I needed to find out what the countersniper plan was, what they had in place. There was this one poor British sniper. He was a senior corporal who had been a sniper years and years ago. He was totally

COME ON FEEL THE NOISE

exhausted. I asked him how things were divided up and he said, "Mate, I've got nothing." He was covering the whole frontage of the British operation. I told him we had three teams available, so why don't we divide up the frontage. One point of interest was this little café near the bridge. That was the heart of the matter. The Serb security forces were working out of that. They had pickets and patrols. It was all controlled by Motorola. They were real trouble makers. The electronic warfare boys were listening in to these guys. They had a van down in the courtyard and a team in a tower. It was a rough environment for them [with all the buildings]. So anyway we split up the frontage, and I briefed the British colonel. And he says, "Right, you have all the snipers in the area, and I'll get you two more teams." So I had four British teams, plus my teams, for a total of seven.

We anticipated a high threat, and that was normal operating mode. The Americans crossed this bridge doing a clearing operation through to the bar and the university. When the Americans got to the university, they got a hostile reception. When they broke into the classrooms, the Serbs started to stone them. They had a running rock battle. The Americans were withdrawing. We heard on the radio that they were coming back across the bridge, and they did. They were flying across it, with a crowd of about two thousand in hot pursuit throwing bottles and rocks at them.

We had other overwatch tasks, and we got to know the city pretty good. The British intelligence guys were anticipating something and wanted information on Kosovar Albanian leaders, where they were hanging out and so on. So we spent a lot of time videotaping and looking for additional OPs. That really paid off when the marches started.[63]

Capt. Andrew Atherton of the Dragoons:

On the twentieth of February we started hearing all sorts of indicators that there was going to be a march or demonstration to push for a unified Mitrovica. Initial reports were that five thousand people were going to do this: they were going to walk from Priština up the main road. We've got to be prepared for something like this. All sorts of checkpoints had to be established to prevent busloads of soccer hooligans and people like that. So it was buildup, buildup, buildup. Brian Power and I (Major Datchko was on leave) decide that if there is going to be a riot up there, we've got to be with our guys there too: Colonel Fenton and everybody is going to be calling me wondering what the hell was going on. We went up the back way. Normally it [is] a forty-minute drive: it took four and half hours. The roads were just chock-a-block with people, thousands of people on these secondary roads. It was totally organized. You could just cut the tension in that town with a knife. We noticed that as we got closer and closer there were all sorts of women and kids, and as you got to the bridge it was all men. We made it to the compound. Originally we were just going to check things out and get out of Dodge, but there was no way out once we were there. We already had two Coyotes there filming everything, so we added one more.[64]

All was not passive on the Kosovar Serb side of the river. The snipers kept a close watch on potential troublemakers:

We had a good feel for this café; it was their security force CP. They were equipped with Motorolas and some had binos. They all wore these soccer jackets, like team jackets. These fellows would confront the French on a daily basis. If the French brought someone across, like an Albanian, God help him. These fellows would be out with rocks and bottles and punching him. And they'd be on the Motorolas. As soon as the Motorolas came out, a crowd would come down. It was quite organized. We had been filming and taping those guys, and the recce got good shots too. They weren't carrying weapons. But we saw them coming in and out of the blocks and the café with paper bags. You couldn't see weapons, but you knew that's what they were. The British electronic warfare guys also heard them deploying snipers. So we knew they were out there. Whenever there was a buildup, they got the snipers, so then we went on alert. We had multiple positions in this building that we could change if we were compromised. And that happened.

You could see the sympathy the French had for the Serbs. It was evident here. The Serbs would not accept any other nation on the bridge. If that happened, rent-a-crowd would show up to protest.

COME ON FEEL THE NOISE

One of my guys saw the French snipers take the scopes off their weapons and hand them to people in the crowd to point out our positions. Whether it was French army or French marines, recce platoon caught them taking money from the Serbs, like payola. It was enough to be captured on video. We never let the French in on anything, and I hate to say it—they were junk. I think they were pro-Serb. The Albanians hated them. We saw this day in and day out. They'd have a little chit-chat and then shake hands. And we videoed exchanges of cash. We gave this to their LOs, but they didn't want to hear about it. It was frustrating. It hampered our operational ability. Everything we did in the beginning, our plans, our traces, it all went over to the French snipers: you know, brothers in arms. They would stand on the roofs, not covering anything, just watching.[65]

Griffons from 430 ETAH followed the progress of the march. Maj. Steve Charpentier:

It looked like twenty thousand people. We flew for eight hours that day, which is the maximum you are supposed to fly in any one day. So we followed the crowd, all the time, and we reported on its progression. We tried to look at everything. Every time we would go to the head of the crowd we would drop down to fifty feet, door open with the door gun and everything, and the crowd would wave at us, "Raaaaahhhhhh!" They were in good spirits; they didn't appear to be mean. So we handled overwatch of the crowd all the way. We had some friction with the French. We landed at Mitrovica. The French were worried about their image, and this French army guy went nuts when he saw us land with two door guns and everything and gave the pilot hell. They didn't like the guns out. They were screaming at Captain Lalancette. They're not like Canadians: they scream and explode. Our guys were shaken up by this treatment and didn't want to go back to deal with these guys, so they didn't for a few days. It was bad enough it went up the chain of command, that the French didn't want to see us anymore. Later we flew in a doctor. We saw the Pioneers: we called them "ZZ Top." I was very proud of them, what they did on the bridge. They really looked the image of the big Canadian bear hunter.[66]

The Pioneer platoon, led by Capt. Jay Harvey and Warrant Officer Rick Duncan, wound up at the focal point of the Mitrovica demonstration. Captain Harvey:

We deployed on 18 February. It started off with a cordon and search operation targeting Kosovar Albanians on the south side. This was a massive KFOR operation, including dropping leaflets from helicopters informing the population that the search was going to be conducted, when, and by whom. It was designed to encourage them to turn over their weapons. We received a briefing from our CO. We were aware from daily O Groups [orders groups] what was going on in Mitrovica. The operation was called Op Bulldog [by MNB (Center)]. We knew there had been rocket attacks and grenade attacks; we were aware of the importance of reintegrating Kosovar Albanians onto the north side. It was a flashpoint and the eyes of the world were looking on. The media was there: their focal point was the Austerlitz Bridge. There were other bridges, but the media set up on this one before the demonstration happened, before all the attacks happened, and as a result, that's where all the people went. So can you tie the presence of the media to where everything happened? Quite probably. In my opinion definitely. The water, which is ankle deep in places, stretches four kilometers through the town of Mitrovica. There were other things behind Op Bulldog too. One was obviously KFOR unity. Brits working with Canadians working with Americans working with the French towards a common goal. It was a show of solidarity within KFOR.

We arrived the evening of 18 February. It was scheduled for that time for obvious reasons. We moved from Priština, flat-bedding our vehicles up the back route to Mitrovica, and off-loaded. We mounted the dozers on our M-113s at the gymnasium. It was the headquarters of the 2nd Battalion, Royal Green Jackets. The media was still in front: they saw us arrive, and all cameras and heads turned. Pioneers were not something the media usually sees. Soldiers are clean cut, clean shaven: we were clean cut but not clean shaven! The beards were unique. From the minute we arrived to the minute we left, all cameras and eyes were trained on us. In that part of the world people who wear beards are usually Spetsnaz,

COME ON FEEL THE NOISE

special forces or Četnik-type people. So when they saw the big, large, burly soldiers with beards, curiosity was definitely piqued.

We were working with British EOD; they had dog teams. There were Royal Military Police and us. There was a small intelligence cell, and there were electronic warfare assets there too. We were sent on a cordon and search to an abandoned soccer field, where there were tunnels and rooms underneath. There was no key, so we used hydraulic power tools to cut off locks and take down obstacles. Nothing was found. We were briefed later by the Green Jackets' CO that a demonstration was starting to form in Priština, and, as a result, all further operations were postponed. We were sitting in the gymnasium when action had to be taken to prevent the crowd from crossing the bridge. It was a coincidence that we were in Mitrovica at the same time. Pioneers do not have a crowd confrontation role: we were tasked to provide security on the building.

The demonstration was supposed to reach Mitrovica by 1430 hours on 21 February. That morning we toured the area with the CO of the Green Jackets: we had expertise in constructing obstacles and that could be useful in stopping the progress of the demonstrators. We got his intent, which was to stop any escalation of the conflict and prevent the use of force in this area. We had a three-layer plan. The first layer was a major junction, eight hundred meters away from the bridge. A platoon of the Green Jackets was to intercept the demonstration and attempt to keep them out of eyesight of the bridge. As soon as you see a target, you want to push to it. This platoon was supposed to identify those who wanted a symbolic crossing and escort them forward. Prior to the main arrival of the demonstration, a smaller local crowd gathered: they used the back roads to push around this first layer. When the platoon learned of this, they contacted the CO, who withdrew them to the second layer. The second layer was to place some wire on the road leading to the bridge and fix it between two buildings. The wire was laid out the morning the demonstrators arrived. However, the speed in which things happened on the twenty-first, [it wasn't ready]. Everything happened extremely quickly. From the moment we heard that a demonstration was formed to when we moved out was ten minutes. We grabbed our kit and moved to protect the building. As soon as we ran out we noticed that our M-113 vehicles parked outside the gym compound were being used as a platform by the demonstrators to taunt the north side of the bridge. With all the supporting vehicles, there was no room in the compound. We had already taken precautionary measures. Our vehicles were stripped of all external equipment and secured inside. The M-113 has a pintle mount for a .50-cal machine gun: we did not want those readily available for the demonstrators to use. All fuel cans were locked up.

The dozer blades usually rest on the ground. Knowing that a crowd was coming we raised the blades to chest level. It provided a solid wall forty feet long that couldn't be pushed through. In order to secure the Canadian vehicles, we moved forward from the building and began to move demonstrators from them. We placed a soldier on top of each one once we cleared it. This was done in a large part by Warrant Officer Rick Duncan. He is an extremely large man who can be very vocal. And that's all it took. He jumped up by himself onto the first one, yelled, and pointed. His presence and appearance and beard provided a little shock value. They quickly left, not a push, not a shove. No physical contact was required. He was an incredible presence and was awarded a CDS Commendation for his actions.

He grabbed one of our soldiers, told him to get on the vehicle and make sure nobody used it, leapt from the first one to the second one, cleared that, leapt to the third and to the fourth. In a matter of less than five minutes. To prevent entry into the building we formed a line in between and beside the vehicles parked out there. The crowd then increased in numbers as the Priština people arrived. Estimates say there were fifty thousand people on the streets of Mitrovica on 21 February. It was a mass surge of bodies against a single line of soldiers. There was no pushing, shoving, or punching. Nobody was trying to break through to cross the bridge at the initial commencement of this demonstration. And then it started to get a bit hairy. Individuals within the crowd started to incite those around them. It was planned: the objective was to reoccupy their homes on the north side. It was a show of resolve. Then the pushing started. The front ranks pushed the Green Jackets. At this time no Canadians were involved in supporting that front line. Individuals started to break through the Green Jackets, and there was nothing to stop them from crossing the bridge other than the French gendarmerie, which was set up on the bridge itself. This was their paramilitary police, which were part of KFOR. The Brits would send small teams to try and grab those who broke through: nobody was arrested or detained by the RMPs: it's a matter of taking those agitators from the front, moving them down an embankment, around through the gym compound, and throwing them back into the crowd. We are talking forty thousand people; it was taking an average of about fifteen or twenty minutes to get back to the front. Then it started to escalate. Pokes were given to British soldiers and pokes were given back to the demonstrators. It was about that time that we realized that unless something was done and fairly quickly, the line would be overwhelmed.

I could reach out and touch a demonstrator from where I was standing. Myself, Capt. Simon Parker from recce platoon, and our LO, Captain Phil [Hunter]. Between the three of us we made a decision. Yes, they required support, and if we didn't do it, they would have pushed through the British line and maimed the British. Se we moved into position to reinforce. Pioneer platoon took the left flank close to our vehicles. Our arrival in the line and the appearance thing played a large factor. The demonstrators realized that we were soldiers, and they lost ground. It was more like a soccer riot, where they start pushing the front gate and the police hold them back. At one minute it was pushing, shoving, occasional blows. At other times it was more amicable. They would offer cigarettes to the front-line soldiers. It was back and forth for a couple of hours. Command and control was extremely difficult. It was chaotic, loud, everybody is yelling, screaming, you're spread out thin. Impromptu situations came up. I was on the front line pushing and shoving next to a private from the Green Jackets and one of my corporals. We didn't know what was happening. Our medic was pushing and shoving in the front line.

In a moment of clarity we sucked back to observe and pass on directions. The crowd continued to ebb and flow. Around 1600 or 1630 they pushed a bit further. It was that time that the French on the bridge, without warning, began launching tear gas into the crowd. The first time it was a complete surprise to all of us: Brits, Canadians, and the crowd. Nobody had gas masks on. There was disorientation and confusion. The crowd started to turn and push back, moving away from the bridge. The French dropped short and the gas landed on our position. The wind helped, but for the most part it landed behind or on us. This one action changed the nature of the crowd from a soccer riot into a beating, kicking, hitting demonstration. This one action escalated it. The demonstrators were now looking for the easiest access away. And that was around our Pioneer vehicles. Our task was still to provide protection to the building.

As soon as the tear gas was launched, [we] run back down that hill, form a line, grab those fleeing, throw them down the line towards the main entrance, and escort them out. It became one big sausage belt. When the gas cleared, they tried to get back to the bridge, then another gas volley would come in. This went on for three hours. Once you use tear gas, you are committed, you cannot take that back. So not only do you have to keep using it, you have to use it in increasing strength. Gas masks: with British ROE, putting on gas masks in a crowd confrontation task is an escalation of force. So is showing riot shields and batons. When some British soldiers put on masks, they were ordered to take them off. You may think this is funny, but it is psychological. Crowd mentality: they're wearing masks, we're not. It also makes the troops look faceless. A gas mask can be used against you. I saw this with the British that put them on. They were grabbed, pulled over eyes, essentially blinding the soldier, exposing him to tear gas. Some were stolen, which gave demonstrators access to them.

When we started out, we were wearing soft hats, like Tilley hats; Brits had their berets. But everybody carried a helmet with them. About suppertime, when things got hairy, we received word that the French snipers on the north side of the bridge were using helmets to identify friendly soldiers on the south side. There was also concern that Serb snipers might fire into the crowd to provoke them. Anyway, helmets went on. This did not have a drastic effect on the crowd's dynamic. The same thing as before continued well into the night. We used vehicles as a barrier: we moved them with British

Warriors to stop the advance of the crowd. One Warrior was going to be used as a barrier: it got caught on a median dividing the road. It was immediately swamped by demonstrators and used as a platform. The crew commander began traversing the turret, using the 30mm cannon to clear the top deck. He got unstuck and formed part of the line. The line blocked the view of the bridge, and that went a long way to calming the crowd. The tear gas stopped. Then one of the French gendarmerie came off the bridge to see what was going on. I threw him back on to the bridge. His presence could have restarted this thing. Helicopters were flying over with Nightsuns to see the crowd. It started to disperse. There was reason for that, no resolution. It just happened. They did their thing, they accomplished their mission. We stood down.[67]

Warrant Officer Rick Duncan:

Mitrovica was an isolated two-week period over the conduct of the tour, but it gained us the most notoriety. We were dispatched to help the British gain entry into derelict buildings. These were supposed to have arms caches in them, or there was questionable traffic coming through. With the UNMIK police in tow, we went to different facilities and we aided the British. This went on for about a week. It was denial, random. Let people know they can't store things in these buildings. It was designed to upset their routine. We got word the march was going to take place. This was no surprise, but the numbers were underestimated. I know that for a fact. So in anticipation there were blocks put on different corridors coming through. And ultimately Canadian soldiers under our mandate by the government are not to be involved in riot situations. The other side of the coin is that we are allowed to do force preservation. Mission essential equipment, we naturally can protect that. We were not dispatched to the riot; the riot came to us. All the Canadians were pulled back to the gymnasium when the word came out that the protesters were coming. We removed all external weapons and equipment from our vehicles and lined them up on this roadway. Anything that was flammable was removed.

There were different catch places along the route where the [demonstration] was going to be stopped. We were getting sitreps:

"It's under control, it's under control." And then, I can't remember the time exactly, we were at a state of alert in the building. The British didn't want to have everybody outside for a show of force outside. They wanted things kept low key. Yes, you're allowed to have your protest going on, and have your symbolic gesture, but there are forces on the other side of the bridge and there would have been deaths, bar none. There was a constant sniper threat out there. The French lost two guys: it was "grassy knoll" time—lots of theories. Movement outside was in helmet and flak jackets. One of the guys who was watching our vehicles came running inside and said, "They're here. No, no, you don't understand, they're here." We went out and our vehicles were covered with protesters. It was like an ant farm. There was women, children, men all shapes and sizes, waving bags, banners. It was like you were at a soccer game and everybody was screaming in Italian but you don't speak Italian and all of a sudden you're put center row. That's what it was like. This was the last line before they went over the bridge. Again, we were not supposed to get involved in the riot situation, but our vehicles were covered and the British had their hands full. They were undermanned and couldn't stop them, so we jumped in. My primary function at the time was to clear the vehicles and put security on them. I did this verbally, but with a definite physical intimidation factor. The average weight and size of the Pioneer over there was approximately two hundred pounds. The beards helped too. I was interviewed by the CBC and the best thing about them was that they were easily seen and not soon forgotten. In their tradition beards were worn by mad bushmen. That's how the locals related to it during the war: they were the guys that came down out of the hills. In their context these were mad Canadian soldiers. We had heard about that before. Anytime we went somewhere we would go rolling in and with our large physiques and helmet and flak jacket, it makes it even more. There was a shock value to it.

I cleared them off: there was some pushing and shoving. There was one photo I saw where I'm carrying away a demonstrator. There were two lines formed: the disruptors and agitators, the hardcore ones, and the people that were just pushing and shoving. The agitators were getting the crowd in a frenzy and they were removed.

That was the process. We locked arms. An individual would pass through: he thought he was getting a lodgment, but once he passed through, the arms would be locked again and he was now on our side of the fence. In this case, he was resisting two British soldiers who were having problems with this fellow, so we simply reached over. Picked him up, carried him over the shoulder, and took him back to hand him over to the British MPs, at which point they would be recycled. As far as you could see there were people. There was an UNMIK Land Rover that was fire-bombed. That was unique: the protesters actually put out the fire. In the Drvar riots everything that could be destroyed was. This was different. There were our guys which showed extreme restraint: one guy beside me had a guy come up and spit right in his face. It doesn't get much more than that, up close and personal. There were level heads in the crowd as well: they were controlling each other, telling people, "You're getting carried away, that's not what we're here for." It could have been worse. There was minimal actual violence. Soldiers had to use force sometimes because they were in danger of losing equipment from their load-bearing vest, but if you locked arm in arm, your kit starts going.

Then we started getting teargased from the French behind us, which was really quite annoying because nobody knew it was coming. The British were ordered not to wear their helmets, but I ordered our guys to. There were lacerations from the canisters that were being fired: they were eight inches long and they go up in the air and explode with these miniature canisters smaller than hockey pucks to disperse the gas. We were questioned after the fact why we didn't wear respirators. The beard, for starters, no tight seal, but if we were arm in arm, the demonstrators would just remove them. Like a horse and a bridle. You're being pushed and all of a sudden an arm from the third row comes out and starts tugging on your face and there's nothing you can do about it. Frag vests: you get yanked around. We noticed that the demonstrators were prepared for the tear gas: they had bags of onions everywhere. I learned from them that you take a slice of onion and put it in each nostril and it counters the effects of gas: you look like a walrus. Low tech and quite effective. They also would cut an onion, put it in a napkin and hold it over their face. I supposed they learned a lot from dealing with the MUP.

Our platoon reacted to this with mixed feelings. Anger, fear naturally, and then a sense of accomplishment when we were completed. The whole thing was accidental, but the soldiers did well and got publicity as a result. There was blood in the water and there was a feeding frenzy. Everybody wanted a piece of Mitrovica. We became a novelty to the press. And it was the *world* press. There were pictures of the "Canadian bushmen" with beards.[68]

Warrant Officer Eric Rolfe of Pioneer platoon:

Mitrovica was the highlight. Recce platoon deployed a week before. We were sent up to break doors and stuff like that as part of a cordon and search. The British were happy to see us; they were in charge of the operation and needed more personnel. We took down doors for them for a couple of days. We were called in around noon. That's when people started to crowd around at the gym. We parked our vehicles along the road in front of the bridge because there was no room in the compound: it was loaded with Warriors. So we had lunch. Now this march had been anticipated for a couple of days, but not the scale. They broke through the first barricades and second, and that's when we came out. We weren't there for riot control; we weren't authorized. So we hung back and tried to help where we could. And then they broke the last barricade and flooded the compound and got on our vehicles. Our ROEs kicked in and we could get involved. Warrant Duncan led the pack, as he always does, and away we went. He climbed up on the APCs: he's a pretty imposing man and it doesn't matter what language he speaks. He was followed by five other guys and they manhandled people off the carriers. When we got them cleared, all hell broke loose. It was a pushing match, that's what it boiled down to, but they outmanned us a million to one. We concentrated on keeping them away from our vehicles, while the British established a human line to keep them back. Warrant Moss from recce platoon, the doc, and the LO captain attached to us started getting mixed in with the British line, and that's when the rest of us poured in to help.

We had arms linked, over the shoulders, whatever worked. We later moved our APCs out in a line across the road to form a vehicle barricade, with the dozer blades up, butted against one another forming a wall. They had to climb over the vehicle to get anywhere, and we had people on them to push them off.

It was a little scary at first, because it was so overwhelming. I mean, there were forty thousand people there. If they wanted to do anything, they were more than capable of doing so. We would have had to open fire, and that was the very, very last option. Just watching it initially was a bit intimidating, let's not underestimate that here. We didn't know what their intentions were, but once we got into it for about an hour, then we understood it was just a pushing match. Okay, so we push for a little while, then they push for a little while. We were, however, doing things to send a message to the crowd. Every now and then we'd pull one over and send him to the MPs. They were getting the hint that we weren't kidding around. The MUP used to shoot into the crowd, segregate individuals, and then do beatings. These guys didn't want to be segregated from their buddies in the crowd. We had to do some manhandling. Everybody around the world saw the picture of Warrant Duncan with the guy over his shoulder. That was classic. That was awesome.

Then they launched the gas and we didn't have our masks on, so we moved down the hill to get out of the gas and we caught people in the compound and manhandled them out back into the crowd. We never hurt anybody the whole time we were there, and there was more than one opportunity. One of the guys was spit at: he cocked his arm and everything, but he showed a tremendous amount of restraint (I would have hit him), but he cocked his arm and walked away. It was similar all the way down the line, for both us and recce platoon. The recce platoon guys came over to help us and give a hand too—the ones who weren't operating the surveillance equipment.

The whole demonstration was totally controlled; it had to have been. If it had degenerated into a mob, there was nothing we could have done to stop them. We were quite proud of ourselves, you know. We got a lot of praise and we couldn't praise our men enough for keeping their heads and whatnot. The CO and RSM [regimental sergeant major] came up later and were quite happy.[69]

Cpl. John Weiss of the Pioneer platoon:

We went up to Mitrovica to kick in some doors. I missed the show: I was one of the drivers. When we came back from the stadium job, there were reporters waiting. When we pulled up I noticed a carload of UCK, or whatever they were being called at the time, with weapons on the front seat. I clicked on my [intercom system] and passed on what I saw: we were told to keep going. The crowd was starting the build and we were going to park [our M-113s] because we weren't supposed to get involved. We parked and let the show start. We knew they were coming. We did something to free up some British troops, so we did security around the building. And then they broke through the line. The demonstrators went after our vehicles and used them as stepping stones and a place to congregate and the warrant [officer] freaked. He got on top of the vehicles and scared them off. It was funny watching him yell. Well, Warrant Duncan's a very big man. It wouldn't take much to motivate these people to get off. I climbed up on one vehicle and a couple of guys cleared the other ones. Now, I didn't have a beard: there is only one member of Pioneer platoon who cannot grow a beard. That's me. I just get patches: it doesn't fill in and I have to comb it over. But the beards on the other guys were useful, like Massey and the other extremely large men. With Massey, you just see him walking around and people moved out of the way. Anyway the British reformed their line and the push started. There was fifty thousand people and two hundred Brits, the scales were all wrong. Then the French fired the tear gas. That was fun. That dispersed the crowd; they reformed and then more gas. Back and forth. Finally it got to the point where the British couldn't hold them back, and the warrant called for us to lend a hand. I stayed on my vehicle for the most part and [pushed people off]. Initially it was pretty scary, like "Oh Jesus!" but it was more like not knowing what was going on. You don't know how the crowd is going to react, like in Drvar: I had a windowpane thrown on my carrier there. At least in this case the anger wasn't directed at us. We were just a stepping stone. Then those of us on the carriers were told to keep a low profile because of snipers: Serb snipers. They shot two French guys the week before, and they had shot at the British. These were in the apartment blocks across the river. So we had snipers in behind us, the crowd in front of us, and the French in between. Then there were Norwegian carriers lined up too, and the French were keeping back another crowd on the other side of the river. I found out later what it was all about, but for the next two hours I didn't care about the big picture. We got hit with gas and jumped off the vehicles, and then we went back on them and said, "Screw it!" We just sat through it. It was a busy day for us. We rotated with the guys in the line. When I got to the crowd, it was more fear and you don't know what's going to happen, and it sort of turned into a big rugby scrum. You'd have the odd person being a pain in the ass, like an agitator. Then the Albanians would pull the guy out and throw him to the back of the crowd. It was an orderly demonstration, near the front. I saw the Albanians giving the British cigarettes during [a lull] and then ten minutes later we were pressed up against the vehicles. Then two Warriors were moved in to block, and the crowd climbed up and bent the 30mm barrel on one. They bent it! You couldn't even see the vehicle there were so many people on it. They figured that they would drive it down the middle and disperse the crowd. It was the funniest thing I'd seen: the driver couldn't see because of the people. He pops open the hatch and all he could see was in front of him. He looks around, sees all the people, then the hatch goes down. Apparently they broke the suspension on it too. I moved my carrier [as part of a blocking wall]. Then one of my own guys locked me in the carrier! I watched the last half hour through my periscopes. They pushed right up. They slowly dispersed.

We were tired. And our beer call was canceled. So we counted our kit. We were only missing a bayonet! Even though they were pulling stuff out of our load-bearing vests. The crowd was good about giving stuff back. One of the guys got pulled up and his mag fell out of his weapon because the release got hit. It was back in his hands in seconds. One of the crowd grabbed it up and threw it back![70]

Members of the Dragoons recce squadron occupying positions next to the bridge also were dragged into the fray. Cpls. Randy Payne and Troy Cleveland:

We were watching the north side when the demonstration started. Things had been pretty quiet. And all of a sudden we hear "Bang! Bang! Bang!" and Payne said "Holy fuck! Look out, we're getting shot at!" None of us had helmets on. This was the French firing tear gas. As the thing progressed there was such a demand for troops that our whole troop plus a lot of guys from the squadron headquarters were there helping at the front gate [of the gym]. The RCR recce platoon had another vehicle monitoring a camera placed on the roof. Everybody was worried about snipers. I personally found one on the north side, the second building from the right of the bridge on the roof. It was a Serbian. At least we think it was. There were no definite markings, but he is on the Serbian side. There were French snipers on the roof also. We were told later to wear helmets so the French snipers could differentiate us [from the demonstrators]. We were looking through the camera [on the Coyote] when the crowd showed up. The British had everything under control. There was an Italian officer here who was also involved. They went down and got the crowd rerouted, to get them running down the back [instead of the road leading onto the brigade]. There was this Italian guy and a British guy. An Albanian general showed up and started to throw his own propaganda thing. We couldn't make out what he was saying, but the crowd was reacting. We saw the Warriors move to block and we saw the Pioneers picking guys up as quick and throwing them over this fence. Then we got involved. Even Captain DeSwert, Corporal Miller, Captain Atherton. It was a rugby scrum. We had twenty guys holding back five thousand, basically. Cleveland was holding on to a rifle barrel on one side and a butt on the other; everything was interlocked. Then the Warrior gun barrel was snapped off. We had wire there: they went over it and fell on it, burying their face in the wire. Power, Cleveland, Snyder, and Payne got the wire back up. Then more gas landed.

Then a kid fell into the wire. He had a gash across his fore-head and another under his eye. This kid just stands up, wipes the blood off, and is ready to go back in. I mean, holy shit! This is a seriously hurt twelve-year-old with a deep gouge. So his father uses sign language for first aid, and there was a Land Rover so we took him over. The guy was doing first aid on a Brit and we asked him to look after the kid, but he said, "He's not a fucking soldier, fuck him, he can bleed."

Then the Serbs started to mass. More French troops arrived in VAB vehicles and started doing crowd control. The British major who was standing on top of a Warrior vehicle barricade with his interpreter: it got to the point where the crowd was getting crazy. He had such a calm demeanor that he had the crowd eating out of his hand. It was amazing. I was listening to what he was saying and I heard the crowd roaring and yelling. The interpreter would say something and the crowd would quiet down. Then they were all cheering and screaming for him. Then they chanted "Canada we love you," "Canadians and British are the best," "France sucks." I mean, there was one French guy who came out of the building and they started throwing rocks at him.

Everything was fine until the French started throwing tear gas, and then it went to hell in a handbasket. One canister hit Corpo-ral Miller in the helmet. If a canister went into the crowd, it was kicked back at us. Payne, Cleveland, and Snyder all got hit with the gas; Warrant Chesterman was trying to get his mask and was blowing snot bubbles. We couldn't see anything. One guy started running backwards and wham! He hit the back of a Warrior.

Haynes was coughing and choking and he wanted to puke, so he stopped at a Land Rover and there was this bottle of water sit-ting on top of it. So he's got his eyes covered and can't see really well, and he was asking, "Can I have a drink of your water?" We're looking at him and thinking, "Who in the hell are you talking to?" So he says, "Ah, fuck it," and he takes the water and douses his face. He gets himself sorted out and tries to clear the gas from his eyes and looks over at the Land Rover to find out who in the hell he was talking to that wouldn't answer him. There was nobody in the Land Rover! So he ran back, got his mask, and stood in the line.[71]

Cpl. Raymond Power:

We had surveillance up with the Coyotes, watching this area, to make sure [the Serbs] didn't get out of control. These guys are getting a bit hyper when there was about fifteen thousand people wanting to cross the bridge and get at them. We were watching these buildings. When it got nighttime we flicked on our thermal. We picked up body heat and we passed it on to the Brit snipers. We monitored those buildings and let them know "okay, we got activity over there." They were moving back and forth, changing each other. If they did fire, we would pick them up for about a minute or two after because of the heat of the barrel. But we could pretty well tell if they were holding a weapon by the way it obstructed the heat signature of the body. So you couldn't actually see the weapon [on thermal] but you could see if they were holding one. It was like Play Station, except real life. Remember, there had been two French guys shot before the demonstration. During the demonstration I think there were three shots that day [at the French], and that's when we were told to put our helmets on so the French snipers wouldn't pick off the wrong people. It was five or six hours of tenseness. Later on in the evening everybody [Serb snipers] across the river disappeared. [Our guys] and the Brits stayed on the roof. Obviously the British were going to fire if they had a visual. I saw a lot of British SAS [Special Air Service] over there. They were walking around in suits. I watched one feller when the smoke was going on. They were trying to get the crowd to go elsewhere. The SAS guys were fanning out in the area. I counted six of them [from the Coyote camera]. They were walking through the crowd. Their main objective was to point out troublemakers. The guys I was on duty with had seen the same thing in Northern Ireland.[72]

The concealed snipers provided overwatch as the demonstration continued to unfold:

I was up on the roof to film the crowd: there were weapons in the crowd. But when I crossed from one position to a hatchway, the French on a building across the river targeted me. There were four of us up there and they called me on the net and told us there was a threat. They had us in their crosshairs. They couldn't recognize the British or Canadian uniforms. We got a message to put on our helmets, that we're being targeted. It was that typical kind of thing that happened over there with the French all the time. I think we feared the French more than the Serbs in the end. The LO who dealt with the French was pretty frustrated. Their snipers, by the way, are controlled at brigade level, who told them where to stand. They had no operational flexibility. So we had seven OPs out and the crowd started coming. The poor Brit platoon was just thrown back. One of our guys was giving this spectacular running commentary on the progress. The CS gas was fired by the French with no coordination. It was quite a mess. I've never seen anything quite like it. There must have been fifteen, twenty gasings. They even managed to get one on our roof. At one point the Albanians caught and disarmed two French soldiers. At one point in the drama, the French went so far as to issue an order to fire into the crowd, and fragmentation grenades were also authorized. The order wasn't relayed to anybody. We heard this from the French guys and we could not believe that they were ready to frag people. They were totally prepared. Two of our guys got to know the French pretty well: the French had the grenades prepared on the wall ready to go. There was no justification for lethal force at that point. It was big and scary and noisy, but there was no justification. The only problem was when somebody set an UNMIK vehicle ablaze. The crowd put it out. They were running with water bottles to put it out. On the other side of the river the Serbs put out huge speakers facing south and were playing patriotic Serbian songs. It would have gotten ugly if the Albanians had made it across the bridge. The Serbs, who are usually vocal, were just standing there quiet. They stood there in line, as if it had been drawn with a ruler. The fellows with the Motorolas in the café, they were really organized and we spent a lot of time taping them. According to int[el] people, a lot of these Serbs were displaced soldiers, irregulars, some MUP, some reserve police, but a lot were just youngsters who were caught up in the whole thing. It was community pride.

I was so disappointed because I'd had an opportunity to work with the French in Sarajevo one time and I really enjoyed the experience. I came here expecting the same thing. But these Marines were okay individually, but collectively there was another agenda at work. It was obvious. When we got the call we were being targeted by the French, it never dawned on me that it might happen.[73]

On 22 February, the day after the demonstration, KFOR HQ asked for additional Canadian elements to be deployed to Mitrovica. The Pioneer platoon went back to the Canadian AOR, where a needless and shameful event unfolded.

A number of fear-filled, skittish bureaucrats at NDHQ in Ottawa panicked when the Pioneers received prominent, worldwide media coverage. Orders were sent to the CO of 1 RCR instructing him to have photographers take mugshots of the members of the Pioneer platoon and to instruct them to shave their beards. These men, who had served so well in the chaos of Mitrovica, were now thoughtlessly treated like common criminals. Why? Apparently these same bureaucrats thought that bearded Canadian soldiers were not the image they wanted to project to the world, and they were furious. In addition they accused the Pioneers of being obese because of the way they looked on television:

> This blindsided us. We thought we had done a good job. Our CO and RSM were happy. We got positive press for the CF. It wasn't Somalia. I was quite shocked, and I asked about what the message traffic said. They were getting questions about what the standard was for beards and why they were so long. Christ, you know if we had shot somebody, they would have concentrated on that more than the beards. There are some dress policies in the CF that have to be enforced, but to pick on us. . . . Corporal Massey was awesome: it was an awesome picture. He's a power lifter, short, stocky, but he was wearing body armor, plus a load-bearing vest. He's very fit. Then there was this magazine where a guy wrote in. This fucking asshole asked what army we represented, that we looked more like Banditos than soldiers and going on and on about skin conditions. You know, Massey always passed the BFT [battle fitness test]. First trim your beards, and then we want to take your pictures because you look like fat fucks. That was disheartening.[74]

COME ON FEEL THE NOISE

Ultimately Warrant Officer Rick Duncan received a CDS Commendation, and the Pioneer and recce platoons were awarded Commander Multinational Brigade (Center) Commendations. It did not compensate for the poor treatment meted out by thoughtless people in NDHQ.

All was not over in Mitrovica, however. The Dragoons, the recce platoon, and sniper assets were still involved in stabilizing the area. Capt. Jonathan DeSwert:

> Two or three days after the riot, the RCR were handing over to us and we were going to take over surveillance in the area. We were watching the café shop. We set up a Coyote here and we had an EO sensor up. Our soldiers were getting targets [on the north side], and we started to pick up some really interesting int[el]. Then one day I was watching and there was a lot of commotion. The guys said, "You'd better get over here, sir." All the groups were crowding out in front of this little shop, and everyone from the other café, The American, came over and started listening and a big crowd started going. We had a British MEWT, a mobile electronic warfare team, listening in on the Motorolas. They started hearing "Moving left. Okay, is there anyone? Yes, I see a Belgian Scimitar. Okay, moving right, I don't have anything right here, call to the Shipskas [shitheads]." That was the Serbs calling to the Albanians. We had the EO sensors and picked up all this information. The MEWT plus what we were seeing, we were able to piece it all together. When the attack came, the Serbs wanted to blame it on the Albanians. It was Oliver Nikolovic. He was the one in the crowd; you could see him. He is a bald thug. What he was trying to do was keep the tension up and keep CNN in the area. So when he started to see the foreign press leave, he needed to escalate the situation. It was then they put an RPG put into a building. No one was killed. We were able to prove who did it, and after that anyone with a Motorola was taken away.
>
> There were 1,400 French soldiers over there and 1,600 Serbs. It was 25,000 Albanians on the south side. And when 1 RCR was there, it was only 150 guys. My troop was able to work with the

MEWT, and we worked with the Swedish EW. We scanned the area, and later on there was a grenade attack. We were able to use the Swede EW teams with the British EW teams, and with the Coyotes we were able to see who was controlling what and once again it was controlled by one person.[75]

The snipers of course saw all: "There was no RPG. They *said* it was an RPG fired from the soccer field. The target building was about a kilometer away. So the 'RPG' miraculously came straight down on top of this building and blew up with such a blast to send the blast another five stories over top of a seven-story building. I saw later the target building had been collapsed on all four corners. They probably put four antitank mines on four corners of the building and dropped it. We could feel the concussions. I've never seen an RPG that could do that."[76]

Maj. Pat Koch:

When we got there the British were responsible for a two-hundred-meter circle just to the south end of the bridge, and they had a company of soldiers. We had the Germans on one flank and some Belgians. It was a mix. We did a recce with digital cameras. . . . We finished an officers' meeting and it was around one in the morning. The ground was littered with CS gas canisters and barbed wire that had been chopped up. I did my estimate. Our mission was changed from crowd confrontation to handling the whole southern portion of the town. Me with my company of eighty-seven guys, with a pack of guys on leave. I had to leave a platoon back in my AOR to secure both camps and patrol. We took a composite platoon from Bravo Company. I had three platoons, two attack dogs from the Norwegian company, plus four of their water cannon. Then the brigade commander made me responsible for a mobile military footbridge which was being installed downstream. We got into town and did a walkaround: As soon as people saw our Canadian flag on our shirts, they were coming up to us and waved, "Hey Canada! Hey Canada! Welcome Canada!"[77]

It was fortunate that the mission changed from crowd confrontation on the Austerlitz Bridge to patrolling. Master Warrant Officer Don Sheppard:

The threat was perceived to be quite high. There were different organizations: we had snipers deployed, we had the Greeks and Belgians in front of us with full riot gear. Small riots could become flashpoints to something bigger. There were CS and smoke canisters all over the place. When the soldiers went in there, their eyes were huge. They were on unfamiliar ground, faced with an unfamiliar threat, and we hadn't trained them for what we were doing. Patrolling was no problem. It was riot control. It could have easily escalated where we might have been involved in something like that. We were not confident we could handle it. We had young platoon commanders that had never done it. We may have had young sergeants who had never done it. I mean, you could have had the greatest OC and sergeant major with all the experience in the world, but once you have a mass in front of you, you can only direct so much. We didn't have the experience. There was a lot of apprehension.[78]

Lt. Eleanor Taylor, platoon commander, cogently explained:

We received no crowd confrontation training and no equipment. I thought we were ill prepared for that. That was a true fear of mine, that we did not know the drills, and if something were to occur we could have been in rough shape. I was going through drills with my section commanders who had received their [internal security] training years and years ago. I was talking with my section commanders about something we might have to do in two hours, which was not a nice position to be in. I know my superiors were in agreement with me, but it was an NDHQ directive [that produced the deficiency]. I can't overemphasize how serious I felt this was, but the response that I was given was, "Well, you have senior NCOs who are experienced." But my response to that is "Bullshit." My section commanders did it ten years ago. And every section commander learned it a different way. The fact that we haven't had a fatality or serious injury in the crowd confrontation situations we were involved in is only sheer luck.[79]

Maj. Pat Koch:

One thing we picked up on was that there was more than one bridge across the river but that there was only ever trouble at one of them, the Austerlitz Bridge. It was on the main drag, and because it was a focal point for the media, you could see in the videos of the riot that when the cameras panned there was a "stadium wave" where people became raucous and then calmed down as the cameras passed. They were very, very intelligent in planning these riots and demonstrations. It was choreographed. The plan was to open the Austerlitz Bridge to traffic, and they were trying to create a balance between the ethnicities on both sides of the river. There were a couple of apartment buildings on the north side where Albanians lived previously, and they were trying to get them to move back into their abode. It was too dangerous to try and have these people go across the main bridge, and it would have been a shooting gallery. The master plan was to put in a footbridge southwest of the main bridge that would give the people in the apartment buildings direct access to the Albanian side. This gave them an enclave on the north side. The French put up significant security forces around there to make sure nothing happened. This was a "Poster Child" operation. There was a military AVLB bridge in there, and a permanent one was being built. I was made responsible for the south end. I wanted to patrol on the north side and along the banks, but the French were not even mildly interested in that. In time they were convinced. We involved the UNMIK police and broke down a lot of barriers. We based it on what we'd done in Glogovac.

The problem now was the Serbs, who were not interested in having Albanians in those buildings. We had a couple of soldiers escort the men who lived in the buildings who were checking to see if their furniture was still there, which of course it wasn't. We had a tent set up and we checked their ID: we had a list of guys who were allowed across because we didn't want insurgents infiltrating the other side and starting something. We had some shields to protect them, but when we got to the north side the French would not allow us to touch ground and they said they'd take over. By that time the Serbs lined up along the road and started pelting them with rocks and bricks and everything else. You know, the people we escorted were older fellows, in their sixties. One was struck with a stone and rolled down the hill. The French were outnumbered. I don't think they really had a plan for that sort of thing, so they protected themselves. My guys went and grabbed the Albanians and got them back across the footbridge and evacuated them to the hospital.[80]

Sgt. Gary Reid of the RCD saw similar events from his Coyote:

I got on shift as the surveillance operator. Everybody on a crew does surveillance, everybody rotates through. I saw this woman come out of an apartment building; she had two girls by hand. She was walking up the street where there were different cafés and bread places, all Serb-controlled. So as she was walking up the road, a woman walks out of one of the cafés and boots her right in the guts. And I mean, she's bent over with the kids in her hands and she stood up and this woman started punching her in the face and booting her and everything, but she didn't let go of the two kids. She just stood there taking these kicks. Now the girl who had done the kicking, you could tell she was militarily trained or trained in some martial art, she knew what she was doing, her stance and everything. I'm an unarmed combat instructor, and I knew by the way she would stand that somebody taught her this. No woman stands that way, you know? This went on for forty-five seconds. The French troops pushed her away from the woman with the kids and she came right back at her; one of the French soldiers went BAM! right in her face. She just dropped. It was impressive: a woman taking all of that holding her kids. They identified the woman later: she was from a Serb faction. Anytime they saw a woman out on the street, she was dispatched out of the café to beat them up.[81]

The sniper detachment:

The French spent about a week putting this little bridge in here, and the whole time the Serbs were gathering and watching them. When they got it up and running, the French would dutifully search [out] the Albanians, who were mostly old men and women, and then send them across the bridge into the waiting arms of the Serbs on the other side. It got ugly. They were stoned: the Serb crowds would form, big ones. They would just pounce. There's a few French soldiers but they seemed generally disinterested in the whole affair. After the first attack, the gendarmes would be in there with gas. The Serb security force wore soccer jackets and they were quite recognizable. The young fellows were in the vanguard. They gave these people a hellacious beating. They would have running battles late into the night. Then we pulled out and the Swedes took over.[82]

Duke's Company conducted presence patrolling to keep everything calm. Sgt. Kevin Earl:

The French never did foot patrols in town. So we did. The French thought we were completely loony, but we started pulling Glogovac-type patrols, night patrols. We went totally black. It started to have an effect. We did several raids based on information we gathered after having only been there three weeks. Our snipers and Coyotes changed their world and how we looked at stuff. High-definition imagery. EW intercepts. The Danes did a fantastic job of controlling the crowds. I saw them break up a demonstration that was getting out of hand on the Serb side. They got out their APC dozers and heaved smoke and flash bangs into the crowd. In five minutes this five-hour demonstration was gone.[83]

Maj. Pat Koch:

Canadians tend to be more accepting of different ideas or different ways of doing things. We sent guys on patrol. Part of their job was to stop at a local café, sit down, take weapons off, put them on the floor, have a Coke, talk to the local owner, talk to the guys in the restaurant, and say, "Hey, you know what, we're just human guys in uniform." We'd get some information that way and plus it gave us a more personal thing. It works both ways. People are less likely to stand there and throw a stone at someone they just had coffee with twenty minutes ago. If you were an army guy and you're always pushing people around, it's much easier to pick up a stone and hurl it at a guy who is patrolling and called you a name or slagged you or whatever. I have some great pictures of my sergeant major, who's quite a hard fellow, walking down the street while on patrol holding a kid in each hand and he's telling them stories and they don't understand a word, but they're smiling and kicking soccer balls back and forth. There was direction given to our soldiers: you *will* smile. They learned a few words, how to say "Hello" "I am fine," and I tell you, it goes a long way. We were having a greater effect with eighty-seven soldiers than the fourteen hundred on the north side.[84]

One of Duke's Company's last missions in Mitrovica was a bit of a surprise. Master Warrant Officer Don Sheppard:

We did a raid. We had the Swedes with the dog teams and they sniffed around. We found a pistol. We were just going to wrap it up, and I turned to Major Koch and said, "I'm going to send one of the sections over to the next house just to see who lives there." It turned out that the guy I sent was 6 feet, 3 inches and about 260 pounds. I said, "I want you to go to the door and explain to him that if he doesn't give up the ammunition or weapons that he has in the house, the dogs will come in and look around." So they knocked on the door and who comes to the door but little Hitler himself! We found three or four grenades on his back porch. . . . He went to jail for thirty days and they let him out. There were a lot of good days, a lot of good days in Mitrovica. The company was happy when the Norwegians started showing up with their female medics. That was a good day too![85]

For the rest of their tour the men and women of 1 RCR battle group continued to conduct presence patrolling throughout their area of operations and prepare for a potential VJ incursion. Nothing was quite like Mitrovica, though, and as the tour wound down in 2000, so did most overt belligerent activity. Indeed in the final weeks boredom set in, and it looked as though peace was at hand in most of the province, save Mitrovica.

ELEVEN

Wait for the Wagon, Jimmy
Supporting Operation Kinetic

> When an army begins an operation, whether it is to attack the enemy
> and invade his theater of war or to take up positions along its own
> borders, it necessarily remains dependent on its sources of supply and
> replenishment and must maintain communications with them.
> They constitute the basis of its existence and survival.
>
> —CLAUSEWITZ, *On War*

Military history on the whole deals with the action-oriented aspects
of any given military operation; this study is no exception. It is
easy in all the hubbub of Coyotes racing around, Griffons flaring
into LZs, and infantry soldiers raiding arms dumps to overlook
the extremely critical but for some less exciting support functions
necessary for those vehicles and their crews to execute their missions. Canadian support personnel are quick to quote the American
general George S. Patton, who once said that amateurs talk about
tactics while professionals think about logistics. Unlike the operations conducted by the recce squadron, the helicopter squadron,
and the battle group, most of the support functions are processes.
The ability to respond to a wide variety of operations conducted
by the combat arms is the spice of their existence: the maintenance of a stable and predictable conveyor belt of information,
ammunition, rations, and POL (petroleum, oil, lubricants) to the
combat units is the goal of the support units. If the process is working, there is little to discuss. When the support system hiccups,
the attention paid to the error tends to be greater because of the
effects on the ability of the combat arms to carry out their mis-

sions, which is the objective of the exercise in the first place. The historical low-level animosity between combat and support personnel is perhaps something that will always exist. In any event it is difficult to do justice to the hard work undertaken by the men and women of the support units.

This chapter therefore examines the support provided by the National Command Element (NCE) and National Support Element (NSE) organizations established for Operation Kinetic, as well as the engineering support to the mission. As with the previous chapters, a description of the NCE and NSE is followed by an examination of what the support processes consist of and the specific challenges that the two organizations encountered during the course of the operation.

Reach Out and Touch Someone:
The National Command Element

Although the role of the Task Force Kosovo commander has been adequately explained in previous chapters, how he carried out his duties has not. In traditional military operations involving brigade- or division-size formations, a brigade or division headquarters will deploy and be the repository of command functions. In the case of Operation Kinetic there were two brigade-level assets (the recce squadron and tactical helicopter squadron) plus a mechanized infantry battle group. All operated under a British brigade headquarters. The NCE looks like a small brigade headquarters, but it is there to ensure that there is an unbroken chain of command back to Canada and to provide specialized forms of national support to the deployed Canadian units—support that could not be turned over to some other nation. One such element, for example, is national intelligence, to which other nations are not necessarily entitled.

The NCE for Operation Kinetic consisted of approximately one hundred personnel and was located in Macedonia. As a unit, the NSE is ad hoc but usually based on an existing brigade headquarters augmented from a variety of other units and formations. In the case of Operation Kinetic the Roto 0 NCE drew on 2 Canadian Mechanized Brigade Group (2 CMBG) from Edmonton, while

Roto 1 had substantial numbers of 2 CMBG personnel from Pet-awawa. The basic G-staff functions mimic those of a brigade head-quarters but with some modification. The G-1 (personnel) section has a visitors' bureau to handle Canadian VIPs. Unlike previous deployments, in Kosovo a military psychologist was also part of the G-1. The G-2 (intelligence) organization acted as a means to pass information back to intelligence organizations in Ottawa, as well as to pass Canadian-eyes-only material forward to the deployed units if needed. It also kept the TFK commander informed so that he could make decisions that were national in scope, like the deci-sion to deploy to Mitrovica or MNB (East). The G-3 (operations) shop was small, since those functions were really part of the Brit-ish brigade commanding MNB (Center). There were, however, numerous Canadian officers embedded in that headquarters, par-ticularly in the intelligence and operations staffs: seven at KFOR HQ and three at HQ MNB (Center). The G-4 (logistics) group was also small, since the National Support Element was responsible for sustaining the force, but there was a force-level comptroller to han-dle Canadian-specific accounting issues. Public affairs, a Canadian national function, was also part of the NCE.[1]

A substantial policing presence existed in the NCE. There were three National Investigative Service (NIS) investigators and twelve military police officers, plus a JAG officer. This was in addition to the Airfield Security Force (ASF) MP platoon of thirty people, plus the seven MPs and RPs (regimental police personnel) in the battle group. This is easily explainable: after the events in Somalia in 1993, there was a tendency to have an increased level of guard-ianship in any deployed Canadian formation or unit.

The problem in Operation Kinetic was not the numbers of MPs: it was how they were employed. The ASF was an ad hoc infan-try platoon mostly made up of air command military police that reported to the KRWAU: it was designed to protect the Griffons. The ASF apparently did not leave the airfield, and the NCE MPs generally stayed in Macedonia. The battle group MPs were clearly overworked, and bureaucratic blocks were placed in their way when they tried to draw on the other two pools of personnel.

The ASF MPs left graffiti in their bunkers at the Camp DK airfield: "Never have so many come so far to do so little"—a clear expression of their frustration at not being allowed to contribute more to the mission.[2] It was in some ways a missed opportunity: a close working relationship between these other MP groups and the UNMIK police in the Canadian AOR would have been beneficial and contributed to stability around Glogovac. On the other hand the ad hoc nature of the ASF and the dubious reasons for its creation produced an attitude at the Task Force Kosovo HQ that was "opposed to enthusiastic mission creep."[3]

The NCE was also the repository of that most critical of national functions: signals. Signals is the essence of national command: no nation should ever permit its communications to be handled by any other entity. The G-6 position in the NCE was responsible to the commander for national command communications and information systems (NCCIS) and acted as a broker of sorts between information systems in Canada and those deployed to the field.

The explosion of computing capabilities and their integration with emergent communication technologies in the mid-1990s radically altered how the Canadian Forces moves information. In essence there were now four types of in-theater communication: radio, cell phone, land-line telephone, and computer, which used one of the other three to "transmit." Operations in the former Yugoslavia in the early 1990s were in many ways only a generation or two removed from the HF communications systems employed in World War II. There had been advances in satellite telephones (cell phones played a major role in belligerent communications systems), but the internet was in its infancy during UNPROFOR.[4]

By the mid-1990s there was considerable evolution but in a qualified way. In terms of tactical-level unit communications this was less obvious: the units were still using Vietnam-era HF radios like the 524 and 77 sets, plus RRB systems that were compatible. There were secure systems that could be added as necessary to augment and provide secure voice communications. The big change was the deployment of the military mobile satellite ground terminal AN/MSC 508, often called "MM."

The MM had been used in Bosnia during SFOR rotations prior to Operation Kinetic but had been improved by the outset of Operation Kinetic. Each MM consisted of a satellite communications system with multiplexing gear capable of handling voice and data. The MMs were loaded into a pod that could be carried by a C-130 Hercules or an eighteen-wheeler. It had a ten-foot dish. The MM generally is operated by eight signalers. The MM detachments were part of 79 Communication Regiment (79 Comm Regt), based in Kingston, Ontario, and were attached to Canadian NCEs throughout the world.[5] There were two MMs deployed in Operation Kinetic: MM 8 to the NCE in Skopje and MM 6 to Camp Donja Koretica in Kosovo.

The MMs were the primary communication system between the camps and NDHQ. Inmarsat B and Irridium were backups. Inmarsat B is essentially a briefcase with a commercial satellite telephone inside: air time is purchased by National Defence from the company, which owns a communications satellite constellation. Inmarsat B has limitations: it is difficult to use on the move and in built-up areas. Irridium was a similar system: the Canadian contingent had ten Irridium systems, but the company went bankrupt during the Kosovo operation. This left the contingent with what the signals personnel called "ten large paperweights."

The need for redundant communications systems in an environment like Kosovo is self-evident. For example, the RRB antennas on Mount Goleš were vulnerable to wind: RRB detachments had never quite seen anything like it. Another was the Kačanik defile: it was a communications nightmare. Cell phones and satellite phones refused to work in what signalers called the "dead zone."

In addition to the MMs, several local area network (LAN) detachments were deployed to support the headquarters. In addition to regular clerical and administrative functions, the LAN detachments disseminated secure information and some meteorological data to the force. Internet service was also provided. The importance of email for morale cannot be underestimated. As Capt. Dave Yarker from 79 Comm Regt was quick to point out, "There was no surer way to piss off the soldiers than to have the internet go down. . . . When there were major internet outages in the United States that went on for a week [due to solar flares or other phenomena], we were the most hated men in the theater."[6]

Finally, signals personnel laid good old land line. Camp DK was connected to the infantry company in Glogovac with a telephone system that went right to the MM switch. Cell phone use was limited: there were some cell towers, but the system originally went through Greece and was considered to be insecure and unreliable.

Canadian signals personnel were also involved in communications reconstruction in Kosovo. One problem that emerged was that the existing (surviving) cell phone system in the province was owned by criminally oriented groups in Belgrade connected to Slobodan Milošević. Even if the system was reconstituted under NATO and UNMIK control in Kosovo, roaming fees and other revenues would accrue to companies in Belgrade. This was in part due to the Yugoslavia area code assigned to the phones in Kosovo (in addition to economic considerations, there were obvious security aspects to this problem). In order to generate revenue that would feed into the new Kosovo economic system, a decision was made to borrow one of Monaco's unused area codes and encourage the development of Kosovar-owned cell phone companies.[7]

The new vistas opened by the proliferation of and reliance on computers and the internet became a new battlefield unto itself. Cyberwarfare was also a factor during Canadian operations in Kosovo, though a highly secretive one. In broad terms cyberwarfare is the use of computer systems to attack other computer systems as a component of information operations: it could be described as a cross between the more traditional fields of electronic warfare and propaganda but expressed through computer systems.

Cyberwarfare was conducted in the run-up to Operation Allied Force and throughout the air campaign. The Serbian group Crna Ruka, which essentially acted as the Milošević regime's hacker battalion, defaced NATO-member websites, damaged or disrupted the email accounts of key NATO-member decision makers, and launched an email campaign called YugoSpam. The official NATO web server was attacked with a successful "ping" campaign and shut down.[8] After the Chinese embassy was bombed, China permitted its cyberwarriors to attack American internet targets.[9] That action probably had a spillover effect on some Canadian systems. An operation called Moonlight Maze, thought to be Russian, went after naval codes and missile guidance systems.[10]

During the Allied Force air campaign, it appears as though there were successful cyberattacks against the Serbian air defense system. NATO special information operations were apparently used on a limited basis for a number of reasons: "the lack of integration into campaign planning, uncertainty as to the legality of such operations, disagreement between intelligence and military personnel over whether to exploit or attack networks [and] limited Serbian reliance on vulnerable networks."[11]

Canada's hacker regiment is called the Canadian Forces Information Operations Group (CFIOG). During Allied Force and Kinetic, Canadian cyberwarriors, who are rated second in NATO next to the Americans, were involved in protecting Canadian Forces information systems from Serbian and other hostile attacks. Canadian declaratory cyberwarfare policy is defensive in nature. CFIOG monitored Canadian systems and concluded that there was no successful penetration attack that could be detected during the two operations, though the CF website was defaced. Other NATO allies were probed and attacked, and Canada assisted them in defensive measures. A virus was loosed on the NCE computers at one point, but it was not believed to be a deliberate cyberattack on the systems by enemy forces: it was collateral damage from something that was infecting systems worldwide.[12]

The KFOR experience also marked the first time that space operations were acknowledged by the Canadian Forces as an institution at the highest levels. Operation Kinetic was the departure point for interest in the tactical exploitation of space (TES). The CF was only starting to think about the tactical exploitation of space in 1998 and had been caught out of phase when the other three ABCA members signed a memorandum of understanding on access to GPS data while Canada remained mired in bureaucracy over space policy. The main proponent of TES, Lt. Gen. George Macdonald, eventually signed off on a report that concluded that Canada needed to take space more seriously; shortly thereafter, the Kosovo conflict escalated with Op Allied Force.[13]

In essence space operations are a force enhancer in five areas: GPS accuracy, satellite imagery support, theater ballistic missile early warning, satellite communications, and space situational awareness. During Operation Kinetic the primary area where Canada exploited space was in satellite imagery. Access to this imagery was critical for the combat mapping staffs that supported the battle group, recce squadron, and tactical helicopter deployments. For Allied Force the capability was used to analyze bomb damage assessments and look for targets of opportunity. In the main Canada relied on access to American systems but also exploited commercial imagery products. There was no detachment deployed to the Op Kinetic contingents: "reach back" was achieved through the NCE and the DCDS in Ottawa. Theater ballistic missile defense issues were handled from the NATO early warning office in Sarajevo and most likely from U.S. Navy Aegis cruisers in the Adriatic.[14]

Service Second to None: The National Support Element

Like the NCE, the National Support Element or NSE is an ad hoc organization. If a brigade group were to be deployed, the support functions would be provided by a service battalion that might have 500 to 700 people. Since the Canadian units were assigned to a British brigade group, the NSE was geared to providing materials and supporting Canadian equipment unique to the Canadian Forces. For Operation Kinetic the NSE had approximately 275 people and some ninety vehicles.[15]

As with the NCE, the NSEs for the two rotations were drawn from the service battalions of 1 and 2 CMBGs plus individual augmentation. The NSE had a headquarters platoon of twenty-three people and was divided into five sub-units: a transport platoon, supply platoon, maintenance platoon, composite logistics platoon, and an engineer troop. The transport platoon included a movement control section and a POL section in addition to handling the 5/4-ton LSVW, 2.5-ton MLVW, and the 10-ton HLVW transport trucks. The supply platoon had a rations section incorporated into its structure, as well as a field kitchen. The maintenance platoon was split into vehicle, fire control system, and recovery sections. The composite platoon included a postal section, a pay section, and a welfare section (all very important for morale), an accounts section, and a medical section. Another medical detachment was supposed to be assigned to the British field hospital, which was part of the British support structure that Canada plugged into.[16]

"Sustain" is one of the six combat functions and permits combat units to plug into several Canadian sustainment systems. These include the replenishment system, the land equipment management system, the personnel support services system, and the health services support system. These are strategic systems based in Canada, and they include program development and integration: at the tactical level, they merge into one unit or units and are generally called service support. The forward-deployed sustainment elements providing direct support for combat units are called combat service support. Replenishment and land equipment management are further grouped and called logistics, while health and personnel support are collectively called personnel administration. The third element is sustainment engineering. In Canadian military doctrine sustainment is a combination of military administration and civilian support. For example, host nation support, like that provided by the Macedonians, is a critical contribution to the Canadian sustainment effort.[17]

In ideal terms the sustainment effort should provide a seamless system of support, from Canada to wherever soldiers are. It should support the combat effort as far forward as possible. It must support, as opposed to hinder, the commander's operational plan, and it must be forward thinking, to assure maximum flexibility in operational situations. Sustainment also recognizes that a Canadian formation or unit operating in a coalition context will always require specific and unique Canadian equipment and support.[18]

In any operation the area is physically divided into a combat zone (which in the case of Operation Kinetic was Kosovo) and a communications zone (Comm Z); the Comm Z for Op Kinetic included Macedonia, Greece, and Albania. Deployed Canadian contingents generally have five units in the Comm Z: the NCE (as described above), a Canadian support group, a Canadian medical group, an engineer support unit, and a military police unit. In the case of Op Kinetic these functions were provided by units that were a slice of those that would have been deployed with a brigade group and in some cases, like the medical function, that were handed over to coalition partners. The reasons for integration with allied formations can be varied. In the case of Task Force Kosovo the size of the Canadian force being supported in the combat zone was about the size of a very large battalion. Consequently it would have been expensive and unnecessary to deploy a vast sustainment organization when the opportunity existed to integrate with a British brigade.

The levels of support to a Canadian formation or unit correspond to the tactical, operational, and strategic: these replaced the older terminology of first-, second-, and third-line support. For Op Kinetic the strategic level of support related to getting the forces from Canada to Kosovo. That involved, as we have seen, the employment of alternate service delivery, or ASD. To save money and labor, the Department of National Defence decided to contract out numerous functions to private contractors. Strategic lift was one such item. Companies operating beat-up 747 aircraft and rusting Ukrainian RO-RO ships won the bids to deploy Canadian soldiers. The efficacy of these decisions has already been discussed in previous chapters in the words of the soldiers who had to deal with these challenges. In the case of the GTS *Katie* (see the epilogue) these contractors virtually held the Canadian government hostage, threatened Canadian sovereignty, and wasted taxpayer money.[19]

Another deficiency at the strategic level of sustainment related to a policy implemented in the early 1990s. The decision to close all Canadian bases in Germany and repatriate all Canadian personnel (save a small personnel support group in Geilenkirchen) by 1993 removed Canada's long-standing strategic support base. This shortsighted decision was made for ideological reasons as much as perceived cost savings.[20] It meant that some operational-level sustainment activities had to be conducted from 3 Canadian Support Group, located in Montreal, which ran against some sustainment doctrinal tenets. If CFB Lahr or CFB Baden had been retained and a Canadian battle group had still been stationed there, it could have practically driven (or entrained) to Italy and then moved by ferry to Kosovo as the UNPROFOR contingents did to Bosnia and Croatia in 1992. Canada would not have had to subject its soldiers to unreliable and dangerous ASD activities, and considerable taxpayer money might have been saved.

The ability of 3 Canadian Support Group (3 CSG) to handle preparations for the Operation Kinetic deployment was cause for concern. It could have been catastrophic in the case of the TOW under armor units and the lack of machine guns for the Leopard tanks and other vehicles. The interference by 3 CSG personnel with tanks that were already "shot in" and personally loaded by their crews could have been a factor in decreasing confidence in the vehicle's reliability in the event that the Strathcona's tank troop had to deploy into battle. The possibility that foreign nationals could have prolonged access to the Coyote vehicles and their capabilities by sending them on an ASD ship from a non-NATO nation should have been more closely examined. These deficiencies are the products of a peacetime mentality as much as anything, as well as of a business mentality as opposed to an operational one.[21]

The operational and tactical levels of support in Operation Kinetic appear to have functioned well. There will always be comments from soldiers that the NSE should be called the "Canadian Self-Support Group," but these can be chalked up to the time-honored rivalry between combat and support troops that has existed as long as there has been warfare.[22]

First In, Last Out: The Royal Canadian Engineers

The structure of the engineer units in Operation Kinetic underwent some evolution: some resources were part of the NSE, while others were incorporated into the battle group under the battle group engineer advisor. In addition to the combat engineer assets assigned to the battle group the NSE had the services of 15 Engineer Squadron in the early days of Operation Kinetic. Totaling some 160 personnel, 15 Engineer Squadron had several disparate sections. There was a detachment from 1 Construction Engineer Unit and another from 141 Airfield Engineering Force. These sections were responsible for the construction of camp accommodations and the repair and maintenance of the runway at Camp DK.

A four-member firefighter detachment was deployed, with its fire truck, with the KRWAU, while a signals line section was squeezed into the squadron since there was no autonomous in-theater signals unit. The squadron also had a reverse osmosis water purification unit (ROWPU), which was set up at Camp DK. The field engineer troop, which included a heavy equipment section, rounded out the squadron. Fifteen Engineer Squadron moved from Skopje to Kosovo halfway through June 1999.[23]

The tasks undertaken by the engineers mostly related to siting the Canadian camps, constructing them, and building defensive positions for them. Once these tasks were completed, engineers were involved in a wide array of CIMIC activities alongside the battle group's Pioneer platoon. Mobility support was absolutely critical given the poor state of the roads in Kosovo. In some cases heavy equipment had to be rented from local contractors, which provided an economic benefit to the community.[24]

With regard to mine clearance the engineers could undertake operations as part of force protection, but the extensive demining required in the country meant that NATO- or UN-contracted demining companies were ultimately employed. EOD disposal was generally left up to the British EOD unit when practicable, though sometimes Canadians provided EOD support to ICTY staff working on mass grave exhumation.[25] The ROWPU was a significant presence in a land where the basic infrastructure was decayed: it was used to supply clean water to the residents of Glogovac as well as the battle group.[26]

As with the other support functions, many engineering resources belonged to the British brigade or the British NSE equivalent. For example, 15 Engineer Squadron had a close working relationship with 7 Squadron, Royal Engineers, in Macedonia, and with 6 Gurkha Squadron and 21 Engineer Regiment, Royal Engineers in Kosovo. Another unit with which Canadian engineers had close contact was 21 Explosive Ordnance Disposal Squadron.

After 15 Engineer Squadron redeployed to Canada in December, 23 Engineer Squadron replaced it. Structured differently, it consisted of two field engineer troops, plus a heavy equipment troop. Some of the other function units were retained, including the ROWPU and the firefighting unit.

The engineers were also the last Canadians to leave Kosovo in the spring of 2000. Once Operation Kinetic ended, the teardown of the camps, the packing of the remaining equipment, and the final close-out of accounts ended a process called "Balkans rationalization," which ironically had begun at the same time as the initial planning for Operation Kinetic in the spring of 1999.

The decision to commit Canadian forces to Kosovo back in the spring of 1999 had been made with a clear understanding that Canada could not indefinitely sustain contingents in Bosnia with SFOR and in Kosovo with KFOR. The primary motivator appears to have been cost, which was driven up by the need to sustain two commitments that were geographically separated. There were two NCEs, two NSEs, and two engineer structures. At the same time, NATO was examining how it would approach the region militarily and which forces should be deployed where. The British were also committed to SFOR and KFOR: Canadian units were part of the coalition structures they led and were dependent on many forms of support, so there was some impetus from them to work out some arrangements. Consequently the process called "Balkans rationalization" was implemented.[27]

The policy world wanted Canada to be visible in both Bosnia and Kosovo. However, the reality was that the Canadian Forces could not maintain the same level of logistics, medical, engineer, and military police support to two theaters beyond six months. Alternate service delivery might decrease some of the pressure on logistics functions, but it would be impossible to keep a Canadian combat force deployed in these active theaters without adequate national sustainment. The Canadian Forces, quite simply, was too small.[28]

The planners were confronted with few options. One was to maintain the status quo, which would be "untenable" after six months. Second, there could be a "main effort," with a battle group in one theater and a sub-unit representing Canada in the other. A variant of this was to have a "main effort" battle group in one theater, with a "leadership role" (brigade group headquarters and brigade-level resources) plus a sub-unit in the other theater. Finally, there was a "rotating main effort" option in which Canada became responsible for a brigade headquarters for one year (within a three-year rotation with other troop contributors) in one theater, plus a sub-unit in the other theater.[29]

Brig. Gen. R. S. Richard, Canada's military attaché in the United Kingdom, put it most cogently:

> I suggest that the Canadian presence in the Balkans must be clearly visible. I believe that this is a key strategic issue. At present we are subordinate to the UK in both Bosnia and Kosovo (my recent visit confirms that our flag does not appear on the map in the UK Permanent Joint HQ nor in SFOR HQ). Our contribution is significant in total, but has been "piece-meal" [which] reduces overall visibility. There is a risk that more "piece-mealing" will occur . . . [SFOR will soon reduce from twenty-two battle groups to nine]. Canada has an opportunity to take on more leadership responsibilities by actively participating in NATO HQs and commanding a [SFOR] Sector on the ground (we can do this with less troops). This should be a clear strategic objective.[30]

The political decision-making process that resulted in the withdrawal of the Operation Kinetic forces in the spring of 2000 and the subsequent Canadian acceptance of command of SFOR's Multinational Division (Southwest) in Bosnia in 2001 closely followed the views expressed by Brigadier General Richard.

The withdrawal of the Canadian Forces from Kosovo was unfortunately marred by the GTS *Katie* affair. An alternate service delivery contract RO-RO vessel, GTS *Katie*, was hired to retrieve the 580 Operation Kinetic vehicles (the Griffons were transferred to serve with the Operation Palladium commitment to SFOR in Bosnia) and 390 sea containers from the port of Thessaloniki. On 28 June 2000 the *Katie* sailed from Greece on its way to Bécancour, Quebec. A contract dispute between subcontractors erupted on 7 July and the ship stopped in the middle of the Atlantic and started to drift west of the Azores. On 18 July the owners ordered the *Katie* to turn from its course to Canada because of the contract dispute. It then anchored off Newfoundland. Soon it was heading toward

Quebec again as negotiations continued between the government of Canada, the contractors, and the subcontractor.

When negotiations broke off again, the Canadian government made the decision to board and secure the ship. Operation Megaphone was initiated on 2 August: the frigate HMCS *Montreal* and destroyer HMCS *Athabaskan* with their helicopters and naval boarding parties, took over GTS *Katie* and put it on course for Quebec. The bizarre spectacle of Canada and its armed forces being held hostage by a shady shipping agent and the crew of a rusting RO-RO ship was finished.[31]

Epilogue

> Your circles shrink: first you judged your friends according to their
> views on the wars in Croatia and Bosnia and you fell out with some of
> them, then you judged them on Kosovo, which was a test for many people
> who opposed the war in Bosnia but then thought Albanians should be
> killed. Then you judged them on the NATO bombing—OK, I didn't
> approve of it, but I could not say, "Oh, the West is crazy," because
> I could understand the rationale behind it.
>
> —DUSKA ANASTASIJEVIC, Belgrade journalist

Throughout 2000 Serbian opposition to the Milošević regime, exemplified by the Otpor movement and supported by the persuasive and creative staff at Radio B92, coalesced. In October the man who had led the former Yugoslavia into the heart of darkness, misusing Serb nationalism as his unholy banner, was removed from power.[1] The sequence of events and the exact causes remain under debate and will be for decades. Was it growing discontent among the young, who were being increasingly dragooned into violently suppressive adventurism? Was that discontent stimulated from outside Serbia? Was it the 1999 air campaign and its calculated effects on the Serb population that got the ball rolling? How about international sanctions and economic stagnation? It was probably the synergistic effects of all of these factors.[2]

The intervention and stabilization of Kosovo likely played a role as well. Up until 1999 the Milošević regime behaved with impunity and repeatedly humiliated the international community. By standing up to the regime with pervasive KDOM and KVM surveillance, by using coercive force from both airpower and the threat of a ground intervention, by finally standing up to Belgrade's machinations, NATO members demonstrated that it was in fact possible to coerce dictators and get them to cease their genocidal activity. That psychological moment in early 1999 was essentially consolidated from late 1999 and into 2000 when it was evident to Milošević, his supporters, and the Serbian people as a whole that KFOR was not leaving Kosovo and UNMIK was coming in to govern the province. Belgrade's inability and/or unwillingness to mount any counteroperations at a low level throughout 2000 further demonstrated to the broader audience that their bolt had been shot—and it missed. There would be no going back. Lame Serb attempts at provocation in 2004 and successful Serb attempts at parallel governance in the northern part of the province up to and after 2008 are but echoes of what could have been a more serious impediment to the consolidation of international community governance in Kosovo and with it a semblance of social peace.[3]

Indeed successor KFOR commanders after 2001 continued with their surveillance of the Kosovar Albanian side of the divided house. Gen. Fabio Mini, KFOR commander from October 2002 to October 2003, dismantled KFOR's partnership with the TMK/KPC and "considered organized crime networks, Kosovo Albanian traditional social structures, the KLA and its successor structure, the KPC, as largely interchangeable."[4]

The war of words between aggrieved Serbs and smug Albanians did not cease in the 2000s. Critics argued that NATO and the UN had created structures that essentially legitimized and protected Albanian organized crime networks that had their tentacles all over Europe. Their position was that if the "antiterrorist" measures undertaken in 1998 to destroy these criminal networks had not been interfered with, Kosovo would be a peaceful place under Belgrade's benign hand. It would have been a desired outcome for the Serbs of course but not the million and a half or so refugees destabilizing the southern Balkans neighborhood. And, as one report put it, the Albanians didn't have the hammerlock on regional illicit activity: "[the] Serbs of Mitrovica are pawns in the nationalist game played by Belgrade and hostages to organized crime."[5] Indeed "the combination of wartime smuggling and sanctions-busting created a new social class in Serbia, a wealthy criminal cabal which was intimately linked to the political, military, and bureaucratic elite."[6]

As Churchill once said, however, it is better to jaw-jaw than to war-war. The mastication has not ceased and probably never will. The gruesome 2010 allegations that the UÇK had lured three hundred Serb mental patients to a makeshift clinic in Albania for organ harvesting for rich Turks was pounced on and held up by the uncritical and the credulous as "proof" that NATO should not have intervened (other reports suggest that a handful of people from a variety of ethnicities, not just Serbs, were victimized, and it was unclear exactly what role the UÇK leadership had played, if any). These allegations remain unproven as of 2017 and should be folded into the ongoing war of words. The idea that this alleged incident is somehow the moral equivalent of what Serb security forces were doing to the Kosovar Albanian population for six months in 1999 beggars belief and challenges the very concept of rational discourse.[7]

For critics of the 1999 NATO intervention and the ensuing stability operations, neither will ever be viewed in a positive light, regardless of the facts. Critics have not suggested any other alternative or solution to the intervention that would have stopped the high levels of ethnic violence instigated and supported by Belgrade and the re-destabilization of the Balkans that followed.

One has to ask the question: even if there are Kosovar Albanian organized crime networks interwoven with their governance system, and there are, was it morally right to summarily drive an entire population from its homes with the intention of denying them the basics of life? Surely not all one and half million refugees were criminals, terrorists, and organ harvesters. Yet those who are critical of the intervention seem to believe that suppression and expulsion of the Kosovar Albanians was somehow legitimate, and they continuously fall back on simplistic legalities to confuse the issues. For comparative purposes that would be the functional equivalent of expelling the entire Italian population of New Jersey into Delaware because of the existence of Mafia-run casinos in Atlantic City. We know that not every New Jersey Italian is Tony Soprano. Not every Kosovar Albanian is engaged in Adriatic cigarette smuggling or international car theft. And even if they are, do they deserve to die en masse as a people because of it? Once again, perspective and consequences are important in the war of words: that sort of thinking belongs in the Soviet Union in 1932 or Germany in 1935 (or 20 January 1942 at Wannsee for that matter), not in the second decade of the twenty-first century in Europe.

The connection between the 1999 intervention, the 1999–2000 stabilization operations, and the status quo today is relatively linear. Despite the spike in violence during 2004, here we are more than a decade later working toward a compromise that would permit Kosovo, Serbia, and the overlapping jurisdictions of northern Kosovo to enter into the European Union and the cornucopia of economic benefits that the various stakeholders hope will result from that relationship. That is a far cry from the days of January to June 1999 when, as reflected in the ICTY indictment,

> Slobodan Milosevic, Milan Milutinovic, Nikola Sainovic, Dragoljub Ojdanic and Vlajko Stojiljkovic planned, instigated, ordered, committed or otherwise aided and abetted in a campaign of terror and violence directed at Kosovo Albanian civilians living in Kosovo in the FRY . . . The campaign of terror and violence directed at the Kosovo Albanian population was executed by the VJ, the police force of the FRY, police forces of Serbia and paramilitary units acting at the direction with the encouragement, or with the support of Slobodan Milosevic. . . . The operations targeting the Kosovo Albanians were undertaken with the objective of removing a substantial portion of the Kosovo Albanian population from Kosovo in an effort to ensure continued Serbian control over the province. . . . The forces of the FRY and Serbia intentionally created an atmosphere of fear and oppression through the use of force. . . . The forces of the FRY and Serbia engaged in a systematic campaign of destruction. . . . This was accomplished through the widespread shelling of towns and villages; the burning of homes, farms and businesses. . . . Policemen, soldiers, and military officers per-

sistently subjected Kosovo Albanians to insults, racial slurs, degrading acts, beating and other forms of physical mistreatment based on their racial, religious, and political identification. . . . Actions were undertaken in order to erase any record of the deported Kosovo Albanian[s]' presence in Kosovo and to deny them the right to return to their homes.[8]

Certainly the awkward compromises that slowly emerge today in Kosovo are better than that state of affairs. And, shaky as they are, they were built on the foundation of KFOR and Operation Kinetic.

> I decline utterly to be impartial as between the fire brigade and the fire.
>
> —WINSTON CHURCHILL

NOTES

For security reasons, some interviewees are not identified by name or place and date of interview.

Introduction

1. See Lawrence, *Messages to the World*.

2. Graham, *By His Own Rules*, 382.

3. Bojana Barlovac, "Putin Says Kosovo Precedent Justified Crimea Succession," *BalkanInsight*, 18 March 2014, http://www.balkaninsight.com/en/article/crimea-secession -just-like-kosovo-putin. See also Vladislav B. Sotirovic, "Kosovo Precedent and the Ukrainian Crisis," *Modern Diplomacy*, 26 May 2016, http://moderndiplomacy .eu/index.php?option=com_k2&view=item&id=1450:kosovo-precedent-and-the -ukrainian-crisis&Itemid=771.

4. An example is Vladimir Kozin, "Countering NATO Propaganda on Russia: NATO Intervention in Afghanistan, Kosovo, Libya, Ukraine," *Global Research*, 8 February 2015, http://www.globalresearch.ca/countering-nato-propaganda-on-russia -nato-intervention-in-afghanistan-kosovo-libya-ukraine/5430008. At the 2015 Spur Festival, an annual gathering devoted to politics, art, and ideas in Canada, in what was supposed to be an academic discussion of NATO's future, one panelist dominated the discussion by repeatedly pushing a carbon copy of the Russian view from the *Global Research* website while the chair, Stephanie Levitz, actively blocked rebuttal by panel members who had had direct experience with NATO in the Balkans.

5. UNHCR Global Report 1999, "Kosovo Emergency," UNHCR, http://www .unhcr.org/publications/fundraising/3e2d4d5f7/unhcr-global-report-1999-kosovo -emergency.html.

6. International Commission on Missing Persons, "Batajnica Summary Report: Forensic Monitoring Activities, April 2004," http://www.ic-mp.org/wp-content/uploads /2008/02/icmp-fsd-16-04-2-doc.pdf. See also "Kosovo Albanian Mass Grave Found under Car Park in Serbia," *Guardian*, 10 May 2010, https://www.theguardian.com /world/2010/may/10/kosovo-albanian-mass-grave-serbia.

7. See Bruce Jackson and Wladyslav Stepniak, "General Assessment of the Situation of Archives in Kosovo," UNESCO Restricted Technical Report, RP/1998–1999/ IV.2.2, 2000, http://www.unesco.org/webworld/publications/jackson_report.rtf; and Andras Riedlmayer, "Destruction of Cultural Heritage in Kosovo: A Postwar Assess-

ment," Conservation OnLine, 21 September 2000, http://cool.conservation-us.org /byform/mailing-lists/cdl/2000/1124.html.

8. "Kosovo Assault 'Was Not Genocide,'" *BBC News*, 7 September 2001, http:// news.bbc.co.uk/2/hi/europe/1530781.stm.

9. On issues surrounding the Serb Orthodox holy places in Kosovo, see Avramovic et al., *Predicament of Serbian Orthodox Holy Places in Kosovo and Metohia*.

1. The Balkans

1. Kinross, *Ottoman Centuries*, 47–49; Crnobrnja, *Yugoslav Drama*, chap. 1.

2. Cohen, *Broken Bonds*, 1–6; Glenny, *Balkans*, chap. 2.

3. Lampe, *Yugoslavia as History*, chaps. 7 and 8; Vickers, *Between Serb and Albanian*, chaps. 6 and 7.

4. Lampe, *Yugoslavia as History*, chaps. 1 and 11; Crnobrnja, *Yugoslav Drama*, chap. 1.

5. Maclaren, *Canadians behind Enemy Lines*, chap. 11. See also Street, *Parachute Ward*.

6. For an exposition on the Canadian Army and NATO, see Maloney, *War without Battles*.

7. Nuti, "Italy and the Defence of NATO's Southern Flank 1949–1955." See also Heinemann, *Vom Zusammenwachsen des Bündnisses*.

8. "USAREUR Intelligence Estimate Supplement," 15 February 1965, National Security Archive, George Washington University, Washington DC.

9. Crnobrnja, *Yugoslav Drama*, 3–7; Glenny, *Balkans*, 43.

10. Ramet, *Balkan Babel*, xiii, 1–2, 26.

11. Ramet, *Balkan Babel*, 40–42, 243.

12. Kaplan, *Balkan Ghosts*, xvii, xviii.

13. Ramet, *Balkan Babel*, 243.

14. Cohen, *Broken Bonds*, chap. 3 (quote); Lampe, *Yugoslavia as History*, 6–7.

15. Glenny, *Fall of Yugoslavia*, 153.

16. Lampe, *Yugoslavia as History*, 6, 332, 345.

17. Winchester, *Fracture Zone*, 8–10.

18. Silber and Little, *Yugoslavia*, 25.

19. Silber and Little, *Yugoslavia*, 82–87.

20. Silber and Little, *Yugoslavia*, 25–26.

21. The events in Slovenia are covered in Harris, *Somebody Else's War*; and Meier, *Yugoslavia*.

22. Meier, *Yugoslavia*, 2–5.

23. Meier, *Yugoslavia*, 4.

24. Meier, *Yugoslavia*, 6–19.

25. Meier, *Yugoslavia*, 6.

26. Crozier, *Rise and Fall of the Soviet Empire*, 411–13, 416–22.

27. Crozier, *Rise and Fall of the Soviet Empire*, 411–13, 416–22.

28. Maloney, *Operation BOLSTER*, 5–7.

29. Maloney, *War without Battles*, chap. 7; Maloney, "Missed Opportunity," 37–46; Maloney, *Operation BOLSTER*, 19.

30. Maloney, *Operation BOLSTER*, 19, 35, 39.

31. Maloney, "Helpful Fixer or Hired Gun."

32. Crozier, *Rise and Fall of the Soviet Empire*, esp. the epilogue; Odom, *Collapse of the Soviet Military*, chaps. 15 and 16; and particularly Pry, *War Scare*.

33. See Directorate of Land Strategic Concepts Report Number 99-2, *The Future Security Environment*, August 1999.

34. Adm. William Smith, USN, interview by author, 22 August 1995, Washington DC; confidential interviews.

35. Ash, *History of the Present*, 42–46.

36. Glenny, *Balkans*, 637.

37. Glenny, *Fall of Yugoslavia*, 112.

38. United Nations, "Vance Plan," 3.

39. Maloney, *War without Battles*, chap. 7.

40. United Nations, *United Nations and the Situation in the Former Yugoslavia*, 4, 56–59.

41. Pry, *War Scare*, 208–12.

42. See Maloney, *Operation BOLSTER*; UN documentation message, Wahlgren to Annan, "Report of the Secretary General Concerning UNPROFOR's Deployment and Activities in Former Yugoslav Republic of Macedonia (FYRM)," 11 June 1993.

43. See Maloney, *Canada and UN Peacekeeping*.

44. See Maloney, *Hindrance of Military Operations Ashore*.

45. Holbrooke, *To End a War*, 215–16; J-3 Operations, "Technical Briefing-Canadian Participation in the NATO-Led Peace Implementation Force."

46. J-3 Operations, "Technical Briefing-Canadian Participation in the NATO-Led Peace Implementation Force."

47. Holbrooke, *To End a War*, 216–19. See also Campbell, *Road to Kosovo*.

48. By the late 1990s a system had been established in which the British, Dutch, and Canadians rotated command of Multinational Division (Southwest).

49. Williams, "From Coercion Back to Consent—SFOR's Endgame," 3–10; Marteinson et al., *Royal Canadian Armoured Corps*, 408–9.

50. See esp. Ash, *History of the Present*; and Freeland, *Sale of the Century*.

2. Kosovo

1. Judah, *Serbs*, 30.

2. Vickers, *Between Serb and Albanian*, chap. 2.

3. Kinross, *Ottoman Centuries*, 52–53; Judah, *Serbs*, 34–40.

4. Vickers, *Between Serb and Albanian*, chap. 4.

5. Judah, *Serbs*, 132–33.

6. Judah, *Serbs*, 365.

7. Malcolm, *Kosovo*, xxx.

8. Vickers, *Between Serb and Albanian*, 42–44; McAllester, *Beyond the Mountains of the Damned*, chap. 4.

9. Vickers, *Between Serb and Albanian*, 44–49.

10. Vickers, *Between Serb and Albanian*, 62–70.

11. Malcolm, *Kosovo*, 253.

12. Vickers, *Between Serb and Albanian*, 79–80.

13. See Schmidl, "International Operation in Albania, 1913–14."

14. Vickers, *Between Serb and Albanian*, 85.

15. Vickers, *Between Serb and Albanian*, 88.

16. Vickers, *Between Serb and Albanian*, 89–92.

17. Vickers, *Between Serb and Albanian*, 97.

18. Vickers, *Between Serb and Albanian*, 99–120.

19. Vickers, *Between Serb and Albanian*, 121–30.

20. Vickers, *Between Serb and Albanian*, 146–48.

21. Malcolm, *Kosovo*, 314.

22. Malcolm, *Kosovo*, 317–18.

23. Malcolm, *Kosovo*, 318.

24. Malcolm, *Kosovo*, 320.

25. Malcolm, *Kosovo*, 324–30.

26. Fonseca, *Bury Me Standing*, 28.

27. See *Colours* magazine's February–March 2001 special issue on the Roma in the Balkans, as well as Fonseca, *Bury Me Standing*, for a discussion of the elimination of the Roma by Nazi Germany.

28. Malcolm, *Kosovo*, 334–36; Lampe, *Yugoslavia as History*, 321–22.

29. Meier, *Yugoslavia*, chap. 2; Silber and Little, *Yugoslavia*, chap. 1.

30. Doder and Branson, *Milosevic*, chap. 2.

31. Judah, *Kosovo*, 62

32. Thomas, *Serbia*, 4–5, 22–23.

33. Thomas, *Serbia*, 4–5, 22–23.

34. Thomas, *Serbia*, 4–5, 22–23.

35. See Maloney, *Hindrance of Military Operations Ashore*; and Maloney, *Operation BOLSTER*, for details of Greek malfeasance. See also "Why the Orthodox Are Heterodox," *Economist*, 14 March 1998.

36. Thomas, *Serbia*, 24; "Why the Orthodox Are Heterodox," *Economist*, 14 March 1998.

37. "Serbia and Montenegro: Mountain Unrest," *Economist*, 25 October 1997.

38. Judah, *Kosovo*, 64–66. The information on Rugova and Bukoshi was acquired in a confidential interview. See also Chiclet and Ravenel, *Kosovo*, 229–40.

39. Judah, *Kosovo*, 68–70, 81. For comparison with the Sinn Fein/IRA, see M. L. R. Smith, *Fighting for Ireland?*, chap. 2; and Coogan, *IRA*, chap. 1.

40. Judah, *Kosovo*, 113–15. The information on Agim Çeku was acquired in a confidential interview. Chiclet and Ravenel do note in their book *Kosovo: Le piège* that Çeku was involved in the Medak Pocket, where Canadian and French UNPROFOR troops opposed a Croatian army ethnic cleansing operation directed against the Krajina Serbs. Singer notes in *Corporate Warriors* that Çeku received training from MPRI, an American private military corporation that assisted the Croatian army. Assertions from some quarters that Çeku is or was an American covert "asset" have yet to be proven, however. Receiving training does not automatically demonstrate control.

41. Judah, *Kosovo*, 124, 126. See also Holbrooke, *To End a War*, for the specific sequence of events leading up to Dayton.

42. See Raufer with Quéré, *La mafia albanaise*; and Chiclet and Ravenel, *Kosovo*, 229–40.

43. Confidential interviews. The effectiveness of the al Qaeda–UÇK link is questioned by one observer who was present for some of the infighting. See Collins, *My Jihad*, 147–216. See also Jacquard, *In the Name of Osama Bin Laden*, 70–72.

44. Vickers and Pettifer, *Albania*, 3–7; Milivojević, *Wounded Eagle*, 29.

45. Vickers and Pettifer, *Albania*, chaps. 6 and 7.

46. Vickers and Pettifer, *Albania*, 142, 148–53; Judah, *Kosovo*, 127–28. During a research trip to Kosovo I had a series of discussions with Kosovar Albanian members of the Kosovo police service, all of whom had previously served with various intelligence branches of Yugoslavia's interior ministry before being fired by Belgrade in the early 1990s. They confirm that there has been and still is a certain clan-based animosity between the Albanian and Kosovar Albanian people. It is also an ideological holdover from the Cold War standoff between Albania and Yugoslavia.

47. Milivojević, *Wounded Eagle*, 5; Maloney, *Hindrance of Military Operations Ashore*.

48. United Nations Development Programme, "Italy: Peace-Keeping Operations," UNDP, accessed 2001, http://www.undp.org/missions/italy/key/peace.htm; Husson, *Encyclopédie des forces spéciales du monde*, 266–84; Wesley K. Clark, "NATO: Facing the Challenges Ahead," CSIS, 27 February 2001, http://www.csis.org/hill/ts010227clark .html; Fabian Schmidt, "1997 in Review: From Anarchy to an Uncertain Stability in Albania," Radio Free Europe/Radio Liberty, 9 December 1997, http://www.rferl.org /nca/features/1997/12F.RU.97129121715.htm.

49. "Albania, Berisha Beckons," *Economist*, 18 May 1996; "Albania: Bad for Berisha, Bad for the West," *Economist*, 1 June 1996; "Albania Not So Bad," *Economist*, 26 October 1996.

50. "Serbia and Montenegro: Mountain Unrest," *Economist*, 25 October 1997; "Rebuke by US Adds to Woes of Milosevic," *Times* (London), 16 January 1998; "Milosevic Plays the Full Montenegro," *Economist*, 17 January 1998; "The Two Culprits," *Economist*, 24 January 1998. See also McAllester, *Beyond the Mountains of the Damned*, 27.

51. Judah, *Kosovo*, chaps. 3 and 4. See also Raufer with Quéré, *La mafia albanaise*; and Chiclet and Ravenel, *Kosovo*.

52. Judah, *Kosovo*, 138–61; "US Alarmed as Mujahadin Join Kosovo Rebels," *Times* (London), 26 November 1998. The information on the Krajinan Serbs was acquired in a series of discussions with rank-and-file members of Serb extremist groups in Mitrovica during a 2001 research trip to Kosovo.

53. "Albanian Angst," *Economist*, 24 January 1998; Lampe, *Yugoslavia as History*, 394–96.

54. "Macedonia's Protection Racket," *Economist*, 6 March 1998.

55. Cappelli, "Macedonian Question . . . Again."

3. Clash of the Damned

1. The same must be said for the ins and outs of all the backroom diplomatic maneuvering that was going on at the time. Such things will perhaps have to wait for the next generation of historians.

2. Tom Walker, "Kosovo Guerrillas Take Strategic Mine," *Globe and Mail*, 25 June 1998; Tom Walker, "Serbs Recapture Critical Coal Mine," *Globe and Mail*, 30 June 1998; Judah, *Kosovo*, 169; "Macedonia Fears Spread of Violence," *Times* (London), 3 February 1998.

3. "Arkan, Perhaps Sighted, Surely Wanted," *Economist*, 31 January 1998.

4. The description of the Serbian organization here was derived from a series of confidential discussions the author conducted in Kosovo with knowledgeable personnel.

5. The confusing number of agencies involved reflects the totalitarian nature of Yugoslavia in that a balance of power among the security forces is necessary to prevent the overthrow of the state by one dominant agency. Special police can thus fight the army if need be, while the special operations capabilities are spread out across three different organizations so they can counter each other if necessary.

6. McAllester, *Beyond the Mountains of the Damned*, 32.

7. The description of the UÇK organization presented here was derived from a series of confidential discussions the author conducted in Kosovo with knowledgeable personnel.

8. Note that the ECMM had maintained a small presence in Serbia dating back to the early 1990s. See Maloney, *Operation BOLSTER*.

9. Maisonneuve, "Canadian Foreign Policy and the Kosovo Crisis of 1998" (unpublished paper); Daalder and O'Hanlon, *Winning Ugly*, 27.

10. Clark, *Waging Modern War*, 107–8.

11. "Belgrade to Negotiate with Ethnic Albanians," *Times* (London), 12 March 1998; "Kosovo: Its War," *Economist*, 2 May 1998; "Kosovo Sliding Towards Ethnic War," *Globe and Mail*, 9 May 1998.

12. Human Rights Watch, "Under Orders: War Crimes in Kosovo," 2001, http://www.hrw.org/reports/2001/kosovo/undword.htm.

13. "British Troops May Join Albanian Force," *Times* (London), 15 May 1998; "Canada Would Back UN Role in Kosovo," *Globe and Mail*, 18 May 1998; Clark, *Waging Modern War*, 114–15.

14. Peterson, *Me against My Brother*, part 1; Melvern, *People Betrayed*; Huband, *Skull beneath the Skin*.

15. See Rohde, *Endgame*; and Honig and Both, *Srebrenica*.

16. Gen. Maurice Baril, interview by author, Ottawa, 27 November 2001.

17. See Campbell, *Road to Kosovo*.

18. UN Secretary General, "High Representative for Implementation of the Peace Agreement in Bosnia Herzegovina: Seventh Report," 16 October 1997; UN Secretary General, letters from the Secretary General of the North Atlantic Treaty Organization to the UN Secretary General regarding Security Council Resolution 1088, dated 13 December 1997, 16 January 1998, 5 February 1998, 16 March 1998, 8 April 1998, 11 June 1998, 17 June 1998, 16 July 1998, 10 August 1998, 28 September 1998, and 13 November 1998.

19. UN Secretary General, "High Representative for Implementation of the Peace Agreement in Bosnia Herzegovina: Report for the Months October–December 1998," February 1999.

20. UN Secretary General, Secretary General of the North Atlantic Treaty Organization, letter to the UN Secretary General regarding Security Council Resolution 1088, 17 July 1998.

21. NATO SFOR Backgrounder, "Operation JOINT GUARD Exercise DYNAMIC RESPONSE 98."

22. UN Secretary General, Secretary General of the North Atlantic Treaty Organization to the UN Secretary General regarding Security Council Resolution 1160, 2 July 1998.

23. UN Secretary General, "High Representative for Implementation of the Peace Agreement in Bosnia Herzegovina: Report for the Months July–September 1998," October 1998.

24. These aspects are discussed in Chandler, *Bosnia*, particularly chap. 8.

25. Naumann, "NATO: A Chairman's Perspective" (undelivered address).

26. Critics of NATO intervention in Kosovo from the left and right of the political spectrum have placed far too much emphasis on deciphering the surface rhetoric of Pres. Bill Clinton's administration and on NATO pronouncements during the war. These were tools designed to shape public opinion and maintain consensus while the alliance and its leaders were under pressure. They did not necessarily reflect policy or the detailed behind-the-scenes workings and objectives that the media and political science communities do not see. For two such collections of criticism, see Ali, *Masters of the Universe?*; and Carpenter, *NATO's Empty Victory*.

27. See Maloney, *Canada and UN Peacekeeping*, chap. 10, for insight into the Cyprus crisis and its effects on NATO.

28. Sezer, "Turkey's New Security Environment, Nuclear Weapons, and Proliferation"; Hickok, "Hegemon Rising."

29. Naumann, "NATO: A Chairman's Perspective" (undelivered address).

30. See Butler, *Greatest Threat*.

31. Bugajski, "Close to the Edge in Kosovo," 19–21 (quote, 19).

32. ACE Mobile Force was created during the Cold War in the early 1960s as a rapid reaction force to demonstrate NATO resolve to adversaries adjacent to peripheral areas like Norway, Italy, Greece, and Turkey. AMF(L) exercises were conducted regularly in those areas to demonstrate the force's capability and to bolster NATO members if they believed they were experiencing undue diplomatic or military pressure from the Soviet Union or its allies.

33. Gen. Sir Mike Jackson, interview by author, Wilton, UK, 19 February 2001; Lt. Col. James Cade, interview by author, Ottawa, 31 January 2001.

34. NATO memo briefing note, 6 August 1998.

35. Maisonneuve, "Canadian Foreign Policy and the Kosovo Crisis of 1998" (unpublished paper).

36. "Milosevic Again," *Economist*, 6 June 1998; Judah, *Kosovo*, 176–77.

37. "NATO to Train in Albania and Macedonia for Raids on Serb Targets," *Times* (London), 11 June 1998; "NATO Ministers Weighing Options in Kosovo," *Globe and Mail*, 11 June 1998; "Defence Ministers Give Go Ahead for NATO Air Strikes," *Times* (London), 12 June 1998; "RAF in NATO Show of Force," *Times* (London), 15 June 1998; "NATO Flights to Proceed without Canadian Aircraft," *Globe and Mail*, 15 June 1998.

38. "UN Envoy Urges Swift NATO Action to Prevent Another Bosnia," *Times* (London), 23 June 1998; Clark, *Waging Modern War*, 128.

39. Judah, *Kosovo*, 176–77.

40. The story of Canada's participation in KDOM will be the subject of a separate study.

41. "NATO Exercise Sends Warning to Belgrade," *Times* (London), 18 September 1998; "The Balkans: A Dangerous Chain Reaction," *Economist*, 19 September 1998; "Italy Plotted Power Switch in Tirana," *Times* (London), 1 October 1998.

42. "Russia Rejects NATO Push for Kosovo Military Move," *Globe and Mail*, 8 August 1998.

43. Jackson interview.

44. KDOM, Belgrade, message to NDHQ, "Kosovo: VJ/MUP Ops," 22 September 1998.

45. Human Rights Watch, "Under Orders: War Crimes in Kosovo," 2001, http://www.hrw.org/reports/2001/kosovo/undword.htm.

46. "NATO Jets to Hit Serbia," *Times* (London), 25 September 1998; Judah, *Kosovo*, 176–77; "Pulling Out of Kosovo," *Globe and Mail*, 3 October 1998.

47. "Reprisals Promised If Air Strikes Hit Yugoslavia," *Globe and Mail*, 5 October 1998.

48. "Serb Missiles Pose Threat to NATO Jets," *Times* (London), 7 October 1998; "Attacks by NATO Becoming Likelier," *Globe and Mail*, 7 October 1998; "US Sends Envoy to Belgrade with Warning," *Globe and Mail*, 9 October 1998.

49. Aspects of this are covered in Halberstam, *War in a Time of Peace*.

50. Baril interview.

51. Confidential interview.

52. KDOM, Belgrade, message to External Ottawa, "Kosovo: Belgrade's Response to UNSC 1199," 29 September 1998.

53. Clark, *Waging Modern War*, 138–47; "UN Holds Emergency Session on Kosovo Massacre," *Globe and Mail*, 1 October 1998; "NATO Ready for Air Strikes on Serbia," *Times* (London), 1 October 1998; "Pressure Mounts to Attack Yugoslavia," *Globe and Mail*, 2 October 1998; "Milosevic Pulls Back from the Brink," *Times* (London), 3 October 1998; Maisonneuve, "Canadian Foreign Policy and the Kosovo Crisis of 1998" (unpublished paper).

54. OSCE KVM, "KVM Verification Standards Directive," 5 February 1999.

55. Maj. Gen. Michel Maisonneuve, interview by author, Ottawa, 27 November 2001. Canada's role in the KVM will be the subject of a separate and more detailed study.

56. Lt. Col. Walter Semianow, memo to Chief of Land Staff, 5 February 1999; Maisonneuve interview.

57. Jackson interview; Naumann, "NATO—A Chairman's Perspective" (undelivered address).

58. Briefing provided to the author on Operation Joint Guarantor. See also J-3 memo, "Kosovo Extraction of OSCE Verifiers," 13 November 1998; and Brig. Colin Tadier, interview by author, Priština, Kosovo, 28 May 2001.

59. Jackson interview.

60. Jackson interview.

61. Lt. Col. David Fraser, interview by author, Kingston, 28 November 2000.

62. "A Dummy's Guide to Kosovo Verification," J-3 fact sheet.

63. Fraser interview.

64. Oliviero, "Operation DELIVERANCE."

65. Baril interview.

66. Lt. Gen. William Leach, interview by author, Ottawa, 28 November 2001.

67. KDOM reports, 13 October 1998, 28 October 1998, 13 November 1998.

68. "US Alarmed as Mujaheddin Join Kosovo Rebels," Times (London), 26 November 1998.

69. Gall and de Waal, Chechnya, 194–95, 294; S. Smith, Allah's Mountains, 74–78, 154.

70. Butler, Greatest Threat, chaps. 12 and 13; Patrick, "United States, Europe, and the Security of the Gulf"; Armed Forces Press Service, "US Strikes Aimed at Iraqi Weapons of Mass Destruction," 16 December 1998, http://www.defenselink.mil/news/Dec1998/n12171998_9812172.html.

71. OSCE, KVM memo, head RC Prizren to NDHQ, "First Impressions, RC Prizren KVM," 23 December 1998.

4. In NATO's Vanguard

1. OSCE KVM, "Briefing: Significant Violent Activities, January 1999."

2. OSCE KVM, RC Prizren, "Update 4 KVM," 16 January 1999.

3. Maj. Gen. Michel Maisonneuve, interview by author, Ottawa, 27 November 2001; Gen. Sir Mike Jackson, interview by author, Wilton, UK, 19 February 2001.

4. OSCE KVM, "Briefing: Significant Violent Activities, January 1999"; Halberstam, War in a Time of Peace, 409–10; Clark, Waging Modern War, 158.

5. OSCE KVM, "Briefing: Significant Violent Activities, January 1999."

6. OSCE KVM, "Rogovo Incident: Assessment," 30 January 1999; OSCE KVM, "Briefing: Significant Violent Activities, January 1999."

7. "UN Chief Backs Use of Force," Times (London), 29 January 1999; "Canada Joins NATO in Drawing Swords in Kosovo," Globe and Mail, 30 January 1999.

8. OSCE Media Monitoring Section, "Statement by the North Atlantic Council on Kosovo," 30 January 1999.

9. OSCE KVM memo, Deputy Head of Mission to OSCE, "Rambouillet Talks: The Requirement to Anticipate Changes to the KVM," 10 February 1999; OSCE KVM, message from Wilson to Walker, "Letter from Rambouillet," 9 February 1999. See also Daalder and O'Hanlon, Winning Ugly, 79–84.

10. Confidential interview.

11. Daalder and O'Hanlon, *Winning Ugly*, 79–84. Halberstam's *War in a Time of Peace* and Clark's *Waging Modern War* both catalog the problems in Washington during this period.

12. Director of Land Force Readiness memo, Semianow to Chief of Land Staff, "Chronology of Events in Planning Process," 5 February 1999; Deputy Canadian Military Representative letter, W. E. Morton to J. O. M. Maisonneuve, 3 February 1999.

13. Director of Land Force Readiness memo, Semianow to CLS, "Chronology of Events in Planning Process," 5 February 1999; Lt. Col. David Fraser, interview by author, Kingston, 28 November 2000; Lt. Col. James Cade, interview by author, Ottawa, 31 January 2001.

14. Lt. Gen. William Leach, interview by author, Ottawa, 28 November 2001.

15. Director of Land Force Readiness, "Kosovo Force Options," 6 February 1999; Fraser interview.

16. Brig. Gen. Andrew Leslie, interview by author, Ottawa, 18 April 2001.

17. Director of Land Force Readiness, "Kosovo Force Options," 6 February 1999; Fraser interview; Leach interview; Gen. Maurice Baril, interview by author, Ottawa, 27 November 2001.

18. Fraser interview.

19. Leach interview.

20. Fraser interview.

21. Fraser interview; Maj. Paul Fleury, interview by author, Ottawa, 4 June 2000.

22. Leach interview; Fraser interview; Brig. Colin Tadier, interview by author, Priština, Kosovo, 28 May 2001.

23. "Canada, Allies Gear for Attack on Yugoslavia," *Globe and Mail*, 19 February 1999; Maisonneuve, "Canadian Foreign Policy and the Kosovo Crisis of 1998" (unpublished paper).

24. DCDS/CLS/CAS message, "WNG O 01–Potential CF Contribution to NATO-led Kosovo Force (KFOR)–Op KINETIC," 4 March 1999.

25. OSCE KVM, "Briefing: Significant Violent Activities, February 1999," January 1999.

26. *Air Forces Monthly*, NATO Air Power Special Edition, 2000, 30.

27. "ALLIED FORCE–Balkans Rats," *Air Forces Monthly*, November 1999, 56–61; DCDS, "Briefing to Airmen Talks North 99: Lessons Learned Task Force Aviano," 7 July 1999.

28. Daalder and O'Hanlon, *Winning Ugly*, 115–24; Cordesman, *Lessons and Non-Lessons of the Air and Missile Campaign in Kosovo*, 1–10.

29. Human Rights Watch, "Under Orders: War Crimes in Kosovo," 2001, http://www.hrw.org/reports/2001/kosovo/undword.htm; Amnesty International, *Annual Report 2000: Yugoslavia*, http://www.web.amnesty.org/web/ar2000web.nsf/countries/445feb9.

30. "Kosovo Atrocities: Reported Atrocities 15 Jan 1999 to 20 Jun 1999," UK Ministry of Defense, http://www.kosovo.mod.uk/atrocities.htm.

31. Human Rights Watch, "Under Orders: War Crimes in Kosovo," 2001, http://www.hrw.org/reports/2001/kosovo/undword.htm,

32. U.S. State Department Report, *Ethnic Cleansing in Kosovo: An Accounting*, December 1999, http://www.state.gov/www/global/human_rights/kosovoii/homepage.

33. Jackson interview.

34. UN Secretary General, "High Representative for Implementation of the Peace Agreement in Bosnia Herzegovina: Report for the Months January–March 1999," March 1999; Secretary General of the North Atlantic Treaty Organization to the UN Secretary General, letter regarding Security Council Resolution 1088, 14 April 1999; Secretary General of the North Atlantic Treaty Organization to the UN Secretary General, letter regarding Security Council Resolution 1088, 8 July 1999. Gen. Wesley Clark confirms in his book that the events in Banja Luka were orchestrated from Belgrade. Clark, *Waging Modern War*, 206.

35. Clark, *Waging Modern War*, 209.

36. Leach interview.

37. Poulton, *Who Are the Macedonians?*, 170.

38. Capt. David Travers, interview by author, Kingston, 12 April 2002.

39. Yeltsin, *Midnight Diaries*, 60.

40. Freeland, *Sale of the Century*, 10, 73, 94, 99, 285–309; Kotkin, *Armageddon Averted*, 15–16, 146; Brzezinski, *Grand Chessboard*, 143–48.

41. Yeltsin, *Midnight Diaries*, 167–68; Freeland, *Sale of the Century*, 306–9.

42. Yeltsin, *Midnight Diaries*, 259. See also Andrei Kortunov, "NATO Enlargement and Russia: In Search for an Adequate Response," in Haglund, *Will NATO Go East?*

43. Yeltsin, *Midnight Diaries*, 259. Keep in mind that this was the man who had used state security forces against a satirical puppet show called "Kukly" because it critiqued his policies during the Chechen War. See Hoffman, *Oligarchs*, 294.

44. "It Disagrees about Kosovo. Ah, Yes," *Economist*, 27 March 1999; Clark, *Waging Modern War*, 206–12, 226; confidential interview.

45. Baril interview.

46. "AFOR: NATO's Humanitarian Mission to Albania, April–September 1999, Operation ALLIED HARBOUR," NATO, September 1999, http://www.afsouth.nato.int/operations/harbour/.

47. J6IO letter to J-3, "Implementation of NATO Information Operations in Kosovo," 31 May 1999.

48. "AFOR: NATO's Humanitarian Mission to Albania, April–September 1999, Operation ALLIED HARBOUR," NATO, September 1999, http://www.afsouth.nato.int/operations/harbour/.

49. DND, "DCDS Media Update," 11 April 1999; Mitch Gillett, "CF Part of Aid Airlift to Balkans," *Maple Leaf* 2, no. 8 (1999).

50. UK Select Committee on Defense, "Examination of Witness General Klaus Naumann," 7 June 2000.

51. Travers interview.

52. Jackson interview.

53. Jackson interview.

54. Travers interview.

55. Clark, *Waging Modern War*, 261; "Cabinet Hawkish on Ground Troops," *Globe and Mail*, 8 April 1999; "Eggleton Line Jarred Pentagon," *Globe and Mail*, 10 April 1999; "Don't Let the Endgame Be His," *Economist*, 10 April 1999; "Canadians Back Bombing Campaign," *Globe and Mail*, 12 April 1999.

56. J610 letter to J-3, "Implementation of NATO Information Operations in Kosovo," 31 May 1999.

57. J-3, "Command and Liaison Visit Op KINETIC 5–9 May 1999," 12 May 1999.

58. J-3, "Command and Liaison Visit Op KINETIC 5–9 May 1999," 12 May 1999.

59. Col. Michael Ward, interview by author, Kingston, 11 August 2000; J-3, briefing note to the CDS, "Force Options for an Addition to the CF Contribution to KFOR," 24 May 1999.

60. DCDS, message to distribution list, "Op FORTITUDE," 1 April 1999.

61. Fraser interview; Cade interview.

62. Fraser interview; Cade interview; Leach interview.

63. Leslie interview.

64. Leslie interview; Fraser interview; Leach interview.

65. Leslie interview. See also 1 CMBG Brigade Command to distribution list, "Left and Right of Arcs for 1 CMBG Commanding Officers," 16 July 1997.

66. Leslie interview.

67. Confidential interviews.

68. Fraser interview; Leach interview.

69. J-3 memo, COSJ-3 to DCDS, "BN for CDS-Force Options for an Addition to the CF Contribution to KFOR," 20 May 1999.

70. J-3 memo, COSJ-3 to DCDS, "BN for CDS-Force Options for an Addition to the CF Contribution to KFOR," 20 May 1999.

71. J-3 memo, COSJ-3 to DCDS, "BN for CDS-Force Options for an Addition to the CF Contribution to KFOR," 20 May 1999.

72. DCDS briefing note to the CDS, "Force Options for an Addition to the CF Contribution to KFOR, 24 May 1999; DCDS briefing note to the CDS, "Force Options for an Addition to the CF Contribution to KFOR," 5 May 1999.

73. Briefing slides, "Additional Canadian Contribution to a Peace Implementation Force in Kosovo," 1 June 1999.

74. Director of Land Force Readiness briefing note for DGLFR, "Op KINETIC (PLUS)–Battle Group Less Armoured Squadron," 4 June 1999.

75. Director of Land Force Readiness briefing note for DGLFR, "Op KINETIC (PLUS)–Battle Group Less Armoured Squadron," 4 June 1999.

76. Director of Land Force Readiness briefing note for DGLFR, "Op KINETIC (PLUS)–Battle Group Less Armoured Squadron," 4 June 1999.

77. DCDS memo to CDS, "Options in Lieu of an Infantry Battle Group to the NATO Implementation Force in Kosovo," 4 June 1999.

78. Fraser interview.

79. Leach interview.

80. Maj. Barbara McInnis, interview by author, Sarajevo, May 2001.

81. J-3 briefing note to CDS, "Proposed Augmentation of KFOR-Delayed Deployment of an Infantry BG," 9 June 1999.

5. Into the Breach, Dear Friends

1. Yeltsin, *Midnight Diaries*, 255–60.

2. Talbott, *Russia Hand*, 300–303.

3. Clark, *Waging Modern War*, 294.

4. Talbott, *Russia Hand*, 310–11, 453.

5. TFK message, Task Force Kosovo, "ASSESSREP 02," 30 May 1999.

6. Talbott, *Russia Hand*, 322.

7. Talbott, *Russia Hand*, 323–24.

8. Clark, *Waging Modern War*, 348; Talbott, *Russia Hand*, 324. Note that the partition argument was not accepted as gospel by all participants. See Gen. Sir Mike Jackson, interview by author, Wilton, UK, 19 February 2001.

9. TFK message, Task Force Kosovo, "ASSESSREP 01," 29 May 1999; TFK message, Task Force Kosovo, "ASSESSREP 02," 30 May 1999.

10. TFK message, Task Force Kosovo, "ASSESSREP 01," 29 May 1999; TFK message, Task Force Kosovo, "ASSESSREP 02," 30 May 1999.

11. Clark, *Waging Modern War*, 327.

12. UK Select Committee on Defense, "The Conduct of the Campaign: The End of the Campaign," *Fourteenth Report: Lessons of Kosovo*, 24 October 2000.

13. McAllester, *Beyond the Mountains of the Damned*, 75; confidential interviews.

14. Confidential interviews. See also Shiner, "Predator," 1; Harris, "Operation DETERMINED FORCE in Mazedonien."

15. Gen. Maurice Baril, interview by author, Ottawa, 27 November 2001.

16. Confidential interviews.

17. Confidential interview.

18. Jackson interview.

19. Jackson interview.

20. Confidential interview.

21. TFK, 4 (UK) Armoured Brigade OPO 3/99, June 1999.

22. Jackson interview; Brig. Bill Rollo, interview by author, Bovington, UK, 23 February 2001.

23. TFK, "Brief to Colonel Ward," 6 May 1999.

24. TFK, "Brief to Colonel Ward," 6 May 1999; Rollo interview.

25. TFK, "Command Liaison Visit (Op KINETIC) 5–9 May 1999," 9 May 1999. Although shoulder patch style might seem to be an insignificant issue, it was an important one for national identity and pride: the recce party recommended that "Canadian shoulder patches should be red and white to more visibly distinguish us from other English-speaking allies. Both the US and UK have coloured patches."

26. TFK, "DCDS' Intent for Comd Task Force Kosovo-OP KINETIC," 17 May 1999.

27. TFK, "DCDS' Intent for Comd Task Force Kosovo-OP KINETIC," 17 May 1999.

28. Clark, *Waging Modern War*, 299.

29. TFK message, TFK to NDOC, "ASSESSREP 01," 29 May 1999; TFK message, TFK to NDOC, "ASSESSREP 02," 30 May 1999.

30. Rollo interview; UK Ministry of Defense, "Briefing by the Armed Forces Minister Mr. Doug Henderson and the Chief of Joint Operations Admiral Sir Ian Garnett," 12 June 1999.

31. Jackson, "KFOR: The Inside Story"; Sell, *Slobodan Milosevic and the Destruction of Yugoslavia*, 306, 308–9. See also Collin, *Guerrilla Radio*.

32. TFK, memo to DCDS, "Commander's Message to DCDS," 4 June 1999.

33. TFK, memo to DCDS, "Commander's Message to DCDS," 4 June 1999.

34. Op Agricola was named after Gnaeus Julius Agricola (AD 40–93), the Roman senator and governor of Britain from AD 78 to 93. Under his tenure Rome extended control over Scotland and Wales.

35. TFK, "4 Armd Bde Op AGRICOLA Wngo 01 CONPLAN (Revised) (Entry into Kosovo)," 7 June 1999.

36. TFK, "4 Armd Bde Op AGRICOLA Wngo 01 CONPLAN (Revised) (Entry into Kosovo)," 7 June 1999.

37. TFK message, TFK to NDOC, "ASSESSREP 11," 9 June 1999.

38. TFK message, TFK to NDOC, "ASSESSREP 11," 9 June 1999.

39. Confidential interview; Col. Michael Ward, interview by author, Kingston, 11 August 2000.

40. Ward interview.

41. Discussions with Col. Geoff St. John.

42. Discussions with Col. Geoff St. John; Canadian Forces Attaché Rome message, St. John to J-4 Log, 2 June 1999.

43. NDHQ message to DL, "Operation KINETIC: CDS Op O for the CF Contribution to the NATO-led Force in Kosovo," 11 June 1999.

44. TFK message, TFK to NDOC, "ASSESSREP 11," 8 June 1999; TFK message, TFK to NDOC, "ASSESSREP 12," 9 June 1999.

45. TFK message, TFK to NDOC, "ASSESSREP 11," 8 June 1999.

46. TFK message, TFK to NDOC, "ASSESSREP 11," 8 June 1999; TFK message, TFK to NDOC, "ASSESSREP 12," 9 June 1999.

47. Daalder and O'Hanlon, *Winning Ugly*, 274–78.

48. Jackson, "KFOR: The Inside Story"; Maj. Paul Fleury, interview by author, Ottawa, 4 June 2000.

49. Fleury interview.

50. Ward interview.

51. Capt. Trevor Gosselin, interview by author, Ottawa, 1 June 2000.

52. Capt. Mark Connolly, interview by author, Ottawa, 1 June 2000.

53. Capt. Barbara Palmer, interview by author, Edmonton, 13 June 2000.

54. Capt. Erik O'Connor, interview by author, Edmonton, 13 June 2000.

55. Capt. David Travers, interview by author, Kingston, 12 April 2002.

56. Clark, *Waging Modern War*, 385.

57. Confidential interview.

58. Travers interview.

59. Jackson interview.

60. Ward interview.

61. Rollo interview.

62. Yeltsin, *Midnight Diaries*, 266.

63. NDOC information note, 28 June 1999.

64. The basic information on the Russian aircraft and their weapons is derived from Cochran et al., *Nuclear Weapons Databook*, vol. 4.

65. Lt. Gen. George Macdonald, email correspondence with author, 29 April 2002.

66. Jackson interview.

67. Baril interview.

68. Confidential interviews.

69. Confidential interviews.

70. Discussions with senior KFOR HQ personnel, Priština, Kosovo, June 2001.

6. Warrior Politics

1. United Nations Security Council Resolution 1244 (1999), 10 June 1999.

2. United Nations Security Council Resolution 1244 (1999), 10 June 1999.

3. "Military Technical Agreement between the International Security Force (KFOR) and the Governments of Federal Republic of Yugoslavia and the Republic of Serbia," 9 June 1999.

4. "Military Technical Agreement between the International Security Force (KFOR) and the Governments of Federal Republic of Yugoslavia and the Republic of Serbia," 9 June 1999.

5. "Military Technical Agreement between the International Security Force (KFOR) and the Governments of Federal Republic of Yugoslavia and the Republic of Serbia," 9 June 1999.

6. 1 PPCLI, "COMKFOR Directive," 20 July 1999.

7. 1 PPCLI, "COMKFOR Directive," 20 July 1999.

8. Lt. Col. Shane Brennan, interview by author, Edmonton, 16 June 2000.

9. 1 PPCLI, "Undertaking of Demilitarisation and Transformation by the UCK," 21 June 1999.

10. 1 PPCLI, "Undertaking of Demilitarisation and Transformation by the UCK," 21 June 1999.

11. 1 PPCLI, "Undertaking of Demilitarisation and Transformation by the UCK," 21 June 1999.

12. 1 PPCLI, "Undertaking of Demilitarisation and Transformation by the UCK," 21 June 1999.

13. 1 PPCLI, "COMKFOR Guidance on the Undertaking of Demilitarization and Transformation by UCK," 21 June 1999.

14. Brennan interview.

15. Brennan interview.

16. 1 PPCLI, "The Transformation of the UCK: A Bridge to the Future," 18 July 1999.

17. 1 PPCLI, "The Transformation of the UCK: A Bridge to the Future," 18 July 1999; Brig. Bill Rollo, interview by author, Bovington, UK, 23 February 2001; Gen. Sir Mike Jackson, interview by author, Wilton, UK, 19 February 2001.

18. 1 PPCLI, memo COMKFOR, August 1999.

19. The terms "Desert Rats" and "Puking Panthers" refer to British soldiers' affectionate names for their brigade flashes: 4 and 7 Brigades each have a desert rat (black for 4, red for 7) since these formations have lineage to those that conducted operations in Egypt and Libya during World War II. Nineteen Mechanised Brigade has a lion wreathed in flame, but it looks like a "puking panther" according to Brig. Peter Pearson.

20. Rollo interview. See also NDOC, "4 Armd Bde Op AGRICOLA OPO 03 (Entry into Kosovo)," 9 June 1999.

21. Rollo interview.

22. Rollo interview.

23. Rollo interview.

24. J-3 fax, "KFOR CONPLAN 16 to OPORDER 04-Defence against FRY-Non-compliance with MTA," July 1999.

25. J-3 fax, "KFOR CONPLAN 16 to OPORDER 04-Defence against FRY-Non-compliance with MTA," July 1999.

26. Rollo interview; J-3, fax "KFOR CONPLAN 16 to OPORDER 04-Defence against FRY-Non-compliance with MTA," July 1999.

27. Rollo interview.

28. Rollo interview.

29. Rollo interview.

30. Rollo interview.

31. Rollo interview.

32. Note that there was some overlap: elements of some 4 (UK) Armoured Brigade infantry units stayed for some weeks after 19 (UK) Mechanised Brigade took over before rotating home.

33. Brig. Peter Pearson, interview by author, Wilton, UK, 21 February 2001; Briefing package, Pearson to Maloney, "Combined International Action in Kosovo."

34. Pearson interview.

35. Pearson interview.

36. Pearson interview.

37. Pearson interview.

38. Pearson interview.

39. Pearson interview; Briefing package, Pearson to Maloney, "Combined International Action in Kosovo."

40. Pearson interview.

41. Pearson interview.

42. Pearson interview.

43. Brennan interview.

44. Pearson interview.

45. Brennan interview.

46. 408 THS, "CONPLAN THUNDERING KROW," 18 November 1999.

47. 408 THS, "CONPLAN THUNDERING KROW," 18 November 1999.

48. 408 THS, "CONPLAN THUNDERING KROW," 18 November 1999.

7. The Coyote Howls

1. I am indebted to Lt. Col. Ross Carruthers for putting his reminiscences and a chronology of the Coyote development project on paper for me (cited hereafter as Carruthers notes to Maloney). See also David, "LAV-Recce 25mm Ammunition and Cannon" and Carruthers letter; plus J. DeCarufel, "The LAV-25 as an Armoured Reconnaissance Vehicle," *Armour Bulletin*, Spring 1993 for early discussions of LAV-Recce.

2. Carruthers notes to Maloney.

3. Carruthers notes to Maloney.

4. Carruthers notes to Maloney.

5. The development of ISTAR was a complicated process with many, many inputs: it warrants a separate study. The introduction of ISTAR in the Canadian Army was rife with professional as well as personal disagreements, turf fights, and legitimate constructive criticism. My intention is to merely sketch the salient points. I have relied on discussions with several members of DAD and others with an interest in ISTAR for this section: Lt. Col. Rick Bowes, Maj. Gord Ohlke, Maj. John Grodzinski, Maj. Clark Beamish, Col. Chuck Oliviero, and Col. Ray Wlasichuk.

6. This section was synthesized from sections of the DAD draft publication "Armoured Reconnaissance," 11 July 1997.

7. DAD discussions; DAD, "RISTA Working Group Gagetown 10–12 March 1997—Final Report," 28 April 1997.

8. DAD discussions; DAD, "RISTA Working Group Gagetown 10–12 March 1997—Final Report," 28 April 1997.

9. I am indebted to Maj. Daryld Cross, the officer commanding the RCD recce squadron; his second in command, Capt. Tim Halfkenny; and all the members of Second Troop, particularly Trooper John Nickerson, M.Cpl. Kevin Smith, Cpl. Eric Winkles, Warrant Officer Ben Aubin, and Cpl. Pat Hogan for bringing me up to date on all aspects of Coyote operations during Exercise Running Bear in 2002.

10. Cpl. Jason Parteger, interview by author, Ottawa, 1 June 2000.

11. Trooper John Nickerson, interview by author, 2002.

12. Cpl. Steven Haynes, interview by author, Petawawa, 28 November 2000.

13. Cpl. David Horne, interview by author, Ottawa, 4 June 2000.

14. Cpl. Kevin Malost, interview by author, Petawawa, 28 November 2000.

15. Maj. Paul Fleury, interview by author, Ottawa, 4 June 2000.

16. Master Warrant Officer Pierre Whelan, interview by author, Petawawa, 27 November, 2000; Warrant Officer Joseph Ramsay, interview by author, Ottawa, 1 June 2000; Fleury interview; Capt. Mark Connolly, interview by author, Ottawa, 1 June 2000; Warrant Officer Mike Brabant, interview by author, Petawawa, 28 November 2000; Maj. Tim Datchko, interview by author, Petawawa, 27 November 2000.

17. Brabant interview.

18. Fleury interview.

19. Fleury interview.

20. Capt. Chris Hunt, interview by author, Ottawa, 1 June 2000.

21. Capt. Trevor Gosselin, interview by author, Ottawa, 1 June 2000.

22. Capt. Chris Hunt, interview by author, Ottawa, 1 June 2000.

23. Gosselin interview.

24. Gosselin interview.

25. Hunt interview.

26. Lt. Derek Chenette, interview by author, Ottawa, 1 June 2000.

27. Gosselin interview.

28. Parteger interview.

29. Chenette interview.

30. See, for example, Bercuson and Wise, *Valour and the Horror Revisited*, which dissects the popular mythology generated in part by the McKenna brothers' docudrama of the same name. Brereton Greenhous and Brian Villa have explained that the command situations in both operations were far more complicated than sheer British arrogance. See Villa, *Unauthorized Action*; and Greenhous, *"C" Force to Hong Kong*.

31. This is detailed in my own books: *War without Battles: Canada's NATO Brigade in Germany, 1951–1993* and *Chances for Peace: Canadian Soldiers in the Balkans, 1992–1995; An Oral History*.

32. KRWAU memo, "Information Requirements," 7 September 1999.

33. CDS, "Operation KINETIC–Recce Squadron Command and Control," 27 July 1999.

34. Fleury interview; Datchko interview.

35. Fleury interview; Datchko interview; Capt. Andrew Atherton, interview by author, Petawawa, 27 November 2000.

36. Ramsay interview.

37. Connolly interview.

38. Sgt. Gary Reid, interview by author, Petawawa, 28 November 2000.

39. Connolly interview.

40. Whelan interview.

41. Hunt interview.

42. Ramsay interview.

43. Whelan interview.

44. Cpl. Kevin Malost, interview by author, Petawawa, 28 November 2000.

45. LdSH, "Daily Situation Report," 23 June 1999.

46. LdSH, "Daily Situation Report," 23 June 1999.

47. Fleury interview.

48. Gosselin interview.

49. Horne interview.

50. Chenette interview; Hunt interview.

51. Gosselin interview.

52. TFK Situation Report 150, 24 November 1999.

53. TFK Situation Report 009, 26 December 1999.

54. LdsH Daily Situation Report, 2 July 1999.

55. Hunt interview.

56. Gosselin interview.

57. J-9 KFOR, "Ethnic Breakdown by Municipality: MNB (Centre)," September 2000.

58. Datchko interview.

59. Gosselin interview.

60. TFK Situation Report 69, 10 August 1999.

61. Parteger interview.

62. Hunt interview.

63. Atherton interview; Malost interview.

64. J-9 KFOR, "Ethnic Breakdown by Municipality: MNB (Centre)," September 2000.

65. It would take time: it was only in mid-April 2000 that the Gračanica Serbs joined the IAC, amid great criticism from their counterparts in Mitrovica. See TFK Situation Report 95, 11 April 2000.

66. Gosselin interview.

67. TFK Situation Report 023, 5 January 2000.

68. Cpls. Randy Payne and Troy Cleveland, interview by author, Petawawa, 27 November 2000.

69. Brabant interview.

70. Malost interview.

71. Parteger interview.

72. Capt. Brian Power, interview by author, Petawawa, 28 November 2000.

73. Warrant Officer Carl Cox, interview by author, Petawawa, 27 November 2000.

74. Atherton interview.

75. Atherton interview.

76. Malost interview.

77. Datchko interview.

78. TFK Situation Reports, November 1999–May 2000.

79. TFK Situation Report 147, 21 November 1999.

80. Hunt interview.

81. Parteger interview.

82. Whelan interview.

83. Capt. Brian Power interview.

84. Datchko interview.

85. Capt. Jonathan DeSwert, interview by author, Petawawa, 27 November 2000.

86. Fleury interview.

87. Hunt interview.

88. DeSwert interview.

89. Capt. Brian Power interview.

90. DeSwert, Hunt, and Capt. Brian Power interview.

91. Rollo, Fleury, Datchko, DeSwert, and Atherton interviews.

92. TFK Daily Situation Reports for 13–16 December 1999, 18 December 1999, 17 January 2000, and 30 January 2000.

93. Cpl. Raymond Power, interview by author, Petawawa, 28 November 2000.

94. TFK Situation Report, 11 December 1999.

95. Capt. Brian Power interview.

96. TFK, "Commander's Periodic Report #2-Op KINETIC 15-Jan–5 Mar 00," 4 March 2000.

97. Col. Ivan Fenton, interview by author, Petawawa, 27 April 2001.

98. TFK message, NDHQ to TFK, "Authority for Out of MNB Deployment–Op SPECTATOR," 7 January 2000.

99. Confidential interview.

100. TFK Situation Report 75, 15 March 2000.

101. Payne and Cleveland interview.

102. Cpl. Steven Haynes interview.

103. The organization underwent at least two names changes in the spring of 2000. By April 2000 KFOR was referring to it as the UCPMB [(UÇPMB].

104. This information was collected by the author during a research trip to the region in 2001, when KFOR conducted a series of operations designed to disarm the UÇPMB just prior to Operation Essential Harvest, established by NATO to disarm the NLA force in Macedonia.

105. Confidential interview.

106. TFK Situation Report 41, 30 January 2000.

107. TFK Situation Report 51, 13 February 2000.

108. TFK Situation Report 53, 15 February 2000.

109. TFK Situation Report 73, 13 March 2000.

110. See note 104.

111. See note 104.

112. See note 104.

113. Datchko interview.

114. Atherton interview.

115. Reid interview.

116. Cpl. Ray Power, interview by author, Petawawa, 28 November 2000.

117. Cpl. Steven Haynes interview.

118. Datchko interview.

119. Confidential interview.

120. Capt. Brian Power interview.

121. Numerous personnel commented on these matters and were particularly baffled by the overzealous American operational security, particularly when Canadian systems provided better, more up-to-date, and more accurate information. National pride should never be underestimated as a motivating factor and is usually a more likely scenario than conspiracy. But then again, this is the Balkans.

122. Confidential interview.

123. See note 104.

124. Ramsay interview.

8. As the KRWAU Flies

1. VCDS, "Canadian Forces Utility Tactical Transport Helicopter (CFUTTH) Acquisition Project: Statement of Operational Requirement," 21 April 1993.

2. Maj. Duart Townshend, interview by author, Kingston, 11 March 2002.

3. An informal number-crunching exercise carried out in Canada's defense establishment at the time (and subsequently ignored by the politically motivated) concluded that for the cost of 100 Griffons Canada could have purchased 150 UH-60 Blackhawks and 50 Seahawks from the Americans. Obviously several thousand people in Quebec would not have been employed, nor political obligation extracted. Confidential interviews.

4. VCDS, "Canadian Forces Utility Tactical Transport Helicopter (CFUTTH) Acquisition Project: Statement of Operational Requirement," 21 April 1993.

5. The Jet Rangers were better-powered training aircraft from the CF base at Portage La Prairie and had been hastily modified for the command-and-liaison role. Note that Kiowas were not used because they were underpowered and had problems operating in the humid and mountainous tropical conditions.

6. I would like to thank Maj. Gil McCauley for providing me with information on Tac Hel operations in the 1990s.

7. Discussions with Maj. Fred Bigelow pursuant to research for Maloney, *Hindrance of Military Operations Ashore*, 64.

8. Information provided by Maj. Gil McCauley on Tac Hel operations in the 1990s.

9. One may speculate about the deeper motives within the tactical helicopter community. Perhaps some relate to rivalry within the air force—fighter pilots versus maritime air versus tactical helicopter, the competition for money, and thus competition for continued existence. There is as yet no material available that would shed light on such thinking.

10. 10 TAGHQ memo, Comd to distribution list, "CH-146-Operational Roles and Capabilities," 31 January 1997; Director General Land Forces Readiness memo, Baril to distribution list, "CH-146-Operational Roles and Capabilities," 22 February 1997; Maj. Scott McLeish, briefing for the author, "CH-146 Griffon Electro-Optical Reconnaissance, Surveillance, and Target Acquisition (ERSTA) Mission Kit."

11. CF Land Doctrine Reconnaissance Working Group, "CH-146 Griffon Helicopter Equipped for Reconnaissance, Intelligence, Surveillance, Target Acquisition (RISTA) and Fire Support Tasks," 12 March 1997.

12. VCDS, "Canadian Forces Utility Tactical Transport Helicopter (CFUTTH) Acquisition Project: Statement of Operational Requirement," 21 April 1993; 10 TAGHQ, "Statement of Capability Deficiency—Reconnaissance, Surveillance and Target Acquisition System for the CH-146," 16 April 1997; 10 TAGHQ memo, Pennie to distribution list, "Statement of Capability Deficiency-Reconnaissance, Surveillance and Target Acquisition System for the CH-146," 18 April 1997.

13. McLeish briefing for author, "CH-146 Griffon Electro-Optical Reconnaissance."

14. I am indebted to Warrant Officer Jake Boucher of 430 ETAH for an intimate examination and explanation of the Griffon's capabilities.

15. Cpl. Aaron Nickerson, interview by author, Edmonton, 13 June 2000.

16. Sgt. Robert Wheatley, interview by author, Edmonton, 13 June 2000.

17. McLeish briefing for author, "CH-146 Griffon Electro-Optical Reconnaissance."

18. Maj. Jim MacAlese, interview by author, Edmonton, 13 June 2000.

19. Briefing provided to the author, "Kosovo Rotary Wing Aviation Unit."

20. Capt. Denis Boucher, interview by author, Valcartier, 25 January 2001.

21. Capt. Barbara Palmer, interview by author, Edmonton, 13 June 2000.

22. Capt. Andrea Andrachuk, interview by author, Valcartier, 24 January 2001.

23. The Airfield Security Force remains a sensitive issue among the people I interviewed, and these people were hesitant to go on the record about it. To some the ASF was a needless imposition and a blatant political move by a cadre of ambitious people. Critics viewed it as interference in the functioning of the tactical helicopter squadrons. It generated significant friction between the military police serving in the battle group and those serving with the NCE in Skopje. This should by no means be taken to denigrate the ASF members themselves or their willingness to serve in Kosovo or their professionalism in carrying out their assigned in-theater tasks.

24. Capt. Erik O'Connor, interview by author, Edmonton, 13 June 2000.

25. Cpl. Aaron Nickerson interview.

26. Cpl. Terry Merritt, interview by author, Edmonton, 13 June 2000.

27. Palmer interview.

28. O'Connor interview.

29. Cpl. Aaron Nickerson interview.

30. O'Connor interview.

31. Merritt interview.

32. Lt. Col. Serge Lavallée, interview by author, Valcartier, 25 January 2001.

33. Gen. Maurice Baril, interview by author, Ottawa, 27 November 2001.

34. MacAlese interview.

35. Discussions with Warrant Officer Jake Boucher of 430 ETAH, 25 January 2001.

36. Cpl. Aaron Nickerson interview.

37. Maj. Steve Charpentier, interview by author, Valcartier, 25 January 2001.

38. Capt. Erick Simoneau, interview by author, Valcartier, 24 January 2001.

39. MacAlese interview.

40. For another impressionistic overview of KRWAU operations in Kosovo, see the excellent article by Jonathan Knaul, "Memories of Kosovo," *Air and Space*, December 2000–January 2001, 26–33.

41. Charpentier interview.

42. Capt. Peter Lyon, interview by author, Edmonton, 13 June 2000.

43. Lyon interview.

44. Sgt. Robert Wheatley, interview by author, Edmonton, 13 June 2000.

45. Lavallée interview.

46. Simoneau interview.

47. Capt. Pierre Lalancette, interview by author, Valcartier, 25 January 2001.

48. Confidential interviews.

49. Isby, *Weapons and Tactics of the Soviet Army*, 351–52, 364–65.

50. Capt. Les Beothy, interview by author, Edmonton, 13 June 2000.

51. Warrant Officer Robert Boucher, interview by author, Valcartier, 26 January 2001.

52. Nickerson interview.

53. Lalancette interview.

54. Confidential interviews.

55. Confidential interviews.

56. Confidential interviews.

57. Note that laser beams can be seen if there is enough moisture in the air.

58. TFK message, TFK to NDOC, "Significant Incident Report–Grn Fire Engagement (Laser/Tracers) Close to Aircraft," 13 July 1999.

59. O'Connor interview.

60. Cpl. Aaron Nickerson interview.

61. Confidential interview.

62. Beothy interview; TFK message, TFK to NDOC, Situation Report 91, 2 September 1999.

63. Confidential interview.

64. Confidential interview.

65. Gertz, *Betrayal*, chap. 2.

66. 408 THS memo, CO to 408 THS, "Op KINETIC Rotary Wing Aviation Unit C&L/Recce Report," 9 May 1999.

67. 408 THS memo, CO to 408 THS, "Op KINETIC Rotary Wing Aviation Unit C&L/Recce Report," 9 May 1999.

68. MacAlese interview.

69. Simoneau interview.

70. Maj. Christian Drouin, interview by author, Valcartier, 25 January 2001.

71. KRWAU memo, "Information Requirements," 7 September 1999.

72. Warrant Officer Robert Boucher interview.

73. MacAlese interview.

74. Wheatley interview.

75. O'Connor interview.

76. Nickerson interview.

77. Charpentier interview.

78. Drouin interview.

79. Simoneau interview.

80. Wheatley interview.

81. KRWAU, KRWAU Situation Report No. 9924, 7 July 1999.

82. Wheatley interview.

83. MacAlese interview.

84. Lalancette interview.

85. Charpentier interview.

86. Cpl. Aaron Nickerson interview.

87. TFK Situation Report 83, 20 August 1999.

88. Lyon interview.

89. Cpl. Aaron Nickerson interview.

90. Cpl. Aaron Nickerson interview.

91. MacAlese interview.

92. TFK Situation Report 67, 5 August 1999.

93. Wheatley interview.

94. Lalancette interview.

95. Simoneau interview.

96. Charpentier interview.

97. MacAlese interview.

98. Simoneau interview.

99. Quote recalled in Charpentier interview.

100. Cpl. Nathalie Castonguay, interview by author, Valcartier, 25 January 2001.

101. Andrachuk interview.

102. Chief Warrant Officer Mike Guay, interview by author, Valcartier, 26 January 2001.

103. Sgt. Sylvain St-Gelais, interview by author, Valcartier, 25 January 2001.

104. Merritt interview.

105. Guay interview.

9. Finger on the Pulse

1. Maj. Alan Bolster, telephone interview by author, 13 November 1999.

2. Warrant Officer Steve Brown, interview by author, Petawawa, 27 April 2001.

3. Warrant Officer Lee Humphrey, interview by author, Edmonton, 14 June 2000. The Wolf designation for the Bison mortar variant was later changed to Dragon.

4. Warrant Officer Hubert Kenney, interview by author, Edmonton, 14 June 2000; Sgt. Hayward Russell, interview by author, Petawawa, 27 April 2001.

5. Warrant Officer Rick Duncan, interview by author, Petawawa, 25 April 2001; Warrant Officer Drago Ranisavljevic, interview by author, Edmonton, 16 June, 2000.

6. Capt. Jay Harvey, interview by author, Petawawa, 25 April 2001.

7. Maj. Chris Stec, interview by author, Edmonton, 16 June 2000.

8. Confidential interviews. I was politely asked at several levels to refrain from identifying specialist personnel for personal security reasons and to refrain from detailing certain capabilities to protect specific operational capabilities.

9. CLS, "CLS Mounting Guidance–Op KINETIC Plus," 16 June 1999.

10. Lt. Col. Steve Bryan, interview by author, Ottawa, 19 April 2001.

11. Maj. Jerry Walsh, interview by author, Edmonton, 14 June 2000.

12. Maj. Stu Sharpe, interview by author, Edmonton, 14 June 2000.

13. A Company Situation Report to RGJ, 14 July 1999.

14. Bryan interview.

15. Maj. Jerry Walsh interview.

16. Capt. Don Senft, telephone interview by author, 3 March 2000.

17. Capt. Mason Stalker, interview by author, Edmonton, 14 June 2000.

18. Humphrey interview.

19. Maj. David Corbould, interview by author, Edmonton, 15 June 2000.

20. Capt. Todd Hisey, interview by author, Edmonton, 15 June 2000.

21. This analysis was compiled from several sources during a research trip to Kosovo by the author.

22. 1 PPCLI, "114 Bde, Drenica OZ," 17 September 1999.

23. Confidential interview.

24. 1 PPCLI, "113 Bde, Drenica OZ," 17 September 1999.

25. Confidential interview.

26. Confidential interview.

27. Confidential interview.

28. Company Sgt.M. Ed Haines, interview by author, Edmonton, 14 June 2000.

29. Senft telephone interview.

30. Lt. Mike Onieu, interview by author, Edmonton, 12 June 2000.

31. Cpl. Scott Marshall, interview by author, Edmonton, 12 June 2000.

32. Warrant Officer Hubert Kenny, interview by author, Edmonton, 14 June 2000.

33. TFK Daily Situation Report, 15 August 1999.

34. Maj. Jerry Walsh interview.

35. Stalker interview.

36. Sgt. Richard Walsh, interview by author, Kingston, 18 May 2000.

37. Cpl. Barb Hays, interview by author, Edmonton, 15 June 2000.

38. Cpl. Brent Richards, interview by author, Edmonton, 15 June 2000.

39. Trooper Melissa Dubbs, interview by author, Edmonton, 12 June 2000.

40. Capt. Jeffrey Gill, interview by author, Edmonton, 14 June 2000.

41. Corbould interview.

42. Humphrey interview.

43. Haines interview.

44. Senft telephone interview.

45. Lt. Col. Shane Brennan, interview by author, Edmonton, 18 June 2000.

46. A Company Situation Report to RGJ, 28 July 1999.

47. Bryan interview.

48. A Company Situation Report to RGJ, 30 July 1999.

49. Bryan interview.

50. 1 PPCLI, Daily Situation Report, 7 August 1999.

51. Bryan interview.

52. Bryan interview.

53. Maj. Jerry Walsh interview.

54. Maj. Jerry Walsh interview.

55. KRWAU memo, "Information Requirements," 7 September 1999.

56. Maj. Jerry Walsh interview.

57. Hisey interview.

58. Brennan interview. The replacement of Lieutenant Colonel Bryan with Lieutenant Colonel Brennan requires some explanation. A disciplinary situation developed with Lieutenant Colonel Bryan, and the TFK commander, Col. Mike Ward, decided to remove him. The nature of the situation is a matter of public record, is discussed elsewhere, and does not affect an analysis of how the battle group was structured or how it conducted operations in Kosovo. It is to his credit that Lieutenant Colonel Bryan

chose to speak with me and was in my opinion perfectly candid about his experiences in Kosovo. I am of the opinion after numerous interviews and discussions that the concept of operations was sound regardless of what happened later. I have opted not to go into the details of the incident: continued public humiliation serves absolutely no purpose here.

59. Hisey interview.

60. Hisey interview.

61. Hisey interview.

62. A Company Situation Report to RGJ, 19 July 1999.

63. 1 PPCLI, "CCKFOR BG CIMIC Cell Organization," 12 August 1999; D. E. Delaney, "CIMIC Operations during OP KINETIC" (draft paper); Maj. Doug Delaney, interview by author, Edmonton, 16 June 2000.

64. Delaney interview.

65. Brigitte Deschenes, interview by author, 2001.

66. Delaney interview.

67. Steven Salewicz, interview by author, Hull.

68. Delaney interview;

69. Salewicz interview.

70. Delaney interview.

71. Deschenes interview.

72. Delaney interview.

73. Delaney interview.

74. Hays interview.

75. Deschenes interview; Salewicz interview (block quote).

76. 1 PPCLI, "Operations Order Op COMFORT," 15 September 1999.

77. Ranisavljevic interview.

78. Hays interview.

79. B Company, "OC B Coy's Weekly Assessment," 1 September 1999.

80. Stec interview.

81. Bryan interview.

82. Senft telephone interview.

83. A Company Situation Report to RGJ, 17 July 1999.

84. Sharpe interview.

85. Stalker interview.

86. Hays interview.

87. A Company Weekly Summary, 11 September 1999.

88. Maj. Jerry Walsh interview.

89. Hisey interview.

90. 1 PPCLI, CCKFOR Daily Situation Report, A Company, 29 July 1999.

91. 1 PPCLI, Daily Situation Report, 31 July 1999.

92. Brennan interview.

93. Sharpe interview.

94. Senft telephone interview.

95. A Company Weekly Summaries, 5 September–22 October 1999.

96. Warrant Officer Rick Oliver, interview by author, Kingston, 19 May 2000.

97. A Company, "Post-Operation Report–Op WOLVERINE 01," October 1999.

98. Sgt. Richard Walsh interview.

99. Confidential interview.

100. Confidential interviews.

101. Corbould interview.

102. Corbould interview.

103. B Company, "OC B Coy's Weekly Assessment," 1 September 1999.

104. Richards interview.

105. Haines interview.

106. Sgt John Devine, interview by author, Edmonton, 15 June 2000.

107. Haines interview.

108. B Company, "OC B Coy's Weekly Assessment," 4 September 1999.

109. Corbould interview.

110. B Company, "OC B Coy's Weekly Assessment," 2 October 1999.

111. Bryan interview; Maj. Jerry Walsh interview.

112. Bryan interview.

113. Corbould interview.

114. Senft telephone interview.

115. Onieu interview.

116. Onieu interview.

117. Dubbs interview.

118. Onieu interview.

119. Corbould interview.

120. Haines interview.

121. Capt. Jeffrey Gill, interview by author, Edmonton, 14 June 2000.

122. Sharpe interview.

123. Confidential interview.

124. Gill interview.

125. Senft telephone interview.

126. Confidential interview.

127. Sgt. Richard Walsh interview.

128. Confidential interview.

129. This was an ongoing problem, reported by Canadian soldiers as early as July 1999. See, for example, A Company Situation Report to RGJ, 22 July 1999.

130. Confidential interview.

131. Humphrey interview.

132. Confidential interview.

133. B Company, "OC B Coy's Weekly Assessment," 1 September 1999.

134. Confidential interview.

135. Confidential interview.

136. Confidential interview.

137. B Company, "OC B Coy's Weekly Assessment," 1 September 1999; TFK Situation Report 98, 13 September 1999.

138. Corbould interview.

139. 1 PPCLI, "Draft FRAGO for Company Deployment to K. Mitrovica," 31 October 1999.

140. Col. Mike Ward, interview by author, Kingston, 11 August 2000.

10. Come On Feel the Noise

1. Cpl. Alan Spencer, interview by author, Petawawa, 26 April 2001.

2. TFK, Roto 1 Situation Report 002, 16 December 1999.

3. TFK, "Commander's Periodic Report #1–Op KINETIC: 15 Dec 1999–14 Jan 00," 15 January 2000.

4. Spencer interview.

5. TFK, Roto 1 Situation Report 005, 20 December 1999; Situation Report 006, 21 December 1999; Situation Report 007, 22 December 1999; Situation Report 008, 23 December 1999.

6. Maj. Pat Koch, interview by author, Petawawa, 26 April 2001.

7. TFK, "Commander's Periodic Report #2–Op KINETIC: 15 Jan 00–5 Mar 00," 4 March 2000. See also Eyre, "Civil Disorder and the Canadian Soldier Overseas."

8. Lt. Col. Bruce Pennington, interview by author, Petawawa, 24 April 2001.

9. Maj. Omer Lavoie, interview by author, Petawawa, 26 April 2001. See also 1 RCR Operations Briefing provided to the author, 24 April 2001.

10. Maj. Rob MacIlroy, interview by author, Petawawa, 26 April 2001.

11. Koch interview.

12. Koch interview.

13. Capt. Jon Herbert, interview by author, Petawawa, 25 April 2001.

14. Sgt. Kevin Earl, interview by author, Petawawa, 25 April 2001.

15. MacIlroy interview.

16. Koch interview.

17. MacIlroy interview.

18. MacIlroy interview.

19. Anonymous Op Soap Box sniper, interview by author

20. Warrant Officer Eric Rolfe, interview by author, Petawawa, 26 April 2001.

21. Warrant Officer Rick Duncan, interview by author, Petawawa, 25 April 2001.

22. Herbert interview.

23. Lavoie interview.

24. Sgt. John MacDougall, interview by author, Petawawa, 27 April 2001.

25. Warrant Officer Steve Shirley, interview by author, Petawawa, 25 April 2001.

26. Sgt. Hayward Russell, interview by author, Petawawa, 27 April 2001.

27. Earl interview.

28. MacDougall interview.

29. MacDougall interview.

30. 1 RCR Operations Briefing, provided to the author, 24 April 2001.

31. MacIlroy interview.

32. Master Warrant Officer Paul Mason, interview by author, Petawawa, 25 April 2001.

33. Snipers interview.

34. Spencer interview.

35. Mason interview.

36. Russell interview.

37. Capt. Jay Harvey, interview by author, Petawawa, 25 April 2001.

38. DNSP memo Thorp to Fulton, "Meeting to Discuss TAV Discrepancies," 18 April 2000.

39. Harvey interview.

40. Harvey interview.

41. There is a discussion of the DU disinformation controversy in Dunnigan, *Next War Zone*, 74–76. See also Andrews, "Depleted Uranium on the Battlefield." Dr. Andrews specifically notes that "most small arms rounds (until recently) contained lead, a known toxic element. Further, the WHA warheads [standard tank ammunition since World War II], as already noted, contain tungsten and cobalt, which are more of a toxicological hazard than uranium (especially DU) is a radiological hazard" (44–45).

42. TFK Roto 1 Situation Report 036, 23 January 2000; quote from TFK Roto 1 Situation Report 044, 2 February 2000.

43. Lt. Alex Haynes, interview by author, Petawawa, 25 April 2001.

44. Lt. Eleanor Taylor, interview by author, Petawawa, 24 April 2001.

45. MacIlroy interview.

46. Lt. Alex Haynes interview.

47. Taylor interview.

48. Pennington interview.

49. Snipers interview.

50. Mason interview.

51. TFK Situation Report 044, 2 February 2000; TFK Situation Report 045, 3 February 2000.

52. TFK Situation Report 056, 6 February 2000; MNB (Center), FRAGO 569 "Op MITROVICA," 7 February 2000; MNB (Center), "Op VALKYRIE," 7 February 2000.

53. TFK Situation Report 048, 8 February 2000; TFK Situation Report 050, 10 February 2000.

54. TFK Situation Report 051, 10 February 2000.

55. Col. Ivan Fenton, interview by author, Petawawa, 27 April 2001.

56. MNB (Center) memo, COS to COMD, "Canadian Capabilities," 8 March 2000.

57. Fenton interview.

58. Pennington interview.

59. Snipers interview.

60. Spencer interview.

61. Capt. Brian Power, interview by author, Petawawa, 28 November 2000.

62. TFK Situation Report 56, 20 February 2000.

63. Snipers interview.

64. Capt. Andrew Atherton, interview by author, Petawawa, 27 November 2000.

65. Sniper interviews.

66. Maj. Steve Charpentier, interview by author, Valcartier, 25 January 2001.

67. Harvey interview.

68. Duncan interview.

69. Rolfe interview.

70. Cpl. John Weiss, interview by author, Petawawa, 26 April 2001.

71. Cpls. Randy Payne and Troy Cleveland, interview by author, Petawawa, 27 November 2000.

72. Cpl. Raymond Power, interview by author, Petawawa, 28 November 2000.

73. Snipers interview.

74. Pioneer interviews.

75. Capt. Jonathan DeSwert, interview by author, Petawawa, 27 November 2000.

76. Snipers interview.

77. Koch interview.

78. Master Warrant Officer Don Sheppard, interview by author, Petawawa, 27 April 2001.

79. Taylor interview.

80. Koch interview.

81. Sgt. Gary Reid, interview by author, Petawawa, 28 November 2000.

82. Snipers interview.

83. Earl interview.

84. Koch interview.

85. Sheppard interview.

11. Wait for the Wagon, Jimmy

1. CLS, "CLS Mounting Guidance–Op KINETIC Plus," 16 June 1999. Note that the specific numbers of personnel in each G staff position changed throughout the planning process, so the numbers used here are approximate.

2. Unfortunately the air staff would not provide me access to the relevant files on the ASF and were visibly skittish when asked about how it was created, who created it, and what its purpose was. The high level of anxiety displayed when presented with straightforward questions indicates that the ASF remains a sensitive subject. It is clear from discussions with military police personnel involved in Operation Kinetic that there was a lot of frustration among the deployed MPs in the ASF and NCE and that many would have been quite happy to work in the Canadian AOR with the battle group MPs. It is equally clear from discussions with battle group MPs that they were overworked.

3. Director of Land Force Readiness memo, Warren to Fraser, 21 May 1999; see esp. minute number 2 from Col. M. J. Ward. Regarding the reasons for creating the ASF, see CLS, "CLS Mounting Guidance–Op KINETIC Plus," 16 June 1999.

4. The information on signals operations was derived from an interview with Capt. David Yarker, Kingston, 28 March 2001; and from CLS, "CEOI 005/99-Op KINETIC," 25 June 1999.

5. During Op Kinetic 79 Comm Regt was disbanded and its functions incorporated into the Joint Signal Regiment just prior to Roto 1.

6. Yarker interview.

7. I am indebted to Maj. Luke Angolini for this information.

8. Vegh, "Classifying Forms of On-Line Activism," 81.

9. Dunnigan, *Next War Zone*, 70–72.

10. Nonie C. Cabana, "Cyber Attack Response: The Military in a Support Role," *Air and Space Power Chronicles*, 4 April 2000, http://www.airuniversity.af.mil. See also Jamie Shea, "Lessons of the Kosovo Conflict: Communications Strategy in Modern Warfare," CEPS *Web Notes*, 13 March 2000, http://www.ceps.be.

11. Andrew Rathmell, "Final Report: Strategic and Organisational Implications for Euro-Atlantic Security of Information Operations," 10, RAND Europe, www.randeurope.org. See also Bob Brewin, "Kosovo Ushered in Cyberwar," *Federal Computer Week*, 27 September 1999, https://fcw.com/articles/1999/09/27/kosovo-ushered-in-cyberwar.aspx; and Dan Verton, "DOD Redefining Info Ops," *Federal Computer Week*, 29 May 2000, https://fcw.com/articles/2000/05/29/dod-redefining-info-ops.aspx.

12. The information on CFIOG was obtained from Brig. Gen. Andrew Leslie, who commanded the organization that was in charge of CFIOG after Operation Kinetic, and it is used with his permission. The sensitive nature of CFIOG operations precludes a more detailed discussion.

13. Maj. Andrew Godefroy, interview by author, Kingston, 24 June 2003.

14. Godefroy interview.

15. CLS, "CLS Mounting Guidance–Op KINETIC Plus," 16 June 1999.

16. CLS, "CLS Mounting Guidance–Op KINETIC Plus," 16 June 1999.

17. This information was provided by Lt. Col. Al Morrow and is in part derived from Directorate of Army Doctrine, B-GL-300-004/FP-001, *Land Force Sustainment*, 18 January 1999.

18. Directorate of Army Doctrine, B-GL-300-004/FP-001, *Land Force Sustainment*, 18 January 1999.

19. Attempts to discuss these issues with personnel from the J-4 branch at NDHQ or to be permitted access to their records merely to confirm dates and places were met with obstruction and a lack of cooperation. The material requested under Access to Information and provided to the author was next to useless.

20. Maloney, *War without Battles*, 481–85.

21. Repeated attempts to contact (including by voice mail and email messages) the commander of 3 Canadian Support Group from this period to discuss these issues, and thus offer another perspective, have been ignored. Lt. Col. Alain Cote penned a letter to the editor of *Canadian Military Journal* (printed in 1, no. 4 [Winter 2000]) in response to comparatively mild criticism by Col. Mike Ward, TFK commander, in his article "Task Force Kosovo: Adapting Operations to a Changing Security Environment," which appeared in the very first issue of CMJ. This response by Lieutenant Colonel Cote does not acknowledge that the TFK encountered problems with the TUA, Leopards, or Coyotes nor does his letter betray any recognition of the possible lethal consequences of the deficiencies in the logistics system.

22. For an examination of that mentality, see Kindsvatter, *American Soldiers*, chap. 10: "Dwellers beyond the Environment of War."

23. Maj. Chris Stec, interview by author, Edmonton, 16 June 2000.

24. Stec interview; TFK Situation Report 74, 11 August 1999.

25. Stec interview.

26. TFK Situation Report 44, 11 July 1999.

27. Director of Land Force Readiness, "Regional Force Generation Issues: DCDS Joint Staff Planning Guidance," July 1999.

28. Director of Land Force Readiness, "Regional Force Generation Issues: DCDS Joint Staff Planning Guidance," July 1999.

29. Director of Land Force Readiness, "Regional Force Generation Issues: DCDS Joint Staff Planning Guidance," July 1999.

30. Director of Land Force Readiness memo, Richard to VCDS, "Balkans Theatre Rationalization," 8 July 1999.

31. NDHQ, MND press briefing: "Canadian Navy's Boarding of a Ship Carrying Canadian Military Equipment," 3 August 2000.

Epilogue

Epigraph: Anastasijevic quoted in Collin, *Guerrilla Radio*, 185.

1. See Collin, *Guerrilla Radio*; and Bujosevic and Radovanovic, *Fall of Milosevic*.

2. See Schulte, "Regime Change without Military Force"; Byman and Waxman, "Kosovo and the Great Air Power Debate"; Albert Cevallos, *Whither the Bulldozer? Nonviolent Revolution and the Transition to Democracy in Serbia*, United States Institute of Peace Special Report, 6 August 2001, https://www.usip.org/publications/2001 /08/whither-bulldozer-nonviolent-revolution-and-transition-democracy-serbia; "The Year Life Won in Serbia: The Otpor Movement against Milosevic," Tavaana Case Study, https://tavaana.org/en/content/year-life-won-serbia-otpor-movement -against-milosevic-0.

3. International Crisis Group, "Collapse in Kosovo: 22 April 2004," ICG Europe Report No. 155; International Crisis Group, "UNMIK's Kosovo Albatross: Tackling Division in Mitrovica: 3 June 2002," ICG Balkans Report No. 131.

4. International Crisis Group, "Collapse in Kosovo: 22 April 2004," ICG Europe Report No. 155.

5. International Crisis Group, "UNMIK's Kosovo Albatross: Tackling Division in Mitrovica; 3 June 2002," ICG Balkans Report No. 131.

6. Collin, *Guerrilla Radio*, 69.

7. For two views see "Senior Kosovo Guerrillas Face Crimes against Humanity Cases," *Balkan Transitional Justice*, 29 July 2014, http://www.balkaninsight.com/en /article/kosovo-liberation-army-organ-trafficking-report; and "The Bloody Yellow House," https://thebloodyellowhouse.wordpress.com/. See also Paul Lewis, "Kosovo PM Is Head of Human Organ and Arms Ring, Council of Europe Reports," *Guardian*, 14 December 2010; "Former Kosovo Rebel Describes Removing Prisoner's Heart for Black Market Sale," *Telegraph*, 11 September 2012; and Nicholas Schmidle, "Bring Up the Bodies," *New Yorker*, 6 May 2013.

8. ICTY Case No. IT-99-37-I, "The Prosecutor of the Tribunal against Slobodan Milosevic, Milan Milutinovic, Nikola Sainovic, Dragoljub Ojdanic, and Vlajko Stojiljkovic: Amended Indictment 29 June 2001." Note that the ICTY's largely symbolic return of no verdict on Milošević in 2016, ten years after his death, does not alter the facts underlying the indictment itself.

BIBLIOGRAPHY

This book benefited from a variety of primary sources that were provided to the author by the Department of National Defence of Canada and from units that deployed with KFOR. In addition, individuals in command positions, other national forces, and international organizations conducting operations in Kosovo provided other material to the author during travel to the Balkans on numerous occasions.

Ali, Tariq, ed. *Masters of the Universe? NATO's Balkan's Crusade.* New York: Verso, 2000.

Andrews, William. "Depleted Uranium on the Battlefield, Part 1: Ballistic Considerations." *Canadian Military Journal* 4, no. 1 (Spring 2003): 41–46.

Ash, Timothy Garton. *History of the Present: Essays, Sketches, and Dispatches from Europe in the 1990s.* New York: Random House, 1999.

Avramovic, Sima, et al. *The Predicament of Serbian Orthodox Holy Places in Kosovo and Metohia: Elements for a Historical, Legal and Conservational Understanding.* Belgrade: University of Belgrade Faculty of Law, 2010.

Bercuson, David J., and S. F. Wise, eds. *The Valour and the Horror Revisited.* Montreal: McGill-Queen's University Press, 1994.

Brzezinski, Zbigniew. *The Grand Chessboard: American Primacy and Its Geostrategic Imperatives.* New York: Basic Books, 1997.

Bugajski, Janusz. "Close to the Edge in Kosovo." *Washington Quarterly,* Summer 1998, 19–21.

Bujosevic, Dragan, and Ivan Radovanovic. *The Fall of Milosevic: The October 5 Revolution.* New York: Palgrave Macmillan, 2006.

Butler, Richard. *The Greatest Threat: Iraq, Weapons of Mass Destruction, and the Crisis of Global Security.* New York: PublicAffairs, 2000.

Byman, Daniel L., and Matthew C. Waxman. "Kosovo and the Great Air Power Debate." *International Security* 24, no. 4 (2000): 5–38.

Campbell, Greg. *The Road to Kosovo: A Balkan Diary.* Boulder CO: Westview Press, 1999.

Cappelli, Vanni. "The Macedonian Question . . . Again." *Washington Quarterly,* Summer 1998, 129–34.

Carpenter, Ted Galen, ed. *NATO's Empty Victory: A Postmortem on the Balkan War.* Washington DC: CATO Institute, 2000.

Chandler, David. *Bosnia: Faking Democracy after Dayton.* 2nd ed. London: Pluto Press, 1999.

Chiclet, Christophe, and Bernard Ravenel. *Kosovo: Le piège.* Paris: L'Harmattan, 2000.

Clark, Wesley K. *Waging Modern War.* New York: PublicAffairs, 2001.

Cochran, Thomas B., et al. *Nuclear Weapons Databook.* Vol. 4, *Soviet Nuclear Weapons.* New York: Harper and Row, 1989.

Cohen, Lenard J. *Broken Bonds: The Disintegration of Yugoslavia.* Boulder CO: Westview Press, 1993.

Collin, Matthew. *Guerrilla Radio: Rock 'n' Roll Radio and Serbia's Underground Resistance.* New York: Thunder's Mouth Press, 2001.

Collins, Aukai. *My Jihad.* Guilford CT: Lyons Press, 2002.

Coogan, Tim Pat. *The IRA: A History.* Niwot CO: Roberts Rinehart Publishers, 1994.

Cordesman, Anthony H. *The Lessons and Non-Lessons of the Air and Missile Campaign in Kosovo.* Washington DC: Center for Strategic and International Studies, 1999.

Crnobrnja, Mihailo. *The Yugoslav Drama.* Kingston ON: McGill-Queen's University Press, 1994.

Crozier, Brian. *The Rise and Fall of the Soviet Empire.* Rocklin CA: Prima Publishing, 1999.

Daalder, Ivo, and Michael E. O'Hanlon. *Winning Ugly: NATO's War to Save Kosovo.* Washington DC: Brookings Institution, 2000.

David, Denis. "LAV-Recce 25mm Ammunition and Cannon," and R. F. Carruthers, letter to the editor. *Armour Bulletin* 27, no. 1 (1994): 4, 11–15.

Doder, Dusko, and Louise Branson. *Milosevic: Portrait of a Tyrant.* New York: Free Press, 1990.

Dunnigan, James F. *The Next War Zone: Confronting the Global Threat of Cyberterrorism.* New York: Citadel Press, 2002.

Eyre, Wayne. "Civil Disorder and the Canadian Soldier Overseas: What Do We Do? The Palladium Experience." *Army Doctrine and Training Bulletin* 4, no. 2 (Summer 2001): 24–30.

Fallows, James. *Breaking the News: How the Media Undermine American Democracy.* New York: Vintage Books, 1996.

Fonseca, Isabel. *Bury Me Standing: The Gypsies and Their Journey.* New York: Vintage Books, 1995.

Freeland, Chrystia. *Sale of the Century: Russia's Wild Ride from Communism to Capitalism.* Toronto: Doubleday Canada, 2000.

Gall, Carlotta, and Thomas de Waal. *Chechnya: Calamity in the Caucasus.* New York: New York University Press, 1998.

Gertz, Bill. *Betrayal: How the Clinton Administration Undermined American Security.* Washington DC: Regnery Books, 1999.

Glenny, Misha. *The Balkans: Nationalism, War, and the Great Powers 1804–1999.* London: Granta Books, 1999.

———. *The Fall of Yugoslavia: The Third Balkan War.* London: Penguin Books, 1992.

Gow, James et al. *Bosnia by Television.* London: British Film Institute, 1996.

Graham, Bradley. *By His Own Rules: The Ambitions, Successes, and Ultimate Failures of Donald Rumsfeld*. New York: PublicAffairs, 2009.

Greenhous, Brereton. *"C" Force to Hong Kong: A Canadian Catastrophe, 1941–1945*. Toronto: Dundurn Press, 2008.

Grodzinski, John G. "An Overview of the Army Strategic Planning Process." Unpublished course paper, April 1999.

Haglund, David, ed. *Will NATO Go East? The Debate over Enlarging the Atlantic Alliance*. Kingston ON: Center for International Relations, Queen's University, 1996.

Halberstam, David. *War in a Time of Peace: Bush, Clinton, and the Generals*. New York: Scribner Books, 2001.

Harris, Paul. "Operation DETERMINED FORCE in Mazedonien." *Barett Internationales Militarmagazin*, May–June 1999, 50–55.

———. *Somebody Else's War: Frontline Reports from the Balkan Wars*. Stevenage, UK: SPA Books, 1992.

Hayes, Dale, and Gary Wheatley, eds. *Peace Operations: Haiti—A Case Study*. Washington DC: NDU Press, 1995.

Heinemann, Winfried. *Vom Zusammenwachsen des Bündnisses: Die Funktionsweise der NATO in ausgewählten Krisenfällen 1951–1956*. Munich: Oldenbourg, 1998.

Hickock, Michael Robert. "Hegemon Rising: The Gap between Turkish Strategy and Military Modernization." *Parameters* 30, no. 2 (Summer 2000): 105–19.

Hoffman, David E. *The Oligarchs: Wealth and Power in the New Russia*. New York: PublicAffairs, 2002.

Holbrooke, Richard. *To End a War*. New York: Random House, 1998.

Holman, Fraser. "The State of the Canadian Forces: The Minister's Report of March 1997." *Canadian Defence Quarterly*, Summer 1997, 32–34.

Honig, Jan Willem, and Norbert Both. *Srebrenica: Record of a War Crime*. New York: Penguin Books, 1996.

Hope, Ian. "Misunderstanding Mars and Minerva: The Canadian Army's Failure to Define an Operational Doctrine." *Army Doctrine and Training Bulletin* 4, no. 4 (Winter 2001–2): 16–35.

Huband, Mark. *The Skull beneath the Skin: Africa after the Cold War*. Boulder CO: Westview Press, 2003.

Husson, Jean-Pierre. *Encyclopédie des forces spéciales du monde*. Vol. 1. Paris: Histoire et Collections, 2000.

Isby, David C. *Weapons and Tactics of the Soviet Army*. 2nd rev. ed. London: Jane's Information Group, 1988.

Jackson, Sir Mike. "KFOR: The Inside Story." *RUSI Journal*, February 2000, 13–18.

Jacquard, Roland. *In the Name of Osama Bin Laden: Global Terrorism and the Bin Laden Brotherhood*. Durham NC: Duke University Press, 2002.

Jarymowycz, Roman. "Doctrine and Canada's Army—Seduction by Foreign Dogma: Coming to Terms with Who We Are." *Army Doctrine and Training Bulletin* 2, no. 3 (August 1999): 48–52.

Jockel, Joseph T. *The Canadian Forces: Soft Power, Hard Choices*. Toronto: CISS, 1999.

Judah, Tim. *The Serbs: History, Myth and the Destruction of Yugoslavia*. New Haven CT: Yale University Press, 1997.

Judah, Tim. *Kosovo: War and Revenge*. [New Haven CT]: Yale University Press, 2000.

Kaplan, Robert D. *Balkan Ghosts: A Journey through History*. New York: St. Martin's Press, 1993.

Kinross, Lord. *The Ottoman Centuries: The Rise and Fall of the Turkish Empire*. New York: Morrow Quill, 1997.

Knaul, Jonathan. "Memories of Kosovo." *Air and Space*, December 2000–January 2001, 26–33.

Kortunov, Andrei. "NATO Enlargement and Russia: In Search of an Adequate Response." In *Will NATO Go East? The Debate over Enlarging the Alliance*, edited by David G. Haglund, 69–92. Kingston ON: Center for International Relations, Queen's University, 1996.

Kotkin, Stephen. *Armageddon Averted: The Soviet Collapse, 1970–2000*. Oxford: Oxford University Press, 2001.

Lampe, John R. *Yugoslavia as History: Twice There Was a Country*. 2nd ed. New York: Cambridge University Press, 2000.

Land Forces Command. *Canada's Army: We Stand on Guard for Thee*. Ottawa: DND, 1998.

Lawrence, Bruce, ed. *Messages to the World: The Statements of Osama Bin Laden*. London: Verso, 2005.

MacInnis, John A. "Peacekeeping at the Crossroads (But Who Cares?)." *Canadian Defence Quarterly*, December 1995, 10–12.

Maclaren, Roy. *Canadians behind Enemy Lines 1939–1945*. Vancouver: UBC Press, 1981.

Maisonneuve, Michel. "Canadian Foreign Policy and the Kosovo Crisis of 1998: A Policy of Engagement." Unpublished paper.

Malcolm, Noel. *Kosovo: A Short History*. London: Macmillan, 1998.

Maloney, Sean M. *Canada and UN Peacekeeping: Cold War by Other Means, 1945–1970*. St. Catharines ON: Vanwell Publishing, 2002.

———. "Helpful Fixer or Hired Gun: Why Canada Goes Overseas." *Policy Options* 22, no. 1 (January–February 2001): 59–65.

———. *The Hindrance of Military Operations Ashore: Canadian Participation in Operation SHARP GUARD, 1993–1996*. Halifax NS: Dalhousie University, 2000.

———. "Insights into Canadian Peacekeeping Doctrine." *Military Review*, March–April 1996, 12–23.

———. *Operation BOLSTER: Canada and the European Community Monitor Mission in the Balkans, 1991–1994*. Toronto: CISS, 1997.

———. *War without Battles: Canada's NATO Brigade in Germany 1951–1993*. Toronto: McGraw-Hill Ryerson, 1997.

Marteinson, John et al. *The Royal Canadian Armoured Corps: An Illustrated History*. Toronto: Robin Brass Studios, 2000.

McAllester, Matthew. *Beyond the Mountains of the Damned: The War inside Kosovo*. New York: New York University Press, 2002.

Meier, Viktor. *Yugoslavia: A History of Its Demise*. New York: Routledge, 1999.

Melvern, Linda. *A People Betrayed: The Role of the West in Rwanda's Genocide*. London: Zed Books, 2009.

Milivojević, Marko. *Wounded Eagle: Albania's Fight for Survival*. London: Institute for European Defense and Strategic Studies, 1992.

Moeller, Susan D. *Compassion Fatigue: How the Media Sell Disease, Famine, War and Death*. New York: Routledge, 1999.

Naumann, Gen. Klaus. "NATO: A Chairman's Perspective." Undelivered address to the Council on Foreign Relations, 31 March 1999.

Nuti, Leopoldo. "Italy and the Defence of NATO's Southern Flank 1949–1955." In *Das Nordatlantische Bündnis 1949–1956*, edited by Klaus A. Maier and Norbert Wiggershaus, 197–212. Munich: Oldenbourg, 1993.

Odom, William E. *The Collapse of the Soviet Military*. New Haven CT: Yale University Press, 1998.

Oliviero, Charles S. "Operation DELIVERANCE: International Success or Domestic Failure?" *Canadian Military Journal* 2, no. 2 (Summer 2001): 51–58.

Oliviero, Chuck. "Trust, Maneuver Warfare, Mission Command and Canada's Army." *Army Doctrine and Training Bulletin* 1, no. 1 (August 1998): 24–28.

Patrick, Neil. "The United States, Europe, and the Security of the Gulf." *RUSI Journal* 145, no. 2 (April 2000): 44–48.

Pearson, Lester B. *Democracy in World Politics*. Princeton NJ: Princeton University Press, 1955.

Peterson, Scott. *Me against My Brother: At War in Somalia, Sudan, and Rwanda*. London: Routledge, 2000.

Poulton, Hugh. *Who Are the Macedonians?* London: C. Hurst and Company, 2000.

Pry, Peter. *War Scare: Russian and America on the Nuclear Brink*. London: Praeger, 1999.

Ramet, Sabrina Petra. *Balkan Babel: The Disintegration of Yugoslavia from the Death of Tito to Ethnic War*. 2nd ed. Boulder CO: Westview Press, 1996.

Raufer, Xavier, with Stéphane Quéré. *La mafia albanaise: Un menace pour l'Europe*. Lausanne, Switzerland: Editions Favre, 2000.

Robins, Robert S., and Jerrold M. Post. *Political Paranoia: The Psychopolitics of Hatred*. New Haven CT: Yale University Press, 1997.

Rohde, David. *Endgame: The Betrayal and Fall of Srebrenica*. New York: Farrar, Straus and Giroux, 1997.

Schmidl, Erwin A. "The International Operation in Albania, 1913–14." *International Peacekeeping* 6, no. 3 (Autumn 1999): 1–10.

Schulte, Gregory L. "Regime Change without Military Force: Lessons from Overthrowing Milosevic." *Prism: A Journal of the Center for Complex Operations* 4, no. 2 (2013): 45–55.

Sell, Louis. *Slobodan Milosevic and the Destruction of Yugoslavia*. Durham NC: Duke University Press, 2002.

Sezer, Duygu Bazogl. "Turkey's New Security Environment, Nuclear Weapons, and Proliferation." *Comparative Strategy* 14, no. 2 (1995): 149–72.

Shacochis, Bob. *The Immaculate Invasion*. New York: Penguin Books, 1999.

Shiner, Linda. "Predator: First Watch." *Air and Space*, April–May 2001, 48–57.

Silber, Laura, and Allan Little. *Yugoslavia: Death of a Nation*. New York: Penguin USA, 1996.

Singer, P. W. *Corporate Warriors: The Rise of the Privatized Military Industry*. Ithaca NY: Cornell University Press, 2003.

Smith, M. L. R. *Fighting for Ireland? The Military Strategy of the Irish Republican Movement*. London: Routledge, 1995.

Smith, Sebastian. *Allah's Mountains: The Battle for Chechnya*. London: I. B. Taurus, 2001.

Stotzky, Irwin P. *Silencing the Guns in Haiti: The Promise of Deliberative Democracy*. Chicago: University of Chicago Press, 1997.

Street, Brian. *The Parachute Ward: A Canadian Surgeon's Wartime Adventures in Yugoslavia*. Toronto: Lester and Orphen Dennys, 1987.

Talbott, Strobe. *The Russia Hand: A Memoir of Presidential Diplomacy*. New York: Random House, 2002.

Thomas, Robert. *Serbia: Still Europe's Pariah?* London: Institute for European Defense and Strategic Studies, 1996.

UK Select Committee on Defense. *Fourteenth Report: Lessons of Kosovo*. 24 October 2000.

United Nations. *The United Nations and the Situation in the Former Yugoslavia*. UN Reference Paper, 15 March 1994. [New York]: UN Department of Public Information, 1994.

———. "Vance Plan: Concept for a United Nations Peace-Keeping Operation in Yugoslavia, November–December 1991." In *The United Nations and the Situation in the Former Yugoslavia*. UN Reference Paper, 15 March 1994. [New York]: UN Department of Public Information, 1994.

U.S. State Department. *Ethnic Cleansing in Kosovo: An Accounting*. December 1999.

Vegh, Sandor. "Classifying Forms of Online Activism: The Case of Cyber Protests against the World Bank." In *Cyberactivism: Online Activism in Theory and Practice*, edited by Martha McCaughey and Michael D. Ayers, 71–96. New York: Routledge, 2003.

Vickers, Miranda. *Between Serb and Albanian: A History of Kosovo*. New York: Columbia University Press, 1998.

Vickers, Miranda, and James Pettifer. *Albania: From Anarchy to a Balkan Identity*. New York: New York University Press, 1997.

Villa, Brian. *Unauthorized Action: Mountbatten and the Dieppe Raid*. Oxford: Oxford University Press, 1989.

White, Linda, Peter Dawson, and Andrea Dawson. *Albania: A Guide and Illustrated Journal*. 2nd ed. Chalfont St. Peter, UK: Brandt Publications, 1995.

Williams, P. G. "From Coercion Back to Consent—SFOR's Endgame." *British Army Review*, no. 122 (Autumn 1999): 3–10.

Winchester, Simon. *The Fracture Zone: A Return to the Balkans*. New York: HarperCollins, 1999.

Yeltsin, Boris. *Midnight Diaries*. New York: PublicAffairs, 2000.

INDEX

Multinational Brigade (South), 197
Multinational Brigade (West), 373
"Mystery Mortar Man," 186–87

narcotics trade, 26, 40–41, 58, 181, 355
National Command Element (Canadian), 100, 112, 115, 174, 407–13
National Liberation Army (Macedonia), 207, 214, 215, 413–16
National Support Element (Canadian), 98, 100, 112, 115, 119, 226, 279
Naumann, Klaus, 65, 90
Netherlands, 21, 30, 56; air ops, 86; forces, 68, 93, 197
NGOs, 285, 292, 294, 296, 298, 332, 347
19 (UK) Mechanized Brigade, 139, 145, 146
Nis Express, 191, 193
NORAD, 125
North Atlantic Council, 61, 65, 67, 77, 78
North Atlantic Treaty Organization (NATO): 15, 16, 20, 22–23, 43, 53–54, 56–57, 58; air campaign, 64, 66; Cold War, 6–7; maritime interdiction ops, 42; Military Committee, 65; objectives in Kosovo, 92–93; and UN, 62
Northern Frontier Boundary Commission, 30–31
Norway, 93; forces, 146, 186, 320
nuclear weapons, 17–18, 125, 127; threats to use, 104, 125

Obilic power plants, 26, 49–50, 144, 145, 233, 357
1 Canadian Air Group, 15
1 Canadian Mechanized Brigade Group, 80, 98
1 Combat Engineer Regiment, 258, 262
Operation Agricola, 114
Operation Alba, 42–43
Operation Alliance, 22
Operation Allied Force, 83, 88, 91, 106, 115, 118, 127
Operation Allied Harbor, 89–90
Operation Arrow, 105, 108
Operation Bulldog, 382
Operation Calliope, 198
Operation Cobra, 260
Operation Collaborative Assembly, 62, 89
Operation Comfort, 336, 350

Operation Constant Resolve, 193, 196, 197
Operation Cordon, 70
Operation Deliberate Force, 55
Operation Desert Fox, 71
Operation Eagle Eye, 67, 69
Operation Echo, 83
Operation Essential Harvest, 215
Operation Fortitude, 94, 110
Operation Goliath, 190, 191
Operation Grasshopper, 304, 305
Operation Guarantor, 69
Operation Harmony, 18
Operation Joint Endeavor, 21
Operation Joint Guardian, 79, 86, 111
Operation Kimono, 69
Operation Kinetic, 80, 82
Operation Lombardo, 339
Operation Market Day, 183
Operation Megaphone, 420
Operation Millennium, 339
Operation Northern Watch, 58
Operation Othello, 183
Operation Palladium, 22, 79, 95
Operation Perseverance, 69
Operation Quarterback, 309, 311
Operation Salome, 183
Operation Sharp Guard, 21, 37
Operation Soap Box, 348, 349, 350
Operation Southern Watch, 58
Operation Spectator, 200, 203
Operations Plan 10413, 79
Operation Thunderbolt, 330, 333
Operation Trojan, 187, 189
Operation Vandal, 187
Operation Wolverine, 308
organized crime, 37, 40–41, 42, 43, 44, 50, 51, 149, 181, 184, 200, 247, 306, 307, 330, 355, 356, 357, 361, 422, 423
OSCE, 14, 53, 55, 66, 104, 290, 342
OTPOR movement, 113, 421

Pan-Slavism, 103
Partnership for Peace, 54
peacekeeping versus warfighting, 97, 100
Pearson, Peter, 139, 145, 146, 147, 148
Peć, 29, 142
Peel Regional Police Service, 354
Petrovac Training Area, 163
Phoenix UAVs, 91–92, 198

space operations, 412–13

Special Air Service, 122, 242, 332

special operations forces, 106, 137, 213, 214, 215, 248, 328

Specijalna Antiteroristicka Jedinica (SAJ), 50, 63, 76

Srebrenica, 21, 54

Stabilization Force (SFOR), 22, 54, 55–56, 85–86; FRY air attacks, 86; MND (SW), 145; Russian problems, 88, 121

Stambolić, Ivan, 35–36

Stanišić, Jovica, 70

Stevanović, Obrad, 132

Swedish forces, 146, 195, 196, 244, 404

Switzerland, 38, 41

Taliban, 41

Task Force Kosovo, 111, 229

Telemark Battalion, 146

Ten-Day War (Slovenia), 11, 14

Thachi, Hasim, 117, 135–36, 137, 207, 240, 271, 272, 316, 373

Thessaloniki port, 86, 112, 115, 116, 118, 120, 122, 163

3rd Battalion, Princess Patricia's Canadian Light Infantry, 97

3 Canadian Support Group, 276, 277

Tito (Josip Broz), 5, 6, 9, 10, 11, 26, 32, 33, 36

TMK. *See* Kosovo Protection Corps

TOW Under Armour vehicles, 143, 150, 261, 276, 277, 323, 325, 329, 333, 349, 355, 361, 369

Trepča mine, 37, 50

Tudjman, Franjo, 10

TU-142 Bear nuclear bomber, 125, 126

TU-160 Blackjack nuclear bomber, 125, 126

Turkey, 20, 57, 58

22nd Marine Expeditionary Unit, 152

26th Marine Expeditionary Unit, 122

UÇK, 31, 39–40, 43, 49, 59, 117, 135, 167, 168, 172, 235, 245, 268, 269, 270, 283, 287, 291, 324, 328, 340, 345, 360; "Atlantic Brigade," 52; Drenica Operational Zone, 272, 273; kidnappings, 76, 82, 167, 304; legitimacy, 58–59; 121 Brigade, 273; operations, 63, 70, 74, 82, 108; organized crime links, 44; and the Preševo Valley, 205; provoking Russians, 322, 323; 60 (SF) Brigade, 273, 274;

splinter group problem, 178; structure, 51–53, 272, 273; transformation, 138, 148, 182, 271; and VJ withdrawal, 228; ZKZ CI command, 274

UÇK Undertaking of Demilitarization and Transformation, 135–36

UÇPMB (Liberation Army of the Preševo, Medvedja, and Bujanovic), 204, 206, 208, 209, 210, 213, 215, 372

UDB (political police), 12, 33

UH-60 Blackhawk helicopters, 237

United Kingdom, 30, 61, 71; forces, 93, 110

United Nations, 15, 18–19, 59, 65, 77, 113

United Nations Forces in Cyprus, 20, 22

United Nations High Commission for Refugees (UNHCR), 293, 295

United Nations Mine Action Coordination Center, 300

United Nations Mission in Kosovo, 117, 134–35, 271, 285, 293, 342, 348; UNMIK police, 191, 245, 340, 343, 352, 353, 354, 365, 369, 378, 397

United Nations Preventive Deployment, 20, 44–45, 52, 68

United Nations Protection Force (UNPROFOR), 18–19, 20, 54, 96, 140, 178, 188, 247, 281, 350, 375–76

United Nations Protection Force II (UNPROFOR II), 19, 20; NATO air support for, 19, 55

United Nations Security Council, 62, 117

United Nations Special Commission (UNSCOM), 58, 66, 71

United States, 43, 56, 61, 63, 64, 76; diplomacy, 78; forces, 68, 378; legislative constraints on forces, 201, 208; posture, 202

unmanned aerial vehicles, 198, 199, 212

UNSCR 1160 (1998), 53

UNSCR 1199, 64

UNSCR 1244 (1999), 105, 117, 131–32, 136, 142

USAID, 292

Veliki Belaćevac, 309, 301, 312

Vrboche massacre site, 302, 303

Walker, William, 74, 75

Warrior MICV, 387, 394

Weapons Authorization Certificate, 316, 325

Western European Union, 21, 42, 55

Wright, David, 77

Xhinobci, Yemen "Herr Hitler," 355, 356

Yeltsin, Boris, 61, 87–88, 103–4, 121, 124

Y2K, 339

Yugoslav Army (VJ), 50, 52, 54, 91, 142; air defense systems, 235; deception measures, 169, 170; disproportionate force, 61; operations, 63, 64, 70, 72, 84, 105, 268; possible re-intervention, 149, 150, 372, 374; Preševo Valley operations, 204; SOF infiltration, 251; withdrawal from Kosovo, 137, 167, 168, 227, 228

Yugoslavia: collapse, 5, 7–14, 17, 24; deportation of Kosovar Albanians, 33; guerilla warfare, 12; suppression of Albanian language, 33; Territorial Defense Forces, 12–13, 38; World War II, 5, 12, 17–18, 31–33

Yugoslav National Army, 11, 13; counterintelligence service (KOS), 11

Zavarzin, Viktor, 121, 124